GREAT AUSTRALIAN DISSENTS

When judges disagree, those in the minority write a dissenting opinion. This book considers the great dissents in Australian law. Their worth may derive from numerous factors including their rhetorical force as a piece of legal reasoning or emotive power as a judicial lament for the 'error' into which the majority has fallen; the general importance of the issue at stake; as a challenge to the orthodoxy; and, sometimes, the subsequent recognition of a dissenting opinion's correctness and its ultimate vindication. On some occasions, all these features may be strongly present, on others only some. Through a diverse selection of memorable dissenting opinions, this book illuminates the topic of judicial disagreement more generally – not only through examples of instances when minority opinions have been distinctly valuable, but by drawing out a richer understanding of the attributes and circumstances which lead some dissents to become iconic, while so many lie forgotten.

ANDREW LYNCH teaches and researches in the field of Australian constitutional law at the Faculty of Law, University of New South Wales. His co-authored and co-edited publications include *Blackshield & Williams' Australian Constitutional Law and Theory* (2014), *Inside Australia's Terrorism Laws and Trials* (2014), *Tomorrow's Federation – Reforming Australian Government* (2012) and *Counter-Terrorism and Beyond: The Culture of Law and Justice After 9/11* (2010).

GREAT AUSTRALIAN DISSENTS

Edited by

ANDREW LYNCH

CAMBRIDGE
UNIVERSITY PRESS

CAMBRIDGE
UNIVERSITY PRESS

University Printing House, Cambridge CB2 8BS, United Kingdom

One Liberty Plaza, 20th Floor, New York, NY 10006, USA

477 Williamstown Road, Port Melbourne, VIC 3207, Australia

4843/24, 2nd Floor, Ansari Road, Daryaganj, Delhi – 110002, India

79 Anson Road, #06-04/06, Singapore 079906

Cambridge University Press is part of the University of Cambridge.

It furthers the University's mission by disseminating knowledge in the pursuit of education, learning and research at the highest international levels of excellence.

www.cambridge.org
Information on this title: www.cambridge.org/9781107158535

First published 2016

A catalogue record for this publication is available from the British Library.

ISBN 978-1-107-15853-5 Hardback

CONTENTS

CONTRIBUTORS

GABRIELLE APPLEBY is an Associate Professor and Co-Director of The Judiciary Project, Gilbert + Tobin Centre of Public Law at the School of Law, University of New South Wales.

SEAN BRENNAN is an Associate Professor and the Director of the Gilbert + Tobin Centre of Public Law at the School of Law, University of New South Wales.

A J BROWN is Professor of Public Policy and Law and programme leader, Public Integrity & Anti-Corruption in the Centre for Governance and Public Policy, Griffith University.

ANNE CARTER is a PhD candidate at Melbourne Law School, University of Melbourne.

MICHAEL COPER is a Professor of Law at the ANU College of Law, Australian National University.

SIMONE DEGELING is a Professor at the School of Law, University of New South Wales.

JEREMY GANS is a Professor at Melbourne Law School, University of Melbourne.

MATTHEW GROVES is a Professor at the Faculty of Law, Monash University.

OLIVER JONES is a Barrister, New Chambers, Sydney.

ANDREW LYNCH is a Professor and Co-Director of The Judiciary Project, Gilbert + Tobin Centre of Public Law at the School of Law, University of New South Wales.

BARBARA MCDONALD is a Professor of Law in the Faculty of Law, University of Sydney.

STEPHEN MCDONALD is a Barrister at Hanson Chambers and an Adjunct Senior Lecturer at the University of Adelaide.

JOE MCINTYRE is a Senior Lecturer at the School of Law, University of South Australia.

HEATHER ROBERTS is a Senior Lecturer at the ANU College of Law.

OSCAR ROOS is a Senior Lecturer at the School of Law, Deakin University.

AMELIA SIMPSON is an Associate Professor at the ANU College of Law.

PETA STEPHENSON is a PhD Candidate at the TC Beirne School of Law, University of Queensland.

ADRIENNE STONE is a Professor and the Director of the Centre for Comparative Constitutional Studies, Melbourne Law School, University of Melbourne.

KRISTEN WALKER is a Queens Counsel at the Victorian Bar and a Principal Fellow at the University of Melbourne.

GREG WEEKS is a Senior Lecturer at the School of Law, University of New South Wales.

GEORGE WILLIAMS is the Anthony Mason Professor, a Scientia Professor and Foundation Director, Gilbert + Tobin Centre of Public Law, Faculty of Law, University of New South Wales; Australian Research Council Laureate Fellow; and Barrister, New South Wales Bar.

FIGURE

TABLE

ACKNOWLEDGMENTS

I am grateful to all the contributing authors for their participation at the two day research workshop in June 2015 at which these chapters were first presented and discussed. It has been my great pleasure to work with them since in preparing this book. The workshop and this publication would not have been possible without the support of the Faculty of Law at the University of New South Wales and the Gilbert + Tobin Centre of Public Law. I particularly thank the Centre's Director, Associate Professor Sean Brennan, for his unstinting encouragement and material assistance in the realisation of this project. I appreciated the interest and support of my other colleagues in the Centre, especially those who contributed chapters and also Professor Rosalind Dixon and Dr Ben Golder, who chaired sessions at the workshop and contributed generously to its proceedings.

I also thank the simply invaluable Anna Reinstra for her excellent and thoughtful editorial assistance in readying the full manuscript for delivery to the publisher. I thank Lucy Russell at Cambridge University Press in Australia for her enthusiastic response to the book proposal, and Finola O'Sullivan and all the team at Cambridge University Press in the United Kingdom for their work on this publication.

Andrew Lynch

We would like to thank Joshua Gani for his excellent research assistance and Stephen McDonald, James Lee and Rosalind Dixon for their helpful comments on earlier drafts. We would also like to thank Andrew Lynch for his insightful comments and suggestions, together with all of the participants at the Great Australian Dissents workshop.

Gabrielle Appleby and Heather Roberts

We are grateful for the comments of Rosalind Dixon, Matthew Harding, Jessica Hudson and Barbara McDonald and the research assistance of Eftim Ancev. All errors are our own.

Simone Degeling and Greg Weeks

I would like to thank Emma Cunliffe for her advice on the Chamberlain case and her feedback on a draft of my chapter.

Jeremy Gans

I would like to thank David John Jones MA (Oxon); Dip Lib, PhD (UNSW) for his research assistance.

Oliver Jones

I am most grateful to Professor Andrew Lynch especially and to other participants at the Great Dissents workshop for their insightful comments on the draft chapter, and also for the most resourceful legal and historical research and comments of Daniel Farinha.

Barbara McDonald

We would like to thank Gabrielle Appleby for her helpful comments on an earlier draft. We are also grateful to Andrew Lynch and the other participants at the Great Australian Dissents workshop for their insights and suggestions.

Stephen McDonald and Anne Carter

I wish to thank all the participants at the Great Australian Dissents workshop for their insightful comments on the draft chapter, and for the animated discussion of that workshop that has influenced this chapter is so many ways. In particular, I am most grateful for the support and guidance of Professor Andrew Lynch in guiding this book to fruition.

Joe McIntyre

In addition to the Great Australian Dissents workshop participants, Oscar would like to thank Professors Jeff Goldsworthy and Greg Taylor for their comments on an earlier draft of the chapter.

Oscar Roos

Thanks to Leighton McDonald, Fiona Wheeler, Anthony Hopkins and the participants in the Great Australian Dissents workshop for valuable comments.

Amelia Simpson

I would like to thank Sir Anthony Mason for generously reading and commenting on an earlier draft of this chapter. I am also grateful to Jonathan

Crowe, Oscar Roos and Benjamin Saunders for their helpful suggestions and the participants at the Great Australian Dissents workshop for their insights, feedback and encouragement.

Peta Stephenson

Thanks are due to Alexandra Harrison-Ichlov for her excellent research assistance.

Adrienne Stone and Kristen Walker QC

I thank Horace Ng for his research assistance.

George Williams AO

TABLE OF CASES

1

Introduction – What Makes a Dissent 'Great'?

ANDREW LYNCH

I Introduction

The delivery of dissenting opinions is such a familiar phenomenon of appellate court decision-making in common law systems as to often go unremarked. Outside the United States of America, in which judicial dissent has long been viewed with a pronounced romanticism and has amassed a vast literature, direct scholarly attention has been limited. This is certainly true in Australia. Additionally, what judicial and academic discussion there is on the topic typically falls into one of two camps. In the first are contributions that engage in a fairly abstract weighing of the benefits of judicial dissent against its costs to the institutional authority and efficiency of the courts; these reflections are predominantly sourced from the judiciary. In the second is academic research with an empirical focus, in which determining the frequency of judicial disagreement and the identification of regular coalitions and dissenters on the bench feature as dominant objectives.

Despite the value of these different contributions, an important gap in our understanding of this topic remains: specifically, when and how has dissent *really mattered*? A full appreciation of the practice of judges writing minority opinions – what motivates them to do so, the adoption of a particular tone or style, and the impact of disagreement upon the work and standing of the court and the later development of the law – can only be gained through a substantive discussion about the value and significance of particular examples. This book aims to fill this gap by presenting a diverse collection of such opinions in which the circumstances and consequences of judicial dissent are explored in detail.

At the same time, *Great Australian Dissents* is, as its title unambiguously indicates, a celebration of the genre. The contributing authors were invited to nominate a minority opinion they believe merits inclusion in the pantheon – but pointedly, they were not offered any pre-determined criteria for that purpose. Many of the dissents here will be ones widely anticipated by those who have studied and worked in the law, some may surprise, and the inclusion of others again may be hotly contested – just as they were at the two day workshop in which the chapters of this book were initially presented and discussed. The common purpose of the 21 authors across the 17 chapters that follow is to justify their selection to the reader. In doing so, they place the dissenting opinion in context so that its novelty and impact may be appreciated against the majority's approach and the existing law. The authors detail the opinion's immediate attractions and enduring appeal, if not vindication. In this way, the chapters of the book work in dialogue with each other to illuminate the topic of dissent more generally – not simply by providing instances when minority opinions have been distinctly valuable, but by also constructing a holistic understanding of those attributes and circumstances which lead some dissents to stand out as significant, even to become iconic, while so many lie forgotten.

The purpose of this chapter is to introduce this highly varied collection and also the central themes that emerge from it – the many different ways in which a minority opinion may, despite losing the day when the case was decided, nevertheless make some claim to greatness.

II Recognising Dissent

The precise origins of the practice of judicial dissent are unclear. Although the significance of the right to make speeches in the Appellate Committee of the House of Lords has been pointed to as providing a constitutional basis for the practice of judicial dissent in English law,[1] this is not the same as an historical explanation for the emergence of the practice.[2] Sir John Baker has described the transition from a seemingly open-ended search for judicial consensus in the late medieval period, which could produce stasis, to a willingness by the end of the 16th century to accept decisions by majority in order to achieve an authoritative judicial pronouncement of the law.[3] Minority opinions, it is clear from Baker's account, were not

[1] John Alder, 'Dissents in Courts of Last Resort: Tragic Choices?' (2000) 20 *Oxford Journal of Legal Studies* 221, 233; Alan Paterson, *The Law Lords* (Macmillan, 1982) 98.

[2] Chris Young, 'The History of Judicial Dissent in England: What Relevance does It have for Modern Common Law Legal Systems?'(2009) 32 *Australian Bar Review* 96; Cf Michael Kirby, 'Judicial Dissent – Common Law and Civil Law Traditions' (2007) 123 *Law Quarterly Review* 379, 385–6.

[3] John Baker, *The Oxford History of the Laws of England, Vol VI 1483–1558* (Oxford University Press, 2003) 49–51.

suddenly permitted, but are just the natural consequence of the seriatim practice of judgment delivery employed in the English courts for centuries, by which individual judges announced their opinion on the case in order of seniority.[4] Although Lord Mansfield briefly enforced a practice of unanimous opinion delivery upon his appointment as Lord Chief Justice in the second half of the 18th century,[5] the English tradition has otherwise been unbroken, although fluctuations in the relative levels of unanimity and dissent have certainly occurred over time.[6] The seriatim practice of judgment delivery, with its inherent capacity for explicit judicial disagreement was exported throughout the common law world.

A notable exception was the Judicial Committee of the Privy Council, which heard appeals from Britain's former colonial possessions. The Privy Council's rigid requirement of unanimity was something strongly disdained by Australia's Sir Garfield Barwick, and his part in ending that institutional practice is discussed in chapter 7 – that dissent is a curiosity in this collection for although its author was an Australian judge, it was not delivered in an Australian case. It should also be noted that there has been a lingering wariness around the delivery of dissent in criminal appeal matters due to the serious consequences for the accused.[7] In some jurisdictions this has taken the form of a statutory instruction to the courts to strive for unanimity. The dissent examined in chapter 8 provides an example of a dissenting judge having to overcome that sort of pressure for conformity in order to deliver an opinion that proved hugely influential on the English criminal law.

The use of seriatim opinions by the United States Supreme Court was short-lived. The Court's fourth Chief Justice, John Marshall, imposed the practice of near constant unanimity on his colleagues in order to secure its fledgling authority.[8] The resistance of Justice Johnson, emboldened by Thomas Jefferson behind the scenes, prevented Marshall CJ from

4 M Todd Henderson, 'From Seriatim to Consensus and Back Again: A Theory of Dissent' (2007) *The Supreme Court Review* 283, 292–4.

5 Ibid 294–303.

6 With respect to decision-making trends in the United Kingdom's final court since the 1970s, see Alan Paterson, *Final Judgment – The Last Law Lords and the Supreme Court* (Hart Publishing, 2013).

7 Alder, above n 1, 242.

8 Henderson, above n 4, 305–25; John P Kelsh, 'The Opinion Delivery Practices of the United States Supreme Court 1790–1945' (1999) 77 *Washington University Law Quarterly* 137, 143–52.

eradicating the potential for judicial dissent.[9] But the result was what the current court's Justice Bader Ginsburg has called a 'middle way':

> [There are] three patterns of appellate judgments by collegial courts: seriatim opinions by each member of the bench, which is the British tradition; a single anonymous judgment with no dissent made public, which is the civil law prototype; and the middle way familiar in the United States – generally an opinion for the court, from which individual judges sometimes disassociate themselves in varying degrees.[10]

While that description basically holds, the early 1940s was a watershed between the consensus driven approach instigated by Marshall and the rise again of individual expression on the Supreme Court through separate concurrences and dissents.[11] The delivery of an opinion 'for the Court' means that identification of both concurring and dissenting judgments is not only a much simpler task when reading the case reports of the United States Supreme Court, but it may be thought to assume a greater significance in the process of judicial deliberation and composition of judgments. A Justice who is disinclined to join the Court's opinion has the option of writing a separate concurring opinion or a dissent. Either represents a formal and deliberate breaking away – a disassociation 'in varying degrees' – from the central judgment which represents the views of the majority. By contrast, the status of judgments in the seriatim tradition was so indistinct as to baffle American observers:

> A judge may in fact be dissenting from his panel's disposition, but the reports never say so. Similarly, a judge may in fact be concurring – he may agree with the disposition but disagree with the reasoning of a majority of the panel – but the reports never say that he's concurring. You have to read through all the judgments in order to discover that any one of them is a concurrence. Indeed, there could not as a logical matter be dissents or concurrences in the English system, because no appellate panel ever adopts a single judgment as the judgment of the court . . . [12]

9 Meredith Kolsky, 'Justice William Johnston and the History of Supreme Court Dissent' (1995) 83 *Georgetown Law Journal* 2069, 2069–81.

10 Justice Ruth Bader Ginsburg, 'Remarks on Writing Separately' (1990) 65 *Washington Law Review* 133, 134.

11 Henderson, above n 4, 325–41; Mervin I Urofsky, *Dissent and the Supreme Court: Its Role in the Court's History and the Nation's Constitutional Dialogue* (Pantheon Books, 2015), 209–26.

12 Arthur J Jacobson, 'Publishing Dissent' (2005) 62 *Washington and Lee Law Review* 1607, 1609.

That observation has less purchase as the trend towards more unanimous or joint judgments increasingly supplants the pure seriatim practices which were the historical norm in the English and Australian courts.[13] But it relevantly highlights a consideration that explains the historical tendency to less strident expression of dissent in the English and Australian courts – often what ended up as a minority opinion was not consciously written as such, but was simply the judge's opinion on the case. What made it a dissent was nothing more than the failure of a majority of the bench to agree with it; the opinion possessed no inherent properties as a dissent. The dissent of Justice Anthony Mason in *Hospital Products Ltd v United States Surgical Corporation*,[14] discussed in chapter 12, is a very good example and about which its author has said:

> At the time I wrote it I thought it could end up as the judgment of the Court or a judgment that formed part of a majority in the Court. But it didn't turn out that way. So, though not written as a dissenting judgment, it became a dissenting judgment.[15]

Some cases throw up issues that make consensus difficult to obtain, and the judges will resort to the highly individualised mode of expression in the seriatim tradition. The result can be that a crisp line between the majority that determines the High Court's orders and those who disagree simply does not exist. The cases discussed in chapters 10 and 13 are each of this description, and show a bench fragmented across a range of different issues. On such occasions, the dissents under examination will also be unlikely to make any overt display of their minority status – and indeed on some aspects of the case they may share substantial agreement with the reasoning of the majority or even the orders of the Court.[16] The United States Supreme Court has experience of partial dissents, even under circumstances where no solid majority sustains the 'opinion of the Court',[17] but an American audience would probably be surprised by the identification of such opinions, from which the reader has to draw out

[13] See respectively, Paterson, above n 6, 99–110 and Justice Susan Kiefel, 'The Individual Judge' (2014) 88 *Australian Law Journal* 554, 557.

[14] (1984) 156 CLR 41.

[15] Katy Barnett, 'Sir Anthony Mason Reflects on Judging in Australia and Hong Kong, Precedent and Judgment Writing' on Melbourne Law School, *Opinions on High* (28 July 2014) <http://blogs.unimelb.edu.au/opinionsonhigh/2014/07/28/barnett-mason/>.

[16] See Andrew Lynch, 'Dissent: Towards a Methodology for Measuring Judicial Disagreement in the High Court of Australia' (2002) 24 *Sydney Law Review* 470, 492–502.

[17] Mark A Thurmon, 'When the Court Divides: Reconsidering the Precedential Value of Supreme Court Plurality Decisions' (1992) 42 *Duke Law Journal* 419.

the author's differences from the rest of the Court, as 'great dissents'. If they barely look like a dissent, how can they be truly great?

III Great Dissenters; Great Dissent?

The whole notion of 'greatness' is a complex one, strongly linked to judicial reputation. Occasionally, Justices of the High Court of Australia have acquired the sobriquet of 'Great Dissenter'. In chapters 3 and 5 we are reminded that, though long forgotten now, Sir Owen Dixon wore this label in his first decade on the Court, in reference to his regular minority opinions on the interpretation of the constitutional guarantee of freedom of inter-state trade and commerce. He soon shed the title when his views attracted the support of others and his swift emergence as the dominant force on the Court was assured. By contrast, a reputation for dissent defines the judicial careers of two later Justices – Lionel Murphy and Michael Kirby. The status of both as a minority voice on the bench shapes scholarly assessment of their contribution.[18] Invaluable as those personal studies are, it would be misguided to seek to understand the phenomenon of minority opinions, much less its significance, through the prism of any particular individual. To do so is not merely insufficient, but also risks distorting or limiting an appreciation of dissent as a broader experience.

These dangers are acutely apparent when one asks what the identification of an individual as a 'Great Dissenter' is supposed to signify. The title is an imported one, having a long lineage in the appraisal of Justices of the United States Supreme Court. The first Justice John Marshall Harlan was referred to as the Great Dissenter on account not only of 'the sheer number of his separate opinions, but for their importance in helping to shape the country's constitutional development'.[19] Undoubtedly, Harlan J's most famous dissent stands also as one of the Court's – his objection to the constitutional validity of the 'Jim Crow' segregation laws of the Southern states in *Plessy v Ferguson*.[20] But Harlan J's influence, on this and other constitutional issues, was far from apparent at the time, with the importance of his legacy only emerging several decades after

[18] Michael Coper and George Williams (eds), *Justice Lionel Murphy – Influential or Merely Prescient* (Federation Press, 1997); Ian Freckelton and Hugh Selby (eds), *Appealing to the Future: Michael Kirby and his Legacy* (Thomson Reuters, 2009); and Scott Guy and Kristy Richardson, 'Justices Murphy and Kirby: Reviving Social Democracy and the Constitution' (2010) 22 *Bond Law Review* 26.

[19] Urofsky, above n 11, 105. [20] 163 US 537 (1896).

his death. In the meanwhile, the title of Great Dissenter was even more memorably attached to Justice Oliver Wendell Holmes Jr, not due to his rate of dissent, which was modest, but because of his persuasive oratory when in disagreement with a majority of the Court on questions of great significance.[21] Since then, the title has been invoked in respect of others (including Harlan J's grandson who also served on the Court)[22] – but it clearly refers to more than the mere fact of disagreement, pointing also to a discernible judicial attitude or a philosophy which is plaintively or persistently raised against the mainstream of the Court's opinion.

A similar flavour is found in Australian appellation of the 'Great Dissenter', although it is arguable that popular usage tends to emphasise the quantity of an individual's dissent over more specific qualities of judicial style or outlook. So far this century, the Australian media have identified Kirby J and then Heydon J in quick succession as the Great Dissenter on the High Court.[23] In many respects the conferral is not inapt. There is no doubt that Kirby J and Heydon J were distinct outliers on the bench for at least some of their time at the High Court; both had two consecutive years towards the end of their respective tenures in which they dissented in over 40 per cent of cases while all other judges had a dissent rate of less than 10 per cent.[24]

More importantly, Kirby J and Heydon J appeared to embrace their outlier status, speaking candidly and persuasively about the value of judicial

[21] Allen Mendenhall, 'Holmes and Dissent' (2011) *The Journal Jurisprudence* 679, 681. Schwartz links these two aspects of Holmes J's reputation, saying he would forego dissent except when in disagreement on 'great cases': Bernard Schwartz, *A Book of Legal Lists: The Best and Worst in American Law* (Oxford University Press, 1997) 107.

[22] See, eg, Tinsley E Yarbrough, *John Marshall Harlan: Great Dissenter of the Warren Court* (Oxford University Press, 1992); Michael Mello, *Against the Death Penalty – The Relentless Dissents of Justices Brennan and Marshall* (Northeastern, 1996); and Thomas F Shea, 'The Great Dissenters: Parallel Currents in Holmes and Scalia' (1997) 67 *Mississippi Law Journal* 397.

[23] See, eg, Chris Merritt, 'It's unanimous: Kirby still the great dissenter' *The Australian* (Sydney) 16 February 2007; and Harriet Alexander, 'Great dissenter takes a swipe at "closed minds" of the bench' *The Sydney Morning Herald* (Sydney) 16 March 2013.

[24] Regarding Kirby J: Andrew Lynch and George Williams, 'The High Court on Constitutional Law – the 2006 Statistics' (2007) 30 *University of New South Wales Law Journal* 188, 196; Andrew Lynch and George Williams, 'The High Court on Constitutional Law – the 2007 Statistics' (2008) 31 *University of New South Wales Law Journal* 238, 245. Regarding Heydon J: Andrew Lynch and George Williams, 'The High Court on Constitutional Law – the 2011 Statistics' (2012) 35 *University of New South Wales Law Journal* 846, 855; Andrew Lynch and George Williams, 'The High Court on Constitutional Law – the 2012 Statistics' (2013) 36 *University of New South Wales Law Journal* 514, 522.

individualism and the importance of dissent.[25] Further, they each maintained a distinctive vision of the judicial role which not only underpinned their disagreement with the rest of the Court but was something they articulated at length in public speeches and articles.[26] Lastly, both took full advantage of the liberty that is afforded the judge writing alone in dissent, free from the deadening effects of compromise and the responsibility to lay down the law with colleagues in the majority, to compose highly memorable opinions replete with 'passages of great force, eloquence, and ardor'.[27] Justices Kirby and Heydon proved to be highly adept at delivering what, in the former's judgments, were referred to as 'kicks' against the positions adopted by their colleagues.[28]

In Kirby J's case, his biographer, Professor A J Brown, noted that the kicks became 'increasingly poetically drafted, and increasingly noticed', but they were 'primarily tactical weapons in his battle for public opinion'.[29] In chapter 17, Brown reflects on the different audiences that apparently explain the stark differences between Kirby J's dissent and that of Chief Justice Gleeson in the unsuccessful challenge to Australia's immigration detention law in *Al-Kateb v Godwin*.[30] The appeal to an external audience is a noted feature of some judicial opinions.[31] While that strategy may be particularly understandable in a dissent,[32] Professor Melvin I Urofsky claims that, 'unless it can show convincingly how wrong the majority is, it will never – no matter how well it may be written – be more than an angry tirade or enter into the constitutional dialogue'.[33] In his contrasting of

[25] See Kirby, above n 2; J D Heydon, 'Threats to Judicial Independence: The Enemy Within' (2013) 129 *Law Quarterly Review* 205; J D Heydon, 'Japanese War Crimes, Retroactive Laws and Mr Justice Pal' (2011) 85 *Australian Law Journal* 627.

[26] See, eg, Michael Kirby, *Judicial Activism – Hamlyn Lectures, 2003* (Sweet & Maxwell, 2004); J D Heydon, 'Varieties of Judicial Method in the Late 20th Century' (2012) 34 *Sydney Law Review* 219.

[27] Alan Barth, *Prophets with Honor – Great Dissents and Great Dissenters in the Supreme Court* (Knopf, 1974) xii. See also Justice Antonin Scalia, 'The Dissenting Opinion' (1994) *Journal of Supreme Court History* 33, 42.

[28] A J Brown, *Michael Kirby – Principles/Paradoxes* (Federation Press, 2011), 391–2, 396, 399.

[29] Ibid 392, 399. See also Gavan Griffith and Graeme Hill, 'Constitutional Law: Dissents and Posterity' in Freckelton and Selby, above n 18, 217, 217.

[30] (2004) 219 CLR 562.

[31] Lawrence Baum, *Judges and their Audiences – A Perspective on Judicial Behaviour* (Princeton University Press, 2006); Nuno Garoupa and Tom Ginsburg, 'Judicial Audiences and Reputation: Perspectives from Comparative Law' (2009) 47 *Columbia Journal of Transnational Law* 451.

[32] Lani Guinier, 'The Supreme Court, 2007 Term – Foreword: Demosprudence Through Dissent' (2008) 122 *Harvard Law Review* 4.

[33] Urofsky, above n 11, 407.

the opinions in *Al-Kateb v Godwin*, Brown explores whether the decision to write for the public sacrifices a dissent's appeal to the Court on a later occasion.

Justice Heydon may not have as deliberately employed 'kicks' but his personal style also tended to forthrightness; his flair for acerbity avoided the strident hyperbole of Justice Antonin Scalia's dissents, while being no less quotable.[34] In chapter 18, the authors examine Heydon J's very final judgment and highly distinctive dissent in the context of earlier disagreements with the Court and his broader advocacy of a particular conception of judicial legitimacy, going back over several years. Once again, the issue of audience is a clear focus.

Despite all that, it is unclear whether either Kirby J or Heydon J will be regarded as a Great Dissenter by future generations. Although, their reputation for judicial disagreement is undoubtedly cemented in a way that was not the case for the young Dixon J of the 1930s, the ultimate indicium of a Great Dissenter is to speak to posterity. The question of subsequent influence, rather more nuanced than may first appear, is discussed in Part IV below, but in the context of whether an individual is aptly acknowledged as a Great Dissenter, only time can really tell. Although an opinion of Kirby J and Heydon J each appears in this collection, it is just too soon to know whether these or their other prominent dissents will endure, let alone prevail.

In any case, this is a book about great dissents, not Great Dissenters. While we might assume the former emanate from the latter, this need not be so. For one thing, those who are mythologised as dissenters may leave a plentiful, but nevertheless thin, legacy. Professor Mark Tushnet confronted this paradox when he explained the omission from his personal selection of great dissents of the United States Supreme Court of any opinions by Justice William O Douglas.[35] Douglas was the Court's longest ever serving Justice, its most prolific dissenter, and was regarded as a Great Dissenter in his lifetime.[36] But Tushnet described Douglas J's dissents as diminished not only by a 'somewhat slapdash' writing style but more significantly, as 'curiously time-bound'.[37] In short, they were of

[34] 'Scalia has perfected the "opinion as attack ad" rhetoric': Mark Tushnet, *I Dissent – Great Opposing Opinions in Landmark Supreme Court Cases* (Beacon Press, 2006) xxii. As one commentator remarked on Scalia J's criticisms of the majority reasoning in cases from the Court's 2014–15 term: 'Welcome to the era of the judicial dissent as body slam': Dahlia Lithwick, 'Sunday Book Review: "Dissent and the Supreme Court" by Melvin I Urofsky' *The New York Times* (21 October 2015).

[35] Tushnet, above n 34. [36] Schwartz, above n 21, 106. [37] Tushnet, above n 34.

little value beyond the immediate case itself. Professor George Williams has offered a similar explanation for Murphy J's lack of influence in the High Court's development of implied constitutional rights, despite his pioneering opinions in the area, most especially with respect to the freedom of political communication. Williams said that Murphy J's legal method 'ensured that his decisions would not likely be repeated and would not be capable of being developed'.[38] Two opinions of Justice Murphy do appear in chapters 11 and 13 of this collection, though his idiosyncratic style is certainly acknowledged in assessing the impact of his views and the very limited extent to which they have been attributed by judges who came after him.

Conversely, it is clear that great dissents have been written by judges who enjoy no particular reputation for dissent. This should not be nearly as surprising as the previous observation. Judges who are the intellectual leaders of the court may find themselves occasionally in the minority, but the qualities that explain their usual ability to attract, if not actually shape, majority support amongst their colleagues can hardly be expected to have deserted them. Whether due to the high regard in which the judge is held, or the strength of reasoning in the particular dissent (indeed, probably a powerful combination of both), such opinions may stand over time as important ones. Their place on the legal landscape must be acknowledged by later generations, even if they are never simply adopted. Reputation clearly plays a part here also, but in this instance it lends the dissent an authority that might otherwise be lacking. It is no accident that many of the chapters in this book nominate as 'great dissents' opinions authored not by a Great Dissenter, but simply by a great judge.

Perceptions of judicial greatness matter because reputation is inevitably an aspect of subsequent citation and influence.[39] This is so generally not just in respect of dissents, but the latter depend much more on an appeal to 'greatness' – or, more prosaically, 'correctness' – if they are to have some future relevance. It seems unduly cynical to suggest that 'greatness', even 'heroism', is occasionally constructed by Justices with a view to the redemption of a minority opinion to support their preferred outcome in a

[38] George Williams, 'Lionel Murphy and Democracy and Rights' in Coper and Williams, above n 18, 63. See also George Winterton, 'Murphy: A Maverick Reconsidered' (1997) *University of New South Wales Law Journal* 204, 206.

[39] Russell Smyth, 'Who Gets Cited? An Empirical Study of Judicial Prestige in the High Court' (2000) 21 *University of Queensland Law Journal* 7; and Russell Smyth, 'Judicial Prestige: A Citation Analysis of Federal Court Judges' (2001) 6 *Deakin Law Review* 120.

later case.[40] However, it is necessary to appreciate that greatness may take diverse forms. In his 2012 book *Laughing at the Gods: Great Judges and How They Made the Common Law*, Professor Allan Hutchinson expressed the following understanding of judicial greatness:

> Great judges seek to make a critical accommodation with the legal tradition by combining heresy and heritage in a playful judicial style; they refuse to be hampered by customary habits of judicial mind. For them, law is not something to be mastered. It is a sprawling tableau of transformation in which experimentation and improvisation are valued as much as predictability and faithfulness to existing rules and ideas. They see possibilities and make moves that others overlook. Great judges flaunt conventional standards in the process of remaking them; their judgments are the exceptions that prove the rule. And, once they have done what they do, others are less able to view the world in the same way again.[41]

So far as Hutchinson's description emphasises the quality of true independence of mind, both from the views of one's colleagues and the weight of existing legal authority, he identifies what is, obviously, essential to the practice of dissent. However, the passage resonates with a particularly romanticised view of judicial dissent[42] – and thus sits awkwardly with many of the opinions for which the claim of greatness is made in this book. Certainly, many of those opinions are innovative, some possibly bold, and the charge of heresy has even long been levelled at one of them.[43] But it seems an overstatement to say that they are the product of a refusal 'to be hampered by customary habits of judicial mind', while it is even more doubtful that any might be described as 'playful'. Hutchinson's apparent equation of greatness with radicalism is not necessarily inaccurate but it is incomplete and, in the Australian legal tradition, decidedly marginal. Consider, by way of contrast, Chief Justice Murray Gleeson's perspective on judicial decision-making as a tonic to Hutchinson's further suggestion that great judges 'take an almost daredevilish approach':[44]

40 Richard A Primus, 'Canon, Anti-Canon, and Judicial Dissent' (1998) 48 *Duke Law Journal* 243, 259–64.

41 Allan C Hutchinson, *Laughing at the Gods: Great Judges and How They Made the Common Law* (Cambridge University Press, 2012) 15.

42 Consider the parallels with Mendenhall's remark that, 'Holmes hammered out succinct, hard-hitting prose that smacked of urgency and playfulness at once . . . The language of Holmes's dissents was acrobatic': above n 21, 680–1.

43 Justice Dixon's opinion in *Re Foreman & Sons Pty Ltd; Uther v Commissioner of Taxation* (1947) 74 CLR 508.

44 Hutchinson, above n 41.

'Only someone given to mock heroics or lacking a sense of the ridiculous could characterise differences of judicial opinion in terms of bravery'.[45]

What is striking about the dissents gathered here is how they collectively challenge the stereotype of great dissents as those 'that soar with passion and ring with rhetoric . . . that, at their best, straddle the worlds of literature and law'.[46] To be sure, the Australian canon of dissent *does* have examples of that sort, most famously Justice Herbert Vere Evatt's heartfelt opinion in *Chester v Waverley Corporation*, discussed in chapter 4.[47] But far more commonly disagreement is expressed with simple, we might even say quiet, effectiveness. Two otherwise sharply contrasting examples in the collection demonstrate this point. In chapter 9, Justice Ninian Stephen's dissent in *Henry v Boehm* from the Court's neutered interpretation of the constitutional guarantee of freedom from discrimination on the basis of state residency was delivered with zero theatricality.[48] This reflected the author's general sentiment that it was 'not a matter of great zeal and enthusiasm that my view should prevail'.[49] Yet prevail his dissent ultimately did, receiving unanimous vindication on the next occasion the High Court considered the question.[50] The tone of Stephen J's opinion is not markedly distinct from the dissent celebrated in chapter 15, that of Justice Dawson in *Langer v Commonwealth*.[51] In that case, Dawson J was not seeking to break away from the constitutional mainstream, but rather to urge a consistent application of a newly developed principle that in earlier decisions he had gone so far as to reject. The opinion has not been later approved, and as the authors of that chapter surmise, is most unlikely ever to be so. In their specific features and later influence the two dissents could not be more different, but they share at least this: they eschew the clichéd image of a 'great dissent' as a self-consciously radical act.

Where Hutchinson's reflection on greatness serves this collection better is his more straightforward statement that great judges 'are not afraid to take a stance and will not always get it right . . . Even if their views do not always prevail or carry the day entirely, they manage by dint of their example and efforts to change the legal world and the way others think

[45] Murray Gleeson, *The Rule of Law and the Constitution* (ABC Books, 2000) 136.
[46] Justice W J Brennan, 'In Defense of Dissents' (1986) 37 *Hastings Law Journal* 427, 431.
[47] (1939) 62 CLR 1. [48] (1973) 128 CLR 482.
[49] Stephen J quoted in Michael Coper, *Encounters with the Australian Constitution* (CCH, 1987) 152.
[50] *Street v Queensland Bar Association* (1989) 168 CLR 461. [51] (1996) 186 CLR 302.

about the judicial role'.[52] That claim, neutral as it is on matters of style, is a more accommodating idea and transposes easily to the specific topic of judicial dissent. So far as that view connects judicial greatness with a willingness to forge one's own path or resist the pull of conformity then dissent offers the clearest manifestation of this. But Hutchinson also refers to the change that the individual effectuates through his or her independence, a consideration that arose in the earlier mention of posterity. It is time now to consider impact.

IV Vindication, Influence and Importance

To be a great dissent, an opinion must hold some future importance. It may never be agreed with but it cannot be ignored. This is even true of what is probably the most controversial inclusion in this collection, the dissent of Chief Justice John Latham in the High Court's most iconic decision, *Australian Communist Party v Commonwealth*.[53] In chapter 6, George Williams acknowledges that Latham CJ's dissent 'has been eclipsed by the brilliance of the majority position', but suggests that it remains important in offering essentially a counter-factual of what might have been had the *Communist Party Dissolution Act 1950* (Cth) been upheld. In other words, the dissent remains relevant in underscoring the correctness of the majority decision. The preference for some aspects of Latham CJ's dissent that was expressed by Justice Ian Callinan over 50 years later only shows that the opinion has not disappeared from view.[54]

The question of a dissent's potential influence over the later development of the law will never be more lyrically expressed than by the United States' Chief Justice Evan Hughes:

> A dissent in a court of last resort is an appeal to the brooding spirit of the law, to the intelligence of a future day, when a later decision may possibly correct the error into which the dissenting judge believes the court to have been betrayed.[55]

In *Federation Insurance Limited v Wasson*, a joint judgment of the High Court echoed this view by saying that a 'dissenting judge will often see his or her judgment as an appeal to the brooding spirit of the law, waiting for

[52] Hutchinson, above n 41, 14. [53] (1951) 83 CLR 1.
[54] *Thomas v Mowbray* (2007) 233 CLR 307, 484–6.
[55] Charles E Hughes, *The Supreme Court of the United States* (Columbia University Press, 1928) 68.

judges in future cases to discover its wisdom'.[56] To imagine dissent as an appeal to 'the intelligence of a future day' is one thing, but to talk of it as judicial prophecy, of which there is a rich tradition in the United States,[57] obscures the important role which the dissent itself may play in prompting a later change in the law.[58] It seems preferable to describe dissents, where appropriate, as 'foreshadows of the law'[59] or 'prescient',[60] than as acts of prophecy.

Even then, taken as a whole this collection suggests that ultimate and unambiguous vindication is far from an essential criterion when looking for greatness in Australian dissents. Only in chapter 9 of this book does the express and lasting vindication of a dissent see the reversal of the court's earlier decision. Some other dissents have enjoyed later adoption but they in turn have fallen victim to new winds of change or are presently under siege from critics. Fascinating examples are provided in chapters 5 and 8, and in chapter 13 Jeremy Gans charts the rise and fall of judicial opinion on key aspects of the criminal trial over almost a century. Other dissenting views have been woven into the fabric of the law almost by stealth – either because they have, over time, emerged from the chaos of an earlier case with no clear majority, as chapter 10 argues in respect of Mason J's influential opinion in the *Australian Assistance Plan Case*,[61] or because lower courts have been cautious about being seen to depart from the majority decision in favour of a view that was expressed in dissent. The latter is notable in the subsequent treatment of Murphy J's dissent on public interest standing, considered in chapter 11, and Mason J's account of the essence of a fiduciary relationship in dissent in *Hospital Products Ltd v United States Surgical Corporation*, discussed in chapter 12.

However, most of the time, the spirit of the law continues to brood rather than act. Some of the dissents in this book may yet meet with a favourable, albeit delayed, reception. As an examination of a path in the law that was not taken, chapter 16's consideration of Justice Anthony North's dissent in the Federal Court of Australia on native title extinguishment highlights the lost opportunities in this contentious area, so

[56] (1987) 163 CLR 303, 314 (Mason CJ, Wilson, Dawson and Toohey JJ).

[57] Barth, above n 27; Felix Frankfurter, 'Mr Justice Holmes and the Constitution – A Review of his Twenty-Five Years on the Supreme Court' (1927) 41 *Harvard Law Review* 121, 162; Percival E Jackson, *Dissent in the Supreme Court – A Chronology* (1969) 3.

[58] See Tushnet, above n 34, 99.

[59] Donald E Lively, *Foreshadows of the Law – Supreme Court Dissents and Constitutional Development* (Praeger, 1992).

[60] Coper and Williams, above n 18.

[61] *Victoria v Commonwealth* (1975) 134 CLR 338.

critical to Australia's relationship with its Indigenous peoples and to redressing their dispossession by colonisation. The chapter concludes by noting recent signs that the High Court may turn back from the path upon which it set in the case of *Western Australia v Ward* over a decade ago.[62] Whether the Court will head in the direction that was signalled by North J or develop some other route remains to be seen. But it is not hard to appreciate that the existence of a clearly stated alternative may enrich the Court's reassessment of the previously dominant approach.

A quite different role is played by the joint dissent of Dixon and Evatt JJ in *R v Federal Court of Bankruptcy; Ex parte Lowenstein*,[63] which is considered in chapter 3. That opinion has been followed, but only by later dissenters who shared its authors' rejection of the orthodox interpretation of the right to trial by jury in section 80 of the *Commonwealth Constitution*. Successive majorities have not been swayed from their acceptance of the traditional view. But the stream of dissent has had an influence all the same, prodding the defenders of the status quo to give a better account of their position. This cannot have been the ambition of the dissenting Justices, and looks like defeat rather than vindication, but in this way their dissents have exerted a positive influence. In their failure, there is still greatness to be found, if only because it offers such a strong illustration of the value of judicial disagreement.

The path not taken is also a feature of the dissents in chapters 2 and 14. In the relevant cases, the Court fractured over a question of the judges' fundamental constitutional vision. These are not small disagreements; the dissents present a challenging alternative. In chapter 2, Justice Edmund Barton's conception of judicial power in Chapter III of the *Commonwealth Constitution* is revisited a century after his opinion was delivered. Given the contemporary dissatisfaction with the complexity of Chapter III jurisprudence and its oft-noted practical inconvenience, Barton J's principled yet pragmatic commitment to legal pluralism rather than formalist rigidity holds strong appeal to modern readers. As chapter 14 shows, the joint dissent of Justices William Deane and John Toohey in *Leeth v Commonwealth* features its own highly original vision – of a constitutional principle of equality that would be supported through judicial review.[64] Amelia Simpson reviews the vitriolic reaction to the boldness of that vision before defending the opinion as a clear instance of the value of dissent as 'crucial to the vitality of common law courts' dialectical and transparent approach to decision making'. Considerable odds are stacked

[62] (2002) 213 CLR 1. [63] (1938) 59 CLR 556. [64] (1992) 174 CLR 455.

against the redemption of either of these dissents, but this does not negate the fact that both possess a certain grandeur as articulations of a parallel constitutional future. As such, their vindication would indeed be a triumph, but at the same time it would augment rather than establish their greatness.

V Great *Australian* Dissents

Having spoken to both the identification of opinions as 'dissents' and the diverse ways in which 'greatness' may be understood, it would be remiss to ignore the third basic qualifying criterion – that these are *Australian* dissents. As already noted, while one of the opinions is not delivered in an Australian case, all are authored by Australian judges and we may say, recognising the Privy Council's place at one time in the Australian court hierarchy, in an Australian court. That might be thought sufficient, but it is possible to argue that there are specific national characteristics discernible in these dissents.

Consider, for instance, Peta Stephenson's discussion of Mason J's opinion in the *Australian Assistance Plan Case* on the scope of the executive power of the Commonwealth as the national government in the Australian federation. Stephenson places this dissent firmly in the historical context of the loosening of Australia's ties to the United Kingdom in the final decades of the 20th century. Another example is provided by Sean Brennan's focus on judicial disagreement in native title law, as the courts confront the reverberations of the *Mabo* decision[65] – a unique legal, social and cultural turning point for Indigenous Australians and their relationship with the state.

Different evidence of an Australian sensibility appears in Evatt J's evocation of the settler's dread of losing a child in the bush in his dissent awarding Mrs Chester damages for nervous shock upon the death of her son. Barbara McDonald discusses '"the lost child" as a recurring motif in Australian literature' and artworks in her reflection on Evatt J's dissent. This aspect of the national psyche also goes a long way to explaining the Australian public's fascination with the legal ordeal of Lindy and Michael Chamberlain following the tragic taking of their daughter Azaria by a dingo at Uluru in 1980. In chapter 13, Jeremy Gans contrasts the three very different minority views in the Chamberlains' unsuccessful High Court appeal against conviction.

[65] *Mabo v Queensland [No 2]* (1992) 175 CLR 1.

More generally, it should be very apparent from the discussion above that the dissents assembled here are of a different ilk from those which might comprise a similar collection in another country. This is most obviously so when one considers the opinions that regularly feature in American compilations of 'great dissents'.[66] There are a number of reasons for this. One already canvassed is simply the different practices of judgment delivery between the two jurisdictions and one effect of seriatim opinions being often to render the writing of a dissent a far less deliberate and self-conscious exercise than in the United States. This in part seems to account for differences in style and tone. But additionally, the centrality of the Bill of Rights in America's political and social discourse ensures that many of the Supreme Court's decisions are assured of a much wider audience outside the Court and beyond the particular parties to litigation. The dominance of rights questions before the Court lends itself to grand rhetoric and invests many decisions, concerned as they often are with protest, religion, race, sex, life and death, with an obvious dramatic potential.

The Australian setting and mood is different. But it is a mistake to assume that by comparison it is dull. Despite the lack of a national bill of rights supported by judicial review, many of the cases in this book squarely concern civil liberties – the freedoms of political speech and association, protection from indefinite detention by the state, freedom from discrimination, and the right to trial by jury. Others focus on the rights of the accused in criminal proceedings. The deeper distinction with the United States lies in the more subtle, even elusive, way that judicial disagreement in Australia exerts an influence upon the law. This undoubtedly makes for less theatricality as a general rule and, as a consequence, dissent is not so heavily mythologised in Australian legal culture.[67] This is despite the fact that the rate of dissent in the High Court over the last four decades has been more on par with that of the United States Supreme Court than with the final courts of Canada, South Africa and the United Kingdom.[68] This book amply demonstrates that the more subdued complexity and variety

[66] See Barth, above n 27; Lively, above n 59; Schwartz, above n 21; Tushnet, above n 34; and Urofsky, above n 11.

[67] The same appears true in the United Kingdom where collections of significant dissenting opinions also bear little resemblance to the many American examples of the genre: see Neal Geach and Chris Monaghan, *Dissenting Judgments in the Law* (Wildy, Simmonds and Hill Publishing, 2012); and Frederick Reynold, *Disagreement and Dissent in Judicial Decision-making* (Wildy, Simmonds and Hill Publishing, 2013).

[68] Paterson, above n 6, 113.

of judicial dissent in Australia is no less fascinating than the American experience.

VI Matters of Opinion – and Omission

Lastly, it is necessary to acknowledge that this book is obviously the product of the subjective opinions of its many contributors – they have chosen the dissents they wish to champion. Adopting a collective approach seemed a more robust way of devising such a list than through selection by a single author – which risks idiosyncrasy or repetition of the 'usual suspects'.[69] But inevitably, with the compilation of any list, there will be inclusions that some dispute and omissions that others decry. Stimulating debate about both is not unintended.

That said, at the workshop at which contributors presented and discussed earlier drafts of these chapters, there was discussion of particular opinions that could easily also be included in the pantheon of great Australian dissents. Amongst these were the minority opinions of Justices Isaacs and Higgins that were spectacularly vindicated in the High Court's pivotal decision on constitutional interpretation in *Amalgamated Society of Engineers v Adelaide Steamship Co Ltd*.[70] The memorable dissents, over several cases in the early 1980s but culminating in *Commonwealth v Tasmania* ('*Tasmanian Dams Case*'),[71] objecting to the expansion of the Commonwealth's powers to make laws with respect to corporations and external affairs were also noted as strong contenders for inclusion, as was Justice McHugh's dissent on the *persona designata* exception to the separation of judicial power in *Grollo v Palmer* in 1995.[72] The vast dissent of Callinan J in *New South Wales v Commonwealth* ('*Work Choices Case*') – the longest opinion in the history of the Court – was also recognised as one with a claim to greatness, if only for its elegiac quality.[73] At a different time and with different contributors, these and other dissents might just as likely appear on a list of this kind.

Saying that in no way diminishes the claims that are made for the opinions that are featured in the chapters that follow. On the contrary, it emphasises that their nomination has been hard won and not without some agonising. The collection is a rich and diverse one – spanning almost a century of legal decisions with only the 1900s and the 1920s unrepresented. While, as might be anticipated, the bulk of the dissents

[69] The latter danger is illustrated by the titles above n 66. [70] (1920) 28 CLR 129.
[71] (1983) 158 CLR 1. [72] (1995) 184 CLR 348. [73] (2005) 229 CLR 1.

are found in the decisions of the High Court, three other courts each contribute an opinion – the Privy Council, the Supreme Court of South Australia and the Federal Court of Australia. Only three dissenting judges appear on the list more than once – Justices Dixon, Mason and Murphy.

Ultimately, there is enormous variety in the Australians dissents gathered here and presented as great. It is impossible to view them as limited – whether as the product of particular judicial personalities, or to a specific era in Australian legal history, or as displaying a certain rhetorical or self-conscious style, or to having a similar effect upon the law's subsequent development. No two dissents are the same in even essential respects, excepting one common characteristic: they are not forgotten. Just why that is so I leave to the authors of each chapter to explain. But as a collection, the greatness of these dissents undoubtedly lies not only in their continued significance years after the cases that gave rise to them, but also in what they tell us about the work of Australian courts and the important benefits that judicial disagreement has brought to the evolution of Australian law.

2

Justice Barton and the Demise of the Inter-State Commission in the *Wheat Case* (1915)

OSCAR ROOS

I Introduction

Justice Isaacs, for one, was in no doubt about the significance of *New South Wales v Commonwealth* ('*Wheat Case*').[1] He commenced his reasons in the case by acknowledging that: 'Questions of vast importance present themselves for consideration'.[2] What proceeds from that opening sentence is one of the most significant judgments in the High Court's history, seminal in the development of the modern doctrine of the separation of powers. However, a century later, it is the minority judgment in the *Wheat Case* of a far less feted member of the High Court, Justice Edmund Barton, which deserves to be celebrated as a great Australian dissent.

A Barton dissent was, of itself, a rare event; a far more typical Barton judgment was a brief concurrence with Griffith CJ, contributing to a probably undeserved reputation for judicial indolence.[3] While 'Tosspot Toby', as Barton was colloquially known, may have lacked Sir Isaac Isaacs' intellectual fervour, this chapter seeks to demonstrate that in the *Wheat Case* he was correct, in terms of the original meaning of the *Constitution*, about two related and important constitutional issues that have had an enormous impact upon High Court litigation. The first of those issues concerns the role of the Inter-State Commission ('ISC') and s 92 of the *Constitution*, and the second concerns the separation of powers.

1 (1915) 20 CLR 54. 2 Ibid 82.

3 Geoffrey Bolton and John Williams, 'Barton, Edmund' in Tony Blackshield, Michael Coper and George Williams (eds), *The Oxford Companion to the High Court of Australia* (Oxford University Press, 2001) 54; Sir Anthony Mason, 'Reflections on the High Court: Its Judges and Judgments' (2013) 37 *Australian Bar Review* 102, 103; Robert G Menzies, 'Foreword' in John Reynolds, *Edmund Barton* (Angus and Robertson, 1948) vii–ix. See also *Official Record of the Debates of the Australasian Federal Convention*, Melbourne, 27 January 1898, 213 (Edmund Barton).

However, this chapter does not argue that Barton J's dissent in the *Wheat Case* is great merely because it, and not the majority judgments, delivers on the basic hermeneutic premise of the entire Court that the *Constitution* should be interpreted in accordance with the intentions of its framers.[4] Nor is this chapter a simple lament for the constitutional lost opportunity of the ISC – history records that the *Wheat Case* eviscerated the ISC and it was effectively disbanded by 1920,[5] the year of Barton's death. Rather, this chapter argues that Barton J's dissent serves as a testament to the historical realities underlying the separation of judicial power in Chapter III of the *Constitution* and provides a foundation for a more flexible and coherent approach to a separation of powers principle which has rarely been questioned.[6]

II The *Wheat Case*

The Inter-State Commission Act 1912 *(Cth)*

Section 101 of the *Constitution* provides that:

> There shall be an Inter-State Commission, with such powers of adjudication and administration as the Parliament deems necessary for the execution and maintenance, within the Commonwealth, of the provisions of this *Constitution* relating to trade and commerce, and of all laws made thereunder.

In 1912 the Commonwealth Parliament exercised what it believed to be its powers under s 101 and enacted the *Inter-State Commission Act 1912* (Cth) ('*ISC Act*') to set up the ISC. It was clearly intended to be both an administrative body and a court.[7] The ISC was simultaneously given broad investigatory powers under pt III of the *ISC Act* and judicial powers under pt V. Specifically, under pt V the ISC was constituted under s 23 as a court of record with jurisdiction 'to hear and determine any complaint, dispute or question . . . on any matter arising as to' a range of matters relating to inter-state trade and commerce.[8] It had the power to award damages,

[4] *Wheat Case* (1915) 20 CLR 54, 62 (Griffith CJ), 71, 73–6, 79 (Barton J) 83–4, 88, 90, 93 (Isaacs J), 103–4 (Gavan Duffy J), 106 (Powers J), 109–10 (Rich J).

[5] Michael Coper, 'The Second Coming of the Fourth Arm: The Role and Functions of the Inter-State Commission' (1989) 63 *Australian Law Journal* 731, 734.

[6] See James Stellios, 'Reconceiving the Separation of Judicial Power' (2011) 22 *Public Law Review* 113, 114.

[7] See, eg, Commonwealth, *Parliamentary Debates*, House of Representatives, 13 December 1912, 7066 (William Hughes).

[8] *ISC Act* s 24.

issue injunctions, declare a state regulation void, and impose summary fines for disobedience of its orders made within its jurisdiction.[9] Section 35 provided for an order of the ISC to be made and enforced as an order of the High Court and, under s 36, the ISC was generally conferred with the powers, right and privileges of the High Court.

The Constitutional Challenge

The constitutional validity of pt V of the *ISC Act* was challenged in the *Wheat Case.* Pursuant to powers vested in him by the *Wheat Acquisition Act 1914* (NSW) ('*NSW Act*'), the New South Wales Inspector-General of Police confiscated several quantities of wheat in New South Wales which were to be delivered to purchasers in Victoria. The Commonwealth alleged that the *NSW Act* violated s 92 and went to the ISC seeking an injunction. The ISC found that the *NSW Act* was constitutionally invalid, granted the injunction and ordered the defendants to pay the Commonwealth's costs.[10]

New South Wales and the New South Wales Inspector-General then appealed to the High Court and argued that pt V of the *ISC Act* was invalid. In the High Court it was not disputed that the *ISC Act* constituted the ISC as a court exercising both judicial and executive powers;[11] the question was whether the existence of such a hybrid body was constitutionally permissible.

The High Court found that the *NSW Act* did not breach s 92 of the *Constitution* and that consequently no injunction should have been issued by the ISC. On that question, the Court was unanimous; this chapter is not concerned with that aspect of its decision. The ongoing significance of the *Wheat Case* rests primarily on what the Court said about the Parliament's power to constitute the ISC as a court and the separation of judicial power in Chapter III more generally. It is on those issues that Barton J dissented with Gavan Duffy J, from a majority made up of Griffith CJ, Isaacs, Powers and Rich JJ all writing separately.

The Majority Judgments

The majority invalidated the whole of pt V of the *ISC Act.* In summarising the four majority judgments, it is necessary to distinguish between

[9] Ibid ss 30–4. [10] *Wheat Case* (1915) 20 CLR 54, 56.
[11] Ibid 82–3 (Isaacs J), 101 (Gavan Duffy J), 106 (Powers J), 110 (Rich J).

the narrower institutional question which fell to be determined, that is, whether the Parliament has the capacity under s 101 to constitute the ISC as a court, and the broader abstract question of whether the 'general frame of the *Constitution*'[12] embodies a separation of powers which prevents the Parliament from vesting judicial power in bodies which are not courts. On the narrow question, the majority Justices arrived at their conclusion that s 101 did not permit the Parliament to constitute the ISC as a court primarily by reference to the text of s 101, and the context provided by s 103 and Chapter III.

In relation to the text of s 101, the majority argued that (a) the expression 'powers of adjudication' in s 101 was ambiguous,[13] such that it did not stamp the ISC with the character of a court;[14] and (b) the 'dominant words in s 101 were "the execution and maintenance of the provisions of the *Constitution* relating to trade and commerce and of all laws made thereunder"'[15] and that those words were 'practically a repetition of the phraseology of s 61',[16] indicating that the ISC could only exercise a subset of the Commonwealth's general executive powers under s 61.[17]

In relation to the context provided by s 103 and Chapter III, the majority argued that the ISC could not be a federal court because (a) Chapter III was exhaustive, in that no 'excrescent court of justice'[18] could exist outside of it;[19] (b) there was a 'marked distinction'[20] between s 72 of the *Constitution*, which places no temporal limit on the tenure of Justices of 'other courts created by the Parliament', and s 103, which imposed a seven-year term on ISC Commissioners;[21] and (c) s 73 made separate provision for appeals from the ISC, as opposed to appeals from a 'federal court', and limited appeals from the ISC to questions of law.[22]

If one excludes the slight contribution of Powers J from consideration, support for a broader separation of powers doctrine is only found in the judgments of Isaacs J and Rich J. Both emphasised the separate vesting of legislative, executive and judicial powers in Chapters I, II and III of the *Constitution*. However, for Rich J it was merely 'a clear distinction – well known in all British communities',[23] such that the creation of a 'body which might at once be an executive department and a court of

[12] Ibid 88 (Isaacs J). [13] Ibid 63–4 (Griffith CJ), 83–7 (Isaacs J), 109 (Rich J).
[14] Ibid 63–4 (Griffith CJ), 87 (Isaacs J). [15] Ibid 92–3 (Isaacs J).
[16] Ibid 91 (Isaacs J). See also at 93 (Isaacs J).
[17] Ibid 62–4 (Griffith CJ), 92–3 (Isaacs J) 109–10 (Rich J). [18] Ibid 94 (Isaacs J).
[19] Ibid 62 (Griffith CJ), 89, 93 (Isaacs J). [20] Ibid 109 (Rich J).
[21] Ibid 62 (Griffith CJ), 93 (Isaacs J), 109 (Rich J). But see at 107 (Powers J).
[22] Ibid 110 (Rich J). See also at 62 (Griffith CJ), 87–8, 90 (Isaacs J). [23] Ibid 108.

law'[24] would be 'curiously anomalous'.[25] By contrast, Isaacs J conflated the narrow and broad questions distinguished above[26] to go much further, and he did so by making overtly originalist claims. He inferred from the triadic distribution of power in Chapters I, II and III that the framers intended to embody the 'manifest aim and object of the constitutional separation of powers'[27] as 'the fundamental structure and scheme of the *Constitution*'[28] and its 'dominant principle of demarcation'.[29]

The asserted ambiguity in s 101 did not therefore indicate:

> 'uncertainty about general principle, but to that difficulty in obtaining ready agreement about phrases which attends the drafting of legislative measures by large assemblages'. When the fundamental principle of the separation of powers as marked out in the *Australian Constitution* is observed and borne in mind, it relieves the question of much of its obscurity.[30]

Consequently, 'Chapter III . . . vests the judicial power of the Commonwealth . . . in specific organs, namely Courts strictly so called'[31] such that 'the distinct command of the *Constitution* is that whatever judicial power . . . is to be exerted in the name of the Commonwealth must be exercised by these strictly so called judicial tribunals'.[32] This principle was subsequently confirmed as the 'first limb of the *Boilermakers* doctrine',[33] after the High Court's iconic 1956 decision of *R v Kirby; Ex parte Boilermakers' Society of Australia* ('*Boilermakers*').[34]

Justice Barton's Dissent

Justice Barton and Gavan Duffy J, in separate dissents, found that s 101 did allow the Parliament to constitute the ISC as a court and that pt V of the *ISC Act* was wholly valid. Of the two opinions, it is Barton J's that bears the authority of a key framer of the *Constitution* and which contains

[24] Ibid 109. [25] Ibid. [26] Ibid 83, 88. Cf at 110 (Rich J).

[27] Ibid 93. [28] Ibid. [29] Ibid 90.

[30] Ibid 88, quoting the Privy Council in *John Deere Plow Co Ltd v Wharton* [1915] AC 330, 338.

[31] Ibid 89. [32] Ibid 89–90.

[33] Gabrielle Appleby, 'Imperfection and Inconvenience: Boilermakers and the Separation of Judicial Power in Australia' (2012) 31 *University of Queensland Law Journal* 265, 267.

[34] (1956) 94 CLR 254. See especially at 270–1, 277 (Dixon CJ, McTiernan, Fullagar and Kitto JJ). See generally Fiona Wheeler, 'The Boilermakers Case' in H P Lee and George Winterton (eds), *Australian Constitutional Landmarks* (Cambridge University Press, 2003) 160.

the most powerful alternative account of the constitutional role of the ISC and of Chapter III.[35]

Justice Barton disagreed with the majority in three respects. First, in relation to 'the true construction of [s 101], considered by itself',[36] he maintained that s 101 did not require the ISC's 'powers of adjudication' to be subordinated to its 'powers . . . of administration'. Rather, both powers could be exercised by the ISC 'as the Parliament deems necessary for a particular and specific purpose, namely, the execution and maintenance with the Commonwealth of the trade and commerce provisions of the *Constitution* and of all valid laws made by virtue of these provisions'.[37] Second, in relation to s 103, Barton J argued that the difference between the terms and conditions of appointment of ISC Commissioners under s 103 and those of federal judges under s 73 did not indicate that the ISC could not be established as a court.[38]

Third, in relation to the 'controlling context' of Chapter III, Barton J observed that:

> Chapter III relates to the composition, attributes and functions of the general judiciary, whether the tribunal in question be . . . the High Court, or some other federal court created by the Parliament, or any other court not created by Parliament, but invested by it with federal jurisdiction.[39]

He then stated that 'the general judiciary system of the Commonwealth' established under Chapter III 'has no relation to tribunals instituted or appointed for special purposes and confined in their jurisdiction to the enforcement and upholding of any special and limited class of laws'.[40]

III Original Meaning – Why Justice Barton Was Right

It is unsurprising that Barton J dissented in the *Wheat Case* and, according to one of his biographers, reacted to the majority's decision with dismay.[41] He had been involved in the disputes between the pre-1901 colonies over trade and tariff policies and cherished the ISC as a 'new province for law and order'.[42] In a speech delivered as Prime Minister-designate on 17 January 1901, Barton had described the ISC as a 'body next in importance to High Court' and observed that 'these two great

[35] Cf *Wheat Case* (1915) 20 CLR 54, 103 (Gavan Duffy J). [36] Ibid 71.
[37] Ibid 70. See also at 101–2 (Gavan Duffy J).
[38] Ibid 76. See also at 103 (Gavan Duffy J).
[39] Ibid 72. See also at 103 (Gavan Duffy J). [40] Ibid 73.
[41] Geoffrey Bolton, *Edmund Barton* (Allen & Unwin, 2000) 319. [42] Ibid.

tribunals will give confidence to citizens everywhere that justice will be secured to them';[43] it was the Barton ministry that in 1901 introduced into the Parliament the first, ill-fated Bill to establish the ISC.[44] Justice Barton's disappointment with the *Wheat Case* decision also had considerable justification as a matter of legal principle: he was right, in terms of the *Constitution*'s original meaning, in relation to each of the three issues about which he disagreed with the majority. The first two of these are focused on the narrower, institutional question concerning the ISC specifically, while the third is focused more broadly on the scope and significance of Chapter III and the separation of powers.

Sections 101 and 103

Professor Colin Howard was characteristically blunt in his assessment of the way the majority in the *Wheat Case* interpreted the expression 'powers of adjudication' in s 101 to invalidate pt V of the *ISC Act*: 'The court disposed of this invasion of its own area of interest by deciding that s 101 did not mean what it said'.[45] Even if it is conceded that there is some slight ambiguity in the *literal* meaning of the expression 'powers of adjudication',[46] the contextual evidence provided by ss 73 and 103 of the *Constitution*, the Convention Debates[47] and other contemporaneous materials[48] make it clear that it contemplated the establishment of the ISC as a court.

The framers understood that the United States Inter-State Commission was not a 'judicial body' with the power to enforce its decisions[49] and,

[43] Andrew Bell, 'Inter-State Commission' in Blackshield, Coper and Williams (eds), above n 3, 353.

[44] Bolton, above n 41, 243.

[45] Colin Howard, *Australia's Constitution* (Penguin, 1985) 40.

[46] *Wheat Case* (1915) 20 CLR 54, 63–4 (Griffith CJ), 83–4 (Isaacs J), 101 (Gavan Duffy J).

[47] See, eg, *Official Record of the Debates of the Australasian Federal Convention*, Melbourne, 11 March 1898, 2277 (Richard O'Connor), 2281 (George Reid), 2282 (George Reid, Frederick Holder and Richard O'Connor), 2284 (Richard O'Connor), 2391 (George Reid); *Official Record of the Debates of the Australasian Federal Convention*, Melbourne, 16 March 1898, 2458 (Edmund Barton and Charles Kingston); *Official Record of the Debates of the Australasian Federal Convention*, Melbourne, 17 March 1898, 2503 (Alfred Deakin).

[48] See, eg, Sir John Quick and Robert Garran, *Annotated Constitution of the Commonwealth of Australia* (Angus & Robertson, 1901) 202, 899–900; A Inglis Clark, *Studies in Australian Constitutional Law* (Legal Books, first published 1901, 1997 ed) 186–8; W Harrison Moore, *The Constitution of the Commonwealth of Australia* (John Murray, 1902) 205–9, 280–1. Cf Sir W Harrison Moore, *The Constitution of the Commonwealth of Australia* (Sweet & Maxwell, 2nd ed, 1910) 574–6, 586.

[49] *Official Record of the Debates of the Australasian Federal Convention*, Melbourne, 11 March 1898, 2280–1 (Patrick Glynn and Frederick Holder).

in stark contradiction to the claims of Isaacs J,[50] specifically framed s 101 to avoid so limiting the powers of the ISC under the *Constitution* and rendering the ISC 'impotent'.[51] Consistently with their confidence in parliamentary supremacy, the framers gave 'the Parliament full power to declare what the duties of the Commission are'.[52] The first paragraph of s 73, which expressly embraced High Court appeals from the 'judgments, decrees, orders and sentences' of Chapter III courts and the ISC in a trio of subparagraphs, only confirms that the ISC could be established as a court.

Justice Barton was also right that the seven-year limit on the tenure of ISC Commissioners under s 103 did not indicate that the ISC could not be established as a court. As he tellingly observed, s 103 'is, save in one particular, couched in terms substantially, and almost verbally identical with those of s 72'.[53] Moreover, the Convention Debates reveal that the time limit was inserted into s 103 out of concern for 'needless expense'[54] if the 'necessity for the Commission died out',[55] not to detract from the ISC's potential status as a court.[56] The insertion of a time limit is consistent with what was then normal practice: specialist bodies were commonly established for limited periods to resolve specific problems.[57]

Chapter III and the 'General Judiciary'

The third point of disagreement between Barton J and the majority was on the broader questions about the design and separation of Chapter III. Justice Barton's claim that Chapter III relates to the composition,

50 *Wheat Case* (1915) 20 CLR 54, 92, 94.

51 *Official Record of the Debates of the Australasian Federal Convention*, Melbourne, 11 March 1898, 2281 (Frederick Holder). See also at 2282 (Henry Higgins, George Reid and Richard O'Connor), 2284 (Richard O'Connor).

52 Ibid 2394 (William McMillian). See also at 2394 (Edmund Barton); Moore (1902), above n 48, 207; Clark, above n 48, 188. Cf *Wheat Case* (1915) 20 CLR 54, 92, 109 (Rich J).

53 *Wheat Case* (1915) 20 CLR 54, 76.

54 *Official Record of the Debates of the Australasian Federal Convention*, Melbourne, 25 February 1898, 1530 (Edmund Barton).

55 Ibid 1531 (Edmund Barton).

56 Ibid 1529–32 (George Reid, Adye Douglas, Edmund Barton, Sir Edward Braddon and William Moore), 1534–5 (Adye Douglas, Edmund Barton and Sir George Turner); *Official Record of the Debates of the Australasian Federal Convention*, Melbourne, 16 March 1898, 2457–60 (Edmund Barton, Sir Edward Braddon and Josiah Symon), 2462 (Edmund Barton). See also *Official Report of the National Australasian Convention Debates*, Adelaide, 14 April 1897, 1114–17 (Sir William Zeal, Henry Dobson, Josiah Symon and Charles Grant).

57 Chantal Stebbings, *Legal Foundations of Tribunals in Nineteenth-Century England* (Cambridge, 2006) 102–3.

attributes and functions of the 'general judiciary' is corroborated by the text and structure of the *Constitution* read in its historical context.

'New Legal Pluralism' versus Legal Formalist Ideology

The late 19th century was marked by a contrast between the claims of constitutional theory and the offerings of legal reality. The reformist Parliaments which emerged in the 19th century were sensitive to the limitations of superior courts and the vested interests of the magistracy in responding to the appalling social problems which had emerged as a result of increased industrialisation, population and urbanisation.[58] Consequently, and as was noted in the *Wheat Case*,[59] from around the enactment of the *Factories Act 1833*[60] onwards, parliaments throughout the British Empire exercised their plenary powers of legislation to create a diversity of statutory dispute resolution bodies, or 'tribunals',[61] to achieve complex socio-economic public policy ends by flexible administrative means.[62] These tribunals were novel because, although there was a long history of the exercise of administrative functions by judicial bodies (notably by justices of the peace),[63] the judicial and administrative functions of those judicial bodies were internally distinct; by contrast, tribunals integrated their judicial and administrative functions, albeit that their powers of adjudication were exercised, unlike courts, to service their predominant administrative function.[64]

The tribunals of the 'new legal pluralism'[65] had a number of distinctive features. Typically, they had a subject-specific jurisdiction strictly

[58] H W Arthurs, *'Without the Law': Administrative Justice and Legal Pluralism in Nineteenth-Century England* (Toronto, 1985) 95, 101, 130, 140, 158–60; Stebbings, above n 57, 10–22, 27, 41–63, 74–6, 292–3, 314.

[59] (1915) 20 CLR 54, 63–4 (Griffith CJ), 70 (Barton) 84–6 (Isaacs J).

[60] 3 & 4 Will IV, c 103.

[61] As noted by Chantal Stebbings, the term 'tribunal' is not a term of art nor does it have a clear meaning in law: Stebbings, above n 57, 3, 71. In this chapter the term 'tribunal' is used (a) generally, to refer to any dispute-resolution body, other than 'regular' or 'ordinary' courts of law; and (b) specifically, in the Australian Commonwealth context, to refer to Commonwealth dispute-resolution bodies which are not Chapter III courts. It would therefore include the ISC and a number of the institutions of the so-called 'integrity branch', for which, see generally, A J Brown, 'The Integrity Branch: A "System", an "Industry", or a Sensible Emerging Fourth Arm of Government?' in Matthew Groves (ed), *Modern Administrative Law in Australia: Concepts and Context* (Cambridge, 2014) 301.

[62] Stebbings, above n 57, 5–7, 26–30, 74–5, 94–7, 103–4, 147.

[63] Ibid 279–80, 303.

[64] Ibid 148–51, 166–7, 173–4, 182, 255, 281, 294–6, 309.

[65] Arthurs, above n 58, 163–4.

circumscribed by statute[66] and were staffed (like the ISC)[67] with lay persons possessing expertise in the area of regulation.[68] They exercised their judicial functions 'without the law', that is, they administered 'their own particular statutory regime of law'[69] consisting of 'novel rules that were often technical and promulgated in the context of a clear social policy'[70] outside of many or all of the constraints of the common law.[71] That these tribunals often exercised judicial powers was not in doubt: members were bound by oath to act judicially;[72] tribunals passed sentence and inflicted penalties;[73] their decisions could be made as effective and binding as judicial decisions;[74] and some even had the power to punish for contempt.[75]

The specialist tribunals of the new legal pluralism were creatures of statute and their exercise of judicial powers was legitimised by a robust belief in parliamentary sovereignty.[76] However, the legal formalist ideology of the late Victorian period refused to incorporate the emergence of a new legal pluralism into its centralist paradigm of British constitutionalism and the rule of law. It extolled only the virtues of 'ordinary law' and the 'ordinary courts', with their theoretical monopoly on dispute resolution.[77] As Chantal Stebbings has observed, '[b]ecause the adjudicatory function of the tribunals was integral to administrative functions, and because administrative functions were strictly subject specific, the growth in adjudicative powers by organs of central government grew virtually unnoticed'.[78]

Given the influence of that formalist legal ideology at the time the *Constitution* was framed, one would expect the framers to be preoccupied with the establishment and constitutional independence of a 'general judiciary' in framing Chapter III; in short, tribunals were sunk below

66 Stebbings, above n 57, 279, 282, 285–6, 309, 331.

67 Coper, above n 5, 734.

68 Stebbings, above n 57, 39, 274–5, 282, 299, 309. See also H W Arthurs, 'Rethinking Administrative Law: A Slightly Dicey Business' (1979) 17 *Osgoode Hall Law Journal* 1, 33–5.

69 Stebbings, above n 57, 9. See also at 28, 276–9.

70 Ibid 39.

71 Ibid 44, 91, 171, 251–2, 254, 298–9, 316–17.

72 Ibid 299.

73 Ibid.

74 See, eg, *Local Government Board v Arlidge* [1915] AC 120. See also *Wheat Case* (1915) 20 CLR 54, 64–5 (Griffith CJ), 87, 94 (Isaacs J).

75 The Railway Commissioners under s 25 of the *Railway and Canal Traffic Act 1873* (UK) 36 & 37 Vict, c 48 and their successor, the Railway and Canal Commission, under s 18(1) of the *Railway and Canal Traffic Act 1888* (UK) 51 & 52 Vict, c 25. See also Stebbings, above n 57, 299.

76 See, eg, the United Kingdom Railway and Canal Commissioners and their successor, the Railway and Canal Commission, discussed in Stebbings, above n 57, 34.

77 Ibid 105–9. See Arthurs, above n 68, 11–14.

78 Stebbings, above n 57, 290.

'Dicey's Plimsoll Line'.[79] The framers' concern about maintaining the independence of Chapter III courts is also consistent with proposition that Chapter III had nothing to do with the work of tribunals in their specialist jurisdictions, as that work was seen as politicised and thus a threat to both the perception and reality of judicial independence.[80]

The Text and Structure of the Constitution

In terms of the text and structure of the *Constitution*, at least three provisions can be identified which expressly or impliedly empower the Parliament to create courts of specialist jurisdiction, namely s 47 concerning courts of disputed returns, s 51(xxxv) concerning courts of conciliation and arbitration, and s 101 concerning the ISC. All three provisions were placed outside of Chapter III.[81]

In terms of the text and structure of Chapter III itself, s 73 defines the High Court's appellate jurisdiction. This appellate jurisdiction was clearly modelled on that of the Judicial Committee of the Privy Council,[82] and in a series of cases in the second half of the 19th century the Privy Council had determined that it would not hear appeals when Parliament by statute 'was creating a new and unknown jurisdiction for the purpose of vesting in a particular court [a] very peculiar jurisdiction'.[83] This line of authority was adopted by the early High Court in 1906 in *Holmes v Angwin*[84] in dismissing an appeal from the Western Australian Supreme Court sitting as Court of Disputed Returns. The framers' assumption that s 73 was

79 Arthurs, above n 68, 14. (The 'Plimsoll Line', named after 19th century politician and social reformer, Samuel Plimsoll, is a load line on the hull of every cargo ship which indicates the maximum depth to which the ship can be safely and legally loaded). See, eg, *Official Record of the Debates of the Australasian Federal Convention*, Melbourne, 11 March 1898, 2284 (Richard O'Connor). See also *Official Record of the Debates of the Australasian Federal Convention*, Melbourne, 22 February 1898, 1265 (Henry Higgins); Moore (1902), above n 48, 281.

80 See, eg, *Official Record of the Debates of the Australasian Federal Convention*, Melbourne, 11 March 1898, 2283 (Josiah Symon).

81 See *Wheat Case* (1915) 20 CLR 54, 73 (Barton J).

82 See, eg, *Official Report of the National Australasian Convention Debates*, Sydney, 6 March 1891, 126–7 (Sir Patrick Jennings); *Official Report of the National Australasian Convention Debates*, Adelaide, 23 March 1897, 25 (Edmund Barton); *Official Report of the National Australasian Convention Debates*, Adelaide, 25 March 1897, 130 (Josiah Symon), 272–3 (George Reid); *Official Report of the National Australasian Convention Debates*, Adelaide, 31 March 1897, 369 (Edmund Barton); *Official Record of the Debates of the Australasian Federal Convention*, Melbourne, 4 March 1898, 1890–1 (Richard O'Connor).

83 *Théberge v Laudry* (1876) 2 App Cas 102. See, eg, *Moses v Parker* [1896] AC 245.

84 (1906) 4 CLR 297.

concerned only with appeals in general jurisdiction is also consistent with the insertion of subpara (iii) into the first paragraph of s 73 (which gives the High Court a specific jurisdiction to hear appeals on questions of law from the ISC), notwithstanding their clear assumption that the ISC could exercise judicial powers.[85]

Of course, the High Court also has an original jurisdiction, but it would strain the text and structure of Chapter III beyond breaking point to maintain that its original jurisdiction encompassed specialist jurisdiction if its appellate jurisdiction did not. The drawing of such a radical distinction runs against the grain of late 19th century legal thought, which placed *less* emphasis on the difference between appellate and original jurisdiction than is placed today.[86] It is also inconsistent with the opening section of Chapter III, s 71, which vests 'the judicial power *of the Commonwealth*' in the High Court and other Chapter III courts as a single conception, not as a hybrid. Moreover, and most importantly, in the 19th century, the exercise of judicial powers by tribunals was *not* perceived to be an exercise of, or a component of, the judicial power *of the state*;[87] rather, tribunals were firmly regarded as part of the executive branch of government.[88]

Chapter III and Tribunals

Justice Barton's statement that Chapter III 'has no relation to tribunals instituted or appointed for special purposes *and confined in their jurisdiction to the enforcement and upholding of any special and limited class of laws*' (emphasis added) is correct, in terms of the *Constitution*'s original meaning for two reasons.

First, it accurately describes the conventional legal relationship between courts of general jurisdiction and tribunals of specialist jurisdiction at the time the *Constitution* was framed. At the time the *Constitution* was framed generalist courts had no relationship with tribunals of specialist jurisdiction *provided that* those tribunals acted within their jurisdiction. Where tribunals transgressed their jurisdiction, it was well established that generalist superior courts would strive to confine them to their jurisdiction

85 See also *Official Record of the Debates of the Australasian Federal Convention*, Melbourne, 11 March 1898, 2279 (Richard O'Connor); Quick and Garran, above n 48, 202.

86 See generally Mark Leeming, *Authority to Decide: The Law of Jurisdiction in Australia* (Federation Press, 2012) 287–90.

87 Stebbings, above n 57, 106–7, 281, 288, 294–5, 297, 300, 306–10, 326, 329.

88 Ibid 8, 63, 229, 281, 288, 294–5, 297, 300, 304, 306, 308, 311, 313–14, 324–7, 334.

through the use of the prerogative writs.[89] Although privative clauses were a common feature of many of the Acts underpinning the new legal pluralism, by the latter part of the 19th century superior courts would almost invariably read those clauses down to ensure that they did not protect decisions made without jurisdiction, or at least those flawed by a 'manifest defect of jurisdiction'.[90] By contrast, the writ of certiorari for non-jurisdictional error had fallen into disuse.[91]

Second, the *Constitution* did not alter that relationship. The meaning of the expression 'to make laws for peace, order and good government', which introduces the heads of Commonwealth legislative power under s 51, is a conferral of legislative power 'as plenary and as ample . . . as the Imperial Parliament in the plenitude of its power possessed and could bestow'.[92] If the *Constitution* altered the conventional relationship between Chapter III courts, as generalist courts, and tribunals of specialist jurisdiction, such as to trench upon what would be the Parliament's plenary power to create specialist tribunals with judicial powers within its areas of legislative responsibility, it must have done so by implication, rather than express provision.

Implications which are inherent in the *Constitution* can be identified by their obviousness to the framers' contemporaneous audience imbued with general legal knowledge.[93] The Convention Debates and the evidence of the contemporaneous extrinsic materials on the separation of powers are so inconsistent and scant that it is impossible to identify any 'hard edged' implications inherent in the *Constitution* which limit the Parliament's powers to confer judicial powers on tribunals of specialist jurisdiction.[94]

89 Arthurs, above n 58, 147, 149.

90 Oscar I Roos, 'Accepted Doctrine at the Time of Federation and *Kirk v Industrial Court of New South Wales*' (2013) 35 *Sydney Law Review* 781, 795, 801–5.

91 Lisa Burton, 'Why Those Three? The Significance of the Selection of Remedies in Section 75(v) of the Australian Constitution' (2014) 42 *Federal Law Review* 253, 261–3.

92 *Hodge v The Queen* (1883) 9 App Cas 117, 132.

93 Jeffrey Goldsworthy, 'Implications in Language, Law and the Constitution' in Geoffrey Lindell (ed), *Future Directions in Australian Constitutional Law* (Federation Press, 1994) 168–70.

94 See, eg, *Official Report of the National Australasian Convention Debates*, Sydney, 3 April 1891, 688–9 (Charles Kingston and Sir Samuel Griffith); *Official Report of the National Australasian Convention Debates*, Sydney, 6 April 1891, 780–3 (Charles Kingston, Duncan Gillies and Sir Samuel Griffith), 785 (Charles Kingston); *Official Report of the National Australasian Convention Debates*, Adelaide, 17 April 1897, 782 (Henry Higgins), 790–1 (Josiah Symon and Charles Kingston); *Official Report of the National Australasian Convention Debates*, Adelaide, 22 April 1897, 1174–6 (Josiah Symon, Charles Kingston, Sir

Importantly, the fact that the framers laboured over the insertion of the ISC into Chapter IV of the *Constitution* does not establish the existence of an implication inherent in the *Constitution expressio unius est exclusio alterius* that no body outside of Chapter III, other than the ISC, could exercise judicial power. It cannot be concluded that such an implication was obvious to the framers' contemporaneous audience. The debates concerning the ISC were largely conducted without reference to the separation of powers, with opposition to the ISC focussed primarily 'on the view that the supervision of inter-State trade, railways and rivers should be left to the Federal Parliament'.[95] Also, the framers clearly contemplated that a body constituted under what became the industrial relations head of power (s 51(xxxv)) could exercise judicial power, notwithstanding that that provision was also placed outside of Chapter III.[96]

IV Why Justice Barton's Dissent Is Relevant Today

As Professor Michael Coper observed in 1989, the advent of the *Cole v Whitfield* free trade interpretation of s 92 means that the execution and maintenance of s 92 is particularly suited to the mixed investigatory and

George Turner and Isaac Isaacs); *Official Record of the Debates of the Australasian Federal Convention*, Melbourne, 27 January 1898, 182–3 (John Quick), 185–6 (Charles Kingston), 187–9 (Sir John Downer and Isaac Isaacs), 190–1 (Josiah Symon and Isaac Isaacs), 193 (William Trenwith), 197 (William Trenwith and Sir Joseph Abbott); *Official Record of the Debates of the Australasian Federal Convention*, Melbourne, 1 February 1898, 355–70 (Frederick Holder, Sir George Turner, Sir John Forrest, Richard O'Connor, Henry Higgins, William McMillan, George Reid, Sir John Downer, James Walker, Bernard Wise, William Trenwith, Alexander Peacock and Edmund Barton); *Official Record of the Debates of the Australasian Federal Convention*, Melbourne, 11 March 1898, 2341–3 (Frederick Holder, Henry Higgins and George Reid); Moore (1902), above n 48, 280–1. See also J M Finnis, *The Idea of Judicial Power, with Special Reference to Australian Law* (PhD Thesis, University of Oxford, 1965) 5.9; Fiona Wheeler, 'Original Intent and the Doctrine of the Separation of Powers in Australia' (1996) *Public Law Review* 96, 97–8.

95 J M Finnis, 'Separation of Powers in the Australian Constitution' (1968) 3 *Adelaide Law Review* 159, 172–3.

96 See, eg, *Official Report of the National Australasian Convention Debates*, Sydney, 9 March 1891, 164 (Charles Kingston); *Official Report of the National Australasian Convention Debates*, Sydney, 3 April 1891, 688–9 (Charles Kingston and Sir Samuel Griffith); *Official Report of the National Australasian Convention Debates*, Sydney, 6 April 1891, 780 (Charles Kingston); *Official Report of the National Australasian Convention Debates*, Adelaide, 17 April 1897, 782 (Henry Higgins); *Official Record of the Debates of the Australasian Federal Convention*, Melbourne, 25 January 1898, 182 (John Quick); *Official Record of the Debates of the Australasian Federal Convention*, Melbourne, 27 January 1898, 185 (Charles Kingston).

administrative powers of the ISC.[97] To that apposite blend, one can add the ISC's potential judicial powers. If ever there is a 'third coming of the fourth arm'[98] and the ISC is re-established as a body exercising judicial powers, the *Wheat Case* should be overruled in relation to the construction of s 101 specifically. Since *Cole v Whitfield* in 1988 the High Court has permitted the use of the Convention Debates as an extrinsic aid to constitutional interpretation and these reveal that Barton J's construction of s 101 was right. Consequently, even if the general principle that Chapter III precludes the exercise of judicial power by institutions which exist outside of it is to remain undisturbed, the powers of adjudication which can be conferred on the ISC by the Parliament under s 101 should operate as a specific exception to it.

However, Barton J's dissent is relevant today for reasons that go well beyond the resurrection of the ISC. While the case for the exercise of judicial powers by institutions outside of Chapter III is strongest in relation to the ISC – given s 101 and the constitutional safeguard of tenure provided by s 103 – the case can also be made that other specialist tribunals with strong statutory safeguards of independence should be able to exercise *some* judicial powers, if not the full panoply of judicial powers that the framers envisaged the ISC could exercise under s 101.

Chapter III and Constitutional Implications

As stated at the beginning of this chapter, it is Isaacs J's judgment in the *Wheat Case* which has been seminal in the development of the modern doctrine of separation of powers. As Professor John Finnis observed in 1965, by adhering to Isaac J's reasoning in the *Wheat Case* 'that the *Constitution* was intended to embody a three-way "dominant principle of demarcation" . . . the High Court has absolved itself from further inquiry into actual intentions'.[99] However, today it is increasingly difficult for the Court to shrug off that task, not only because the Court has lifted its embargo on the use of the Convention Debates, but also because the Court's contemporary pronouncements on constitutional implications and Chapter III call for such an inquiry. Moreover, the emergence of the fourth 'integrity branch of government'[100] (such as

[97] Coper, above n 5, 744–6. See *Cole v Whitfield* (1988) 165 CLR 360.

[98] The ISC's second coming has already been and gone: see generally Coper, above n 5, 747–50.

[99] Finnis, above n 94, 5.23–5.24.

[100] See generally Brown, above n 61.

the various independent commissions against corruption) unsettles the 'well-recognised dogma'[101] of triadic separation. As Professor A J Brown has observed, parliaments have deliberately granted a higher degree of independence to those 'fourth branch' institutions and (akin to the ISC) 'chosen, in those bodies, to create some unique mixing and blurring of what would otherwise be considered the three traditionally separate types of governmental power'.[102]

In 1997 in *Lange v Australian Broadcasting Corporation* the High Court stated that constitutional implications 'can validly extend only so far as is necessary to give effect . . . only to what is inherent in the text and structure of the *Constitution*'.[103] The Court has increasingly employed originalist reasoning in interpreting Chapter III.[104] In *South Australia v Totani* in 2010 French CJ went so far as to state that Chapter III implications are to be drawn from assumptions which are 'historical realities'.[105] The conclusion that Barton J was correct in the *Wheat Case* in terms of the original meaning of the *Constitution* should therefore prompt a reassessment of the absolute a priori rule that specialist tribunals cannot exercise judicial power. Bluntly put, Isaacs J's dogmatic claims about 'the fundamental scheme and structure of the *Constitution*' are 'tenuous and unreal'[106] and it is Barton J, not Isaacs J, who emerges as a far more reliable witness to 'historical realities'.[107] The first limb of the *Boilermakers'* doctrine is thus exposed by the veracity of Barton J's dissent as an implication which the Court has chosen to imply *into* the *Constitution*, as opposed a 'crucial foundation principle'[108] 'which is inferentially *expressed by* ss 1, 61 and 71 of the *Constitution*'.[109]

Significant consequences flow from this conclusion. If the a priori rule that only Chapter III courts can exercise judicial power is the product of judicial choices we should not pretend that those choices do not exist or

101 *R v Trade Practices Tribunal; Ex parte Tasmanian Breweries Pty Ltd* (1970) 123 CLR 361, 390 (Windeyer J).

102 Brown, above n 61, 314. 103 (1997) 189 CLR 520, 567.

104 See, eg, *Kirk v Industrial Court of New South Wales* (2010) 239 CLR 531.

105 (2010) 242 CLR 1, 37.

106 *Boilermakers'* (1956) 94 CLR 254, 274 (Dixon CJ, McTiernan, Fullagar and Kitto JJ).

107 It is conceded that subsequently in *Waterside Workers' Federation of Australia v J W Alexander Ltd* (1918) 25 CLR 434, 450, Barton J seemingly adopted the position of the *Wheat Case* majority. However, I maintain that the only plausible explanation for this shift is Barton J's commitment to *stare decisis*.

108 *Wilson v Minister for Aboriginal and Torres Strait Islanders Affairs* (1996) 183 CLR 1, 39 (Kirby J).

109 *Grollo v Palmer* (1995) 184 CLR 348, 376 (McHugh J) (emphasis added).

that they do not explain the rule's existence.[110] Moreover, we might insist that such 'spurious'[111] (or perhaps more felicitously 'judicial') implications are malleable and should only be inserted into the *Constitution* to the extent that it is necessary to achieve some constitutional purpose.[112] The general judicature was established under Chapter III for three purposes: first, to protect the federal compact; second, to protect individual legal rights; and, third, to provide a check on the other branches of the Commonwealth government.[113] Of those three purposes, the federal purpose does not require the judiciary to insert an implication into the *Constitution* excluding non-Chapter III institutions a priori from the exercise of judicial power as a matter of practical necessity.[114] As argued by Finnis, the only implication which can be *necessarily* inferred from federalism is that the High Court (or, at most, the general federal judicature) must be kept independent and free for purely judicial activities.[115] While it may be strongly arguable that the other two purposes justify the insertion of such an implication into Chapter III *in the absence of an entrenched minimum standard of judicial review of specialist tribunals*, the contemporary High Court decisions of *Plaintiff S157/2002 v Commonwealth* ('*Plaintiff S157*')[116] and *Kirk v Industrial Court of New South Wales* ('*Kirk*')[117] now remove the vital precondition of any such argument.

In *Plaintiff S157* the High Court declared that s 75 of the *Constitution* entrenched a minimum standard of judicial review of Commonwealth executive decision-making where the decision-maker is alleged to have made a jurisdictional error. Subsequently, in *Kirk* the Court endorsed a conception of jurisdictional error which 'is almost entirely functional: it is used to validate review when review is felt to be necessary'.[118] These two landmark decisions increase the power of judges and serve to consolidate what Ronald Sackville has described as an 'Age of Judicial Hegemony'.[119] However, they also render an inflexible a priori prohibition on specialist tribunals exercising judicial power undesirable, if judicial hegemony is to

[110] See Sir Anthony Mason, 'The Role of a Constitutional Court in a Federation: A Comparison of the Australian and the United States Experience' (1986) 16 *Federal Law Review* 1, 5.

[111] Jeffrey Goldsworthy, 'Constitutional Implications Revisited' (2011) 30 *University of Queensland Law Journal* 9, 18.

[112] Ibid 18–34. [113] Stellios, above n 6, 119–20.

[114] See generally Goldsworthy, above n 111, 20–1. [115] Finnis, above n 95, 167–8.

[116] (2003) 211 CLR 476. [117] (2010) 239 CLR 531.

[118] Ibid 570 (French CJ, Gummow, Hayne, Crennan, Kiefel and Bell JJ), quoting Louis Jaffe, 'Judicial Review: Constitutional and Jurisdictional Fact' (1957) 70 *Harvard Law Review* 953, 963.

[119] Ronald Sackville, 'An Age of Judicial Hegemony' (2013) 87 *Australian Law Journal* 105.

be kept in check, and militate in favour of a more commodious constitutional accommodation of those tribunals which builds on the historical realities identified in Barton J's dissent. The constitutional guarantee of a system of independent courts of general jurisdiction and an entrenched minimum standard of judicial review by those courts based on a 'functional' concept of jurisdictional error is likely to be sufficient to negate the risk that the second and third purposes of Chapter III will be defeated. This is the case, at least, where the tribunal's specialist jurisdiction does not undermine the general jurisdiction of Chapter III courts and the tribunal exercises its limited judicial powers with the statutory safeguard of a high degree of institutional independence. Moreover, the story of the ISC serves as a reminder of both the benefits that can flow from the conferral of a blend of judicial and non-judicial functions on specialist tribunals, and the disbenefits of the excessive judicial constriction of legislative ingenuity.

Lessons from History

The ISC was a product of the new legal pluralism of the 19th century which was, at very least, a qualified success in ameliorating the lives of those who were exploited during the industrial revolution. Despite that success, the new legal pluralism was met with sustained hostility by the established legal profession and the judges of the generalist courts, as well as by the vested economic interests it threatened.[120]

Perhaps the most pertinent example of this success is to be found in the regulation of the railways in the United Kingdom in the second half of the 19th century. From 1853 to 1872 jurisdiction over the railways was given to the generalist Court of Common Pleas and the Court's exercise of that jurisdiction was almost universally regarded as a failure. In 1873 the United Kingdom Parliament transferred the railway jurisdiction of the Court of Common Pleas to expert Railway Commissioners, who exercised a blend of administrative and judicial functions so successfully that in 1888 the Railway and Canal Commission was re-constituted as a superior court of record.[121]

Although the experience of railway regulation in the United Kingdom influenced the framing of s 101,[122] it is speculative to draw parallels

120 Arthurs, above n 58, 164–6.

121 See Stebbings, above n 57, 25, 34, 44–5, 56–7, 127, 134–7, 177–82, 194–6, 206–7, 223–7, 248, 267–8, 278, 287, 290, 298, 300, 324.

122 See Quick and Garran, above n 48, 896–900, 921–2; Moore (1902), above n 48, 205–7.

between that experience and the impact of the demise of the ISC on the interpretation and application of s 92 of the *Constitution* during the 20th century. What we do know is that the High Court eviscerated the ISC in 1915 contrary to the intentions of the framers and then, with its generalist legal expertise, 'thoroughly botched'[123] its self-arrogated adjudicative monopoly over s 92 for the next 70 years. If Barton J's dissent had prevailed, it would have left Parliament free to experiment with alternative ways in which to promote economic unity within the federal system under s 92. We also know that the a priori exclusion of all non-Chapter III decision-makers from the exercise of judicial power has come at a considerable cost. It is 'imperfect and inconvenient',[124] necessitating a focus on 'the issue of mere classification'[125] – the drawing of artificial, abstract and unsatisfactory distinctions between judicial and non-judicial powers and the contrivance of the 'chameleon doctrine'[126] – that distracts from the critical constitutional task of maintaining the strict *institutional* separation of the general judiciary.

Experience should therefore cause us to be cautious about the insertion of implications into Chapter III by judges which complicate and hamper the work of institutions which fall outside of it, lest we act on the same prejudices that motivated the legal profession in the 19th century. Although Barton J almost certainly assumed that Chapter III courts did not have an entrenched jurisdiction to review the decisions of specialist tribunals on the grounds of jurisdictional error,[127] it is his description of the relationship between them – that is, that there is no relation between Chapter III courts and specialist tribunals *confined to their jurisdiction* – and his robust appreciation of the value of specialist tribunals which more closely resembles what should be the new constitutional reality.

[123] See Jeffrey Goldsworthy, 'Australia: Devotion to Legalism' in Jeffrey Goldsworthy (ed), *Interpreting Constitutions: A Comparative Study* (Oxford, 2007) 106, 126.

[124] Appleby, above n 33, 286.

[125] James Stellios, *Zines's The High Court and the Constitution* (Federation Press, 6th ed, 2015) 331.

[126] See generally Appleby, above n 33, 265.

[127] See *Official Record of the Debates of the Australasian Federal Convention*, Melbourne, 4 March 1898, 1877, 1883–5 (Edmund Barton).

3

Unrequited but Still Great – The Dissent of Justices Dixon and Evatt in *R v Federal Court of Bankruptcy; Ex parte Lowenstein* (1938)

ANDREW LYNCH

I Introduction

Section 80 of the *Commonwealth Constitution* provides that 'trial on indictment of any offence against any law of the Commonwealth shall be by jury'. One of the most enduring debates in Australian constitutional law has been whether this constitutional guarantee amounts to a valuable 'right' to be tried by jury or whether it is little more than a hollow procedural requirement. Crucially, that divide has turned on the question of who determines whether a criminal offence is to be tried on indictment – that is by written accusation presented to the Court by the Crown. Is this simply Parliament's decision? Or are there criteria which may be used to objectively classify offences as ones to be tried on indictment, and in this way to distinguish them from those which may be tried summarily by a judge?

As judicial debates go, this one has been distinctly one-sided. The High Court has consistently interpreted s 80 as only requiring a jury when the Parliament decides to attract its operation by stipulating that a criminal offence is to be tried on indictment. Yet, as Bell J recently observed without exaggeration, this view has 'provoked some of the sharpest divisions among Justices of the High Court'.[1] Minority voices over successive generations of the Court have railed against the orthodoxy. The first and most powerful instance of this was in the decision of *R v Federal Court of Bankruptcy; Ex parte Lowenstein* ('*Lowenstein*').[2] Justices Dixon and Evatt, unquestionably the Court's intellectual leaders at the time, joined

[1] Justice Virginia Bell, 'Section 80 – The Great Constitutional Tautology' (2014) 40 *Monash University Law Review* 7, 7.
[2] (1938) 59 CLR 556.

together in dissent to dismiss the prevailing interpretation as a 'mockery' and to insist upon an operation for the provision which was independent of control by the legislature.

That opinion has echoed down through the years to inspire others to challenge the status quo. But it has never triumphed and now looks most unlikely to do so. How then, can any claim be made as to the greatness of the *Lowenstein* dissent? The answer to that question requires us to move beyond a simplistic understanding of judicial dissent as merely an alternative path in the law, the value of which is measured by whether the Court takes it up at some later moment in time. Instead, dissent may be an oppositional force that although unrequited exerts a positive influence upon the decision-making of the institution. The cases concerning the constitutional guarantee of trial by jury are a strong illustration of this phenomenon.

II The *Archdall* Orthodoxy – Exposition Unnecessary

Discerning the content of s 80 was unnecessary in the early case of *R v Bernasconi*,[3] yet Isaacs J signalled its future interpretation by pithily observing that the requirement of a jury trial would simply not apply 'if a given offence is not made triable on indictment at all'.[4]

This asserted capacity of the Parliament to itself determine which offences would be on indictment, and accordingly comply with s 80's requirement of a jury trial, received full affirmation in the later decision of *R v Archdall and Roskruge; Ex parte Carrigan and Brown* ('*Archdall*').[5] In that case the Court upheld sections of the *Crimes Act 1914* (Cth) which enabled trial for an offence attracting a maximum penalty of one year's imprisonment to be by court of summary jurisdiction. The joint judgment of Knox CJ, Isaacs, Gavan Duffy and Powers JJ limited its entire attention to the issue by saying: 'The suggestion that the Parliament, by reason of s 80 of the *Constitution*, could not validly make the offence punishable summarily has no foundation and its rejection needs no exposition'.[6]

Such curtness is simply unthinkable today. With slightly more illumination, Higgins J agreed that 'if there be an indictment, there must be a jury, but there is nothing to compel procedure by indictment'.[7] Justice Starke did not refer to the constitutional issue at all.

Professor Graham Fricke has said that the 'cavalier and dismissive' joint judgment in *Archdall* is emblematic of the prevailing style of the

[3] (1915) 19 CLR 629. [4] Ibid. [5] (1928) 41 CLR 128. [6] Ibid 136. [7] Ibid 139.

Court under Chief Justice Adrian Knox.[8] He argued that this bald pronouncement unaccompanied by any reasons 'had an unfortunate effect in prematurely rigidifying the development of the law'.[9] This assessment seems fair when one surveys the course of subsequent decisions. For despite its brevity on this point, *Archdall* has not only stood the test of time, but also appears to have dissuaded many on the Court from asking more searching questions about the provision and its purpose. Others, however, have been far from satisfied.

III *Lowenstein* – A Guarantee 'drafted in mockery . . . in truth illusory'

It is ironic that, for a case which has assumed such importance in our understanding of s 80, no argument to the Court was made on that provision at all in *Lowenstein*. William Lowenstein had been declared a bankrupt by the Federal Court of Bankruptcy in June 1936. The same body heard Lowenstein's application for an order discharging him from his debts almost a year later in May 1937. In the course of that hearing, the court directed that Lowenstein be charged with the offence in s 209(g) of the *Bankruptcy Act 1924* (Cth) of failing to keep adequate accounting records 'as are usual and proper in the business carried on by him' (as a 'ladies' hairdresser'), sufficiently disclosing his financial position during any period within the five years immediately preceding the date of his bankruptcy. The offence carried a penalty of three years' imprisonment. Under s 217, the Court was empowered to try any offence against the Act summarily, by serving the accused with a copy of the charge and appointing a day for the trial. At that hearing, Lowenstein pleaded not guilty, before his counsel, Garfield Barwick, later Chief Justice of Australia, challenged both the offence and s 217 as ultra vires the powers of the Commonwealth Parliament.

The matter moved to the High Court for the determination of those questions. The dominant issue was the validity of s 217 as investing the Federal Court of Bankruptcy with the power to decide whether a prosecution should be brought. Barwick submitted that not only was it 'the function of the Executive Government to decide whether or not the law should be put in motion against any particular individual', but

[8] Graham Fricke, 'The Knox Court: Exposition Unnecessary' (1999) 27 *Federal Law Review* 121, 125.

[9] Ibid.

it was 'non-judicial and foreign to the concept of judicial power that a judge should, at the one time, be a party to the proceedings and also the judge presiding therein'.[10] These arguments were rejected by a majority of the High Court comprising Latham CJ, Rich, Starke and McTiernan JJ. In this regard, *Lowenstein* is a case very much of its era – predating the crystallisation of a more rigid separation of judicial power in *R v Kirby; Ex parte Boilermakers' Society of Australia*.[11]

Despite not being invoked by Barwick in his challenge to the law, s 80 was not absent from the majority reasons. Chief Justice Latham raised the provision to address whether a prosecution initiated by a court is, as a result, a proceeding brought upon indictment. He decided it was not, also rejecting any significance attaching to the fact that s 217 might commit the bankrupt for trial before another court on indictment.[12] Noting that s 80 'could easily have been better expressed if it was intended that it should have the effect of preventing or limiting the possibility of the Commonwealth Parliament providing for the summary trial of all, or any particular, offences', Latham CJ accepted the authority of *Archdall* that the Parliament enjoys complete discretion to provide for trial summarily or on indictment.[13] Justice McTiernan also referred to s 80, but said no more than 'I consider I am bound by the previous decisions of the court'.[14]

It is important to acknowledge that the disagreement of Dixon and Evatt JJ with the majority is total, including the central issue of whether s 217 is reconcilable with the conception of judicial power. In that respect, it is quite incorrect to say that their dissent has not received subsequent vindication. Their view that the provision was invalid because under the *Constitution* 'judicial power does not include the promotion, prosecution and proof of criminal charges by a court for its own determination',[15] resonates with later jurisprudential developments against which the majority's reasoning looks both remarkably sanguine and difficult to sustain.[16]

But the dissent of Dixon and Evatt JJ is, of course, remembered today for their remarks on s 80. In the most famous passage, they bluntly rejected Higgins J's comment in *Archdall* that 'if there be an indictment, there must be a jury, but there is nothing to compel procedure by indictment':

[10] *Lowenstein* (1938) 59 CLR 556, 559 (Barwick) (during argument).

[11] (1956) 94 CLR 254. [12] *Lowenstein* (1938) 59 CLR 556, 570.

[13] Ibid 570–1. [14] Ibid 591. [15] Ibid 589.

[16] See further Leslie Zines, *The High Court and the Constitution* (Federation Press, 5th ed, 2008) 212–13.

> It is a queer intention to ascribe to a constitution; for it supposes that the concern of the framers of the provision was not to ensure that no one should be held guilty of a serious offence against the laws of the Commonwealth except by the verdict of a jury, but to prevent a procedural solecism, namely, the use of an indictment in cases where the legislature might think fit to authorize the court itself to pass upon the guilt or innocence of the prisoner. There is high authority for the proposition that 'the *Constitution* is not to be mocked.' A cynic might, perhaps, suggest the possibility that sec 80 was drafted in mockery; that its language was carefully chosen so that the guarantee it appeared on the surface to give should be in truth illusory. No court could countenance such a suggestion, and, if this explanation is rejected and an intention to produce some real operative effect is conceded to the section, then to say that its application can always be avoided by authorizing the substitution of some other form of charge for an indictment seems but to mock at the provision.[17]

The power of this language is undeniable. Its cutting and caustic tone contrasts particularly with that usually adopted by Dixon in his judgments. The pithy and forceful proposition that 'the *Constitution* is not to be mocked' is eminently quotable – and indeed the avoidance of 'mockery' has since been invoked in different contexts to justify one interpretation over another.[18]

In saying that they 'should not have taken the view that s 80 was intended to impose no real restriction upon the legislative power to provide what kind of tribunal shall decide the guilt or innocence on a criminal charge', Dixon and Evatt JJ sought to give substance to the identification of an offence as one tried on indictment.[19] This they did by identifying two elements common to the recognised forms of such a procedure and which they regarded as 'of the essence':

> the first of them would be seen to be that some authority constituted under the law to represent the public interest for the purpose took the responsibility of the step which put the accused on his trial; the grand jury, the coroner's jury or the coroner, the law officer or the court. A second element, we think, would be found in the liability of the offender to a term of imprisonment or to some graver form of punishment.[20]

It is obviously the second requirement that introduces an aspect to s 80 that would constrain Parliament's ability to evade its operation. Section

17 *Lowenstein* (1938) 59 CLR 556, 581–2.

18 See, eg, *A-G (Vic) ex rel Black v Commonwealth* (1981) 146 CLR 559, 633 (Murphy J); *Polyukhovich v Commonwealth* (1991) 172 CLR 501, 607 (Deane J); *Kable v DPP (NSW)* (1996) 189 CLR 51, 117 (McHugh J).

19 *Lowenstein* (1938) 59 CLR 556, 583.

20 Ibid.

217 clearly ran afoul of this by providing for the summary trial of an offence punishable by imprisonment for three years.

Justices Dixon and Evatt rather archly professed themselves uncertain as to whether it was possible to reconcile their view on s 80 with *Archdall* since 'no reasons are given for that decision'.[21] Additionally, they said the facts of the earlier case arguably did not require 'a general view that sec 80 was not a real constitutional guarantee at all'.[22] They concluded their discussion of the provision by acknowledging the difficulties of its expression but reiterating their earlier sentiments by saying that 'to treat such a constitutional provision as producing no substantial effect seems rather to defeat than to ascertain its intention'.[23]

IV A Persistent Disquiet[24]

In the sporadic opportunities for reconsideration of s 80 which arose after 1938, the High Court was clearly disinclined to be persuaded by the arguments of the dissenters in *Lowenstein.* Indeed, Dixon CJ declined to avail himself of the opportunity to persist in the view he had expressed with Evatt J in *Lowenstein* when he applied that decision in a brief judgment for the Court in *Sachter v Attorney-General (Cth).*[25] Reliance upon the non-reasons of *Archdall* was the tenor of the Court's approach whenever attention turned to s 80. For example, in *Zarb v Kennedy*, Barwick CJ said simply that 'the proposition that the parliament is unable to provide that any offence shall be tried summarily is untenable' and that he regarded the question as 'long settled'.[26] The other Justices agreed with varying levels of specificity. Certainly there was no hint of dissatisfaction with the *Archdall* approach.

That was not so when s 80 arose for consideration in *Li Chia Hsing v Rankin* 10 years later.[27] Although Barwick CJ led a majority of the Court to confirm the existing authorities, the circumstances of the case, which concerned a fishing offence punishable by a maximum of six months' imprisonment, did not lend themselves to an application of the Dixon and Evatt JJ interpretation. This was acknowledged by Gibbs, Stephen and Aickin JJ, who appeared to suggest that the precedents could have been usefully exposed to more principled scrutiny had the situation been

[21] Ibid 584. [22] Ibid. [23] (1938) 59 CLR 556, 584.

[24] Some of the following discussion draws on Parts 4(B) and (C) of Andrew Lynch, '"The Intelligence of a Future Day": The Vindication of Constitutional Dissent in the High Court of Australia 1981–2003' (2007) 29(2) *Sydney Law Review* 195.

[25] (1954) 94 CLR 86, 88. [26] (1968) 121 CLR 283, 294. [27] (1978) 141 CLR 182.

different.[28] However, Murphy J, while concurring in the result, took the opportunity to advance a view of s 80 which, like that of Dixon and Evatt JJ's, operated independently of the legislature as 'a basic right entrenched in the *Constitution* to trial by jury, at least in serious criminal cases'.[29] In addition to American authorities,[30] Murphy J cited the key passages above from the *Lowenstein* dissent and agreed with the view that exposure to a punishment of imprisonment rendered an offence sufficiently 'serious' in character as to require trial by jury.[31]

In 1985, the majority in *Kingswell v The Queen* ('*Kingswell*') affirmed s 80's limited constraint upon the powers of the Parliament:

> It has been held that s 80 does not mean that the trial of all serious offences shall be by jury; the section applies if there is a trial on indictment, but leaves it to the Parliament to determine whether any particular offence shall be tried on indictment or summarily. This result has been criticized, but the Court has consistently refused to reopen the question and the construction of the section should be regarded as settled . . . [32]

The acknowledgment of critical voices, despite the unbroken chain of authority, is revealing. Why would such criticism not abate? First, there is the persistent disquiet engendered by the *Archdall* interpretation. In the absence of a better explanation, it is an approach which appears to limit s 80 to a merely procedural requirement, so that it might as well be absent from the *Constitution*. For what is the worth of a 'guarantee' interpreted in such a way that it may be completely avoided? The attraction of the *Lowenstein* dissent essentially rests upon its refusal to accept such apparent obtuseness on behalf of the framers.[33] Indeed, Sir Anthony Mason once wryly observed that the appeal of the dissenting opinion in *Lowenstein* lay simply in the fact that it was 'an unusual instance of interpretation of s 80 of the *Constitution*'.[34]

[28] Ibid 193 (Gibbs J), 195–6 (Stephen and Aickin JJ). [29] Ibid 202.

[30] Most notably *Baldwin v New York*, 399 US 66 (1970).

[31] *Li Chia Hsing v Rankin* (1978) 141 CLR 182, 201. This was a more precise endorsement of the *Lowenstein* dissent than Murphy J had offered in his obiter dicta remarks in *Beckwith v The Queen* (1976) 135 CLR 569, 585.

[32] (1985) 159 CLR 264, 276–7 (Gibbs CJ, Wilson and Dawson JJ).

[33] Michael Coper asked of Higgins J's pithy explanation of the provision: 'Can this apparent nonsense have been intended by the founding fathers?': Michael Coper, *Encounters with the Australian Constitution* (CCH, 1988) 300. See also Amelia Simpson and Mary Wood, '"A Puny Thing Indeed" – *Cheng v The Queen and the Constitutional Right to Trial by Jury*' (2001) 29 *Federal Law Review* 95, 107–11.

[34] Sir Anthony Mason, 'The High Court of Australia: A Personal Impression of Its First 100 Years' (2003) 27 *Melbourne University Law Review* 864, 875.

Second, is the identity of the earliest critics of the *Archdall* orthodoxy. Professor Richard Primus has argued that reputations of 'greatness' and even 'heroism' are often constructed by later Justices with a view to redeeming an earlier minority opinion with which they agree.[35] If there are Australian examples of that practice, this is not one of them. We might accept that judicial reputation is a relevant factor in the likely rehabilitation of a minority opinion, but no puffing up is required here. As Stephen McDonald and Anne Carter discuss further in their chapter in this book,[36] Sir Owen Dixon was publicly feted throughout the common law world in a way which no other Australian judge has been before or since[37] and he continues to be held in the greatest regard by the current generation of the High Court.[38] It is doubtful the dissent in *Lowenstein* would have been quite so enduringly attractive had he not been one of its authors.

That is not meant to diminish Evatt. Of Dixon's colleagues on the bench at that time, none would have added to his own reputational allure more than Evatt, given the latter's own obvious intellectual strengths. Professor Michael Coper was surely right when he argued that the *Lowenstein* dissent commands attention due to its 'powerful combination of two divergent legal minds in Dixon and Evatt'.[39] Professor Leslie Zines once considered at some length the complementary qualities that the 'conceptual' Dixon and 'sociological' Evatt brought to the High Court.[40] Yet despite marked

[35] Richard A Primus, 'Canon, Anti-Canon, and Judicial Dissent' (1998) 48 *Duke Law Journal* 243, 259–64.

[36] Stephen McDonald and Anne Carter, '*Uther's Case* (1947): Justice Dixon and the Troubled Legacy of the Commonwealth Immunity Doctrine' in ch 5 of this book.

[37] See Philip Ayres, *Owen Dixon* (Miegunyah Press, 2003) 232; Kenneth Hayne, 'Dixon, Owen' in Tony Blackshield, Michael Coper and George Williams (eds), *The Oxford Companion to the High Court of Australia* (Oxford University Press, 2001) 219. Though Laurence Maher has commented that 'much of the skiting about Dixon is firmly rooted in snobbery and well practiced techniques of mutual admiration': Laurence W Maher, 'Owen Dixon: Concerning his Political Methods' (2003) 6 *Constitutional Law and Policy Review* 33, 35.

[38] See, eg, K M Hayne, 'Sir Owen Dixon' in J T Gleeson, J A Watson and R C A Higgins, *Historical Foundations of Australian Law: Institutions, Concepts and Personalities* (Federation Press, 2013) vol 1, 372. Citation analysis confirms Dixon's stature: Russell Smyth, 'Who Gets Cited? An Empirical Study of Judicial Prestige in the High Court' (2000) 21 *University of Queensland Law Journal* 7, 16.

[39] Michael Coper, 'Commentary' in Michael Coper and George Williams (eds), *Justice Lionel Murphy – Influential or Merely Prescient?* (Federation Press, 1997) 64, 66. See also Mason, above n 34.

[40] Leslie Zines, 'Mr Justice Evatt and the Constitution' (1969) 3 *Federal Law Review* 153, 175–86. See also Geoffrey Sawer, *Australian Federal Politics and Law 1929–1949* (Melbourne University Press, 1963) 222.

differences in approach and technique, Zines claimed the two had a certain amount in common, especially in contrast to their colleagues:

> They were both constitutional lawyers in the grand manner; both responded readily to the call of a former US Chief Justice, John Marshall, not to forget that 'it is a constitution we are expounding'. Both would have scorned the view that because the *Constitution* was a British statute the canons of construction applicable to it were little different from those relevant to the interpretation of any other Act. Both refused to be fettered by the *Engineers'* case in making assumptions as to the form of government presupposed by the *Constitution*. Both were opposed to reducing constitutional provisions to merely formalistic or procedural relevance.[41]

This translated into a high frequency of explicit agreement between Dixon and Evatt JJ by the second half of the 1930s.[42] These similarities are often overlooked, in part because our image of Dixon is refracted through the lens of his further 24 years' service on the Court when, especially as Chief Justice, he unquestionably dominated it. But as Fricke reminds us, while Evatt J's distinctive voice is well remembered from his single decade on the Court, 'it is less generally understood among today's lawyers . . . that during the earlier years Dixon was known as the Great Dissenter'.[43]

In *Kingswell*, Deane J added his name to the roll call of dissenters on s 80. Reflecting the first of the two considerations just raised, he pointed to the inadequate foundations of the orthodox view. While conceding that:

> if one refers to numbers rather than weight of reasoning, the predominant tendency of the views expressed in judgments of members of the Court is plainly enough towards the conclusion that s 80 should be construed [narrowly] . . . [However,] one searches in vain, in judgments favouring the view which would deprive the 'fundamental law' of s 80 of effective operation, for any coherent statement of a line of reasoning leading to that conclusion.[44]

Rather than flatly deny their correctness, Deane J preferred to confine those earlier decisions to their facts. Doing so shaped the substantive operation of s 80 which he went on to advocate.

41 Zines, above n 40, 175.

42 Russell Smyth, 'Judicial Interaction on the Latham Court: A Quantitative Study of Voting Patterns on the High Court 1935–1950' (2001) 47 *Australian Journal of Politics and History* 330, 338–40. Justice McTiernan had a similarly high level of agreement with these judges, to form 'the most frequent successful three-justice coalition' but Smyth explains this was essentially due to his 'good judgment in choosing who to concur with': at 337–8.

43 Graham Fricke, *Judges of the High Court* (Hutchison, 1986) 118.

44 *Kingswell* (1985) 159 CLR 264, 318.

That account owed a debt, which he readily acknowledged, to the dissent of Dixon and Evatt JJ in *Lowenstein.* Justice Deane shared entirely in its reasoning as a basis for rejecting the *Archdall* approach, saying it was 'unnecessary to go beyond [it] to demonstrate the error of their Honours' assertion [in *Archdall*] that the rejection of the argument based on s 80 needed no exposition'.[45] Reflecting more contemporary themes, he said the dissent demonstrated that to interpret the provision without reference to substance over mere form was to fail to apply ordinary principles of constitutional construction.[46] It was very clear that Deane J saw himself as carrying the mantle of the dissenters in Lowenstein.[47]

Justice Deane agreed that seriousness is the key factor which determines the scope of the s 80, arguing that this is what the framers intended through use of the words 'on indictment'.[48] But he was unable to accept Dixon and Evatt JJ's requirement that trial by jury is guaranteed whenever the accused faces punishment by a term of imprisonment. After reviewing the criminal law at the turn of the century, he concluded that the boundary between serious ('indictable') and minor ('non-indictable') offences was not simply the possibility of imprisonment. Instead, the question turns on whether dealing with the offence summarily is appropriate – which is a question of law to be determined by the courts, rather than the legislature.[49] However, in order perhaps to stave off criticism of this as an unworkably vague test, Deane J ultimately laid down a more precise standard:

> the views expressed by Dixon and Evatt JJ in *Lowenstein*, as qualified in the manner which I have mentioned, should be accepted as a correct statement of the effect of the reference to 'trial on indictment' in s 80 of the *Constitution*. . . . [A] particular alleged offence will, for the purposes of characterizing a particular trial as a 'trial on indictment', be a 'serious offence' if it is not one which could appropriately be dealt with summarily by justices or magistrates in that conviction will expose the accused to grave punishment. It is unnecessary, for the purposes of the present case, to seek to identify more precisely the boundary between offences which are not and offences which are capable of being properly so dealt with. I have, however, indicated the tentative view that that boundary will ordinarily be identified by reference to whether the offence is punishable, when

[45] Ibid 311. [46] Ibid 308.

[47] Justice Deane did not directly connect the dissent of Dixon and Evatt JJ nor his own with the opinion of Murphy J in *Li Chia Hsing v Rankin*, reflecting his dismissal of the latter case as not involving an offence 'serious' enough to require trial by jury under s 80: ibid 315–17. This was a point which Murphy J himself had conceded.

[48] Ibid 309. [49] Ibid 310–11.

> prosecuted in the manner in which it is being prosecuted, by a maximum term of imprisonment of more than one year.[50]

Justice Deane's dissent in *Kingswell* is but a slightly modified version of that which had been delivered by Dixon and Evatt JJ. The amendment to use of a jail term of over a year's duration as the identifying feature of a 'serious' offence to be tried on indictment avoided direct contradiction with the result of any previous cases on s 80. In *Cheng v The Queen* ('*Cheng*'), McHugh J made much of Deane J's qualification, saying that between them, Dixon and Evatt JJ, Murphy J and Deane J 'have not been able to agree, however, as to the meaning that should be given to the phrase "trial on indictment" in s 80'.[51] But this is unfair. First, nothing in Murphy J's broad obiter statements is at all discordant with the other opinions. Second, it is a mistake to view the different standard as to seriousness offered by the two dissents from *Lowenstein* and *Kingswell* as amounting to a disagreement which is in any way destructive of the essential consistency of these two minority opinions written almost 50 years apart.

The Court's consideration of s 80 became much more frequent in the 1990s, but this also saw a shift in focus. The cases of *Cheatle v The Queen*,[52] *Re Tyler; Ex parte Foley*,[53] *Byrnes v The Queen*,[54] and *Katsuno v The Queen*[55] did not concern the legislature's freedom to determine the indictable nature or otherwise of offences for the purpose of s 80, but instead the content of the requirement of trial by jury. So it was not until, in responding to the issues raised in *Re Colina; Ex parte Torney* ('*Re Colina*'),[56] that Kirby J emerged as the latest – and so far last – judge to align himself with the earlier dissent of Dixon and Evatt JJ in *Lowenstein*. Justice Kirby also adopted Deane J's dissent in *Kingswell* and included Murphy J's remarks in *Li Chia Hsing v Rankin* as one of the Court's 'dissenting voices' on this question.[57]

Justice Kirby's opinion in *Re Colina* was explicit in its acknowledgment of the earlier dissents:

> I must pay due regard to the opinions of other Justices past and present about the question.... [B]eing convinced of the error of previous authority

[50] Ibid 318–19.

[51] (2000) 203 CLR 248, 295. Chief Justice Gleeson, Gummow and Hayne JJ merely said, '[t]hose who have dissented have disagreed among themselves as to what the section means': at 269.

[52] (1993) 177 CLR 541.
[53] (1993) 181 CLR 18.
[54] (1999) 199 CLR 1.
[55] (1999) 199 CLR 40.
[56] (1999) 200 CLR 386.
[57] Ibid 420.

> on the meaning of the *Constitution*, I have a duty to express what I consider to be its proper construction. I will state my reasons. I can do so briefly because they follow substantially those upon which predecessors, holding the like opinion currently in the minority, have based their conclusions.[58]

In accepting Deane J's modification from *Kingswell* as to a serious offence being one which attracts a maximum penalty of imprisonment over one year, Kirby J avoided contributing to a perception that the challengers were splintered over what precisely 'on indictment' in s 80 is to mean.[59]

The refusal to accept that the framers could have intended s 80 to operate at Parliament's discretion is a strong point of continuity among all these minority voices. The dissent of Dixon and Evatt JJ in *Lowenstein* set the tone for incredulity on that issue. Yet, and while acknowledging its frequent contestability as a resource, the record of the Convention Debates suggests this is misplaced.[60] The first draft of the provision destined to become s 80 was modelled by Andrew Inglis Clark on art III, § 2 of the *United States Constitution*, and later amended by Sir Samuel Griffith.[61] To the extent it was intended to provide some level of protection beyond the control of the legislature, this did not survive the 1898 Convention. Edmund Barton successfully advocated its alteration so as to restrict its application from simply 'all indictable offences' to only those brought before the courts 'on indictment'.[62] His apparent purpose was to preserve the flexibility of summary trial of minor offences, including contempt of court, rather than necessitating trial by jury for any offence which simply *may* be tried on indictment. While this has been seized upon as indicating a distinction in the minds of the framers based upon gravity of offence,[63] it just as likely confirms a determination to ensure that the requirement of a jury trial could be dispensed with when desired.[64] Isaac

58 Ibid 422. 59 Ibid 422–3.

60 The historical record of the Convention Debates rarely provides a 'single collective view' on the intended meaning of a constitutional provision: *New South Wales v Commonwealth* (2006) 229 CLR 1, 96–7 (Gleeson CJ, Gummow, Hayne, Heydon and Crennan JJ) ('*Work Choices Case*').

61 C L Pannam, 'Trial by Jury and Section 80 of the Australian Constitution' (1968) 6 *Sydney Law Review* 1, 2–6; George Williams and David Hume, *Human Rights under the Australian Constitution* (Oxford University Press, 2nd ed, 2013) 356–7.

62 *Official Report of the National Australasian Convention Debates*, Melbourne, 4 March 1898, 1894–5.

63 Simpson and Wood, above n 33, 110.

64 James Stellios, *The Federal Judicature: Chapter III of the Constitution* (LexisNexis, 2010) 523.

Isaacs, while conceding the attractions of Barton's proposal, repeated his opinion that the provision generally was without 'any real effect at all', given Parliament's ability to control it.[65] On an earlier occasion, and in a direct foreshadowing of the *Archdall* orthodoxy he helped to establish 30 years later, Isaacs had insisted that there was 'no fetter on the Federal Parliament, because, when it creates an offence it may say it is not to be prosecuted by indictment, and immediately it does it is not within the protection of this clause of the *Constitution*'.[66]

Both Deane J and Kirby J suggested that Isaacs' remark at the Convention Debates was discredited by the provision's inclusion in the final draft.[67] But while it cannot be simply assumed that other delegates entirely shared Isaacs' opinion of the matter, there is nothing to clearly indicate that they rejected it; his remarks met with no direct rebuttal. To argue otherwise is to take considerable evidence of the framers' understanding of the provision and use it to support the contrary. This suggests a perhaps understandable reluctance to acknowledge the occasional fallibility of the framers in performing their task. In contrast, Dr Clifford Pannam suggested that we must accept s 80's presence in the *Constitution* simply as a result of 'uncritical and seemingly senseless copying of inappropriate American precedent'.[68]

That view is, though, difficult for many judges to swallow. In 1999 Callinan J, even allowing for the apparent clarity of the provision's text and the weight of judicial authority, admitted sharing 'some of the concerns expressed by Dixon and Evatt JJ in *Lowenstein*'.[69] The following year he maintained that it 'is impossible not to feel disquiet about a proposition that might leave it entirely for the legislature to define what is, and what is not to be an offence charged on indictment, and its elements'.[70] But by 2001,[71] he had moved past the need to express such twinges. This minor rumble of dissatisfaction over the *Archdall* orthodoxy from Callinan J illustrates that the orthodoxy requires a stronger ground for its acceptance than precedent alone if it is ever to throw off the doubts about

65 *Official Report of the National Australasian Convention Debates*, Melbourne, 4 March 1898, 1895.

66 *Official Report of the National Australasian Convention Debates*, Melbourne, 31 January 1898, 352.

67 See *Kingswell* (1985) 159 CLR 264, 313 (Deane J); *Re Colina* (1999) 200 CLR 386, 423–4 (Kirby J). See also Simpson and Wood, above n 33, 109–10; cf Bell, above n 1, 13–14.

68 Pannam, above n 61, 24.

69 *Re Colina* (1999) 200 CLR 386, 439.

70 *Cheng* (2000) 203 CLR 248, 344.

71 *Brownlee v The Queen* (2001) 207 CLR 278, 341–2.

its correctness which were so eloquently voiced by Dixon and Evatt JJ. It appears that, after all, exposition is necessary.

V No Queer Intention – Responding to the *Lowenstein* Dissent

Across the High Court's consideration of s 80, two majority judgments are distinguished by the attempt of their authors to dispel the disquiet over the apparent oddity of the framers drafting a provision which was so deferential to the power of the legislature. Both did so by ascribing a purpose to the section which they say has been fulfilled.

In *Brown v The Queen*,[72] Dawson J surmised that the framers' restriction of the right to trial by jury on indictment was designed to avoid the uncertainty of s 80's American precursor, art III § s 2(3), which had required the Supreme Court to draw difficult distinctions between serious and minor offences so as to determine the availability of a jury.[73] While the use of indictment as indicia of seriousness indubitably gave the Commonwealth the ability to grant or withhold trial by jury as it pleased, Dawson J remarked that experience to date had shown responsible use of that power. Consequently, departing from the plain words of the section was unjustified 'merely because theory rather than practice sees weakness in the choice which it offers the Commonwealth in the mode of prosecution to be adopted'.[74]

Arguably, it is McHugh J's defence of the orthodox interpretation in *Cheng*, which is the definitive response to the objections first raised by Dixon and Evatt JJ. In *Cheng*, the Court was invited to reconsider aspects of *Kingswell*. Most of the bench chose simply to accept the earlier decision as authority on the 'wider issue'[75] of Parliament's ability to determine which offences are to be tried on indictment until a more suitable case came along.[76] But McHugh J was moved to consider the arguments,

[72] (1986) 160 CLR 171, 214–15. [73] *Schick v United States*, 195 US 65 (1904).

[74] *Brown v The Queen* (1986) 160 CLR 171, 215–16. This seems to have been O'Connor's view on the effect of the section at the Melbourne sitting of the Convention: *Official Report of the National Australasian Convention Debates*, Melbourne, 31 January 1898, 352–3. See further Bell J's discussion of the similar views of Professor La Nauze: Bell, above n 1, 14–15.

[75] *Cheng* (2000) 203 CLR 248, 268 (Gleeson CJ, Gummow and Hayne JJ).

[76] The objection to these facts as an agent for substantial re-interpretation of s 80 hinged particularly on the defendants having made guilty pleas so that there was 'nothing for a jury to try': ibid 268 (Gleeson CJ, Gummow and Hayne JJ). See also Simpson and Wood, above n 33, 104–5.

perhaps in light of Kirby J's adoption of the dissentient line and Callinan J's expression of sympathy for it, just the year before in *Re Colina*.

Justice McHugh conceded that s 80's literal meaning produces a 'mere procedural provision'[77] but submits that this accords with its purpose. His general agreement with Dawson J's opinion in *Brown v The Queen* is evident:

> When the section is read in the light of its United States counterpart, its drafts and the discussion at the *Constitution* Conventions, it is plain that it took the form that it did to avoid the mischief that would result if Parliament could not determine which offences against the laws of the Commonwealth were to be tried by juries. The words of s 80 were deliberately and carefully chosen to give the Parliament the capacity to avoid trial by jury when it wished to do so. The current and traditional interpretation of s 80, therefore, gives effect to the purpose of the section.[78]

Concluding that s 80 is 'not a great guarantee', McHugh J acknowledged this was 'unlikely to be acceptable to many civil libertarians'.[79] But it is important to appreciate that he and Dawson J did at least insist that the provision *has* a purpose, rejecting the bleak alternative advanced by Pannam,[80] which has probably only encouraged dissentients to actively attribute a function to the section which its words cannot easily bear.

Justice McHugh also emphasised that reading the guarantee as applying to 'serious' offences (in all the various formulations which dissenting judges have used to convey that basic idea) would leave the Court without any objective means of determining when the section was to operate. As noted above, this arguably overstates the extent of disagreement between the dissenting opinions on this question. But his objection is logically anterior to, and thus not answered by, the use of jail terms of varying length as some sort of barometer for this purpose. For on what basis does the qualification of 'serious' enter into our reading of s 80 at all? Dr Dan Meagher has rejected any interpretation that simply 'smuggles the word "serious" into the text of s 80 and permits the court to define what offences fit this category'.[81] Doing so, he says, crosses the line 'that separates legitimate constitutional interpretation from constitutional amendment'.[82]

[77] *Cheng* (2000) 203 CLR 248, 291. [78] Ibid 292. [79] Ibid 295.

[80] Pannam, above n 61, 6.

[81] Dan Meagher, 'New Day Rising? Non-Originalism, Justice Kirby and Section 80 of the Constitution' (2002) 24 *Sydney Law Review* 141, 167.

[82] Ibid.

Ultimately, and despite the hopes of Inglis Clark in seeking to replicate art III § 2 of the *United States Constitution*, the framers adopted an objectively ascertainable criterion ('trial on indictment') under which Parliament has the final say. Only by dismissing that intention can the section be viewed as one into which some other meaning must be poured. But this ignores the cogent argument that the framers' intention was as the text reflects – and is not so queer after all. Parliament decides which offences will be tried by jury, leaving no need for the Court to play the role which the dissenting opinions have insisted that it must.

In *Cheng*, McHugh J argued persuasively that when 'one looks at text, history or purpose, the answer is the same: the approach to the construction of s 80 accepted by the majority in *Kingswell* and . . . in earlier cases is correct'.[83] Any desire, despite the synthesis of these considerations, to confer upon the provision a more independent operation cannot withstand the objections that to do so involves an illegitimate judicial appropriation of power.

To the extent such a desire is born of a fear that otherwise the guarantee held out by the section is 'in truth illusory', more recent jurisprudential developments provide their own answer. As already noted, over a series of cases around the turn of the century, the Court articulated the constitutional content of the requirement that trial be by 'jury'.[84] In contrast to the long history of dissent over what criteria determines the application of s 80, the Court was strikingly unanimous that it, and not the Parliament, has the last say on the rules governing the composition and practices of the 'jury' which the *Constitution* requires for the trial of those offences brought on indictment. Indeed, even the application of starkly different methodological approaches produced no judicial disagreement across these cases on the essential features of the common law conception of 'jury' which are constitutionally guaranteed by s 80. The emergence of these principles has substantially undercut the complaints of those who remain dissatisfied by the orthodox interpretation and continue to lament it as denying s 80 a meaningful role of rights protection.[85] Accordingly, it is difficult to accept a recent comment that Professor Geoffrey's

[83] (2000) 203 CLR 248, 295.

[84] See *Cheatle v The Queen* (1993) 177 CLR 541; *Katsuno v The Queen* (1999) 199 CLR 40; *Brownlee v The Queen* (2001) 207 CLR 278; *Fittock v The Queen* (2003) 217 CLR 508; *Ng v The Queen* (2003) 217 CLR 521.

[85] See, eg, Anthony Gray, 'Mockery and the Right to Trial by Jury' (2006) 6 *Queensland University of Technology Law and Justice Journal* 66.

Sawer's 1967 dismissal of s 80 as '"in practice worthless" remains correct today'.[86]

VI Conclusion

The dissent of Dixon and Evatt JJ in *Lowenstein* has been the spring from which has streamed a long line of opinions containing what Primus would call the 'anti-canon' of s 80's interpretation.[87] In 1997, Coper acknowledged the 'long history of respectable dissent in favour of the broader view' of s 80, commencing with 'Dixon and Evatt through to the modern-day agitators', before voicing his suspicion that 'today's heterodoxy will become tomorrow's orthodoxy'.[88] Justice Kirby, unsurprisingly, remained confident that redemption of the minority view would 'eventually' occur.[89] A few years later, Mason opined that the *Lowenstein* judgment was 'so persuasive that one wonders why it did not prevail'.[90] Yet the canon – the orthodoxy from *Archdall* – has defied these sceptics, remaining impervious to the blows of judges as diverse as Dixon, Evatt, Murphy, Deane and Kirby JJ.

Understanding the dissatisfaction of those individuals is not difficult. The orthodoxy rested upon some of the thinnest reasoning ever offered by the Court to justify its interpretation of a constitutional provision and this served to fuel dissent.[91] But those deficiencies have, however, now been overcome through more recent majority opinions, particularly that of McHugh J in *Cheng*.[92] This sees the orthodoxy stated in a way which, perhaps for the first time, responds to its detractors by asserting a clear purpose to the text as it appears. That the Court was able, on this occasion, to freely consider the evidence of the Convention Debates as an aid to understanding the provision, only strengthens that consideration of the issue. Consequently, the flow of dissent which has been such an enduring

86 Williams and Hume, above n 61, 360.

87 Primus, above n 35.

88 Coper, 'Commentary', above n 39, 66.

89 *Cheung v The Queen* (2001) 209 CLR 1, 38.

90 Mason, above n 33, 875. The comment is somewhat odd given Mason J's disinclination to be moved by its appeal in *Kingswell* (1985) 159 CLR 264.

91 Grant Webster, 'Trial by Jury? Re Colina; Ex parte Torney' (2000) 5 *Deakin Law Review* 217, 224; George Williams, *Human Rights under the Australian Constitution* (Oxford University Press, 1999) 107.

92 Although Bell J, currently serving on the High Court, has admitted to finding McHugh J's explanation of the Convention Debates in *Cheng* as 'not entirely satisfying' (instead preferring Gaudron J's description of s 80 as a 'constitutional command' in the same case) she does not reject the orthodoxy: above n 1, 19, 23.

feature of the Court's engagement with the constitutional guarantee of trial by jury may be finally staunched.[93]

But, this hardly means that the series of dissenting opinions on s 80 have been worthless. While the interpretation they have promoted has consistently found little favour with the Court's members, those opinions have demanded the majority provide more compelling reasons for continued acceptance of the orthodoxy than were offered by the majority – both in *Archdall* itself and in later cases over the years. Ultimately the persistence of their complaint met with success and the Court has finally come to offer a more robust and principled account of the provision. Ironically, this has virtually ensured that the law is now most unlikely to shift in favour of the *Lowenstein* dissent and its progeny.

But there is a realm of influence which lies beyond that of simple vindication. A dissenting opinion is always a challenge issued to the majority of the bench. They fulfil a valuable service in demanding better-reasoned judgments from the majority. This is strikingly illustrated in the present context. The strength of the orthodox position has been improved upon remarkably since the terse, self-satisfied opinions of the *Archdall* decision were delivered in the absence of any contrary view. Although the *Lowenstein* dissent of Dixon and Evatt JJ failed to spur their colleagues to produce a more compelling case for its approach, it ensured a sense of lingering disquiet with the foundations of the traditional position. The failure of the Court to overcome this on later occasions when it turned to s 80 was highlighted by Deane J in *Kingswell* when he seized upon the fact that the *Lowenstein* dissent 'remains unanswered'.[94]

Galvanising the champions of the majority position to give a better account of themselves is an unlikely motivation for those who dissent from their view.[95] But this is not to the point. Those proposing an alternative approach must always make a case for it – even if, unfairly, the majority asserts that their own view 'needs no exposition'. If those dissents happen to elicit a more vigorous and compelling set of reasons from members of the majority for their stance then so be it. That is all to the good. In acting in this way the Court is engaging in protracted and public deliberation

93 Justice McHugh's judgment in *Cheng* overcomes the criticism attracted by the majority's refusal to be drawn on the issue in *Re Colina* which led one commentator to suggest that future judges would follow in the wake of Kirby J's dissent in the latter case: Webster, above n 91, 224, 228.

94 (1985) 159 CLR 264, 318.

95 Mark A Kadzielski and Robert C Kunda, 'The Unmaking of Judicial Consensus in the 1930s: An Historical Analysis' (1983) 15 *University of West Los Angeles Law Review* 43, 55.

among its membership. This productive use of disagreement results in transparent decisions based on stronger reasoning. The dissenters in these cases – starting with Dixon and Evatt JJ – have played an important role in extracting a more principled and convincing explanation of the Court's preferred interpretation of s 80. A minority opinion which has not been ignored cannot be said to have been of no effect upon the law.

It is impossible to say that the jurisprudence of s 80 would be in a more satisfactory state had the Court not heard – and eventually responded to – those voices of dissent which challenged and stimulated the law's development. It is in this sense, rather than vindication, that the minority opinion in *Lowenstein* lays claim to being celebrated as a great dissent.

4

Justice Evatt and the Lost Child in *Chester v Waverley Corporation* (1939)

BARBARA MCDONALD

I Introduction

On 14 August 1937, tragedy struck the Chester family. Seven-year-old Max Chester went missing while playing in the street in the Sydney suburb of Waverley. The Chesters had moved into the street only two weeks before. After searching for Max for several hours, and hearing a report that he had been seen playing by a deep trench of muddy water at the other end of the street, Mrs Chester witnessed his body being dragged by police from the trench. Efforts were made for three-quarters-of-an-hour by local surf lifesavers to resuscitate him, to no avail. As a result of this experience, Mrs Chester suffered severe nervous shock and a consequent psychiatric illness.

The trench had been dug by the defendant Council. It was known that children played in the street.[1] The trench was up to eight feet deep, and not well guarded: the railing placed by the Council around the trench was such that children could easily slip under it, and it was capable of removal by children, as it lay nearby at the time. The Council had also placed sand along the side of the trench, a further attraction to children.

The plaintiff's claim was non-suited at first instance and the Full Court of the Supreme Court of New South Wales dismissed her appeal. She appealed to the High Court. It was a novel case: Rich J describes the plaintiff as arguing for a 'hitherto unknown cause of action'.[2] The majority dismissed her appeal. Justice Evatt dissented.

[1] *Chester v Council of the Municipality of Waverley* (1939) 62 CLR 1, 23 (Evatt J) ('*Chester*'). A reasonable person in the situation of the defendant council would have 'regard to the unfortunate but notorious fact that children of workpeople are frequently compelled to play in the streets'.

[2] Ibid 11.

The dissenting judgment of Evatt J was noteworthy and powerful in many respects. First, its lengthy and comprehensive treatment of the arguments contrasted sharply with the judgments of the majority. Justice Evatt himself noted 'the great importance of the present case' and stated that because of this, he had set out his reasons at length. His dissenting judgment alone extended to 34 pages, when at that time the average length of a High Court judgment was only five pages.[3] Justice Evatt recognised the legal and social significance of the extension of liability that he favoured, and clearly felt that he had to deal comprehensively with every argument that had been raised against the plaintiff's case in the courts below, in argument and by the majority, and even with arguments that had not.

He dealt also with many hypothetical situations,[4] in order, perhaps, to counter fears that the suggested legal principles would spawn or support unmeritorious claims. Although obiter dicta, this discussion was important to mark the limits or restrictions of the potential new liability. As the majority stated, limits on liability for negligence must be set: a defendant cannot realistically owe a legal duty and liability to the world.

However, it is not the comprehensive treatment of the arguments that marks out Evatt J's dissent for greatness. It is, after all, a feature of many dissenting judgments that they must deal comprehensively with the arguments: the dissenter in that respect has a more difficult task of persuasion and justification than the judges in the majority who have the comfort and force of shared opinions.

What made the judgment exceptional and what has most underpinned its fame among generations of law students[5] and lawyers was Evatt J's use of strong, empathic and persuasive language, with support from literature, to describe the natural – and therefore foreseeable – anguished state of the *plaintiff as the mother* of the lost child. Additionally, the openness that he showed in his legal reasoning to the further development of the common law contrasted sharply with the rigidity of the majority judgments. The opinion is notable too for the extensive citation of scholarly works and

[3] Matthew Groves and Russell Smyth, 'A Century of Judicial Style: Changing Patterns in Judgment Writing on the High Court 1903–2001' (2005) 32 *Federal Law Review* 255, 259.

[4] Such as what if the plaintiff's fear, although realistic, turns out to be unfounded, because the victim is unharmed, as in some rescue cases: *Chester* (1939) 62 CLR 1, 42.

[5] Geoffrey Robertson writes that as a law student he was first impressed with 'the Doc' (as Evatt was popularly known) when he came across his judgment in *Chester*: Geoffrey Robertson, *Dreaming Too Loud: Reflections on a Race Apart* (Random House Australia, 2013) 36. See below text accompanying n 49 for his comment on the judgment.

American case law. Finally, what secures the judgment's place in this collection is the immediate impact it had on statute law and its eventual but forceful significance for the modern common law of both Australia and England.

These features and Evatt J's legal arguments will be examined below, after a consideration of the legal context of the case and the majority views.

II The Legal Context of the Case

In 1939, when *Chester v Council of the Municipality of Waverley* ('*Chester*')[6] was decided, judges in the common law world were still grappling with the implications of the House of Lords' momentous decision in *Donoghue v Stevenson*, decided only seven years earlier, in which Lord Atkin and others had set out a new generalised concept of when a legal duty of care would arise.[7] That decision, and its recognition of a duty of care in tort outside the bounds of privity of contract, had been recognised and accepted as part of Australian law by the Privy Council in *Grant v Australian Knitting Mills Ltd* in 1936[8] and implicitly by the High Court in *Bunyan v Jordan* in 1937.[9] These were the only two cases in the intervening period before *Chester* in which the High Court had to decide whether a duty of care existed. Perhaps not all judges were sanguine with the task ahead of them of defining the limits of Lord Atkin's 'neighbour principle' in particular cases. Justice Rich in *Chester* described the law of tort as in its 'present amorphous condition',[10] while two years before in *Victoria Park Racing and Recreation Grounds Co Ltd v Taylor*, he had quoted Salmond who had recently said that '[t]he action on the case for negligence has no

6 The case is so frequently referred to as '*Chester v Waverley Corporation*' (see, eg, Gaudron J in *Tame v New South Wales* (2002) 211 CLR 317, 339) that this has been used in the title to this chapter.

7 [1932] AC 562.

8 [1936] AC 85. The Privy Council found for the plaintiff. Justice Evatt had dissented from the majority decision for the defendant manufacturer in the High Court in *Australian Knitting Mills Ltd v Grant* (1933) 50 CLR 387, 440–3, applying the principles on a manufacturer's duty of care from 'the *Snail Case*' and from the New York Court of Appeals in *MacPherson v Buick Motor Co*, 217 NY 382 (1916).

9 (1937) 57 CLR 1, 10 (Latham CJ), rejecting a suggested cause of action which would be independent of any intention to injure the plaintiff, any negligence or any special relationship between the parties to found a legal duty.

10 *Chester* (1939) 62 CLR 1, 11. Despite *Donoghue v Stevenson*, foreseeability was not yet established as the 'touchstone' of liability in negligence. See further below n 60 on remoteness rules then applied.

limits set upon its territory, save by previous decisions upon such specific relationships as have come before the courts'.[11]

Chester presented the High Court with a specific issue – the extent of any duty in negligence to avoid causing illness from nervous shock – on which there *were* already previous decisions. However, unlike cases of injury caused by physical impact where there were already many recognised categories of duties of care, there had been few successful actions in negligence for illness or injury caused by shock by 1939. The 1888 decision of the Privy Council in *Victorian Railways Commissioners v Coultas*,[12] rejecting a claim for nervous shock and 'still binding on all Dominion courts',[13] was seen as a formidable hurdle to any nervous shock claim in Australia.

In that case, the plaintiff had suffered shock when she saw a train approaching as she and her husband crossed the tracks in their horse and buggy at a level crossing, allowed through by the negligent gatekeeper. Although they crossed the track just in time, she suffered severe nervous shock out of fear for their safety. The Privy Council had held that 'damages arising from mere sudden terror unaccompanied by an actual physical injury, but occasioning a nervous or mental shock, cannot under such circumstances . . . be considered a consequence which, in the ordinary course of things, would flow from the negligence of the gatekeeper'.[14] The decision was long interpreted as holding that nervous shock was not a kind of injury that could form the basis of a negligence claim.

Chester was significant in the recognition that *Victorian Railways Commissioners v Coultas* was no bar to recovery. In the Full Court of New South Wales, Jordan CJ stated: 'It may be doubted whether that case, if properly understood, decides more than that damages cannot be recovered for proof of mere metal perturbation'.[15]

While the majority in the High Court did not mention the case, Evatt J read down the decision as holding:

> only that damages due to 'mere sudden terror unaccompanied by any actual physical injury' were too remote. It must always be a question of fact whether shock to the nerves causes 'actual physical injury'. To-day it is

[11] (1937) 58 CLR 479, 501, quoting W T S Stallybrass, *Salmond on Torts* (Sweet & Maxwell, 9th ed, 1936) 18–19.

[12] (1888) 13 App Cas 222.

[13] *Chester* (1939) 62 CLR 1, 46 (Evatt J).

[14] *Victorian Railways Commissioners v Coultas* (1888) 13 App Cas 222, 225. The Privy Council did not rule on whether, as the defendant contended, some impact on the plaintiff was required before nervous shock could be recovered.

[15] (1938) 55 WN (NSW) 221, 223.

> known that it does. In 1888 it was widely assumed that it did not.... [I]t has no application to cases like the present where 'shock to the nerves' is another name for actual physical disturbance to the nervous system.[16]

However, removing this bar did not mean that the plaintiff's case was clear. She still had to prove the greatest legal hurdle in a negligence case: the duty of care.

The English courts, not bound by the Privy Council decision, had by 1939 allowed claims for nervous shock in two significant cases. The first was *Dulieu v White & Sons*,[17] where the plaintiff barmaid had been put in immediate fear for her own safety by the negligence of the defendant in driving a pair-horse van into the bar where she was serving. The second case, *Hambrook v Stokes Brothers*,[18] was a more closely analogous one for Mrs Chester to rely on. In that case, the family of a mother recovered damages under the *Fatal Accidents Act 1876*[19] for her illness and subsequent death caused by her nervous shock after she saw a truck careering out of control down a hill and around the corner to an area where she knew her three children were playing. She was immediately fearful of her children's safety and did subsequently discover that one of her children had been injured.

These two English cases were seen as establishing that what was essential for a nervous shock claim by a 'secondary victim', a plaintiff who was not in fear of injury to himself or herself, was that he or she was *somehow involved* in the event, at least as a witness. Further it was stressed that where the cause of shock was merely *being told, afterwards*, of a distressing event such as the death or injury of a loved one, this could not form the basis of a claim. This second limitation remained constant in the law dealing with negligently inflicted nervous shock, and was one which Evatt J clearly accepted.[20]

[16] *Chester* (1939) 62 CLR 1, 47. [17] [1901] 2 KB 669.

[18] [1925] 1 KB 141. [19] 9 & 10 Vict, c 93.

[20] *Chester* (1939) 62 CLR 1, 43. Justice Evatt stated: 'The plaintiff is not disentitled to recover merely because she came to the scene of the fatality after her child had fallen into the trench, provided *that her shock and suffering were due in the main to what she realized from her own unaided senses* during the period I have defined' (emphasis added). See also *Jaensch v Coffey* (1984) 155 CLR 549; but cf *Tame v New South Wales; Annetts v Australian Stations Pty Ltd* (2002) 211 CLR 317 ('*Annetts*'). While judgment in the cases of *Tame* and *Annetts* are reported together, the latter decision is hereafter cited as *Annetts*, because its facts have much greater relevance to this chapter than those in *Tame*.

III The Plaintiff's Case

While in *Chester* it was acknowledged that the Council owed a duty to the neighbourhood children, the case is an early illustration that a plaintiff cannot rely on a duty owed to someone else but must establish that he himself or she herself is owed a duty of reasonable care to avoid causing the type of injury that he or she suffered. This is normally done by showing that he or she is within a class of people to whom a duty was owed by the defendant.

The majority clearly had great difficulty in defining what such a class would comprise in this case. They enthusiastically adopted the 'floodgates' arguments. In particular, a feature of the majority's view, and that of the court below, was that they were clearly not prepared to distinguish mothers of the victim (or presumably parents or other close relatives) from other bystanders who witnessed the discovery of the primary victim's dead body. Chief Justice Latham stated:

> If a duty of the character suggested exists at all, it is not really said that it should be confined to mothers of children who are injured. It must extend to some wider class – but to what class? There appears to be no reason why it should not extend to other relatives or to all other persons, whether they be relatives or not.... [A] person who is guilty of negligence with the result that A is injured will be liable in damages to B, C D and *any other persons* who receive a nervous shock... *at any time* upon perceiving the results of the negligence, whether in disfigurement, physical injury or death.[21]
>
> ...
>
> The question which must be asked... is whether the defendant should have foreseen that a mother would suffer from nervous shock amounting to illness if she saw the dead body of her child where the death had been brought about by the negligence of the defendant towards the child. This mode of formulating the question is very favourable to the plaintiff.... [T]he question should probably be put in a form which substituted the words 'person' and 'another person' for 'mother' or 'child'.[22]

Justice Rich was as undiscriminating as Latham CJ about the relationship of the plaintiff to the primary victim, giving an extreme example to imply

[21] *Chester* (1939) 62 CLR 1, 7–8 (emphasis added), in a passage described by Lord Bridge in *McLoughlin v O'Brian* [1983] 1 AC 410, 18, as an 'interesting' example of the floodgates argument, which found no favour with the House of Lords in that case.

[22] *Chester* (1939) 62 CLR 1, 10.

that to compensate the plaintiff would expose the defendant to liability to an unlimited range of claimants:

> A negligent motorist who caused great facial disfigurement to a pedestrian could not be made liable to every person who throughout the pedestrian's life experienced shock or nausea on seeing his disfigurement.... But the law must fix a point where its remedies stop short of complete reparation for the world at large...[23]

Justice Starke's conclusion in a brief judgment was that the Council could not be liable to the plaintiff because the shock to the plaintiff was 'not within the ordinary range of human experience':[24] it was so remote from the defendant's conduct in creating or guarding the trench that no reasonable person ought to have foreseen it.

IV The Dissent

Language, Literature and Humanity

The desperate plight of the plaintiff as a mother searching for her lost child is powerfully described and constantly referenced by the persuasive use of emotive language in Evatt J's judgment:

> From the moment when the plaintiff discovered her child was missing, she searched for him without intermission... coming with her husband to the side of the trench, the plaintiff was at once beset with fear at the *sinister significance* of the trench, especially when one of the searchers was unable to *plumb the depth* of the water... Like most mothers placed in a similar situation, she was *tortured* between the fear that he had been drowned and the hope that either he was not in the trench at all, or that... quick recovery... and... artificial respiration might still save him from death. In this *agonized and distracted* state of mind and body she remained for about half an hour, when the police arrived and the child's body was discovered and removed.
>
> During this crucial period the plaintiff's condition of mind and nerve can be completely understood only by parents who have been placed in a similar *agony of hope and fear with hope gradually decreasing.* In the present case the half hour of waiting was the culmination of a *long and almost frantic searching* which had already reduced her to a state of nerve exhaustion.[25]

[23] Ibid 11. [24] Ibid 13. [25] Ibid 16–7 (emphasis added).

Later, Evatt J referred to 'the plaintiff's long agony',[26] the 'very terrifying setting of the tragedy . . . attributable to the defendant',[27] the 'special menace of the place',[28] and remarked that 'the law does not assume that all beings can bear a burden too great for many to suffer'.[29]

Justice Evatt's own emotive choice of language is then supplemented by reference to famous literary works, something rarely done in Australian judgments,[30] to support the particular characterisation of the tragedy and the plaintiff's special position in it compared with others. He first quoted William Blake's 'imaginative genius [in portraying] suffering and anxiety of this kind' in *The Little Girl Found*:

> Tired and woe-begone
> Hoarse with making moan
> . . .
> Rising from unrest
> The trembling woman pressed
> With feet of weary woe;
> She could no further go.[31]

He also cited novelist Tom Collins (aka Joseph Furphy) in *Such is Life* on 'the agony of fearfulness caused by the search for a lost child', including the following passage from this iconic Australian novel. It must resonate for parents, like the Annetts,[32] whose 16-year-old son James, after negligent supervision by his employers, disappeared and perished in the Western Australian desert in 1986 and whose remains were only found months later. Many parents of lost children must grapple for long months, or years, or even for the rest of their lives, with the crushing uncertainty Collins acknowledged:

> Bad enough to lose a youngster for a day or two, and find him alive and well; worse, beyond comparison, when he's found dead; but the most fearful thing of all is for a youngster to be lost in the bush, and never found, alive or dead.[33]

26 Ibid 18. 27 Ibid 19. 28 Ibid 23. 29 Ibid 24.

30 Michael Kirby, 'The Literary Desert in Australian Law' (2001) 45(11) *Quadrant* 33, 34.

31 William Blake, 'Little Girl Found' in *Songs of Innocence and Songs of Experience* (R Brimley Johnson, first published 1794, 1901 ed) 42–3, quoted in *Chester* (1939) 62 CLR 1, 17.

32 *Annetts* (2002) 211 CLR 317.

33 Tom Collins, *Such is Life* (Hayes Barton Press, 1975) 238, quoted in *Chester* (1939) 62 CLR 1, 18.

Justice Evatt notes that not only poets and novelists but also those administering 'the common law of England'[34] recognised that shock of the most grievous character can be sustained in circumstances analogous to those of this case.

He might also have invoked a famous Australian painting, which Evatt J, as a keen collector of Australian art, would have known well. Frederick McCubbin's *Lost*, his 1886 haunting painting of a little girl crying beneath thick gum trees in the Australian bush, was and remains one of the most well-known of 19th century Australian impressionist paintings.[35]

Indeed some commentators have identified 'the lost child' as a recurring motif in Australian literature and as a source of constant anxiety underpinning colonial society in a new, strange and vast land.[36] Certainly, there was sympathetic acknowledgement of the newcomer's special fears in Evatt J's description of Mrs Chester as someone who had only resided in the street for 14 days and as a 'woman of Polish extraction, who had special difficulty in narrating the precise nature of her feelings, her fears, her hopes and her sufferings'.[37]

Perhaps Evatt J was affected too by his own experience of his mother's grief at the loss of two sons far away in World War I. Often news of death would follow a period of the person being reported as 'missing in action', a description that would bring the agony of hope and despair and uncertainty. While he himself was rejected for military service because of his poor eyesight, Evatt J's brothers, Ray and Frank had both enlisted. Ray survived Egypt and Gallipoli but was killed in the 1917 Battle of Passchendale on the Western Front. Frank was wounded in that battle but survived to continue fighting through 1918. However, Evatt J's friend and author Kylie Tennant wrote: 'News of his death reached his family after the signing of the Armistice as they were preparing for his return home. Jeanie Evatt fell to the floor unconscious and never fully recovered from the loss of those two sons'.[38]

When Michael Kirby described Australian legal judgments as a 'literary desert' in 2001, with only occasional oases devoted to Shakespeare, the

[34] *Chester* (1939) 62 CLR 1, 18.

[35] See further Malcolm Knox, 'Lure of the Little Child Lost', *The Sydney Morning Herald* (Sydney), 15 August 2009.

[36] Ibid, citing Peter Pierce, *The Country of Lost Children: An Australian Anxiety* (Cambridge University Press, 1999).

[37] *Chester* (1939) 62 CLR 1, 17.

[38] Kylie Tennant, *Evatt: Politics and Justice* (Angus and Robertson, 1970) 23.

Bible or ancient Greek and Roman texts, he singled out Evatt J's judgment in *Chester* as 'the only substantial citation of Australian literature in reasoning in the High Court' in its history.[39] Kirby contrasted the majority's 'orthodox and colourless' prose with the power of the rhetoric in Evatt J's reasons including his invocation of literature to explain Mrs Chester's profound, and natural, suffering.[40]

Unlike the majority, Evatt J gave special attention to the fact the plaintiff was the *mother* of the victim, not merely an unrelated third party caught up in the search for the child or any bystander or passer-by shocked at the sight of his body being dragged from the trench. He quoted the judgment of Jordan CJ in the lower court which described Mrs Chester as 'a person looking for the body of a child then believed to be dead', before offering the correction: 'She was not "looking for the body of a child". She was looking for *her* child'.[41]

Justice Evatt's extensive reliance on the academic writing of influential and well-respected English and American scholars and reference to leading American case law and jurists reinforced the strength and influence of his dissent. His discussion of the law shows how the courts were grappling with the new generalised concept of a duty of care that emerged from *Donoghue v Stevenson* in 1932, and particularly of how to set reasonable limits of legal liability in the tort of negligence. Justice Evatt had dissented in *Australian Knitting Mills Ltd v Grant*[42] by holding that the new principles of *Donoghue v Stevenson* applied to Dr Grant's case, and his dissent was vindicated by the Privy Council on appeal.[43] It is said that Lord Atkin wrote to Evatt J to compliment him on his judgments.[44] Academic commentary on novel cases and concepts was naturally useful at this time of early development of the modern law. Influential too were developments in American case law. Because *Chester* could be seen as somewhat analogous to search and rescue cases, many of which had been decided by the American courts, Evatt J closely considered the decision of the New York Court of Appeals, delivered and surely penned by Cardozo J in *Wagner v International Railway*[45] as well as Professor Goodhart's

[39] Kirby, above n 30, 34. For discussion of the literary features of Heydon J's dissent in *Monis v The Queen* (2013) 249 CLR 92, see Gabrielle Appleby and Heather Roberts, 'He Who Would Not Be Muzzled: Justice Heydon's Last Dissent in *Monis v The Queen* (2013)' in ch 18 of this book.

[40] Kirby, above n 30, 34.

[41] *Chester* (1939) 62 CLR 1, 22 (emphasis added).

[42] (1933) 50 CLR 387.

[43] *Grant v Australian Knitting Mills Ltd* [1936] AC 85.

[44] Tennant, above n 38, 83.

[45] 232 NY 176 (1921).

commentary on that case;[46] and the adoption of its principles in the 1935 English Court of Appeal decision of *Haynes v Harwood*.[47]

The final intrinsic quality of Evatt J's dissenting judgment was the common sense of his legal reasoning and the sense of humanity in his account of the law. Indeed, Evatt J referred directly to these two ideals, concluding that Australian courts should follow the principles by then adopted by the courts of England, 'principles which are not to be rejected or evaded mere because they have introduced into the law an element of humanity and common sense alike'.[48] This contrasted sharply with the rigid, undiscriminating, and arguably arbitrary approach of the majority, who, faced with a claim that the law's boundaries should move by an inch, rejected this as if it attempted to move them by a mile.

Geoffrey Robertson has commented on the sharp contrast between the approach of the majority and Evatt J, stating:

> It was a masterly piece of jurisprudence, infused with humanity, which came in time to be recognised as correct in law as well as in morality. It was an example of Evatt's profound belief that humanitarian principles could be deployed by judges to develop a common law that would meet the needs and challenges of a changing world.[49]

It should not of course be assumed that Evatt J was the only one of the High Court judges hearing *Chester* to be influenced by his life experiences and loss of close family. Justice Starke had also experienced personal tragedy when his mother and sister perished in the *SS Waratah*, which disappeared between Durban and Capetown in 1909. But it appeared that the majority expected the community to be made of sterner stuff than Mrs Chester:

> Death is not an infrequent event, and even violent and distressing deaths are not uncommon. It is, however, not a common experience of mankind that the spectacle, even of the sudden and distressing death of a child, produces any consequence of more than temporary nature . . .[50]

Justice Evatt's Legal Reasoning

Turning to the legal reasoning, which was to have such an influence on the future development of the law, the key issue was whether the defendant

46 A L Goodhart, 'Rescue and Voluntary Assumption of Risk' (1934) 5 *Cambridge Law Journal* 192, 197–8.

47 [1935] 1 KB 146.

48 *Chester* (1939) 62 CLR 1, 46

49 Robertson, above n 5, 37.

50 *Chester* (1939) 62 CLR 1, 10 (Latham CJ).

owed a duty to the plaintiff to avoid causing her nervous shock in the circumstances of this case. Three matters were critical to the finding of a duty of care:

(a) The timing of the shock: If Mrs Chester suffered the shock partly or wholly upon the discovery of her son's body, that is, *after* his death, did this render her shock and subsequent illness not reasonably foreseeable to the defendant and distinguish her case from the successful claim in *Hambrook v Stokes Brothers*?
(b) The 'foreseeable plaintiff': Did the defendant's duty of care extend only towards 'the ordinary normal human being' and not to people who might be categorised as exceptional, '"susceptible and emotional mothers" let us say'?[51]
(c) The special position of parents: Were mothers, or parents of the primary victim, to be treated as no more foreseeable than passers-by and others, so that unless a duty could be proved to the latter, there could be no duty to the former?

Timing

The defendant argued that there was a critical difference between Mrs Chester's situation and that in *Hambrook v Stokes Brothers.* The relevant circumstances were that the plaintiff had spent hours searching for her missing son once she realised he was missing, later heard that he might have fallen into the water-filled trench, and had come to the trench to wait for it to be searched and had then seen his lifeless body recovered. The defendants argued that Mrs Chester suffered shock *after* the death of her son, and not prior to his death; unlike the mother in *Hambrook v Stokes Brothers,* her shock did not arise from *the fear* that he *might* be injured or dead, but from the discovery that he *was.* This put her outside the bounds of reasonable foreseeability.

It seems ridiculous today to the legal reader, and must always have seemed quite incomprehensible to the lay reader, that the law could draw such a fine distinction when deeming a situation reasonably foreseeable or not. However, it was on this basis that the plaintiff had failed in the courts below. The trial judge felt he must find against the plaintiff: as her shock was due to belated cognisance of an injury caused some appreciable time

[51] Ibid 24 (Evatt J).

before, it could not be said to be caused by the negligence.[52] On appeal, Jordan CJ said:

> There is no evidence of a breach of any duty towards the plaintiff, as a person present when the accident occurred, not to cause her [injury] by exposing her to the spectacle of a horrifying accident... The action is an attempt by the plaintiff to obtain damages for the distress which she experienced as the result of learning of her child's death[53] ... [an] attempt to extend what was decided in *Hambrook v Stokes Brothers* to lengths which are unwarranted by either principle or authority.[54]

Justice Evatt first rejected the finding of fact, on which the trial judge based his refusal to put the case to a jury, that the plaintiff's shock was caused merely by the discovery, after the event, that her son was dead. He noted that this took no account of her long agony of waiting and the effect upon her of witnessing the actual removal of his body from the water. He pointed out that she may still have been in an agony of hope and despair[55] because attempts were made for some three-quarters-of-an-hour to resuscitate him,[56] but he failed to respond. In any event, the question of causation was entirely for the jury, which might reasonably have taken into account the critical waiting period and the 'very terrifying setting of the tragedy'.[57] Second, and this is the critical legal point from *Chester*, he took issue with the legal ruling that the defendant should escape liability if the consequences of its negligence to the child had been completed *before* the shock was suffered:

> It seems very unreasonable to make liability depend upon too nice a psychological analysis of the nature and time of the first onset of fear and shock suffered by a mother in circumstances analogous to *Hambrook v Stokes Brothers* ...

[52] As Evatt J pointed out, this is a finding on causation rather than duty but it was then used as the basis for the Full Court's decision on duty: ibid 20.

[53] Damages not recoverable under the *Compensation to Relatives Act 1897* (NSW) ('*Lord Campbell's Act*').

[54] *Chester v Council of the Municipality of Waverley* (1938) 55 WN (NSW) 221, 223.

[55] *Chester* (1939) 62 CLR 1, 19. Justice Evatt notes the circumstances suggested to Mrs Chester and her husband that even at that moment life was not quite extinguished.

[56] Ibid 17. According to Evatt J, 'expert lifesavers had worked on the child's body for some time'. It was reported that members of the Bondi Life Saving Club, the North Bondi Club and Eastern Suburbs Ambulance attempted resuscitation for three-quarters-of-an-hour before the boy was taken to St Vincent's Hospital where he was pronounced dead: 'Boy Drowned in Evacuation: Waverly Tragedy', *Truth* (Sydney), 15 August 1937, 19.

[57] *Chester* (1939) 62 CLR 1, 19.

> It seems indisputable that the jury could have found that the onset of the plaintiff's nervous shock took place at a point of time when the plaintiff, although at the side of the trench, did not know or even believe that her child had been drowned.... She was terrified lest he should have been drowned, was taking notice of little except what her own senses were telling her, was hoping against hope that her very worst fear would not be realised.[58]

The Foreseeable Plaintiff: Only Persons of Normal Fortitude?

The question of whether a defendant owes a duty only if the plaintiff is a person of normal fortitude or whether a defendant owes a duty to the plaintiff only if a person of normal fortitude would foreseeably suffer the relevant injury, is an issue which arises in many contexts in negligence. Immediately it can be seen that there are two alternative questions. In general, the correct question is the second one.[59] Given that, it should not matter if the particular plaintiff has a special susceptibility, as long as the relevant injury might foreseeably be suffered by an ordinary person in the plaintiff's position. Once a breach of *that* duty is shown, the plaintiff can recover in full for any *type* of damage within the bounds of remoteness rules,[60] with the so-called 'eggshell skull' rule that the defendant takes his or her victim as he or she finds them then applying.[61] In other words, the extent of the particular type of damage need not be foreseeable by the defendant, as long as the type of damage is reasonably foreseeable.

The issue of the 'ordinary plaintiff of normal fortitude' as against the 'exceptionally susceptible' plaintiff has long dogged nervous shock

58 Ibid 21–2.

59 *Annetts* (2002) 211 CLR 317, 383 (Gummow and Kirby JJ). Justices Gummow and Kirby stated that attention to the notional person of normal fortitude assists the assessment of the reasonable foreseeability of harm, and does not create a precondition or bar to recovery.

60 The High Court here was still referring to the remoteness rule from *Re Polemis* [1921] 3 KB 560 that the claimed damage be a direct consequence: see, eg, *Chester* (1939) 62 CLR 1, 6 (Latham CJ). It was not until 1961 that that rule was replaced with the 'reasonably foreseeable type of damage' rule of remoteness in *Overseas Tankships (UK) Ltd v Morts Dock and Engineering Co Ltd* [1961] AC 388 ('*The Wagon Mound [No 1]*'). See further n 84 below.

61 *Dulieu v White & Sons* [1901] 2 KB 669, 679 (Kennedy LJ): 'if a man is negligently run over... it is no answer to the sufferer's claim for damages that he would have suffered less injury, or no injury at all, if he had not had an unusually thin skull or an unusually weak heart'. See also *Owens v Liverpool Corporation* [1939] 1 KB 397, 400. Both cases are cited by Evatt J on this point: *Chester* (1939) 62 CLR 1, 26–7.

jurisprudence in the duty context.[62] Justice Evatt was at pains to reject the suggestion implicit in the Full Court's reasoning that only persons in an exceptional category – '"susceptible and emotional mothers" let us say' – would have suffered and that the duty existed *only* to the 'ordinary normal human being'.[63] He felt that the assertion that no type of parent other than a susceptible and nervous mother would suffer shock and illness from such an ordeal was contradicted by all human experience.[64] Further, he stated that any reasonable person is aware that 'all sorts and conditions of men and women' may be found among those involved in or witnessing an accident. He quoted Professor Goodhart that 'we all know that the average man in the street is not necessarily the average man'.[65] Justice Evatt concluded: 'Where a class or group may be endangered by carelessness, the defendant's sphere of duty can seldom be contracted by denying a duty to weak and nervous members of that group'.[66]

The Special Position of Parents in Nervous Shock Cases

It has been noted above that the majority of the High Court, like the Full Court of New South Wales, drew no distinction between the position of the plaintiff as the mother or parent of the primary victim of the defendant's negligence, and that of a stranger who happened upon the scene. At best, parents seemed to be considered no more foreseeable as witnesses than bystanders or passers-by. At worst, it was even implied that a stranger who saw the event itself would be more foreseeable as likely to suffer shock and therefore more deserving of compensation than a mother who later came upon the body of her child.[67]

As noted above, Evatt J showed his and the community's recognition of the special trauma for parents whose child is missing, injured, imperilled or killed. He commented that there lurked a fallacy in the Full Court's reasoning that the principle in *Hambrook v Stokes Brothers* applies only for the benefit of wayfarers or passers-by at the time of the event, declaring, 'I think the law is at once more civilized and more humane'.[68]

62 See, eg, *Wilkinson v Downton* [1897] 2 QB 57; *Jaensch v Coffey* (1984) 155 CLR 549; *Annetts* (2002) 211 CLR 317.

63 *Chester* (1939) 62 CLR 1, 24–5.

64 Ibid 25.

65 Arthur L Goodhart, *Essays in Jurisprudence and the Common Law* (Cambridge University Press, 1931) 126–7, quoted in *Chester* (1939) 62 CLR 1, 26 (Evatt J).

66 *Chester* (1939) 62 CLR 1, 27.

67 *Chester v Council of the Municipality of Waverley* (1938) 55 WN (NSW) 221, 223 (Jordan CJ): 'But she was then there [at the scene] not in the character of a wayfarer startled by a distressing sight, but of a person looking for the body of a child then believed to be dead'.

68 *Chester* (1939) 62 CLR 1, 23.

This fallacy does indeed seem odd in its implication that a mere passer-by, without any involvement in the incident, *might* recover. While it was not until *Bourhill v Young*[69] in 1943 that the House of Lords stressed that the unsuccessful 'fishwife' in that case had no relationship to the party who was killed near her stall, all of the successful nervous shock cases before *Chester* had involved claimants in a close family relationship. In particular, *Hambrook v Stokes Brothers* was a case involving the mother of the primary victims, not a mere passer-by. Even today, it is difficult to think of a case where a mere passer-by, wayfarer or bystander, even as a witness to the event itself, has been able to recover for nervous shock.[70]

It was the failure of the majority to recognise the special relationship of parents to the victim (and thus their greater susceptibility to shock), coupled with the idea that a duty could not be recognised to the former unless it was extended to 'all and sundry',[71] that underpinned fears that allowing the plaintiff to recover would open the 'floodgates' to claims.[72] But as Evatt J pointed out, while the duty could not in principle be limited to parents or relatives, it certainly *extended* to the particular plaintiff, the mother of the child. He drew analogies with well-known 'search and rescue' cases in the United States and England which showed that although rescuers were not limited to anxious family members, they were certainly a highly foreseeable category of rescuer.[73]

This must be right. The difficulty of identifying as a matter of hypothesis or speculation where the outer boundaries of foreseeable plaintiffs might lie should be no reason to deny a duty to someone who, whatever the outer boundaries, was clearly well within them: indeed, to someone who belonged to a class whose members were probably the most foreseeable of all. If it were otherwise, the categories of negligence, far from being 'never closed' as Lord MacMillan had said in *Donoghue v Stevenson*,[74] could never develop.

69 [1943] AC 92.

70 The hurdle in the current *Civil Liability Act 2002* (NSW) in s 30 that a person cannot recover for mental harm *unless* they are a specified family member or a 'witness at the scene of the accident' should not be read as providing that a mere witness *may* recover. See further discussion of bystanders in *Alcock v Chief Constable South Yorkshire Police* [1992] 1 AC 310, 403 (Lord Ackner).

71 *Chester* (1939) 62 CLR 1, 30.

72 *Annetts* (2002) 211 CLR 317, 399 (Hayne J). Justice Hayne, commenting on the floodgates arguments in *Chester*, suggested that floodgates arguments and references to indeterminate liability may actually have been based on unspoken or masked fears about the capacity of the courts to distinguish between cases of real and feigned injury.

73 *Chester* (1939) 62 CLR 1, 41.

74 [1932] AC 562, 619.

V The Impact of the Dissent

Influence on the Legislature

Rarely do dissenting judgments have such an immediate effect on the legislature as Evatt J's did. *Chester* was a case from New South Wales and it was widely reported in the local newspapers and those farther afield.[75] It obviously made its mark on the people of the Sydney suburb of Waverley where the child and his parents lived. It so happened that Mrs Chester's solicitor, Abram Landa, was also the Labor member for the broader Bondi electorate in the New South Wales Legislative Assembly. He became a fierce promoter of legislation to override the decision in the lead up to the next state election, and noted that the people of Bondi had a special reason to appreciate the humanitarian attitude of the government in providing for what Mrs Chester had been unable to obtain from the courts.[76] But it also influenced other state parliamentarians, particularly, but not only, those in the Labor Party.[77] That was of course the party with which Evatt J had a near-lifelong association, both before his appointment to the High Court bench in 1930, and later after his resignation in 1940, when he became Commonwealth Attorney-General and Minister for External Affairs in John Curtin's Labor wartime government.

Soon afterwards, the New South Wales Parliament enacted the *Law Reform (Miscellaneous Provisions) Act 1944* (NSW) ('*1944 Act*'), pt 3 of which introduced a statutory liability for nervous shock suffered by the parent or spouse of a primary victim who had been killed, injured or put in peril by an act, neglect or default of the defendant. The liability also extended to other specified family members but only where they saw or heard the victim being killed, injured or put in peril.

This statutory liability not only relieved the parent or spouse from having to prove that he or she, or the class to which they belonged, was owed a duty of care by the defendant. But most importantly, it removed the requirement of the common law at that time that he or she had witnessed the whole of the accident itself.

[75] See 'Drowning of Child', *The Maitland Daily Mercury* (Maitland), 20 September 1938; 'Death of a Boy', *The Sydney Morning Herald* (Sydney), 1 April 1939; 'Mother's Claim Failed', *The Sydney Morning Herald* (Sydney), 8 June 1939; 'Mother Sees Boy's Body Recovered', *The Advertiser* (Adelaide), 8 June 1939, 22; 'Mother's Claim against Council', *The Singleton Argus* (Singleton), 9 June 1939.

[76] New South Wales, *Parliamentary Debates*, Legislative Assembly, 18 October 1944, 402 (Abram Landa).

[77] Ibid 527–8 (Abram Landa).

On 18 October 1944 the Labor Premier of New South Wales William McKell stated in the New South Wales Legislative Assembly:

> Hon members will all agree that it was to remedy the state of affairs brought about in *Chester v Waverley Council* that that part of the measure was introduced [pt 3]. *Chester v Waverley Council*, as hon members well know, was the case in our own High Court where a mother who had sustained shock through seeing her child's dead body removed from a water-filled trench left unprotected by the council, failed in her action.[78]

Abram Landa commented that the part of this bill dealing with nervous shock had the approval of members on both sides of the House, including 'eminent legal men on the Opposition', despite resistance and an attempted amendment to an earlier version in 'another place' (presumably the Legislative Council) which would have made the bill valueless as a correction of the *Chester* decision. This indicates that there was an earlier unsuccessful attempt to remedy the majority decision in *Chester*, but nevertheless, Landa had persevered.[79]

It cannot be doubted that the *1944 Act* provided a very significant legal right for those who suffered nervous shock due to a tort occurring in New South Wales. However, there does not appear to be any evidence that the statutory liability in New South Wales caused an unbearable, unreasonable or disproportionate burden on defendants and their insurers in New South Wales,[80] or that plaintiffs would regard a nervous shock claim by a parent or a spouse as an easy claim to make. The reason for this is that there was still an essential element built into the Act that served as an important restriction on liability and may have prevented floods of claims. As the Act did not define 'nervous shock', the term was defined by the common law and it was undisputed that, whether at common law or under the statute, a plaintiff could only recover for nervous shock that caused a physical or medically recognised psychiatric *illness*. Mere shock or fright would not do.[81] Justices Gummow and Kirby have since emphasised that the requirement of a recognised psychiatric illness reduces the scope for indeterminate liability and increased litigation.[82]

[78] Ibid 522 (William McKell, Premier and Colonial Treasurer).

[79] Ibid 527–8 (Abram Landa).

[80] See United Kingdom Law Commission, *Liability for Psychiatric Illness*, Consultation Paper No 137 (1995) 65–6 [5.25]. See also the comments on the relatively small potential impact on insurance premiums if liability for psychiatric illness were extended: at 7 [1.13].

[81] See further *Mount Isa Mines Ltd v Pusey* (1970) 125 CLR 383, 394 (Windeyer J); *Jaensch v Coffey* (1984) 155 CLR 549, 564 (Brennan J).

[82] *Annetts* (2002) 211 CLR 317, 496.

The *1944 Act* had no parallel in other states of Australia. While equivalent legislation was enacted in the Australian Capital Territory and the Northern Territory in the 1950s,[83] no other state followed suit. This meant that residents and litigants in those states had to rely on the further development of the common law – and 45 years later the common law followed Evatt J's dissenting judgment.[84]

Influence on the Common Law

Writing in 2001, Michael Kirby commented that Evatt J's opinion

> did not carry the High Court with him. But it has continued to agitate commentators and other lawyers critical of the artificialities of the line which the common law has drawn until now concerning the scope of the legal duty of care where an alleged victim of the default has suffered nervous shock.[85]

Whatever the social or legal unease with the majority decision, the decision could not be reviewed until the right case – and a determined plaintiff and his or her legal advocates – came before the High Court of Australia. That case was *Jaensch v Coffey* in 1984.[86] The High Court overruled the majority decision in *Chester* that a plaintiff could only recover for nervous shock if he or she was in (antecedent) fear of, and witnessed, their loved one *being* killed, injured or put in peril. Chief Justice Gibbs noted that the court is 'not necessarily constrained to follow earlier decisions when they appear to be out of accord with contemporary principles'.[87] He then announced that '*Chester v Waverley Corporation*, which cannot be justified either on the ground that shock in that case was not reasonably foreseeable or on the ground that the requisite proximity was lacking, should no longer be followed'.[88]

Justice Deane, after an extensive review of the law of negligence over the 50 years since *Donoghue v Stevenson*, stated:

83 *Law Reform (Miscellaneous Provisions) Act 1955* (ACT) s 24; *Law Reform (Miscellaneous Provisions) Act* 1956 (NT) s 25.

84 Evatt, it appears, believed his impact had actually occurred earlier. Michael Pelly recounts an amusing tale of Evatt, by now Chief Justice of New South Wales, pressing a young Murray Gleeson, while a student editor of the *Sydney Law Review*, to write about how the Privy Council had vindicated his dissent in its landmark decision in *The Wagon Mound [No 1]*. However, Professor Morison of the University of Sydney Law Faculty, and general editor of the journal, disagreed with this characterisation of the latter case and urged Gleeson to 'just do nothing': Michael Pelly, *Murray Gleeson: The Smiler* (Federation Press, 2014) 28.

85 Kirby, above n 30, 35. 86 (1984) 155 CLR 549. 87 Ibid 554. 88 Ibid.

> The judgments of the majority in *Chester's Case* have not worn well with time. The proposition upon which those judgments [are] based is no longer, if it ever was, acceptable. It is simply out of accord with medical knowledge and human experience to deny that it is reasonably foreseeable that the shock suffered by a mother on seeing the body of her infant child, whom she was seeking, raised from the bottom of a water-filled trench might well be such as to cause psychoneurosis or mental illness. It must now be accepted that the conclusion of Evatt J is, on the facts in *Chester*, plainly to be preferred to that of the majority.[89]

Writing in 2002, Gummow and Kirby JJ in *Tame v New South Wales; Annetts v Australian Stations Pty Ltd* ('*Annetts*') respectfully explained the majority decision in *Chester* as illustrating 'that the determination of what ought reasonably to have been foreseen may differ from one age to the next'.[90]

In *Jaensch v Coffey*, Deane J pointed out that even Evatt J's dissent, limited as it must be to the facts of a plaintiff who was called to the scene and cause of her son's death, did not avail Mrs Coffey, who was called, not to the scene, but to the hospital emergency department where the sight of her husband in a critical state with serious and potentially fatal injuries caused her to suffer a psychiatric illness. The High Court in this case extended liability, as the House of Lords had done, quoting Evatt J's dissent with approval, the year before in *McLoughlin v O'Brian*,[91] to cover nervous shock to a close relative of the primary victim and arising from her own perception of the *immediate aftermath* of the accident.

The speeches in *McLoughlin v O'Brian* show the impact of Evatt J's judgment on the course of the modern English common law. While Lord Wilberforce referred to Evatt J's 'powerful dissent',[92] Lord Bridge admitted to finding Evatt J's 'powerful dissenting judgment . . . wholly convincing' and that 'I cannot for a moment doubt the correctness of his conclusion'.[93] Lord Scarman stated:

> But at each landmark stage common law principle, when considered in the context of developing medical science, has beckoned the judges on. And now, as has been made clear by Evatt J, dissenting, in *Chester's case* in

[89] Ibid 590–1, cited in *Gifford v Strang Patrick Stevedoring Pty Ltd* (2003) 214 CLR 269, 277 (Gleeson CJ).

[90] *Annetts* (2002) 211 CLR 317, 384–5. They acknowledged that the concept can lead to sharply divided views in assessing the evidence, citing the range of opinions in *Bunyan v Jordan* and in *Chester*. But given that the result in *Chester* spurred the legislature in New South Wales to action, the majority's application of the reasonable foreseeability test might be said not even to accord with contemporaneous views.

[91] [1983] 1 AC 410. [92] Ibid 422. [93] Ibid 439.

> the High Court of Australia, by Tobriner J giving the majority judgment in the Californian case of *Dillon v Legg*, and by my noble and learned friend in this case, common law principle requires the judges to follow the logic of the 'reasonably foreseeable test' so as, in circumstances where it is appropriate, to apply it untrammelled by spatial, physical, or temporal limits. Space, time, distance, the nature of the injuries sustained, and the relationship of the plaintiff to the immediate victim of the accident, are factors to be weighed, but not legal limitations, when the test of reasonable foreseeability is to be applied.[94]

The 'immediate aftermath' doctrine and other rigid requirements for liability for nervous shock were finally rejected in turn by the High Court in *Annetts*.[95] The court brought the requirements for a legal duty of care back within the broad principles of negligence that flowed from *Donoghue v Stevenson* and later cases of general application. Justices Gummow and Kirby in the majority commented that unprincipled distinctions and artificial mechanisms such as those that had dominated in the nervous shock cases bring the law into disrepute and impede the emergence of a coherent body of case law.[96]

The majority approach in *Annetts* was similar to that taken by Evatt J in *Chester*. Justice Gaudron referred to the latter's 'seminal dissenting judgment':[97] Evatt J had appreciated the plaintiff's case resting on the reasonable foreseeability of the plaintiff being called to or coming to the scene of her son's then suspected fatality.

VI Conclusion

Unfortunately, the story of Evatt J's dissent in *Chester* does not end with the common sense, logic and humanity shown by the High Court in allowing the Annetts' claim, a result of which he would surely have approved.

In the same year as *Annetts*, the New South Wales government enacted the second tranche of its 'civil liability' tort reforms. Many other states

[94] Ibid 430. There was strong disagreement between the Law Lords as to whether courts could apply 'policy' in drawing a line on liability that foreseeability principles would otherwise allow.

[95] Justice Gaudron and Gummow and Kirby JJ identified the three rules in question operating as control mechanisms as the 'sudden shock' rule, the 'normal fortitude rule' and the 'direct perception' rule: *Annetts* (2002) 211 CLR 317, 339 (Gaudron J), 380 (Gummow and Kirby JJ).

[96] Ibid 380–1.

[97] Ibid 339.

followed the New South Wales example.[98] This second tranche was contained in the *Civil Liability Amendment (Personal Responsibility) Act 2002* (NSW) ('2002 Act'), an Act that was introduced into the House of Representatives by the Labor Premier, Robert Carr, with the comment that it was the most important reform of the laws of negligence in 70 years,[99] seemingly a self-assessment with more than a nod to Lord Atkin.

The 2002 Act's aim, as the title suggests, was to restore the concept of 'personal responsibility' to the law: the personal responsibility of the *plaintiff.* It was enacted without a murmur of objection or amendment by members of the Liberal Party and National Party Opposition or others. It is a pity that there was not a Doc Evatt in the 'House' the day the *2002 Act* was passed. He at least might have had something to say about the responsibility of *defendants.*

The new restrictions on liability would not necessarily stand in the way of Mrs Chester if she were to sue today in the same circumstances.[100] However, in contrast to Evatt J's dissenting judgment, the *1944 Act* and the more expansive views on reasonable foreseeability of psychiatric illness shown by judges of the High Court in recent decisions, these legislated tort 'reforms' can hardly be said to advance the plight of people in Mrs Chester's situation – a plight which Evatt J had described and analysed so eloquently, so humanely, and with such long-lasting influence.

[98] Only Queensland still relies on the common law, while the Northern Territory and the Australian Capital Territory retain a statutory action similar to that in the *1944 Act*: *Law Reform (Miscellaneous Provisions Act) 1956* (NT) s 25; *Civil Law (Wrongs Act) 2002* (ACT) s 36.

[99] New South Wales, *Parliamentary Debates*, Legislative Assembly, 23 October 2002, 5764 (Robert Carr).

[100] She would not be debarred from claiming by *Civil Liability Act 2002* (NSW) s 30, but would have to satisfy the requirements of s 32 and the common law to establish a duty of care. Civil liability statutes and motor accident statutes now tend to limit recovery to those, other than parents, spouses and children of the victim, who have seen or heard the victim 'being killed injured or put in peril' (see, eg, *Civil Liability Act 2002* (NSW) s 31, applied in *Wicks v State Rail Authority of New South Wales* (2010) 241 CLR 60) or who were 'present at the scene of the accident when the accident happened' (see, eg, *Civil Liability Act 1936* (SA) s 53, applied in *King v Philcox* (2015) 89 ALJR 582).

5

Uther's Case (1947): Justice Dixon and the Troubled Legacy of the Commonwealth Immunity Doctrine

STEPHEN MCDONALD AND ANNE CARTER

I Introduction

Sir Owen Dixon has been remembered overwhelmingly as a 'great' judge, and indeed as one of the greatest judges of the 20th century.[1] His dissenting judgment in *Re Foreman & Sons Pty Ltd; Uther v Commissioner of Taxation* ('*Uther's Case*')[2] has, in spite of considerable shortcomings, endured to become a great dissent. In *Uther's Case*, Dixon J rejected the prevailing reciprocal understanding of the relationship between the Commonwealth and the states and instead developed a doctrine that placed the Commonwealth in a privileged position. His conception of the Commonwealth's immunity from state laws, which was ultimately accepted and applied by a majority of the High Court in 1962 in *Commonwealth v Cigamatic Pty Ltd (in liq)* ('*Cigamatic*'),[3] has had a lasting impact. Despite a wealth of academic criticism, the Court has declined[4] to overrule what has been described as a problematic[5] and even heretical[6] doctrine. In this chapter

[1] See, eg, I D F Callinan, 'Comment on Philip Ayres's Article: Dixon's View of the Privy Council' (2003) 24 *Australian Bar Review* 18, 21. David Ritter notes that the quality perhaps most commonly ascribed to Dixon is that of 'greatness', and documents various examples: see David Ritter, 'The Myth of Sir Owen Dixon' (2004) 9 *Australian Journal of Legal History* 249, 253; David Ritter, 'Greatness as Measure? Recent Writings on the High Court of Australia' (2004) 50 *Australian Journal of Politics and History* 434.

[2] (1947) 74 CLR 508. [3] (1962) 108 CLR 372.

[4] Invitations to the High Court to overrule *Cigamatic* were declined in *Maguire v Simpson* (1977) 139 CLR 362 and *Re Residential Tenancies Tribunal (NSW); Ex parte Defence Housing Authority* (1997) 190 CLR 410 ('*Residential Tenancies Tribunal*').

[5] Anne Twomey, 'Federal Limitations on the Legislative Power of the States and the Commonwealth to Bind One Another' (2003) 31 *Federal Law Review* 507, 529.

[6] R P Meagher and W M C Gummow, 'Sir Owen Dixon's Heresy' (1980) 54 *Australian Law Journal* 25.

we examine various factors that have enabled Dixon J's dissent in *Uther's Case* to prevail.

The majority in *Uther's Case* held, consistently with previous cases,[7] that, subject to inconsistent Commonwealth legislation, state laws could validly apply to the Commonwealth. The state legislation in question was a New South Wales Act which provided for a priority order of debts in the case of the winding up of a company.[8] Under the legislation, claims for Commonwealth sales tax and payroll tax were in the class of unsecured debts to be paid after the payment of other specified debts. The majority held that it was within the constitutional competence of New South Wales to restrict or abolish the prerogative right of the Commonwealth in this way. Justice Dixon disagreed, holding that the state legislation was invalid in its application to the Commonwealth. As is explained below, Dixon J's reasoning was underpinned by his comparatively well-formed conception of the Australian federation. Although that was 'necessarily a dual system', in Dixon J's view it was one in which the Commonwealth had 'supremacy' because of the *Constitution*'s affirmative grant of power to legislate with respect to specific topics and the paramountcy accorded to federal laws by s 109 of the *Constitution*.[9]

Fifteen years later, Dixon J's dissent in *Uther's Case* was ultimately adopted by the Court in *Cigamatic*.[10] By that time, Dixon had been Chief Justice for a decade. He was 'perhaps at the height of his powers',[11] and was able to command the support of four other Justices. The facts of *Cigamatic* were very similar to those of *Uther's Case*, and a majority of the Court joined with Dixon CJ in overruling the earlier decision, holding that the state companies legislation could not alter the priority of the Commonwealth in the order of the payment of debts.[12]

In this chapter we explore various interrelated factors that have contributed to the enduring legacy of Dixon J's dissenting reasons. First,

7 See, eg, *Pirrie v McFarlane* (1925) 36 CLR 170; *West v Commissioner of Taxation (NSW)* (1937) 56 CLR 170.

8 *Companies Act 1936* (NSW) s 297.

9 *Uther's Case* (1947) 74 CLR 508, 529.

10 (1962) 108 CLR 372, 378 (Dixon CJ; Kitto and Windeyer JJ agreeing), 389 (Menzies J; Kitto and Owen JJ agreeing), 390 (Windeyer J). See also *Commonwealth v Bogle* (1953) 89 CLR 229, 259–60 (Fullagar J; Dixon CJ, Webb, Kitto and Taylor JJ agreeing).

11 H P Lee, 'Cigamatic Case' in Tony Blackshield, Michael Coper and George Williams (eds), *The Oxford Companion to the High Court of Australia* (Oxford University Press, 2001) 95, 95.

12 (1962) 108 CLR 372. Justices McTiernan and Taylor dissented, holding that the Court should not overrule *Uther's Case*.

we examine Dixon J's conception of the Australian federation, including his conviction concerning the inappropriateness of a state regulating the legal relations of the Commonwealth with its own subjects. Second, we discuss Dixon's influence as Chief Justice of the *Cigamatic* Court, which facilitated the adoption by the Court of what in 1947 had been a minority view. This includes some reflections on Dixon CJ's intellectual leadership of the Court and also the changing dynamics of the Court over this period. Third, and linked to the second point, the continuing reverence for Dixon that continues to the present day has helped to entrench and cement his view of the nature of the federation. Fourth, we consider the centralising imbalance inherent in the doctrine, in contrast to the earlier reciprocal approaches, and how this corresponds with the political reality of the ascendancy of Commonwealth power in the federation. To conclude, we offer a brief examination of the influence of Dixon J's dissent in the cases since *Cigamatic*, contending that despite the possible dilution of the Commonwealth immunity doctrine, Dixon J's reasoning in *Uther's Case*, as accepted in *Cigamatic*, remains important.

II Justice Dixon's Conception of the Federation

According to Dixon J, the state legislation considered in *Uther's Case* sought to regulate the relationship between the Commonwealth and its own subjects. Central to his dissent was the proposition that it is exclusively for the Commonwealth, and not the states, to regulate relations between the Commonwealth government and its subjects: 'to define or regulate the rights or privileges, duties or disabilities, of the Commonwealth in relation to the subjects of the Crown is not a matter for the States'.[13] The appeal of Dixon J's position lies in this simple, fundamental and at least superficially attractive proposition.

Justice Dixon, at least by 1947, seems to have possessed within his own mind a relatively well-formed conception of the Australian federation.[14] As Professor Leslie Zines observed, Dixon J's dissent in *Uther's Case* rested

[13] *Uther's Case* (1947) 74 CLR 508, 528.

[14] The development of Dixon J's views can be traced through his judgments. See, eg, *Australian Railways Union v Victorian Railways Commissioners* (1930) 44 CLR 319, 390; *West v Commissioner of Taxation (NSW)* (1937) 56 CLR 657, 682–3; *Federal Commissioner of Taxation v E O Farley Ltd* (1940) 63 CLR 278, 308; *Essendon Corporation v Criterion Theatres Ltd* (1947) 74 CLR 1, 22.

on his particular theory of federalism,[15] which both built upon and qualified the approach established by *Amalgamated Society of Engineers v Adelaide Steamship Co Ltd* ('*Engineers' Case*')[16] in 1920. That case had, of course, exploded the previously prevailing doctrines of reserved state legislative powers and the implied immunity of state and Commonwealth instrumentalities. The Court instead established a rule that the enumerated grants of legislative power to the Commonwealth were generally to be understood as authorising legislation applying to the states and their agents and instrumentalities. The principle was generally thought to be reciprocal.[17]

We can only speculate as to the genesis of Dixon's federal vision. It appears to have been driven, at least in part, by his dissatisfaction with aspects of the *Engineers' Case*.[18] It may well have been influenced by his experiences and views formed as a barrister appearing in the High Court in the decades either side of the *Engineers' Case*.

Fundamentally, Dixon 'conceive[d] a State as deriving from the law; not the law as deriving from a State'.[19] Australian governments and legislatures were subordinate to the *Constitution* and the rule of law.[20] Each of the states and the Commonwealth were conceived of as 'governments separately organised': '[t]he *Constitution* predicates their continued existence as independent entities'.[21] While neither a states-righter nor an arch-federalist, within this framework Dixon elevated the Commonwealth to a position of superiority over the states and accepted an approach to

15 Leslie Zines, *The High Court and the Constitution* (Federation Press, 5th ed, 2008) 491; Leslie Zines, 'Sir Owen Dixon's Theory of Federalism' (1965) 1 *Federal Law Review* 221.

16 (1920) 28 CLR 129.

17 *Engineers' Case* (1920) 28 CLR 129, 155 (Knox CJ, Isaacs, Rich and Starke JJ); Zines, *The High Court and the Constitution*, above n 15, 488. Keven Booker and Arthur Glass have suggested that, while this is generally how the *Engineers' Case* has been interpreted, the judgment is not definitive on this point: see Keven Booker and Arthur Glass, 'The Engineers Case' in H P Lee and George Winterton (eds), *Australian Constitutional Landmarks* (Cambridge University Press, 2003) 34, 59.

18 Sir Owen Dixon, 'Marshall and the Australian Constitution' in Sir Owen Dixon, *Jesting Pilate and Other Papers*, collected by Severin Woinarski (William S Hein, 2nd ed, 1997) 166, 171; Zines, 'Sir Owen Dixon's Theory of Federalism', above n 15, 223–4; Sir Daryl Dawson and Mark Nicholls, 'Sir Owen Dixon and Judicial Method' (1986) 15 *Melbourne University Law Review* 543, 550.

19 Sir Owen Dixon, 'Sources of Legal Authority' in Sir Owen Dixon, *Jesting Pilate and Other Papers*, collected by Severin Woinarski (William S Hein, 2nd ed, 1997) 198, 199.

20 *Australian Communist Party v Commonwealth* (1951) 83 CLR 1, 193 (Dixon J).

21 *Melbourne Corporation v Commonwealth* (1947) 74 CLR 31, 82 (Dixon J) ('*Melbourne Corporation*').

the interpretation of constitutional grants of power which facilitated the continuing expansion of central power.[22]

Justice Dixon's theory of intergovernmental relations began with the proposition – which is far from self-evident and seemingly in tension with the thrust of the *Engineers' Case*[23] – that '[i]n a dual political system you do not expect to find either government legislating for the other'.[24] However, consistently with the reasoning in the *Engineers' Case*, the existence of express and affirmative grants of legislative power to the Commonwealth was held to displace this basic proposition, as far as Commonwealth legislation binding the states was concerned. The legislative powers of the states, being general and residual, rather than specific and affirmatively granted by the *Constitution*, remained subject to the general proposition against 'legislating for' the Commonwealth.

In his judgment in *Melbourne Corporation v Commonwealth* ('*Melbourne Corporation*'), a decision delivered the day before argument in *Uther's Case* commenced, Dixon J had observed that what a state may do with reference to the federal government and what the Commonwealth might do with reference to the states were 'two quite different questions', affected by different considerations.[25] Although the decision in *Melbourne Corporation* depended upon an implication limiting the legislative power of the Commonwealth to control the states, Dixon J's judgment emphasised the strength of the Commonwealth vis-a-vis the states:

> The position of the federal government is necessarily stronger than that of the States. The Commonwealth is a government to which enumerated powers have been affirmatively granted. The grant carries all that is proper

[22] See, eg, *Australian National Airways Pty Ltd v Commonwealth* (1945) 71 CLR 29, 81, 85 (Dixon J); *Bank of New South Wales v Commonwealth* (1948) 76 CLR 1, 332–4 (Dixon J); *R v Public Vehicles Licensing Appeal Tribunal (Tas); Ex parte Australian National Airways Pty Ltd* (1964) 113 CLR 207, 225–6. But the breadth of federal powers would nevertheless be constrained by textual and purposive considerations: cf *R v Brislan; Ex parte Williams* (1935) 54 CLR 262.

[23] As Anne Twomey has commented, '[i]t is difficult to understand how the majority judgment in the *Engineers' case* can be used to support the proposition that the Commonwealth's enumerated powers can be used to bind the States, without recognizing that it also rejected the proposition that one polity cannot legislate to bind the other': Twomey, above n 5, 526.

[24] *Uther's Case* (1947) 74 CLR 508, 529. Note the use of the second person – a technique employed by Dixon for declamatory effect; cf *R v Kirby; Ex parte Boilermakers' Society of Australia* (1956) 94 CLR 254, 275 (Dixon CJ, McTiernan, Fullagar and Kitto JJ) ('*Boilermakers' Case*').

[25] (1947) 74 CLR 31, 82.

> for its full effectuation. Then supremacy is given to the legislative powers of the Commonwealth.
>
> These two considerations add great strength to the implication protecting the operation of State law affecting the exercise of federal power. But they also amplify the field protected. Further, they limit the claim of the State to protection from the exercise of Commonwealth power.[26]

In his dissent in *Uther's Case* Dixon J gave effect to this reasoning by holding that the powers of the states did not extend to abolishing the Commonwealth's 'fiscal right'[27] to priority in payment of debts. The states, being unable to point to any affirmative grant of power (such as the Commonwealth power to make laws with respect to bankruptcy and insolvency), were thus said to be in a weaker position than the Commonwealth.[28]

In Dixon J's conception, the inability of the states to legislate so as to regulate relations between the Commonwealth and its subjects was not said to be implied from the *Constitution*. Rather, Dixon J focussed, unconvincingly,[29] upon the absence of any affirmative grant of power to the states to legislate for the Commonwealth. Having observed that the general legislative power of the states was 'diminished and controlled' by the *Constitution*, he continued:

> [I]t is not a question whether the power of the Parliament of a Colony becoming a State continues as at the establishment of the Commonwealth. The Colony of New South Wales could not be said at the establishment of the Commonwealth to have any power at all with reference to the Commonwealth. Like the goddess of wisdom the Commonwealth *uno ictu* sprang from the brain of its begetters armed and of full stature. At the same instant the Colonies became States; but whence did the States obtain the power to regulate the legal relations of this new polity with its subjects? It formed no part of the old colonial power. The Federal *Constitution* does not give it. Surely it is for the peace, order and good government of the Commonwealth, not for the peace, welfare and good government of New South Wales, to say what shall be the relative situation of private rights and of the public rights of the Crown representing the Commonwealth, where they come into conflict. It is a question of the fiscal and governmental

26 Ibid 82–3.

27 An expression used by Dixon J in both *Uther's Case* (1947) 74 CLR 508, 531 and *Cigamatic* (1962) 108 CLR 372, 377, 378.

28 *Uther's Case* (1947) 74 CLR 508, 529. See also *Victoria v Commonwealth* (1957) 99 CLR 575, 611–12 (Dixon CJ) ('*Second Uniform Tax Case*').

29 See text accompanying nn 32–43 below.

> rights of the Commonwealth and, as such, is one over which the State has no power.[30]

It is a measure of the influence of Dixon J's reasoning in *Uther's Case* that all of the majority Justices in *Cigamatic*, not just Dixon himself, were content largely to adopt his reasons in the earlier decision without further elaboration.[31] Thus it is essentially Dixon J's initial reasoning in *Uther's Case* that has, through its adoption in *Cigamatic*, had lasting significance.

The resulting '*Cigamatic* doctrine' has prompted a long line of critique from both academic and practising lawyers.[32] The constitutional basis for the doctrine has been questioned repeatedly, with John Doyle QC (when Solicitor-General for South Australia) concluding frankly that 'the basis of *Cigamatic* is unclear, and to the extent it can be discerned, not persuasive'.[33]

Justice Dixon's reasoning, focusing on the absence of any affirmative specific grants of power to the states, failed to acknowledge the true nature of plenary state legislative power.[34] In addition, commentators have pointed out that the 'supremacy' derived from s 109 of the *Constitution* does not support any general implication of Commonwealth superiority or immunity.[35] R P Meagher and W M C Gummow, in their well-known 1980 article, argued that the doctrine represented a 'revival in fresh garb of one aspect of the immunity of instrumentalities doctrine' that was rejected in the *Engineers' Case*.[36]

[30] *Melbourne Corporation* (1947) 74 CLR 31, 82–3.

[31] (1962) 108 CLR 372, 378 (Dixon CJ; Kitto and Windeyer JJ agreeing), 389 (Menzies J; Kitto and Owen JJ agreeing), 390 (Windeyer J).

[32] See, eg, Geoffrey Sawer, 'State Statutes and the Commonwealth' (1961) 1 *University of Tasmania Law Review* 580; W M C Gummow, 'The Nature and Operation of Prerogative Powers in the Federal System: *The Commonwealth of Australia v Cigamatic Pty Ltd*' (1964) 4 *Sydney Law Review* 435; Gareth Evans, 'Rethinking Commonwealth Immunity' (1972) 8 *Melbourne University Law Review* 521; Meagher and Gummow, above n 6, 25; J J Doyle, '1947 Revisited: The Immunity of the Commonwealth from State Law' in Geoffrey Lindell (ed), *Future Directions in Australian Constitutional Law* (Federation Press, 1994) 47; Twomey, above n 5, 526 ff; Zines, *The High Court and the Constitution*, above n 15, 488 ff.

[33] Doyle, above n 32, 49.

[34] See Sawer, above n 32, 585–6; Evans, above n 32, 524–5; Meagher and Gummow, above n 6, 28; Doyle, above n 32, 62–3; Twomey, above n 5, 526; Zines, *The High Court and the Constitution*, above n 15, 497; Ronald Sackville, 'The Doctrine of Immunity of Instrumentalities in the United States and Australia: A Comparative Analysis' (1969) 7 *Melbourne University Law Review* 15, 62.

[35] See, eg, Twomey, above n 5, 528.

[36] Meagher and Gummow, above n 6, 29.

The obscurities surrounding the application of the doctrine have led to it being described as 'almost unworkable'.[37] These difficulties arise because the precise scope of the Commonwealth's immunity which was recognised by Dixon J in *Uther's Case*, and by the majority in *Cigamatic*, was, and has remained, unclear. The absence of a logical foundation for the doctrine in the *Constitution* precludes resolution of such uncertainty by reference to first principles.

In *Uther's Case* itself, Dixon J acknowledged that '[g]eneral laws made by a State may affix legal consequences to given descriptions of transaction and the Commonwealth, if it enters into such a transaction, may be bound by the rule laid down'.[38] Likewise, in *Commonwealth v Bogle*, Fullagar J (Dixon CJ, Webb and Kitto JJ agreeing) maintained that 'the State Parliament has no power over the Commonwealth',[39] yet recognised that '[t]he Commonwealth may, of course, become affected by State laws', giving the example of a contract entered into in Victoria, in which case 'the terms and effect of that contract may have to be sought in the *Goods Act 1928* (Vict)'.[40] And in *Cigamatic*, Dixon CJ distinguished state legislative power 'to control or abolish a federal fiscal right' and state power 'to make some general law governing the rights and duties of those who enter in to some description of transaction, such as the sale of goods, and of the Commonwealth in its executive arm choosing to enter into a transaction of that description'.[41] This 'affected by' aspect of the doctrine was also the subject of much commentary and criticism,[42] and would eventually be rejected.[43]

III Chief Justice Dixon's Influence over the *Cigamatic* Court

By the time of *Cigamatic*, Dixon CJ's influence over the Court was considerable and his conception of the nature of the federation was endorsed by a majority of the Court. Dixon was, by all accounts, a towering figure on the Australian High Court. After being called to the Bar in 1910, he first appeared before the High Court in December 1911 at the age of 25. Dixon quickly developed a formidable reputation and took silk in 1922. Despite

[37] Doyle, above n 32, 47. [38] (1947) 74 CLR 508, 528. [39] (1953) 89 CLR 229, 259.
[40] Ibid 260. [41] (1947) 108 CLR 372, 378.
[42] See, eg, Colin Howard, 'Some Problems of Commonwealth Immunity and Exclusive Legislative Powers' (1972) 5 *Federal Law Review* 31; Grant Donaldson, 'Commonwealth Liability to State Law' (1985) 16 *University of Western Australia Law Review* 135; Zines, *The High Court and the Constitution*, above n 15, 494–6.
[43] *Residential Tenancies Tribunal* (1997) 190 CLR 410.

his success at the Bar, Dixon was hesitant to accept a judicial appointment and in 1926 declined offers of a permanent position on the Supreme Court of Victoria and the role of Chief Judge of the Commonwealth Court of Conciliation and Arbitration.[44] In 1929, aged 42, he somewhat reluctantly accepted appointment to the High Court.[45] He was appointed Chief Justice in 1952 following the retirement of Sir John Latham. Dixon's tenure on the Court spanned 35 years, though it was punctuated by two diplomatic postings: one as Australian Minister to Washington between April 1942 and September 1944, and one as UN-appointed mediator between India and Pakistan in 1950.[46]

Although Dixon disliked judicial work,[47] describing it as hard and unrewarding,[48] his contribution to the Court, and to Australian law, is immense.[49] As a member of the High Court for three-and-a-half decades, Dixon was known and celebrated for many things, most famously, perhaps, his professed judicial method of 'strict and complete legalism'.[50] It is now rarely remembered that in his early days on the Court Dixon was known as the 'Great Dissenter',[51] due mainly to a series of dissents in the 1930s in relation to s 92 of the *Constitution*.[52] But when the entire period of his service on the Court is considered, Dixon was a relatively infrequent dissenter. It has been calculated that in his 35 years on the High Court he

[44] Grant Anderson and Sir Daryl Dawson, 'Dixon, Sir Owen (1886–1972)' in *Australian Dictionary of Biography* (Melbourne University Press, 1996) vol 14; Philip Ayres, *Owen Dixon* (Miegunyah Press, 2nd ed, 2007) 50, 53.

[45] J D Merralls, 'The Rt Hon Sir Owen Dixon, OM, GCMG, 1886–1972' (1972) 46 *Australian Law Journal* 429, 430; Ayres, above n 44, 54.

[46] Kenneth Hayne, 'Dixon, Owen' in Tony Blackshield, Michael Coper and George Williams (eds), *The Oxford Companion to the High Court of Australia* (Oxford University Press, 2001) 218.

[47] See, eg, Ayres, above n 44, 62–3, 70–1, 235. [48] Ibid 219.

[49] See, eg, W M C Gummow, *Change and Continuity: Statute, Equity and Federalism* (Oxford University Press, 1999) xvii.

[50] Sir Owen Dixon, 'Address upon Taking the Oath of Office in Sydney as Chief Justice of the High Court of Australia on 21st April, 1952' in Sir Owen Dixon, *Jesting Pilate and Other Papers*, collected by Severin Woinarski (William S Hein, 2nd ed, 1997) 247, 249. See also Sir Owen Dixon, 'Concerning Judicial Method' in Sir Owen Dixon, *Jesting Pilate and Other Papers* (William S Hein, 2nd ed, 1997) 152, 153–4. For some discussion of Dixon's judicial method, see Dawson and Nicholls, above n 18, 543.

[51] Graham Fricke, *Judges of the High Court* (Hutchinson, 1986) 118. This point is also noted in the discussion of Dixon's reputation in Andrew Lynch, 'Unrequited but Still Great: The Dissent of Justices Dixon and Evatt in *R v Federal Court of Bankruptcy; Ex parte Lowenstein* (1938)' in ch 3 of this book.

[52] See *Willard v Rawson* (1933) 48 CLR 316; *R v Vizzard; Ex parte Hill* (1933) 50 CLR 30; *O Gilpin Ltd v Commissioner for Road Transport and Tramways (NSW)* (1935) 52 CLR 189; *Bessell v Dayman* (1935) 52 CLR 215.

delivered 1699 judgments, and that in just 5.5 per cent of these (94) did he find himself in dissent.[53]

The adoption of Dixon J's dissenting views by a majority of the Court in *Cigamatic* can be explained partly on the basis of the influence that Dixon CJ wielded by that time.[54] While some dissenting judgments can be seen as appealing to the sympathies of a future Court or as recording a defeated argument for the sake of posterity, Dixon's long tenure on the Court and his eventual dominance meant that he personally presided over the vindication of his dissent in *Uther's Case*. By 1962, Dixon had been on the Court for more than three decades, including a decade as Chief Justice. His intellect and legal ability, across all areas of the Court's work, commanded respect and contributed to his 'intellectual dominance' over the Court.[55] Chief Justice Dixon also worked to generate consensus on the Court, in contrast to some of his predecessors. This included the circulation of draft judgments to the other members of the Court.[56] As Sir Douglas Menzies later reflected:

> His authority was, of course, enormous, and when he was concerned that a decision should go in a particular way, his aim was to get his own judgment out first for circulation to other members of the Court. To differ from him was a course always taken with hesitation and never without foreboding.[57]

Chief Justice Dixon's influence was acknowledged in the insightful and prescient observation of Geoffrey Sawer, writing in 1961 about the theory of Commonwealth immunity favoured by Dixon J in *Uther's Case* and by Fullagar J in *Commonwealth v Bogle*:[58]

> In view of the success which Sir Owen Dixon has had in establishing as doctrine what were once *obiter dicta* or dissents in judgments given by him, we may assume that if a suitable case arises, the doctrine will be very strongly pressed, and although the Chief Justice does not hold a position comparable with that of Marshall CJ in his hey-day, there is nevertheless an antecedent probability that a view held by him will command a majority;

53 Matthew Groves and Russell Smyth, 'A Century of Judicial Style: Changing Patterns in Judgment Writing on the High Court 1903–2001' (2004) 32 *Federal Law Review* 255, table 1.

54 Sackville, above n 34, 60.

55 Colin Howard, 'Sir Owen Dixon and the Constitution' (1973) 9 *Melbourne University Law Review* 5, 5.

56 Ayres, above n 44, 57.

57 Sir Douglas Menzies, 'The Right Honourable Sir Owen Dixon, OM GCMG' (1973) 9 *Melbourne University Law Review* 1, 3.

58 (1953) 89 CLR 229.

> its chance of doing so is, to say the least of it, not reduced by its having the support of Fullagar J as well.[59]

In addition, the Court at the time of the *Cigamatic* judgment was a very different place than it had been in earlier years. When Dixon J was appointed in 1929 the Court was divided and fractured.[60] Divisions and disagreement were prevalent, and reportedly Dixon J was for a time the only member of the Court to whom all of the others regularly spoke.[61] Justice Starke was particularly critical of Evatt and McTiernan JJ, referring to them as 'the parrots' on account of their tendency to agree with Dixon J.[62] Justice Starke also refused to discuss or circulate his draft judgments to the other members of the Court, sending his judgments to the Registrar in a sealed envelope with instructions not to open them until the day of judgment delivery.[63] By the time of *Cigamatic*, the composition of the Court had changed considerably and many of the personal divisions between judges had diminished with Dixon CJ at the helm.[64] These changing internal dynamics, combined with Dixon CJ's influence, help to explain why his dissenting judgment – although scarcely an exemplar of the 'strict and complete legalism' which he espoused in 'federal conflicts'[65] – was ultimately adopted by a majority of the Court.

IV Precedent and Continuing Reverence for Sir Owen Dixon

In the decades since *Cigamatic*, the doctrine developed by Dixon J in *Uther's Case* remains accepted by the Court, despite the considerable criticism it has generated. This ongoing legacy can be understood in part, we suggest, by the Court's commitment to precedent, its unwillingness to address constitutional issues unless absolutely necessary, and the reverence for Dixon that continues to the present day.

59 Sawer, above n 32, 583. 60 Ayres, above n 44, 56. 61 Ibid 57.

62 Clem Lloyd, 'Not Peace but a Sword! – The High Court under J G Latham' (1987) 11 *Adelaide Law Review* 175, 181.

63 Sir Anthony Mason, 'The High Court of Australia: A Personal Impression of its First 100 Years' (2003) 27 *Melbourne University Law Review* 864, 874.

64 Ibid 875. Matthew Groves and Russell Smyth have noted that the dissent rate in the Dixon Court was lower than it had been for most of the period that Latham was Chief Justice: Groves and Smyth, above n 53, 271.

65 Dixon, 'Address upon Taking the Oath of Office as Chief Justice of the High Court of Australia', above n 50, 249.

Sir Owen Dixon occupies an almost hallowed place in Australian legal history. During his lifetime he received numerous honours and awards, and the Court over which he presided was well regarded throughout the common law world.[66] Since his retirement and death the accolades have continued, and there is a voluminous academic literature documenting his contribution. His reputation has by now become steeped in mythology, and despite some attempts to present a more nuanced approach by pointing to flaws or criticisms,[67] his reputation remains almost untouchable.[68]

This immense reputation, in combination with the doctrine of precedent, perhaps helps to explain the judicial reluctance to overturn, or even squarely to confront, the Commonwealth immunity doctrine. Although the High Court is not bound by its own decisions, the doctrine of precedent retains importance. The precise relationship between judicial dissent and a willingness to overrule previous decisions is a slippery one, in part because the application of precedent in a final court is fluid.[69] Dixon himself was a strong advocate of the importance of precedent and of the view that the Court should only overrule its own decisions in exceptional circumstances.[70] In *Cigamatic* itself, Dixon CJ only saw the need to depart from *Uther's Case* in relation to the specific issue on which he thought the majority had fallen into 'fundamental error'.[71] Dixon's approach to precedent, enshrined through his exposition of the judicial method, has permeated current conceptions of the judicial task.[72] That Dixon J was the main proponent of the Commonwealth immunity doctrine has certainly enhanced its precedential force.[73]

66 See, eg, Mason, above n 63, 878; Sir Garfield Barwick, 'The Late Sir Owen Dixon' (1972) 126 CLR v, ix.

67 See, eg, Laurence W Maher, 'Tales of the Overt and the Covert: Judges and Politics in Early Cold War Australia' (1993) 21 *Federal Law Review* 151; Dennis Rose, 'Sir Owen Dixon' (2003) 6 *Constitutional Law and Policy Review* 18.

68 Ritter, 'The Myth of Sir Owen Dixon', above n 1.

69 Andrew Lynch, 'Dissent: The Rewards and Risks of Judicial Disagreements in the High Court of Australia' (2003) 27 *Melbourne University Law Review* 724.

70 Dawson and Nicholls, above n 18, 548–52; *Wright v Wright* (1948) 77 CLR 191, 210 (Dixon J).

71 (1962) 108 CLR 372, 377, 379. For another well-known instance in which Dixon CJ refused to adhere to precedent in respect of propositions which he regarded as both 'misconceived and wrong' and 'fundamental', see *Parker v The Queen* (1963) 111 CLR 610, 632.

72 Michael Kirby, 'Judicial Activism? A Riposte to the Counter-Reformation' (2004) 24 *Australian Bar Journal* 219, 221.

73 See *Australian Postal Commission v Dao* (1985) 3 NSWLR 565, 598 (McHugh JA).

After *Cigamatic*, the Court deferred invitations to reconsider that decision through reliance on an expansive construction of s 64 of the *Judiciary Act 1903* (Cth).[74] That section provides:

> In any suit to which the Commonwealth or a State is a party, the rights of the parties shall as nearly as possible be the same, and judgment may be given and costs awarded on either side, as in a suit between subject and subject.

This enables state laws, which might otherwise fall foul of *Cigamatic*, to be applied as if they were Commonwealth laws. By the operation of s 64 the Commonwealth has, in effect, voluntarily placed itself (in most civil cases at least) in the same legal position that would have obtained had the Commonwealth immunity doctrine not existed.

A consequence has been that the Commonwealth immunity doctrine has rarely called for direct application, but has remained an accepted part of Australian constitutional law for decades. By the time the opportunity did arise for reconsidering the doctrine, in a case involving a decision of a state administrative tribunal (rather than a state court exercising federal jurisdiction), and thus not attracting the operation of s 64 of the *Judiciary Act*,[75] the decision in *Cigamatic* had stood for some 35 years.

The result is that Dixon J's fundamental propositions concerning the nature of the federation, which underpin the Commonwealth immunity doctrine, have remained part of the fabric of Australian constitutional law. As such, they have continued to exert a broad influence on the outlook and decisions of the Court, despite the very limited direct application of the doctrine itself.

V Centralising Power and Accord with Political Reality

The resilience of Dixon J's dissent in *Uther's Case* and its progeny, the Commonwealth immunity doctrine, may also be explained in part by its apparent congruity with the political realities of the Australian federation in the modern era.

[74] *Maguire v Simpson* (1977) 139 CLR 362, 390 (Gibbs J), 402 (Mason J), 403–4 (Jacobs J); *Commonwealth v Evans Deakin Industries Ltd* (1986) 161 CLR 254, 267 (Gibbs CJ, Mason, Wilson, Deane and Dawson JJ); cf *Australian Postal Commission v Dao* (1987) 162 CLR 317. See also Keith Mason, 'Has Engineers Reached its "Use-By" Date? A State Perspective' in Michael Coper and George Williams (eds), *How Many Cheers for Engineers?* (Federation Press, 1997) 123, 124–5.

[75] *Residential Tenancies Tribunal* (1997) 190 CLR 410.

The supremacy of Commonwealth legislation by reason of s 109 of the *Constitution* meant that the rejection of the doctrine of implied governmental immunities in the *Engineers' Case* was of 'more benefit to the Commonwealth than the States'.[76] A central tenet of the *Engineers' Case* doctrine was that the express grants of legislative power to the Commonwealth were to be interpreted according to ordinary principles of statutory construction and not subject to any presumption against interference with the states. Thus, with s 109 giving primacy to Commonwealth laws, the *Engineers' Case* had the immediate effect of strengthening the position of the Commonwealth and centralising power.

With some notable but relatively minor exceptions,[77] the trend of subsequent decisions concerning legislative power has been to accept the expansion of federal power through the application of a liberal approach to the construction of the enumerated grants of legislative power to the Commonwealth,[78] at the expense of the states.[79] These developments both supported and reflected the political reality of the gradual ascendancy of central power in Australia. To adopt one aspect of what Windeyer J famously said of the *Engineers' Case*, they have been 'a consequence of developments that had occurred outside the law courts as well as a cause of further developments there'.[80]

The approach adopted by Dixon J in *Uther's Case*, and ultimately the decision in *Cigamatic*, while apparently running counter to the justification given in the *Engineers' Case* itself, is consistent with the trend towards the amplification of central power in the Australian federation. There has been little incentive for High Court judges, regarded generally as

76 Zines, 'Sir Owen Dixon's Theory of Federalism', above n 15, 221–2.

77 See, eg, *New South Wales v Commonwealth* (1990) 169 CLR 482 ('*Incorporation Case*'); *Williams v Commonwealth [No 2]* (2014) 252 CLR 416.

78 See, eg, *R v Public Vehicles Licensing Appeal Tribunal (Tas); Ex parte Australian National Airways Pty Ltd* (1964) 113 CLR 207; *Strickland v Rocla Concrete Pipes Ltd* (1971) 124 CLR 468; *New South Wales v Commonwealth* (1975) 135 CLR 337 ('*Seas and Submerged Lands Case*'); *Murphyores Inc Pty Ltd v Commonwealth* (1976) 136 CLR 1; *Commonwealth v Tasmania* (1983) 158 CLR 1 ('*Tasmanian Dam Case*'); *Grain Pool (WA) v Commonwealth* (2000) 202 CLR 479; *XYZ v Commonwealth* (2006) 227 CLR 532; *New South Wales v Commonwealth* (2006) 229 CLR 1 ('*Work Choices Case*'); *Thomas v Mowbray* (2007) 233 CLR 307; *Commonwealth v Australian Capital Territory* (2013) 250 CLR 441 ('*Same Sex Marriage Case*').

79 This may be contrasted with a more restrictive approach applied to those few legislative powers expressly reserved to the states: *Bourke v State Bank of New South Wales* (1990) 170 CLR 276, 288.

80 *Victoria v Commonwealth* (1971) 122 CLR 353, 396–7 ('*Payroll Tax Case*').

sympathetic to the expansion of central power,[81] to reverse *Cigamatic*. Although it could scarcely be regarded as essential to it, the *Cigamatic* doctrine complements the reality of the gradual evolution towards the dominance of the Commonwealth.

VI Conclusion: The Continuing Legacy of *Uther's Case*

The basic idea espoused by Dixon J in *Uther's Case* – that the relations between the Commonwealth and its subjects are not properly the domain of state legislative power – remains the accepted doctrine of the Court. The doctrine itself and its foundations have been referred to with express or apparent approval in various cases in the decades following the decision in *Cigamatic*.[82]

In *Re Residential Tenancies Tribunal (NSW); Ex parte Defence Housing Authority* ('*Residential Tenancies Tribunal*'), a majority of the Court appeared to accept and reiterate this central aspect of Dixon J's analysis in *Uther's Case*.[83] Despite this, it was accepted that neither 'the Crown nor its agents [presumably meaning the Commonwealth] enjoy any specific immunity from the operation of laws of general application, State or federal'.[84] A majority in *Residential Tenancies Tribunal* took issue with the awkward distinction between state laws that 'bind' the Commonwealth and those merely 'affecting' the Commonwealth,[85] but the new distinction between a law which modifies or impairs Commonwealth executive 'capacities' and a law 'which assumes those capacities and merely seeks to regulate activities . . . which it carrie[s] on in common with other citizens'[86] seems no more satisfactory, and was ultimately defended as resting on the same fundamental principles.

Only time will tell to what extent the *Residential Tenancies Tribunal* represents a 'watered down' version of the Commonwealth immunity

[81] See, eg, Anne Twomey, 'Reforming Australia's Federal System' (2008) 26 *Federal Law Review* 57, 78; James Allan and Nicholas Aroney, 'An Uncommon Court: How the High Court of Australia Has Undermined Australian Federalism' (2008) 30 *Sydney Law Review* 245, 290–1.

[82] See, eg, *Payroll Tax Case* (1971) 122 CLR 353, 373 (Barwick CJ; Owen J agreeing), 410 (Walsh J); *Pape v Commissioner of Taxation* (2009) 238 CLR 1, 85 (Gummow, Crennan and Bell JJ); *Australian Postal Commission v Dao* (1985) 3 NSWLR 565, 595–9 (McHugh JA).

[83] (1997) 190 CLR 410, 424–5 (Brennan CJ), 440–1 (Dawson, Toohey and Gaudron JJ), 451 (McHugh J).

[84] Ibid 443 (Dawson, Toohey and Gaudron JJ).

[85] Ibid 447 (Dawson, Toohey and Gaudron JJ).

[86] Ibid 438–9 (Dawson, Toohey and Gaudron JJ).

doctrine: it appears to remain more than merely a reciprocal application of the *Melbourne Corporation* doctrine.[87] In any event, the foundations underlying Dixonian federal theory appear to have endured.[88]

Justice Dixon's reasoning in *Uther's Case* also remains influential in more subtle ways. Thus, for example, in *Pape v Commissioner of Taxation*, Gummow, Crennan and Bell JJ, referencing *Cigamatic*, spoke of 'the comparative superiority of the position of the Commonwealth in the federal structure' as a 'difficulty' confronting a submission advanced in that case to the effect that the executive power, whether of the Commonwealth or a state, 'continues to be subservient to legislative power irrespective of whether the source of the legislative power is State or Commonwealth'.[89]

In *Hughes v The Queen*, six Justices of the Court accepted, apparently without the need for express justification, the proposition that 'a State by its laws cannot unilaterally invest functions under that law in officers of the Commonwealth'.[90] In the later case of *O'Donoghue v Ireland* it was said that '[a]n important difference between *Hughes* and the present proceedings is that here the officers in question are those of a State, not the Commonwealth, and the conferral of authority is by a law of the Commonwealth, the *Extradition Act 1988* (Cth)'.[91] In the latter case, a majority of the Court accepted that the unilateral imposition by a law of the Commonwealth of *functions* or *powers* on state magistrates was constitutionally permissible, but left open the question whether Commonwealth law could unilaterally impose *duties* on state officers.[92] This lopsided approach to the 'cross-vesting' of executive power can only be explained by reference

[87] See *Residential Tenancies Tribunal* (1997) 190 CLR 410. According to Brennan J, 'the States have no legislative power that can modify a grant of power to the Crown in right of the Commonwealth by a law of the Commonwealth nor any legislative power that can modify a prerogative power conferred by the *Constitution*' and the *Melbourne Corporation* principle 'is irrelevant to the scope of any State legislative power': at 424–6. Justices Dawson, Toohey and Gaudron stated that '[i]n the application of the principle, however, it is necessary to differentiate between the Commonwealth on the one hand and the States on the other': at 440.

[88] Notably, however, Bradley Selway QC expressed the view that '[t]he majority necessarily rejected the reasoning that supported *Cigamatic*, although . . . they were remarkably coy about saying so': Bradley Selway, 'The Nature of the Commonwealth: A Comment' (1998) 20 *Adelaide Law Review* 95, 99.

[89] (2009) 238 CLR 1, 85–6.

[90] (2000) 202 CLR 535, 553 (Gleeson CJ, McHugh, Gaudron, Gummow, Hayne and Callinan JJ).

[91] (2007) 234 CLR 599, 619 (Gummow, Hayne, Heydon, Crennan and Kiefel JJ).

[92] Ibid 614, 623 (Gleeson CJ), 630 (Gummow, Hayne, Heydon, Crennan and Kiefel JJ).

to considerations of the kind that motivated Dixon J's dissent in *Uther's Case.*

Despite its difficulties, Dixon J's conception of federation 'remains of continuing importance'.[93] The Dixonian view of the Australian federation continues to reverberate in contemporary assumptions concerning the relationship between the Commonwealth and the states. Thus has a controversial and imperfect dissent, penned by a great judge, become a great dissent.

[93] Hayne, above n 46, 220.

6

'Lone, vehement and incredulous': Chief Justice Latham in the *Communist Party Case* (1951)

GEORGE WILLIAMS

I Introduction

Australian Communist Party v Commonwealth ('*Communist Party Case*')[1] is often described as the most significant decision handed down by the High Court. At a time when Australia was gripped with a fear of communism, the High Court struck down the *Communist Party Dissolution Act 1950* (Cth) ('*Dissolution Act*'), an attempt to ban the Australian Communist Party ('ACP') and grant the government an unfettered discretion to proscribe other organisations and people linked to communism. In doing so, the Court, and the people voting at a subsequent referendum, prevented the long term damage to Australian democracy that could have resulted from persecuting people on the basis of their ideology and political beliefs.

The High Court's decision applied a number of fundamental legal values, including the rule of law. It reaffirmed the principle that Parliament must operate in accordance with the *Constitution*, and that the High Court possesses the ultimate responsibility of determining the meaning and application of that document. The decision thus had the effect of reinforcing the legal principles that underlie Australian democracy, as well as the central role played by the High Court in the resolution of constitutional disputes.

Two of the judgments in the *Communist Party Case*, those by Dixon J and Fullagar J, stand out as being among the finest expositions of the law by a Justice of the High Court. Indeed, another reason why the case is well remembered is because it contains the most celebrated judgment by Australia's most revered High Court judge, Sir Owen Dixon. In the absence

[1] (1951) 83 CLR 1.

of a bill of rights or other like protection, his decision to strike down the *Dissolution Act* relied upon basal understandings of the *Constitution*. In an oft-quoted passage,[2] he asserted that the *Constitution* was 'framed in accordance with many traditional conceptions', some of which 'are simply assumed'.[3] He went on to say: 'Among these I think that it may fairly be said that the rule of law forms an assumption'.[4] Justice Dixon also warned that communism was not the only danger to Australian democracy:

> History, and not only ancient history, shows that in countries where democratic institutions have been unconstitutionally superseded, it has been done not seldom by those holding the executive power. Forms of government may need protection from dangers likely to arise from within the institutions to be protected.[5]

The judgment of Fullagar J was notable for his analysis of the federal Parliament's defence power in s 51(vi) of the *Constitution*, and also for his appreciation, like Dixon J, of the principles underlying the *Constitution*. Justice Fullagar pinpointed the fundamental flaw of the *Dissolution Act* as being an attempt by Parliament to set itself above the *Constitution*, its own defining instrument, and so to control the operation of the provisions by which it itself is controlled. He rejected this by way of the famous maxim that 'a stream cannot rise higher than its source'.[6] This notion rested upon the principle of judicial review, with Fullagar J stating that 'in our system the principle of *Marbury v Madison* is accepted as axiomatic'.[7]

Justices Dixon and Fullagar were joined by McTiernan, Williams, Webb, and Kitto JJ to form a majority of six judges in favour of striking down the *Dissolution Act*. They were met in dissent only by the Court's Chief Justice, Sir John Latham. In what Zelman Cowen has described as a 'lone, vehement and incredulous dissent',[8] Latham CJ provided a sharp counterpoint to the views of the majority. His judgment is remarkable not

2 See, eg, *Kartinyeri v Commonwealth* (1998) 195 CLR 337, 381 (Gummow and Hayne JJ) ('*Hindmarsh Island Bridge Case*').

3 *Communist Party Case* (1951) 83 CLR 1, 193.

4 Ibid.

5 Ibid 187. This passage has also been referred to many times. See, eg, *Pape v Commissioner of Taxation* (2009) 238 CLR 1, 24 (French CJ).

6 *Communist Party Case* (1951) 83 CLR 1, 258. The statement has again been quoted on many occasions. See, eg, *MacCormick v Federal Commissioner of Taxation* (1984) 158 CLR 622, 640 (Gibbs CJ, Wilson, Deane and Dawson JJ).

7 (1951) 83 CLR 1, 262.

8 Zelman Cowen, *Sir John Latham and Other Papers* (Oxford University Press, 1965) 45.

only for his preparedness to permit the federal Parliament to determine the scope of its own power over defence, but because of how he found himself in sole opposition to the Court that he had led for the prior 15 years.

Reams have been written about the *Communist Party Case* and its significance.[9] By contrast, the dissent of Latham CJ has attracted little attention.[10] Most treatments of the case tend to dismiss it in passing, without subjecting his reasoning to detailed scrutiny. It is perhaps not surprising that Latham CJ's dissent has been eclipsed by the brilliance of the majority position. Nevertheless, his judgment does present an intriguing perspective on what might have been a different result in that case.

After setting out the circumstances that led to the decision, I examine the dissent of Latham CJ and the aftermath of the case. I then explore the surprising way in which his dissent resurfaced in the more recent decision of *Thomas v Mowbray*.[11] That case, handed down more than a half century after the *Communist Party Case*, also involved a challenge to a law directed at a threat to Australia's internal security.

II The *Dissolution Act*

In the aftermath of World War II, tension between the USSR and the United States and the onset of a new Cold War provoked widespread community fear of communist infiltration. Australian reactions to this prospect were visceral and often overblown. They had much in common with the response to 11 September 2001, and President George W Bush's

[9] See, eg, Roger Douglas, 'Cold War Justice? Judicial Responses to Communists and Communism, 1945–1955' (2007) 29 *Sydney Law Review* 43; Roger Douglas, 'A Smallish Blow for Liberty? The Significance of the Communist Party Case' (2001) 27 *Monash University Law Review* 253; George Winterton, 'The Communist Party Case' in H P Lee and George Winterton (eds), *Australian Constitutional Landmarks* (Cambridge University Press, 2003) 108; Leslie Zines, *The High Court and the Constitution* (Federation Press, 5th ed, 2008) ch 11.

[10] For notable exceptions, see David Dyzenhaus, *The Constitution of Law: Legality in a Time of Emergency* (Cambridge University Press, 2008) 78–87; Laurence W Maher, 'Tales of the Overt and the Covert: Judges and Politics in Early Cold War Australia' (1993) 21 *Federal Law Review* 151, 178–83; Kelvin Widdows, *Sir John Latham: Judicial Reasoning in Defence of the Commonwealth* (PhD Thesis, University of New South Wales, 2014) 185–204. See also Frank Moorhouse, *Cold Light* (Vintage, 2011) 318–35, in which the novel's heroine, Edith Campbell Berry, debates the merits of Latham CJ's dissent with him over dinner at the Melbourne Club.

[11] (2007) 233 CLR 307.

statement that 'you're either with us or against us'.[12] Hence, the editorial in *The Sydney Morning Herald* on 7 November 1947 stated:

> Communism is cold, harsh and ruthless, and it is building slowly and inexorably to the day when our democratic Government will be superseded by a Godless, tyrannical Communistic dictatorship in Australia . . . Any Australian born in this country who embraces Communism is a traitor. There is no half way. There has to be a choice between good and evil, and people must be either loyal or disloyal.[13]

The threat posed by the 'red menace', and the prospect of conflict with the USSR, was at the forefront of political debate in Australia in the late 1940s and throughout the 1950s. In 1951, for example, Prime Minister Robert Menzies declared that within three years, Australia must be ready for World War III against the 'communist forces of the world'.[14] Many of the larger moments in Australian political life during this era had their genesis in such concerns, including the Petrov affair and the split in the Australian Labor Party in the mid-1950s.

Attention within Australia focused upon the ACP, and whether it was seeking to pave the way for the overthrow of democracy by developing its influence across the union movement.[15] One frequent response was to suggest that the organisation should be banned. Hence, the Country Party's 1946 federal election policy statement asserted: 'The Country Party regards the Australian communist in the same category as a venomous snake – to be killed before it kills. Therefore, it stands foursquare for declaring the Communist Party an illegal organisation'.[16]

Such questions were a major issue at the federal election held on 10 December 1949. Prior to the poll, Liberal Party leader Menzies joined his coalition partner, the Country Party, in advocating a ban. After a convincing win, Prime Minister Menzies' first significant piece of legislation was the *Dissolution Act*. It was introduced into Parliament on the day the first Australian forces landed in Korea to take part in what became the Korean War. Opposition leader Ben Chifley summed up the circumstances in which the Act was made:

[12] 'You Are Either With Us or Against Us', *CNN* (online), 6 November 2001 <http://edition.cnn.com/2001/US/11/06/gen.attack.on.terror/>.

[13] Phillip Deery (ed), *Labour in Conflict: The 1949 Coal Strike* (Hale & Iremonger, 1978) 21.

[14] 'At Our Peril Must Be Ready', *The Sydney Morning Herald* (Sydney), 3 March 1951.

[15] See generally George Williams, 'The Suppression of Communism by Force of Law: Australia in the Early 1950s' (1996) 42 *Australian Journal of Politics and History* 220.

[16] B McKinlay, *A Documentary History of the Australian Labor Movement 1850–1975* (Drummond, 1979) 691.

> This measure [the *Dissolution Act*] will to some degree be administered in an atmosphere of national hysteria, worked up by politicians and other persons, and by the press... There is great danger that the hysteria and fear complex that has been aroused may result in grave injustices being done to individuals. The multitude can make grave mistakes. It was the multitude, by its vote, that sent Christ to be crucified.[17]

The *Dissolution Act* was an extraordinary piece of legislation. It opened with nine recitals that set out the basis upon which Parliament was acting to suppress communism in Australia. These included the following statements, which *The Sydney Morning Herald* declared to be 'a series of devastating and unanswerable propositions, indicting the communist conspiracy':[18]

> AND WHEREAS the Australian Communist Party, in accordance with the basic theory of communism, as expounded by Marx and Lenin, engages in activities or operations designed to assist or accelerate the coming of a revolutionary situation, in which the Australian Communist Party, acting as a revolutionary minority, would be able to seize power and establish a dictatorship of the proletariat ...
>
> AND WHEREAS it is necessary, for the security and defence of Australia and for the execution and maintenance of the *Constitution* and of the laws of the Commonwealth, that the Australian Communist Party, and bodies of persons affiliated with that Party, should be dissolved and their property forfeited to the Commonwealth, and that members and officers of that party or of any of those bodies and other persons who are communists should be disqualified from employment by the Commonwealth and from holding office in an industrial organization a substantial number of whose members are engaged in a vital industry

Through these recitals, Parliament sought to establish that the operative sections of the Act were necessary for the security and defence of Australia, and so were a valid expression of its powers in the *Constitution* arising under s 51(vi) ('the security and defence of Australia') and the legislative power incidental to s 61 ('the execution and maintenance of the *Constitution* and of the laws of the Commonwealth'). The recitals were an attempt to pre-empt any decision of the High Court to the contrary.

The operative sections of the Act sought to dismantle communism as a political and industrial force in Australia. They did so in s 4 by declaring

17 L F Crisp, *Ben Chifley: A Political Biography* (Angus & Robertson, 1977) 389.

18 'New Bill a Death-Blow to Communist Power', *The Sydney Morning Herald* (Sydney), 28 April 1950.

the ACP to be an unlawful association, providing for its dissolution and enabling the appointment of a receiver to manage its property. Section 7(1) further provided that a person was liable to five years' imprisonment if he or she knowingly committed acts that included continuing to operate as a member or officer of the Party or carrying or displaying anything indicating that he or she was in any way associated with the Party.

Other organisations were also affected. Section 5 applied to entities that supported or advocated communism, were affiliated with the ACP, or had policies substantially shaped by members of the Party or 'Communists'. If the Governor-General was 'satisfied that a body of persons is a body of persons to which this section applies and that the continued existence of that body of persons would be prejudicial to the security and defence of the Commonwealth or to the execution or maintenance of the *Constitution* or of the laws of the Commonwealth', he could declare that body to be an unlawful association. Once unlawful, an association was dissolved under s 6 and a receiver appointed under s 8.

Individuals could also be targeted. Under s 9(2), the Governor-General could declare any person to be a 'Communist' or member of the ACP by exercising a similar discretion to that given by s 5(2). 'Communist' was defined by s 3 to mean 'a person who supports or advocates the objectives, policies, teachings, principles or practices of communism, as expounded by Marx and Lenin'. Once declared, s 10 stated that a person could not hold office in the Commonwealth public service or in industries declared by the Governor-General to be vital to the security and defence of Australia. A person wishing to contest a declaration by the Governor-General could do so under s 9(4), but bore the onus of proof. Section 9(5) provided that 'the burden shall be upon him to prove that he is not a person to whom this section applies'. Accordingly, a person could only escape being declared as a 'communist' if they could prove that they did not in fact support that political belief.

III The High Court Decision

On the day that the *Dissolution Act* came into force, the ACP, 10 unions and several communist union officials lodged a challenge in the High Court. With Latham CJ in sole dissent, the Court held the Act invalid in its entirety. The majority began by rejecting the attempt by Parliament to recite itself into power. It declared unequivocally that the question of whether the Act fell within a head of federal power was one for the Court alone to answer. According to McTiernan J, the 'recitals are in no way decisive of the question whether the Act is valid or invalid, for that is a judicial question which only the judicature has the power to decide finally and conclusively'.[19] Hence: 'If any fact stated in a recital is material to the question whether the Act is valid or invalid, the fact would need to be judicially determined or ascertained'.[20] He concluded that: 'The *Constitution* does not allow the judicature to concede the principle that the Parliament can conclusively "recite itself" into power'.[21]

A focus of the majority reasoning was upon the discretion given to the Governor-General by ss 5(2) and 9(2). At the time, such a discretion was regarded as being unreviewable by any court, and so the effect was to permit the Governor-General to himself determine the ambit of the Act by deciding whether organisations and individuals were 'prejudicial to the security and defence of the Commonwealth or to the execution or maintenance of the *Constitution* or of the laws of the Commonwealth'. This exposed a flaw in the Act, rendering it invalid at what the Court considered was a time of relative peace,[22] because the sections imposed 'legal consequences on a legislative or executive opinion which itself supplies the only link between the power and the legal consequences of the opinion'.[23] In the words of Fullagar J, the Act breached the rule that 'a stream cannot rise higher than its source'.[24]

Both as to the recitals and the Governor-General's discretion, the majority's decision represented a forthright rejection of Parliament's attempt to put such matters beyond the reach of the High Court. The decision can thus be viewed as an assertion of the constitutional role of the Court and of its responsibility to uphold the rule of law by subjecting the other arms of government to the terms of the *Constitution*.

IV The Dissent

Latham was appointed Chief Justice of the High Court in 1935, and had held that position for more than 15 years by the time of the *Communist Party Case*. Indeed, by 1951, he had become the longest serving Chief Justice in the history of the Court. It might have been thought that at this point in his career he was at the height of his powers and influence. The decision demonstrated otherwise, and indeed exposed how Dixon J,

[19] *Communist Party Case* (1951) 83 CLR 1, 205. [20] Ibid. [21] Ibid 205–6

[22] Ibid 196 (Dixon J): 'I think that the matter must be considered substantially upon the same basis as if a state of peace ostensibly existed'.

[23] Ibid 261 (Fullagar J). [24] Ibid 258.

and not Latham CJ, was the intellectual leader of the Court. Perhaps aware of this, Latham CJ unsuccessfully sought to persuade Dixon J to take a holiday upon his return from other duties, rather than to take part in the hearing of the *Communist Party Case*.[25] It is perhaps ironic that Latham once remarked that his finest achievement as Attorney-General was to persuade Dixon to accept a seat on the High Court.[26] He was soon to assist Dixon in another way. Chief Justice Latham announced his forthcoming retirement soon after the *Communist Party Case*, and in 1952 Dixon succeeded him as Chief Justice.

Latham came to the High Court after a long involvement in federal politics, including as Attorney-General in the Bruce Government from 1925 to 1929, opposition leader until 1931 and then Deputy Prime Minister, Attorney-General and Minister for External Affairs in the Lyons Government until 1934. During World War II, while a member of the High Court, he served as First Australian Minister to Japan.[27]

Both prior to his entry into politics, as a Lieutenant-Commander in Naval Intelligence during World War I, and then as a member of Parliament and of the executive, Latham was active in the field of national security. In particular, he was the scourge of radical organisations. His opposition was reflected in his championing in 1926 as Attorney-General of amendments to the *Crimes Act 1914* (Cth) that sought to restrain industrial conduct, facilitate the deportation of agitators and suppress revolutionary and seditious bodies. In a precursor to the *Dissolution Act*, the amendments enabled a body to be declared as an unlawful association where, for example, it 'by its constitution or propaganda or otherwise advocates or encourages . . . overthrow of the *Constitution* of the Commonwealth by revolution or sabotage'.[28] A person found to be a member of an unlawful association was liable to jail for up to one year.[29] These and other actions earned Latham the reputation of being fiercely anti-communist.

Chief Justice Latham's judgment in the *Communist Party Case* was the last major decision he delivered as a member of the High Court. In many ways he produced the result that might have been expected to emerge from the High Court given the enormous political and community pressures upon it to uphold the *Dissolution Act*. Chief Justice Latham's dissent is

[25] Widdows, above n 10, 205–6. [26] Cowen, above n 8, 34.

[27] See Fiona Wheeler, 'Parachuting In: War and Extra-Judicial Activity by High Court Judges' (2010) 38 *Federal Law Review* 485.

[28] *Crimes Act 1926* (Cth) s 30A(1). [29] Ibid s 30B.

notable for a number of reasons. One factor is simply that the dissent is worthy of attention because of the significance of the case in which it was delivered.

Another factor is that Latham, as Chief Justice, found himself in sole dissent. No Chief Justice of the High Court has been a frequent dissenter, though dissent by Chief Justices is not unusual. Sir Harry Gibbs, for example, found himself in dissent in the 1980s in a range of cases dealing with the scope of federal legislative power.[30] He though was not alone, and was joined by judges of a like mind, such as Dawson J, in articulating a vision of more limited federal power than that of a majority usually led by judges such as Sir Anthony Mason. By contrast, Latham CJ was unable to convince any other member of the Court to join his perspective. His dissent is the most dramatic example in history of the High Court of its Chief Justice being at odds with his brethren.[31] The fact that the case was of such importance and attracted enormous political attention further highlights the unusual and exposed nature of Latham CJ's position.

The dissent is also worthy of attention because of its reasoning. The judgment was lengthy for the time in running to 45 pages of the *Commonwealth Law Reports.* For a person regarded as being aloof and somewhat dour, Latham CJ's judgment was also surprisingly impassioned. This was at odds with the rational, logical style that normally characterised his writing. This matter brought to the surface strong feelings and preferences not usually evident in his judgments. This was evident during the 24-day hearing of the case. As I noted in an earlier analysis of those hearings:

> At times, it was only interjections by Latham CJ over the questioning of other judges that enabled [counsel for the Commonwealth Garfield] Barwick to get back on track. For example, at times of intense questioning Latham CJ asked... 'Who determines whether they [defence laws] are essential or not?'... Whether Latham CJ's Dorothy Dix questions were designed to enable Barwick to regain his feet or were out of sympathy for Barwick's subject matter, or both, is unclear. In any event, Latham CJ and Barwick seemed to share a close understanding.[32]

[30] See, eg, *Koowarta v Bjelke-Petersen* (1982) 153 CLR 168; *Hematite Petroleum Pty Ltd v Victoria* (1983) 151 CLR 599; *Commonwealth v Tasmania* (1983) 158 CLR 1 ('*Tasmanian Dam Case*').

[31] A further example of a Chief Justice in sole dissent, though in far less dramatic circumstances, was Sir Gerard Brennan in *Project Blue Sky Inc v Australian Broadcasting Authority* (1998) 194 CLR 355.

[32] George Williams, 'Reading the Judicial Mind: Appellate Argument in the Communist Party Case' (1993) 15 *Sydney Law Review* 1, 9.

On the other hand, Latham CJ clashed with Edward Laurie, counsel for the ACP:

> Latham CJ attacked Laurie's submissions on the basis that they espoused political and not legal principle . . . At several stages argument between the two degenerated into a tussle of political views. At one stage Latham CJ declared that the suppression of an organisation was 'a matter of policy rather than law'. After the support he gave Barwick, Latham CJ's strong attack on Laurie showed that he strongly favoured the Commonwealth's position.[33]

The result was a judgment far from Latham CJ's best. In addition to being prolix, it was a rambling, disjointed engagement with the issues that at times lost the thread of the argument. To the extent there is one theme or perspective that drove his reasoning, it was that matters of national security and the defence of the nation are matters for Parliament and not the courts. Indeed, Latham CJ seemed determined to emphasise this point by way of repetition, as if that might serve to convince his sceptical brethren.

Chief Justice Latham's argument was that the power over defence and the power to make laws to protect the existence of constitutional government in Australia are 'essentially different in character from most, if not all, of the other legislative powers of the Commonwealth Parliament'.[34] In being directed to the preservation of the Commonwealth, they were 'perhaps the most important powers intrusted to the Parliament', and so their exercise took 'precedence over all other matters with which the Commonwealth is concerned. As Cromwell said, "Being comes before well-being"'.[35] As he reiterated soon after, the exercise of these powers 'is a matter of the greatest moment'.[36]

Chief Justice Latham recognised that the extent of these powers must depend upon the circumstances of the time. The greater the threat to the nation, the more they might be relied upon in response. He framed the key question as being: 'Their exercise from time to time must necessarily depend upon the circumstances of the time as viewed by some authority. The question is – "By what authority – by Parliament or by a court?"'[37]

His answer was unequivocal. In matters of defence and national security, the view of the executive and Parliament must prevail. For him,

[33] Ibid 18. Chief Justice Latham reacted similarly to the arguments of Paterson, another counsel representing the ACP: at 19.

[34] *Communist Party Case* (1951) 83 CLR 1, 141.

[35] Ibid. [36] Ibid 142. [37] Ibid.

it was necessary that Parliament have 'the decisive power to determine whether Australia is for communism or against communism, and to legislate in accordance with its decision'.[38] He found that Parliament was not restrained such that it could only do so if 'a court agrees with its decision'.[39]

Chief Justice Latham's thesis was that the preservation of the nation depended upon such power residing unchecked within Parliament. His observations in support of this were peppered with examples from his own national security experience and international affairs. These included observations about how revolutionaries tended to conduct their 'subversive and treasonable activities'.[40] He noted that such activities 'may assume many forms' and that in addition to assisting an enemy in time of war:

> fifth-column work prepares the way for an enemy by undermining the morale of a people and by hindering the exercise of governmental powers in the community. It is a great help to a potential enemy to have inside a country a body (with activities which are ostensible and innocent) which engages in propaganda designed to make people think that potential invaders will be actual liberators. This is a well-established form of revolutionary technique.[41]

In response to such threats, he said later in his judgment: 'Operations against an enemy (external or internal) are conducted by the Executive Government under the control of Parliament and not by courts. They require action. They often require prompt and decisive action'.[42]

His view was that assessments of such matters, including the threat posed to Australia, were not for a court. They were questions of opinion, 'not a question of fact upon which a court can make a decision as to whether the international situation is "set fair" or "stormy" and in what quarter a storm is likely to arise'.[43] In deciding upon such matters, governments necessarily act upon a range of sources, such as diplomatic reports, rumour and even suspicion, things that could not be produced in or considered by a court.

In referring to such material, Latham CJ was at pains to make clear that defence measures, including in regard to communism, were matters of policy and opinion, the determination of which must reside solely within Parliament and the executive. This led to the extraordinary result that Parliament was capable of determining for itself that legislation directed at communism was validly enacted under the *Constitution*. It was also left

[38] Ibid 143. [39] Ibid. [40] Ibid. [41] Ibid. [42] Ibid 161. [43] Ibid 144.

to Parliament to determine the form and content of that legislation. No role was left to the Court to determine the validity of such actions.

The outcome was deeply troubling from the perspective of the rule of law. It left open the possibility that parliamentarians and the executive might manufacture or overstate a threat in order to aggregate power to themselves. This power might then be used, as in this case, to proscribe political and industrial organisations and their members and supporters. Even given Latham CJ's background, the result displayed a surprising insensitivity to basic legal values, and to the constitutional role of the institution he had led for the last 15 years. It suggested a blind spot on his part that he was prepared to depart from these values so readily in the name of the fight against communism.

Chief Justice Latham had developed a reputation in prior cases for taking a permissive attitude towards the capacity of the Commonwealth to use its defence power to prosecute the nation's interests during World War II.[44] However, he was not alone in this regard. Apart from Starke J, the High Court tended to take a highly deferential attitude to legislation during that conflict. Latham CJ took matters several steps further in the *Communist Party Case*, during a period in which Australia was not engaged in anything like a conflict of that magnitude, by granting Parliament unfettered capacity to legislate to combat communism. Indeed, his decision went so far as to be explicable only on the basis that this issue was personal in reflecting his own deeply felt political commitment to the eradication of revolutionary causes.[45] As Laurence Maher has suggested of Latham CJ's dissent:

> In both its structure and execution, it directly reflects the political rhetoric which Menzies had been using steadily since early 1948. It is this writer's view that this is no mere coincidence. This is not to say that Latham deliberately repudiated his judicial oath. It is, however, contended that Latham's willingness to defer to the Parliament on this occasion only makes sense when it is viewed in the context of Latham's long-held set of uncompromising anti-Communist beliefs and his anti-Communist activities prior to his appointment as Chief Justice.[46]

It is interesting that in reaching his conclusions, Latham CJ was at pains to state on a number of occasions that the determination of such issues

[44] Cowen, above n 8, 47, wrote of Latham CJ that 'he leaned towards the State and showed . . . too little regard for quite fundamental liberties'.

[45] Ibid. Cowen states that there is 'little doubt that this was the case in which Latham expressed himself with the deepest personal involvement'.

[46] Maher, above n 10, 178.

should be in no way political. He stated baldly on one occasion, in the context of whether the High Court could determine the correctness of the recitals prefacing the legislation, that: 'The Court should, in my opinion, have no political opinions'.[47] Perhaps aware of the way his own political preferences and sympathy for the position of the Commonwealth was influencing his decision, he was concerned to distance himself from any suggestion that his decision was anything other than a legal treatment of the issues.

Chief Justice Latham's reasoning depended upon creating an extreme scenario whereby the High Court might be required to determine essentially political questions relating to the conduct of defence matters. He viewed the attack on the *Dissolution Act* as necessarily requiring this. Given the binary question ('By what authority – by Parliament or by a court?') posed towards the beginning of his judgment, the unsuitability of the courts to engage in such matters inevitably meant that the authority to determine how to respond to communism was held by Parliament alone.

In reasoning in this way, Latham CJ downplayed the reliance usually placed by the Court on techniques that limited its exposure to political matters. In defence matters, the High Court had during periods such as World War II shown great deference to the legislature.[48] However, such deference had its limits, and did not exclude its capacity and indeed the constitutional duty of the Court to have the final say on the validity of laws. One way of managing this tension was for the Court, rather than engaging in detailed fact finding, to take judicial notice of notorious matters, such as Australia's engagement in war, so as to provide a basis upon which to uphold legislation. This minimised the Court's involvement in issues of policy, while maintaining its role as the arbiter of the *Constitution*.

Hence, in 1944 in *Stenhouse v Coleman*,[49] the Court upheld regulations conferring on the Minister a wide discretionary power to make orders controlling the sale or distribution of 'essential articles'. In doing so, Dixon J noted that whether the measure was connected to the war effort was the product of factors that 'may be of such a nature that they cannot be publicly canvassed without prejudicing the conduct of the war or imperilling the national interest'.[50] In these circumstances,

[47] *Communist Party Case* (1951) 83 CLR 1, 141.

[48] See Brian Galligan, *Politics of the High Court: A Study of the Judicial Branch of Government in Australia* (University of Queensland Press, 1987) 120–9.

[49] (1944) 69 CLR 457.

[50] Ibid 469.

'ordinarily the court does not go beyond matters of which it may take judicial notice'.[51] The effect was that the presumption in favour of the validity of the law was 'reinforced by the respect which the court pays to the opinion or judgment of the other organs of government with whom the responsibility for carrying on the war rests'.[52] However, as 'great as must be the weight given to these considerations, it is finally the court which must form and act upon a judgment upon the question whether the legislation, be it direct or be it subordinate, is a true exercise of the legislative power with respect to defence'.[53]

Such reasoning was a far cry from Latham CJ's suggestion that the argument against the validity of the *Dissolution Act* was akin to saying that 'Parliament cannot legislate against an enemy unless the Court decides on evidence legally admissible (and the Court can have no other evidence) that it is an enemy and that the law is necessary or reasonable'.[54] As he noted, the recent 'decisions to fight Germany and Japan were not made by the Court'.[55] Hence, 'the Court had no authority to review the entirely political decisions in 1914 that Germany was an enemy of the Commonwealth, or in 1939 and 1941 that Germany and Japan constituted a danger to the Commonwealth'.[56] Of course, no one would reasonably suggest that the Court would do this, and so by dismissing these propositions, Latham CJ demolished a straw man.

Chief Justice Latham upheld the *Dissolution Act* in its entirety. This extended to those provisions that provided the Governor-General an unreviewable discretion to declare organisations to be unlawful, and persons to be communists. The leeway given to Parliament to legislate in such areas meant that there could be no problem with such sections. Hence, 'in the case of defence the opinion of those responsible for defence may validly be made by Parliament the crucial matter in determining under a law whether particular action should be taken to protect the community'.[57] Such action may be taken 'sometimes upon suspicion and not upon proved fact'.[58]

V The Aftermath

Menzies responded to the High Court decision by stating: 'This is not the end of the fight against communism, it is merely the beginning'.[59] A week

[51] Ibid. [52] Ibid 470. [53] Ibid. [54] *Communist Party Case* (1951) 83 CLR 1, 151.
[55] Ibid. [56] Ibid 152. [57] Ibid 161. [58] Ibid 165.
[59] *The Age* (Melbourne) 10 March 1951.

later, he called a double dissolution election of Parliament on the basis of the Senate's failure to pass a Bill dealing with the Commonwealth Bank. Communism was, however, the issue of the day, as demonstrated by the Liberal Party's campaign slogan in Tasmania of 'Menzies or Moscow'.[60] Menzies won the poll held on 28 April 1951, and set out immediately to gain the power to ban the ACP. He first sought a referral of power from the states under s 51(xxxvii) of the *Constitution*, but when this was rebuffed by Labor governments in New South Wales and Queensland, he called a referendum.

The referendum put to the people on 22 September 1951 sought to add a new s 51A into the *Constitution*, including in sub-s (1):

> The Parliament shall have power to make such laws for the peace, order and good government of the Commonwealth with respect to communists or communism as the Parliament considers to be necessary or expedient for the defence or security of the Commonwealth or for the execution or maintenance of this *Constitution* or of the laws of the Commonwealth.

This wording reflected Latham CJ's dissent in the *Communist Party Case* by establishing that the capacity to make laws in this area would depend upon Parliament's own judgment as to whether such legislation was needed. The broad nature of the power was further emphasised by the absence of the qualifying words 'subject to this *Constitution*', which exist in regard to the Commonwealth's legislative powers in ss 51 and 52 of the *Constitution*. The referendum failed by a narrow margin, losing the national vote by 2 370 009 'no' votes to 2 317 927 'yes' votes, and winning a 'yes' vote in only three of the six states.[61]

It appears that Latham may have played a role in the wording of the referendum. As Clem Lloyd has revealed, Latham exchanged letters with Country Party leader, and senior minister in the Menzies Government, Sir Earle Page, who 'wrote to Latham praising his judgment because it was realistic and original, the only judgment consistent with "world facts" at that time'.[62] Page then asked Latham: 'At your leisure, I wonder whether you could not advise some constitutional amendment that would enable us to take action during the traditional pre-war period which now

[60] G Starr, *The Liberal Party of Australia: A Documentary History* (Drummond/Heinemann, 1980) 189–91.

[61] See George Williams, Sean Brennan and Andrew Lynch, *Australian Constitutional Law & Theory: Commentary and Materials* (Federation Press, 6th ed, 2014) 874.

[62] Clem Lloyd, 'Not Peace but a Sword! – The High Court under J G Latham' (1987) 11 *Adelaide Law Review* 175, 202.

has become the decisive phase of modern war'.[63] Latham replied: 'As to constitutional amendments I have already had an informal talk with the Prime Minister and have made some suggestions to him'.[64]

People have rightly questioned Latham's integrity and judicial ethics in light of this correspondence.[65] Lloyd has even speculated whether 'Latham's apparent willingness to advise Menzies on Constitutional amendments to snare the Communist Party after dissolution legislation was found invalid' meant that he 'advised the Prime Minister on measures to suppress Communism before the 1949 elections, perhaps even on the *Communist Party Dissolution Act* itself'.[66] Nothing has emerged to substantiate such a suggestion,[67] although Latham did have a long record of providing advice to the Menzies Government behind the scenes on a range of matters. For example, as Fiona Wheeler has detailed:

> On a single day in July 1950, Latham wrote separately to Menzies, urging reform of the income tax treatment of persons in the creative arts; to Page, suggesting that the government provide free hearing aids to persons requiring them; and to the Acting Minister for Defence, Philip McBride, urging greater Asian language training for defence personnel.[68]

It would not be surprising if at some point he also spoke to members of the government about the *Dissolution Act*.

Judges are prone to hoping that a cherished dissent will one day prevail. This is normally on the basis that other members of the Court will come to share their view. In Latham CJ's case, it appears that he was not prepared

[63] Ibid. [64] Ibid.

[65] See T Miller, 'Sir John Latham and the Communist Party Dissolution Act: A Research Note' (1983) 15 *Australasian Political Science Association Newsletter* 2, 2. According to Miller:

> The very concept of a Chief Justice assisting the executive to amend the Constitution after a six to one High Court decision had gone against him raises serious doubts about his integrity and acceptance of major decisions of the Full Bench, quite apart from the fact that it is a judge's job to consider legislation, not to make it. The separation of powers between executive and judiciary was jeopardised.

See also Fiona Wheeler, 'Sir John Latham's Extra-Judicial Advising' (2011) 35 *Melbourne University Law Review* 651, 672. Wheeler notes that Latham's 'subsequent backroom dealings with Menzies over the issue compromised the foundations of his own authority as a judge'.

[66] Lloyd, above n 62, 202.

[67] But see Widdows, above n 10, 207 n 187. Widdows records that 'Latham CJ, in one of his letters to Dixon J in New York during the passage of the Dissolution Bill through Parliament, could not restrain himself… "There was a most successful dinner at the Australian Club… in honour of Menzies. I spent an hour or two with him on Sunday and discussed many matters"'.

[68] Wheeler, above n 65, 669.

to wait to see if this occurred, and so undertook the extraordinary step of advising the government as to how the High Court's decision might be circumvented by way of a referendum. Even though this was a different era in the life of the High Court, when the boundaries between the Court and government were more permeable than they are today, Latham CJ clearly stepped outside of his proper role. Certainly, it is hard to imagine the other members of the High Court supporting his initiative.

VI *Thomas v Mowbray*

The decision in the *Communist Party Case* is of enormous historical and political importance. However, it deals with a narrow set of legal issues arising in extraordinary circumstances. As a result, even where the dicta of particular judges is cited or quoted, the decision tends to have little practical relevance to determining the validity of later statutes. The exception is the decision of the High Court in *Thomas v Mowbray*, which involved a challenge to the control order regime enacted in Australia after the 2005 London bombings.

Division 104 of the *Criminal Code* (Cth) empowered the Australian Federal Police to seek an order imposing restrictions, prohibitions and/or obligations upon an individual (for example, that he or she not communicate with certain people or must reside at a particular address). The order could be made if an 'issuing court' was satisfied, on the balance of probabilities, that the control order would substantially assist in preventing a terrorist act or that the subject of the control order provided training to or received training from a terrorist organisation.[69]

A majority of the High Court held the control order regime to be validly enacted under the defence power in s 51(vi), and not inconsistent with the separation of judicial power brought about by Chapter III of the *Constitution*. In regard to the former issue, the Court deferred to the executive's assessment of the level of the threat posed by terrorism and what action was needed to meet that threat. This reflected the Commonwealth's submission to the Court that there were a number of factors which, taken together, demonstrated something 'new and evil which Australia has to defend [itself] against'.[70] This material, as well as judicial notice of a range of terrorist attacks, including those in the United States on 11 September 2001, was sufficient to ground the legislation in the defence power.

[69] *Criminal Code Act 1995* (Cth) sch 1 s 101.4(1).

[70] *Thomas v Mowbray* (2007) 233 CLR 307, 396.

Of the majority, Callinan J was surprisingly dismissive of the majority judgment in the *Communist Party Case.* He began his analysis of the case by quoting from the dissent of Latham CJ. In doing so, he appeared to give special weight to that judgment in justifying deference to the view of the government and Parliament about the threat faced by Australia. Justice Callinan stated of the evidence in *Thomas v Mowbray* that there was 'an abundance of uncontradicted, cogent, factual and notorious matter, having the character of constitutional and other facts upon which this Court may and should act'.[71] By contrast, commenting on the *Communist Party Case* Callinan J said, 'the Commonwealth sought to rely . . . factually solely on the allegations made in the preamble to the [Act]'.[72] He concluded that the 'particular principle, properly identified and understood' for which the *Communist Party Case* stands is simply that 'it is for the courts, and not the Parliament to have the final say on whether legislation is within constitutional power or not'.[73]

Justice Kirby, in dissent, was scathing of the result reached by the majority, stating:

> I did not expect that, during my service, I would see the *Communist Party Case* sidelined, minimised, doubted and even criticised and denigrated in this Court. Given the reasoning expressed by the majority in these proceedings, it appears likely that, had the *Dissolution Act* of 1950 been challenged today, its constitutional validity would have been upheld. This is further evidence of the unfortunate surrender of the present Court to demands for more and more governmental powers, federal and state, that exceed or offend the constitutional text and its abiding values.[74]

He also took issue with Callinan J's views on Latham CJ's dissent:

> With all respect, I do not accept that Latham CJ's dissent in the *Communist Party Case* gains latter day authority because his political and diplomatic experience exceeded that of his colleagues. Dixon J too had very considerable diplomatic experience both during and after the War, working in wartime in close collaboration with Allied war leaders. He was to prove more aware of the lessons of history involving the misuse of executive powers. He also proved more capable of approaching the issue, as this Court should, as a legal and constitutional one – as guardian of the abiding values that lie at the heart of the *Constitution.*[75]

The decision raises interesting questions about how the dissent of Latham CJ in the *Communist Party Case* should be viewed. It would be wrong in doing so to overstate the extent to which the modern High Court views

[71] Ibid 486. [72] Ibid. [73] Ibid 503. [74] Ibid 442. [75] Ibid 393.

the dissent with favour. Indeed, in *Thomas v Mowbray*, only Callinan J referred to Latham CJ's judgment. And even though the decision in *Thomas v Mowbray* sits uneasily with the landmark decision in the earlier case, it is still a far cry from endorsing the legal principles advocated there by Latham CJ. The more recent decision is an instance of strong deference on the part of the Court to executive and legislative assessments of a threat to Australia's national security. On the other hand, not even Callinan J was prepared to go so far as Latham CJ in suggesting that, when it came to such matters, the validity of legislation rests with Parliament and not the High Court. At best, it might be said that *Thomas v Mowbray*, in holding that the defence power extended to meeting the threat of terrorism, is consistent with the view of Latham CJ that the power must extend to 'defence against internal enemies and against real or suspected internal agents or supporters of actual or potential external enemies'.[76]

VII Conclusion

The *Communist Party Case* is a landmark in Australia's legal history. If only for this reason, Latham CJ's dissent in the case deserves careful analysis. It also provides a revealing insight into Latham, an important figure in Australia's political and legal history, at the end of his tenure on the High Court. That he found himself in sole dissent against the views of the other members of his Court speaks of an unusual level of isolation on his part. This was a reflection of his lengthy background of combating communism, and his strong, indeed overbearing, views about how Australia should combat the threat. No doubt these personal factors played a key role in producing the most extraordinary dissent of his career, and indeed one of the most notable in the history of the High Court.

[76] *Communist Party Case* (1951) 83 CLR 1, 143. See Hernan Pintos-Lopez and George Williams, '"Enemies Foreign and Domestic": *Thomas v Mowbray* and the New Scope of the Defence Power' (2008) 27 *University of Tasmania Law Review* 83.

7

Public Prosecutor v Oie Hee Koi (1968): Not So Humbly Advising? Sir Garfield Barwick and the Introduction of Dissenting Reasons to the Judicial Committee of the Privy Council

OLIVER JONES

I Introduction

For a jurisdiction that has been a model for law and government worldwide, the United Kingdom has a noticeably odd constitution. Institutions with a mediaeval flavour have, more by convention than prescription, assumed modern roles. Some have recently disappeared. In the last two decades, the pace of change and adaptation has been so marked as to prompt talk of Britain's 'new' Constitution.[1] For example, the office of Lord Chancellor no longer exercises senior executive, legislative and judicial functions. Gone too, is a final appellate court existing as a committee of the House of Lords, replaced with the new Supreme Court of the United Kingdom. Yet, amidst all this change, one particular oddity remains: the Judicial Committee of the Privy Council ('Judicial Committee' or, in a given appeal, 'Board').

The Privy Council is a body of advisers to the monarch. However, its Judicial Committee became a final appellate court for the British Empire and, in time, the Commonwealth of Nations. The Board tends not to deliver judgment in the strict sense. Rather, their Lordships deliver reasons and indicate that they will report to the monarch 'humbly advising' that the appeal be allowed or dismissed. There was traditionally a further unorthodoxy to the work of the Judicial Committee. While the Board could decide cases by majority, the publication of dissenting reasons was prohibited.

[1] Vernon Bogdanor, *The New British Constitution* (Hart Publishing, 2009).

There was debate for decades over whether to lift this prohibition. The campaign to allow dissenting reasons in the Judicial Committee ultimately prevailed. Among those involved, Sir Garfield Barwick, who became Chief Justice of Australia and a Privy Counsellor in 1964, looms large. He lobbied hard for the revocation of the prohibition. Soon after, he gave, with Lord Guest, among the first dissenting reasons in *Public Prosecutor v Oie Hee Koi* ('*Oie Hee Koi*').[2] This chapter traces the emergence of dissenting reasons in the Judicial Committee, a development spearheaded by Barwick. It then details the personal significance of *Oie Hee Koi* to Barwick and the nature of his dissent in that case.

II Origins and Development of the Privy Council

The Judicial Committee grew out of the right of a litigant dissatisfied with a decision of a colonial court to petition His or Her Majesty in Council for prerogative relief.[3] The early exercise of this jurisdiction was unimpressive by today's standards. Several decision-makers would hear petitions, typically with only one, the Master of the Rolls, being legally qualified.[4] The modern history of the Privy Council as a judicial body begins with the *Judicial Committee Act 1833* (Imp) ('*1833 Act*').[5] This statute granted the Board the procedural powers of a court.[6] Its reasons were delivered in open court.[7]

There was once fierce discussion of how far the Judicial Committee was a court, rather than an advisory body the views of which could, in an exercise of reserve powers, be rejected by the monarch.[8] Any doubts were dispelled in 1935, when the Board decided *British Coal Corp v The King*.[9] While, under s 3 of the *1833 Act*, the judgments of the Board were a report to the monarch, it was 'unknown and unthinkable that [the monarch]

2 [1968] AC 829.

3 See, eg, *British Coal Corp v The King* [1935] AC 500; *A-G (St Christopher and Nevis) v Rodionov* [2004] 1 WLR 2796; Peter Howell, *Judicial Committee of the Privy Council 1833–1876: Its Origins, Structure and Development* (Cambridge University Press, 1979); David Swinfen, *Imperial Appeal: The Debate on the Appeal to the Privy Council 1833–1986* (Manchester University Press, 1986) ch 1.

4 Swinfen, above n 3, 224.

5 3 & 4 Wm 4, c 41.

6 Swinfen, above n 3, 7, 55; Howell, above n 3, 31–2, 39–40, 58, 155–6.

7 Howell, above n 3, 38–9.

8 Swinfen, above n 3, 225–7; ibid 222–3.

9 [1935] AC 500.

should not give effect to them'.[10] The Board, in other cases, also asserted its independence from Imperial or colonial authorities.[11]

III Prohibition on Public Dissenting Reasons

It must be emphasised that there was never a prohibition on the Judicial Committee making its decisions by majority, with the consequence of a dissenting minority. Section 5 of the *1833 Act* relevantly provided that

> no report or recommendation shall be made to His Majesty unless a majority of the members of such Judicial Committee present at the hearing shall concur in such report or recommendation . . .

The real issue was whether members of the Judicial Committee could, in addition to refraining from voting with the majority on the report or recommendation, express in open court their reasons.[12] From 1833, the problem only rarely arose. Each Board went to great lengths to achieve unanimity. There was an Order in Council of 1627 ('*1627 Order*'), requiring secrecy in deliberations of the Privy Council. Although the *1627 Order* was of doubtful application to the Judicial Committee, it appears to have prompted a conscious decision by that body to reject a practice of delivering separate judgments.[13]

The following process emerged. One member would be assigned the task of preparing draft reasons. The draft would be circulated and revisions considered. The draft would then typically be issued as the unanimous decision of the Board. The principal difficulty, which arose on

[10] Ibid 510–11 (Viscount Sankey LC, for the Board). See also *Hull v M'Kenna* [1926] IR 402, 403 (Viscount Haldane LC, for the Board). The Judicial Committee has a separate function of giving advisory opinions under s 4 of the *1833 Act*: see, eg, *Hearing on the Report of the Chief Justice of Gibraltar* [2009] UKPC 43.

[11] *Ibralebbe v The Queen* [1964] AC 900, 919–21 (Viscount Radcliffe, for the Board); *Independent Jamaica Council for Human Rights (1998) Ltd v Marshall-Burnett* [2005] 2 AC 356, 371 (Lord Bingham, for the Board).

[12] The reference to open court is deliberate. It appears that dissenting reasons were, long before the prohibition on their publication was lifted, privately circulated to the majority: Alan Paterson, *The Law Lords* (Macmillan, 1982) 102. Further, those dissenting reasons and the number of dissenting votes were recorded, but not publicised: Sir Garfield Barwick, Interview with Clyde Cameron (Taped Conversation, 1981) 00:22:44 <http://nla.gov.au/nla.oh-vn2716199>.

[13] Howell, above n 3, 200–1; Swinfen, above n 3, 222. This practice has only recently been abandoned. Separate concurring reasons were given for the first time in 2008: *Raphael Fishing Company Ltd v Mauritius* [2008] UKPC 43. They have been given on several occasions since.

only a few occasions, was when the Board divided evenly. The practice was that the appeal would be reheard before an enlarged or differently constituted Board.[14] This institutional process of judgment production is in vivid contrast with the traditionally individualised work practices and judgment delivery of the High Court of Australia, particularly during the Barwick era.[15]

Peter Howell has recorded occasions from 1833 to the 1870s where the Board would disclose that its report or recommendation was, under s 5 of the *1833 Act*, reached by majority. This was, on rare occasions, accompanied by brief comments from the dissenting members.[16] There appears to have been no controversy during this period as to the prohibition on public dissenting reasons. The members of the Judicial Committee, almost without exception, appeared content that the fact of their dissent had been disclosed before the majority report or recommendation was made to the monarch.[17]

IV Debate over Lifting the Prohibition

All this would soon change. It is important to recall that, in addition to its status as an Imperial court of final appeal, the Judicial Committee had jurisdiction to hear ecclesiastical appeals. It was in this jurisdiction that controversy as to public dissenting reasons first arose. In the 1870s, certain bishops participating in ecclesiastical cases dissented from the opinion of the majority of the Board in two controversial cases.[18] The Church was resentful of the authority of the secular Law Lords. The bishops' reasons for dissenting were not made public, but the fact of their dissent was. The membership by bishops of the Judicial Committee in ecclesiastical cases was presently repealed.[19]

In 1877, there was a third controversial ecclesiastical case. Discord within the Board, including the names of the dissentients, was leaked to the press. A member of the Board and Chief Baron of the Exchequer, Sir Fitzroy Kelly, was quoted in the press condemning the view of the majority. Sir Fitzroy largely admitted the leak and wrote to the Lord Chancellor,

[14] Howell, above n 3, 199–200.

[15] David Marr, *Barwick* (Allen and Unwin, 2005) 215, 221–4, 233, 235. See further the discussion of the High Court's 'consensual norm' in Matthew Groves, 'Justice Murphy's Dissent in *Australian Conservation Foundation v Commonwealth* (1980): The Birth of Public Interest Standing in Australia?' in ch 11 of this book.

[16] Howell, above n 3, 201–3.

[17] Ibid 221.

[18] Swinfen, above n 3, 227.

[19] Ibid 227–9.

Lord Cairns, insisting upon the right to express dissenting reasons. Sir Fitzroy challenged the view that the *1627 Order* denied him this right.[20]

The response of Lord Cairns was swift and perhaps disproportionate. The civilised and summary expression of dissent was replaced with a different regime, comprising a gag. By an Order in Council of 4 February 1878 ('*1878 Order*'), disclosure 'by any man' of any difference of opinion in the Judicial Committee was forbidden. Neither the fact of nor reasons for dissent could thereafter be communicated.[21]

It did not take long for the Australians to get involved, providing the link between the prohibition on public dissenting reasons and the Imperial jurisdiction of the Judicial Committee. In September 1888, Sir Frederick Darley sent to the United Kingdom a series of resolutions as to the Judicial Committee drafted by the Chief Justices of the Australian colonies. One recommended that, when Australian appeals were determined by the Judicial Committee, its members should be free to give dissenting reasons.[22]

The Australian Chief Justices did not provide a justification for their stance. No action was taken. However, the matter was again raised at the Imperial Conference of 1911, which laid the groundwork for the greater autonomy of the dominions, Australia, Canada, Ireland, New Zealand and South Africa. The most cogent argument was put forward by the South African representative, who indicated that the absence of dissenting reasons raised the question of whether the Judicial Committee was an ordinary court of law.[23]

The Imperial authorities stated a preference for maintaining the prohibition and even suggested its extension to the House of Lords.[24] The desire for such an extension was not new. It had been suggested to a committee of inquiry in 1856 that a prohibition on public dissenting reasons advanced the 'great end of having certainty and no element of uncertainty in the law'.[25] In the case of the Judicial Committee, this desire appears to be linked to the 'special advantage' of the authority of their Lordships as an Imperial court.[26]

It must be borne in mind that the Judicial Committee was considered 'an integral part of the system of Imperial government'.[27] It upheld Imperial unity by providing legal uniformity and perhaps even by protecting Imperial interests, whether governmental or commercial.[28] There

[20] Ibid 231–2. [21] Howell, above n 3, 201; ibid 232. [22] Swinfen, above n 3, 234.
[23] Ibid 236. [24] Ibid 237. [25] Ibid 225. [26] Ibid 223.
[27] Howell, above n 3, 14. [28] Swinfen, above n 3, vi, 28, 61.

is ample evidence of the desire of members of the Judicial Committee to pursue uniformity across the various systems of law they were called upon to administer.[29] There is less evidence that the Judicial Committee actively favoured Imperial interests, although the mild-mannered Sir Ninian Stephen would one day, in a shipping case before the High Court, accuse the Board of acting 'in the interests of great fleet-owning nations'.[30]

This conception of the role of the Judicial Committee, at the height of the British Empire, relaxed as decolonisation led to the Commonwealth of Nations. The Judicial Committee came to see itself as compatible with post-colonial independence[31] and, ultimately, a jurisdictionally specific final appellate court.[32] It welcomed local development of the law,[33] although it reserved the right to recognise uniformity where appropriate.[34] In any event, the traditional understanding of the Imperial function of the Judicial Committee is less sinister than it may seem. Certainty or uniformity has always been attractive to foreign investors and explains the contemporary preference for international investment arbitration.[35]

Even so, the preference of the Imperial authorities for the prohibition was not ardent. The Lord Chancellor, Lord Loreburn, indicated that the prohibition could be revoked if the Imperial Conference decided to prefer that course.[36] Indeed, by 1912, there was in circulation a draft Order in

[29] Ibid 63; Lord Atkin, 'Appeal in English Law' (1927) 3 *Cambridge Law Journal* 1, 7; Jean Hall and Douglas Martin, *Haldane – Statesman, Lawyer, Philosopher* (B Rose, 1996) 175.

[30] *Port Jackson Stevedoring Pty Ltd v Salmond & Spraggon (Aust) Pty Ltd* (1978) 139 CLR 231, 258 (Stephen J). This judgment was reversed by the Privy Council, without addressing Stephen J 's allegation: *Port Jackson Stevedoring Pty Ltd v Salmond & Spraggon (Aust) Pty Ltd* [1981] 1 WLR 138.

[31] *Ibralebbe v The Queen* [1964] AC 900, 925.

[32] *Independent Jamaica Council for Human Rights (1998) Ltd v Marshall-Burnett* [2005] 2 AC 356, 363 (Lord Bingham, for the Board).

[33] *Australia Consolidated Press v Uren* [1969] 1 AC 590.

[34] *Hart v O'Connor* [1985] AC 1000, 1017 (Lord Brightman, for the Board); *R v Chan Hak-So* [1988] 1 HKLR 332, 334 (Lord Bridge, for the Board). See also the Judicial Committee's rejection of local attempts to innovate and depart from English authority in *Mutual Life & Citizens Assurance Company Ltd v Evatt* [1971] AC 793; *Port Jackson Stevedoring Pty Ltd v Salmond & Spraggon (Aust) Pty Ltd* [1981] 1 WLR 138; *Red Sea Insurance Co Ltd v Bouygues* [1995] 1 AC 190.

[35] Murray Gleeson, 'The Influence of the Privy Council on Australia' (Speech delivered at the Anglo-Australasian Lawyers Society, Sydney, 31 May 2007) 13–14; Christopher Dugan et al, *Investor-State Arbitration* (Oxford University Press, 2008).

[36] Swinfen, above n 3, 237.

Council revoking the *1878 Order*.[37] All seemed well. Yet, the Australians had evidently underestimated the Canadians.

Former Chief Justice Murray Gleeson has remarked that, in Australia, there was never the widespread depth of feeling about appeals to the Judicial Committee that arose in Canada.[38] It is true that the role of the Privy Council was a stumbling block in the drafting of the *Australian Constitution*, leading to a compromise. Section 74 precluded some constitutional appeals to the Judicial Committee in the absence of a certificate from the High Court.[39] This was influenced by the Canadian experience and, in early disagreements over the scope of s 74, the High Court spoke scathingly of the Judicial Committee's lack of expertise in Australian constitutional cases.[40] However, the somewhat reduced role of the Privy Council provided for by s 74 may have helped prevent acrimony of Canadian proportions.

The Canadians' attitude to the Judicial Committee influenced their opinion on the prohibition on public dissenting reasons. From 1912, they opposed revoking the prohibition, insisting on decisions of the Judicial Committee without public dissenting reasons. The Canadians were sensitive because the Judicial Committee, exercising its unbridled jurisdiction in constitutional cases, consistently favoured the provincial governments over Ottawa. This was spearheaded by Viscount Haldane, including as Lord Chancellor.[41] The Judicial Committee was accused of ignorance of Canadian circumstances. In fairness, on one occasion, the Board lent weight to the accusation by referring to the 'Province of Montreal'.[42]

[37] Ibid. See also John Alder, 'Dissents in Courts of Last Resort: Tragic Choices?' (2000) 20 *Oxford Journal of Legal Studies* 221, 236.

[38] Gleeson, above n 35, 10. This did not mean that some Australian lawyers did not have serious reservations about the Judicial Committee: see, eg, *O'Sullivan v Noarlunga Meat Ltd [No 2]* (1956) 94 CLR 367, 375–6 (Dixon CJ); Phillip Ayres, *Sir Owen Dixon* (Melbourne University Press, 2003) 41–2, 79–80, 238, 246.

[39] The High Court only ever issued one certificate, in *Colonial Sugar Refining Co v A-G (Cth)* (1912) 15 CLR 182. Although s 74 remains in force, no certificate will ever be issued again: *Kirmani v Captain Cook Cruises* (1985) 159 CLR 461.

[40] *Baxter v Commissioner of Taxation (NSW)* (1907) 4 CLR 1087, 1111 (Griffith CJ, Barton and O'Connor JJ).

[41] Frederick Vaughan, *Viscount Haldane: The Wicked Stepfather of the Canadian Constitution* (Toronto University Press, 2010). See also Edward McWhinney, 'Judicial Concurrences and Dissents: A Comparative View of Opinion Writing in Final Appellate Tribunals' (1953) 31 *Canadian Bar Review* 595, 598–9.

[42] Swinfen, above n 3, ch 2; *A-G (Quebec) v Queen Insurance Co* (1878) 3 App Cas 1090, 1096 (George Jessel MR, for the Board).

Whether or not such criticism was wholly justified,[43] it had the following impact on the Canadian attitude to dissenting reasons in the Judicial Committee. In his magisterial work, *Imperial Appeal: The Debate on the Appeal to the Privy Council 1833–1986*, the historian Dr David Swinfen recounts the arguments of the Canadian representative as follows:

> In arguing that a change in current practice would not be in the public interest, the Canadian Minister suggested that the value of the Judicial Committee lay in the 'ultimate and decisive effects of its judgments' in the particular case, and the 'permanent advantage to the profession and to the public generally' of its decisions. While the expression of dissent was of no immediate value to the suitor 'it would serve in the more important aspect of the case, from the public point of view, to affect the interpretation or certainty of a judgment and its quality as a determining precedent'. Many cases brought before the Committee were of a very sensitive character, involving constitutional questions as between the Dominion and the provinces . . . the proposal could not be put into effect 'without in a measure impairing the dignity and influence of a Tribunal which is the ultimate exponent of the law and the constitution'.[44]

Swinfen describes the Canadian justification as pragmatic.[45] This must be right. Given the Canadian sensitivity to the decisions of the Judicial Committee, the path to acceptance of those decisions would only be cluttered by minority reasons expressing why the decision was wrong. Political pragmatism would exclude such own goals in favour of a united front.

In the face of Canadian opposition, the draft Order was not made.[46] However, pragmatism would not ultimately prevail. Canada, after some unsuccessful efforts,[47] abolished criminal appeals to the Privy Council in 1933[48] and civil appeals in 1949.[49] Amazingly, the last Canadian appeal to the Privy Council came as late as 1959.[50] The time was now ripe for change. The Judicial Committee was downplaying its Imperial function and, therefore, had less need to buttress its authority with unanimity. Canadian sensitivities no longer arose.

43 Peter Hogg, 'Canada: From Privy Council to Supreme Court' in Jeffrey Goldsworthy (ed), *Interpreting Constitutions: A Comparative Study* (Oxford University Press, 2006) 75–6; Gleeson, above n 35, 6.

44 Swinfen, above n 3, 238. 45 Ibid 239. 46 Ibid 238–9.

47 *Cushing v Dupuy* (1880) 5 App Cas 409; *Nadan v The King* [1926] AC 482.

48 *British Coal Corp v The King* [1935] AC 500.

49 See, eg, *A-G (Ontario) v A-G (Canada)* [1947] AC 127.

50 *Ponoka-Calmar Oils Ltd v Earl F Wakefield Co* [1960] AC 18. See also W G Morrow, 'The Last Case' (1978) 16 *Alberta Law Review* 1.

Enter Barwick. He had a long association with the Judicial Committee. His biographer, David Marr, goes so far as to say that it was before the Board that Barwick 'made his name'.[51] It was certainly the scene of his most famous, and possibly lucrative, victory in *Commonwealth of Australia v Bank of New South Wales*.[52] Barwick socialised with their Lordships. He perceived warmth from the Judicial Committee that had been withheld, especially by Sir Owen Dixon, in the High Court.[53] So deep was Barwick's affection for the Judicial Committee that he lamented, with some seriousness, the eventual abolition of appeals from Australia and, in particular, being unable to challenge in that forum the 'terrible tosh'[54] of his successors on the High Court in *Cole v Whitfield*.[55]

By 1964, Barwick was Chief Justice of Australia and a Privy Councillor. He thereby joined a long line of overseas common law judges who, since the late 19th century, had been allowed to sit as members of the Board.[56] This enabled Barwick to pursue reform of the prohibition on public dissenting reasons. He proposed that it be revoked. Two grounds appear to have been advanced. The first was that, to the extent the prohibition was referable to the formal procedure of the Judicial Committee advising the monarch, it should be swept away, as the Judicial Committee was, in substance, a court. The second was that, if Commonwealth judges were to sit more frequently as members of the Judicial Committee, the prohibition

[51] Marr, above n 15, 219. [52] [1950] AC 235.

[53] Marr, above n 15, 76–7, 125–6, 129–30.

[54] 'Bar News Interviews Sir Garfield Barwick GCMC', *Bar News* [1989] (Summer) 17. See also Garfield Barwick, *A Radical Tory* (Federation Press, 1995) 61. On the other hand, it has been suggested that, when Chief Justice, Barwick discouraged, even frustrated, an appeal to their Lordships: Keith Mason, *Old Law, New Law* (Federation Press, 2014) 121. Barwick ultimately conceded that the abolition of appeals was appropriate: Sir Garfield Barwick, Interview with Clyde Cameron (Taped Conversation, 1981) 00:40:22 <http://nla.gov.au/nla.oh-vn2716199>.

[55] (1988) 165 CLR 360.

[56] There had been provision, at least formally, for overseas common law judges to sit on the Board since 1895: see Swinfen, above n 3, 77. Regular such members of the Board, including up until when Barwick made his proposal in 1964, were the Chief Justices of Canada Sir Lyman Duff, Sir Charles Fitzpatrick, Sir Henry Strong, Sir Henry Taschereau and, to a lesser extent, Sir Louis Davies, Francis Anglin and Thibaudeau Rinfret; Justice of the Supreme Court of Ceylon L M D de Silva; Chief Justices of South Africa, Sir Henry (later Lord) de Villiers and, to a lesser extent, James Stratford. Other overseas members, who sat less often perhaps due to the distance, were the Chief Justices of Australia Sir Samuel Griffith and Sir Adrian Knox; Justices of the High Court of Australia Sir Edmund Barton, Sir Isaac Isaacs and Sir George Rich; Chief Justices of New Zealand Sir Robert Stout and Sir Michael Myers; and senior New Zealand Justices Sir Joshua Williams and Sir Kenneth Gresson.

should be removed, as it could dissuade such judges, accustomed to giving dissenting reasons, from joining the Board.[57]

The first justification is misplaced. As indicated, s 5 of the *1833 Act* contemplated a single report or recommendation being given to the monarch by majority. It necessarily followed that there was scope for members of the Judicial Committee to vote against the report or recommendation, even if they were prohibited by the *1878 Order* from disclosing that fact. Further, it is apparent that the monarch never received reasons for the advice of the Board in a given case, let alone dissenting reasons. The monarch only received, and by convention was required to make, the proposed orders for the disposition of the appeal.[58] In other words, the procedural formalities of the Judicial Committee, as advisers to the monarch, were blind to whether or not dissenting reasons were published.

The second justification also does not withstand scrutiny. It is the case that Barwick and others had tentative plans to create a Commonwealth Court of Appeal. The Court could have involved an amalgamation of the House of Lords and the Privy Council, possibly with public dissenting reasons, and would have had significant Commonwealth membership.[59] Even in the absence of such a reform, it is easy to imagine Barwick refusing to sit without the right to publish dissenting reasons, in light of his famously independent mind and forthright nature. However, Barwick may not have been the norm. As indicated, overseas common law judges had sat as members of the Judicial Committee, without demur, since the late 19th century.

It is interesting that there does not appear to have been any engagement with the broader notion that the authority of the Judicial Committee was enhanced by unanimity or, conversely, would be undermined by dissenting reasons. As indicated, following the abolition of Canadian appeals and the move away from the status of the Judicial Committee as an Imperial court, the issue may well have been thought simply irrelevant.

In any event, as a justification for the prohibition, the notion that dissent would erode the authority of the Privy Council's decisions was weak. From an Imperial or a Canadian perspective, it was simply a practical concern. It cannot be justified as a matter of principle. Whatever the position in

57 Swinfen, above n 3, 240; Marr, above n 15, 219; Barwick, *A Radical Tory*, above n 54, 222; Sir Garfield Barwick, Interview with Clyde Cameron (Taped Conversation, 1981) 00:22:44 <http://nla.gov.au/nla.oh-vn2716199>.

58 Swinfen, above n 3, 19. The point was confirmed by email correspondence: Email from Registry of Judicial Committee of Privy Council to the author, 7 July 2015.

59 Swinfen, above n 3, 236, 240.

other branches of government, there is no basis in principle for excluding dissenting reasons from a final appellate court. A majority of such a court should have the fortitude to withstand dissent. The court as an institution should be sufficiently at ease with the complexity of its task and the level of choice involved to tolerate minority views. No notion of authority should be so important that dissenting views are excluded.

It is fortunate, therefore, that Barwick's proposal was accepted by Lord Gardiner who, perhaps ironically, was the first Labour Lord Chancellor in some decades, with a vast appetite for law reform.[60] On 4 March 1966, the 'Judicial Committee (Dissenting Opinions) Order 1966' ('*1966 Order*') was pronounced. The *1878 Order* was revoked. The *1966 Order* then read:

> Any member of the Judicial Committee of the Privy Council present at the hearing of any appeal, cause or matter who shall dissent from the opinion of the majority of the members present as to the nature of the report or recommendation to be made to Her Majesty thereon shall be at liberty to publish his dissent in open Court together with his reasons.

It was not long before Barwick would exercise his right to pronounce dissenting reasons.

V Sir Garfield Barwick's Dissenting Reasons

Barwick had not been surprised by the fact of his appointment to the Chief Justiceship. He had indicated to the Prime Minister, Sir Robert Menzies, that he wanted the job. However, the timing of his appointment is said by his biographer, Marr, to have been unexpected. Barwick had a busy period as Minister for External Affairs, at a time when various parts of the Asian region were in turmoil. Immediately before his appointment as Chief Justice, Barwick was ready to depart Australia for a European tour as Minister. The Russian Ambassador had already left to be in Moscow to greet him.[61]

However, it was not to be. The tour had to be cancelled only hours before Barwick was due to depart. Marr claims Barwick complained to friends that 'the old man [Menzies] kicked me out'.[62] Barwick himself strongly denied this.[63] He also denied the central point, namely that he

[60] See generally Muriel Box, *Rebel Advocate: A Biography of Gerald Gardiner* (Gollancz, 1983).

[61] Marr, above n 15, 208. [62] Ibid 209.

[63] Sir Garfield Barwick, Interview with Clyde Cameron (Taped Conversation, 1981) 00:20:46 <http://nla.gov.au/nla.oh-vn2716199>.

left Cabinet for the High Court sooner than he expected.[64] This requires some brief discussion.

Somewhat coincidentally, Barwick's last weeks in ministerial office lay in the events that gave rise to *Oie Hee Koi*. After Indonesian President Sukarno declared a Year of Living Dangerously in 1964, his country and Malaysia were in violent confrontation over whether British Borneo should be incorporated into the latter. Barwick's record of diplomacy in the dispute was impressive. He sought to bring Malaysia and Indonesia together for talks, so as to avoid armed conflict. This involved taking an independent path from that of the United Kingdom on the question.[65] Barwick's approach was uncannily prescient of the more autonomous approach to diplomacy taken a decade later by one of Menzies' successors as Prime Minister, Edward Gough Whitlam.[66]

Barwick almost succeeded. However, his efforts came to be thwarted by an uncompromising United Kingdom, supported by Menzies. Armed conflict between Malaysia and Indonesia ensued. United Kingdom and ANZAC troops became involved. Barwick sought a promise of military support from the United States, as part of the ANZUS alliance.[67] In this respect, Barwick was a far more traditional exponent of Australian foreign relations than Whitlam would become. The Coalition, including Barwick, placed great weight on ANZUS, as a foil to Communism in Asia.[68]

Barwick, having travelled to Washington and having met President John F Kennedy, made some unguarded public pronouncements on his return. They were taken by the United States to overstate the level of support that had been offered. Diplomatic embarrassment ensued. According to Marr, but not Barwick, the result was that Menzies and his Cabinet insisted that Barwick assume the Chief Justiceship immediately.[69]

In mid-1966, Barwick, now Chief Justice, arrived in London to sit as a member of the Judicial Committee. There were several appeals. In two, he delivered the unanimous reasons on behalf of the Board.[70] In

64 Ibid 00:25:23.

65 Marr, above n 15, ch 16. See also Sir Garfield Barwick, Interview with Clyde Cameron (Taped Conversation, 1981) 00:38:07 <http://nla.gov.au/nla.oh-vn2716199>.

66 Whitlam's path, and the rift it caused with President Richard Nixon of the United States, has recently been the subject of detailed scholarship: James Curran, *Unholy Fury: Whitlam and Nixon at War* (Melbourne University Press, 2015).

67 Marr, above n 15, 209. 68 Ibid. 69 Ibid. 207–8.

70 *Inland Revenue Commissioner v Mutual Investment Co Ltd* [1967] 1 AC 587; *Lee Kar Choo v Lee Lian Choon* [1967] 1 AC 602.

the other two, he was party to the unanimous reasons of the Board.[71] A year later, he returned to London to sit as a member of the Board in *Oie Hee Koi*. While Barwick would ultimately, with Lord Guest, deliver public dissenting reasons in that case, they would not be the first to exercise the right to do so under the *1966 Order*.

Lord Donovan, also a former politician, took the honour of delivering the first ever of those reasons in a somewhat dry Australian taxation appeal, *Peate v Commissioner of Taxation (Australia)*.[72] The second public dissenting reasons in the Judicial Committee were delivered by Lord Guest and Lord Devlin in an industrial relations case concerning the separation of powers in Ceylon, *United Engineering Workers Union v Devanayagam*.[73]

Oie Hee Koi was the next occasion for public dissenting reasons in the Board. It was a large criminal case, involving 12 accused, who were separately represented. In addition to Lord Guest, Barwick sat with Lord Hodson, Lord Wilberforce and, it seems uniquely, another Australian, Sir Douglas Menzies. The accused were Chinese Malaysians. They had either been born in or had settled in Malaysia. However, there was no evidence that they had Malaysian nationality or otherwise owed allegiance to Malaysia.

The accused consorted with the Indonesian army and landed in Malaysia by air and sea as members of an armed force under the command of the Indonesian military. They were convicted of offences under the notorious *Internal Security Act 1960* (Malaysia) ('*ISA*')[74] and sentenced to death. On their appeal to the Judicial Committee, they invoked the Geneva Conventions, which were incorporated into Malaysian domestic law. If applicable, the Geneva Conventions would have provided procedural protections to the accused, which had not been observed by the Malaysian courts. The accused also independently challenged whether the *ISA*, properly construed, applied to them.

The majority held that the Geneva Conventions did not apply in relation to persons who were either the nationals of the detaining power or owed allegiance to the detaining power.[75] Lord Guest and Barwick agreed.[76] This conclusion has since been criticised and may no

[71] *Jeffs v New Zealand Dairy Production and Marketing Board* [1967] 1 AC 551; *Frazer v Walker* [1967] 1 AC 569.

[72] [1967] AC 308. [73] [1968] AC 356.

[74] Andrew Harding, *Constitution of Malaysia: A Contextual Analysis* (Hart Publishing, 2001) ch 6.

[75] *Oie Hee Koi* [1968] AC 829, 858 (Lord Hodson, for the majority).

[76] Ibid 863–4 (Lord Guest and Sir Garfield Barwick).

longer represent public international law.[77] In any event, Lord Guest and Barwick parted company from the majority in relation to the *ISA*. The majority held that the *ISA* did not apply to prohibit consorting with members of regular military forces fighting in enemy country. Accordingly, some, but not all, of the charges against the accused under the *ISA* were bad.[78] Lord Guest and Barwick dissented, holding that in such circumstances the *ISA* did apply.[79]

In the result, there was little solace for the accused in the conclusions of either the majority or the minority. Only one of the accused was spared by the majority, on the ground that he alone had discharged his onus of raising the question of the application of the Geneva Conventions, which should have been considered by the Malaysian courts.[80] Lord Guest and Barwick dissented on this point, concluding that this particular accused had not, in fact, raised the Geneva Conventions. Under their dissent, he too would have gone to the gallows.[81]

Despite regularly sitting on the Judicial Committee in subsequent cases, *Oie Hee Koi* appears to be the only occasion where Barwick exercised his entitlement to public dissenting reasons under the reform which he helped bring about.[82]

VI Conclusion

In a book devoted to dissenting reasons for judgment, it is appropriate to have some discussion of whether the institution of dissents is worthwhile. The Judicial Committee of the Privy Council is an excellent vehicle for

77 Ka Ho Tse, 'The Relevancy of Nationality to the Right to Prisoner of War Status' (2009) 8 *Chinese Journal of International Law* 395.

78 *Oie Hee Koi* [1968] AC 829, 860–1 (Lord Hodson, for the majority).

79 Ibid 868 (Lord Guest and Sir Garfield Barwick).

80 Ibid 859–60 (Lord Hodson, for the majority).

81 Ibid 865–6 (Lord Guest and Sir Garfield Barwick). Barwick later indicated that none of the accused were ultimately executed: Sir Garfield Barwick, Interview with Clyde Cameron (Taped Conversation, 1981) 00:28:43 <http://nla.gov.au/nla.oh-vn2716199>.

82 Sir Garfield Barwick delivered the unanimous reasons on behalf of the Board in *Borneo Airways Ltd v Commissioner of Inland Revenue* [1970] AC 929; *Williams v St Lucia* [1970] AC 935. He was party to the unanimous reasons of the Board in *A-G (Guyana) v Nobrega* [1969] 3 All ER 1604; *Sim Lim Investments Ltd v A-G (Singapore)* [1970] AC 923; *Stenhouse Australia Ltd v Phillips* [1974] AC 391; *Walton v The King* [1978] AC 788; *Bhoomidas v Port of Singapore Authority* [1978] 1 All ER 956; *Ross v Henderson* [1979] AC 196; *Port Swettenham Authority v T W Wu & Co Sdn Bhd* [1979] AC 580. He was party to the majority reasons of the Board in *Barton v Armstrong* [1976] AC 104; *Europa Oil (NZ) Ltd v Inland Revenue Commissioner* [1976] 1 All ER 503.

examining that question. For over 100 years, dissenting reasons were prohibited. There was protracted discussion as to whether the prohibition should be lifted. Ultimately, with the work of Barwick, it was.

Dissenting reasons were initially excluded from the Privy Council in light of historical practice. However, the debate over whether to lift the exclusion of such reasons led to an interesting consideration of their merits. The arguments raised in favour of prohibiting dissenting reasons were pragmatic rather than principled. The assertion of Imperial authority, particularly in the delicate Canadian context, was considered to be strengthened by the exclusion of dissenting reasons.

Once the Imperial function of the Judicial Committee had waned, and Canadian appeals were abolished, the pragmatic justification for the prohibition of public dissenting reasons fell away. Barwick, in proposing the introduction of dissenting reasons, did not argue why dissenting reasons should be permitted as a matter of principle. However, there is a principled justification for having dissenting reasons. A final appellate court should be frank and open about not only why the majority has reached its view, but also why the minority considers that view to be wrong. The authority of a court, at least in a post-colonial setting, is not so important that it is enough for the majority to give its reasons, without scope for the contrary reasons of the minority to be heard.

Oie Hee Koi is a fascinating case, with insights into Barwick's career as an internationalist. The majority construction of the Geneva Conventions, in which Barwick and Lord Guest joined, may no longer represent public international law. The dissenting view of Barwick and Lord Guest as to the application of the *ISA* is, however momentous for those concerned, essentially a technical question of statutory construction. But it is the *fact* that Barwick publicly dissented, having lobbied as an Australian member of the Privy Council for the right to do so, that is most important to this book.

8

The Trouble with Duress: The Dissent of Chief Justice Bray in *R v Brown and Morley* (1968)

JOE MCINTYRE

I Introduction

It is rare that a dissent in a criminal law appeal, let alone the lone voice of a state Supreme Court Justice, claims the mantle of greatness. However, the dissent of Chief Justice Bray[1] in *R v Brown and Morley*[2] has a strong claim to such status. In the case, Brown claimed he was acting under duress when aiding Morley to kill a woman by coughing to disguise the noise that he might make on approaching the victim. A majority of the South Australian Supreme Court held that duress could never be a defence to a charge of murder. But in the eight short pages of his erudite dissent, Bray CJ rejected the 'simple proposition that no type of duress can ever afford a defence to any type of complicity in murder'.[3] Chief Justice Bray delivered an example of judicial reasoning of the highest order, striving for a principled resolution to the conflicts of justice, deterrence and policy in a field bereft of clear authority. This masterful example of judge-craft was delivered with admirable restraint and awareness of both the occasional need for a dissent, but also of the limits of function and propriety of such a dissent. In and of itself, it is a great dissent.

This case is, however, that rare example where a lone dissent guides and informs subsequent debate in cases far from home. In *DPP (Northern Ireland) v Lynch* ('*Lynch*'),[4] the House of Lords heard an appeal arising from the Troubles in Northern Ireland. Confronted with a claim of duress as a defence to murder, all five Law Lords referred to the judgment of Bray CJ, and for a generation his dissent was the analytical touchstone on the issue.

[1] See generally John Emerson, *John Jefferson Bray: A Vigilant Life* (Monash University Press, 2015).
[2] [1968] SASR 467. [3] Ibid 499. [4] [1975] AC 653.

Chief Justice Bray's dissent powerfully illustrates not only how a great dissent can be delivered, but why such dissents are important. Its unique form allows insight into judicial decision-making generally, confirming the greater quality, integrity and normative clarity published dissents bring. This chapter explores the decision in *R v Brown and Morley*, and its subsequent reception, to argue that Bray CJ's judgment should, as a matter of judicial theory, be hailed as a truly great Australian dissent.

II A Great Dissent – Form, Substance and Style

By its form as well as its substance, the decision in *R v Brown and Morley* is an extraordinary judgment. The two appellants were convicted over the murder of one Elise Leggett, in whose house Brown lived as lodger with his wife. It was undisputed that Morley had attempted to smother her with a pillow as she lay asleep, before repeatedly stabbing her with a carving knife. The case against Brown was that he was party to some arrangement with Morley whereby Mrs Leggett would be murdered for the purpose of stealing any money she might have, and that he aided Morley by coughing to help hide Morley's approach. The defence of Morley was one of insanity, while Brown claimed that he acted under duress, compelled by the threats of Morley against himself, his wife and his parents.

The appeals were heard jointly, and judgment in the two matters was delivered together. Because of a quirk in the *Criminal Law Consolidation Act 1935* (SA) in operation at the time, this joinder provides a unique insight into the judicial appreciation of the limits and role of the dissenting judgment. Section 349(2) of that Act required that in criminal appeals the decision was to be delivered in a single joint judgment of the Court, unless the Court held it to be appropriate to provide separate judgments.[5] This approach was justified by the particular need for certainty in criminal law cases,[6] and on the basis of not wanting to disappoint an accused who found at least one judge supported him or her.[7] The effect of the provision was

[5] That section was incorporated into South Australian law in the original *Criminal Appeal Act 1924* (SA) s 4(2), and largely mirrored a similar provision in the original United Kingdom Act granting criminal appeals: see *Criminal Appeal Act 1907* (UK) c 23 s 1(4)–(5).

[6] See John Alder, 'Dissents in Courts of Last Resort: Tragic Choices?' (2000) 20 *Oxford Journal of Legal Studies* 221, 242; *R v Howe* [1987] AC 417, 438 (Lord Griffith). See also Kirby J's observations in *Peters v The Queen* (1997) 192 CLR 493, 556.

[7] Michael Kirby, 'Judicial Dissent: Common Law and Civil Law Traditions' (2007) 123 *Law Quarterly Review* 379, 392.

to demand judicial reflection upon both the need and cost of dissenting in such matters, ensuring that any dissent emerged only by deliberate election – and presumably after some internal advocacy. A presumption against dissent requires something more than mere disagreement: there must be some particular intensity in the divergence of views, some broader benefit, so as to justify the pronouncement of separate judgments. By its form, this case illustrates this distinction, with a very different approach being taken for the judgment of Morley, as opposed to that of Brown.

The Court, composed of Bray CJ, Bright and Mitchell JJ, delivered a single judgment dismissing Morley's appeal concerning the adequacy of the directions given with respect to the issues of insanity and alternative verdict of manslaughter. However, while it appears there was consensus on the insanity appeal points, it is clear that the Court was divided on both the issue of whether the judge should have expressly informed the jury about the possibility of returning a verdict of manslaughter and on the consequences of the failure to give such a direction. While the Court unanimously ('we all think') held that no properly instructed jury could, on the evidence, return a verdict of manslaughter,[8] there was disagreement over whether the judge ought nonetheless to have highlighted the jury's legal power to return a verdict of manslaughter ('a majority of us think').[9] A majority of the Court thought that even if there was an error, it was an appropriate case to apply the proviso.[10] One judge, however, thought that the proviso can 'never be applied to a direction which denies the power of the jury to return the so called merciful verdict of manslaughter'.[11] It is not possible, however, to say which judge took this minority view, nor indeed whether there were differently composed majorities for different issues. The judgment remains, in consequence of s 349(2), a single joint judgment. The fact of disagreement is revealed only by the use of language of 'majority' in contrast to the more inclusive 'we all think', 'we agree' or 'in our opinion',[12] and by the phrase '[o]ne member of the Court thinks'.[13] The composition of the majority remains undisclosed, and while there

8 *R v Brown and Morley* [1968] SASR 467, 471. 9 Ibid.

10 Ibid. Criminal appeals are creatures of statute, and the 'proviso' has been a common artefact to such statutes from their earliest days. Under the 'proviso' a court hearing a criminal appeal may dismiss the appeal if it accepts that, although there has been some form of error in the trial, there was no 'substantial miscarriage of justice'. See, eg, *Criminal Law Consolidation Act 1935* (SA) s 353(1). For a useful overview, see Catherine Penhallurick, 'The Proviso in Criminal Appeals' (2003) 27 *Melbourne University Law Review* 800.

11 *R v Brown and Morley* [1968] SASR 467, 473. 12 Cf ibid 471, 476. 13 Ibid 473.

was disagreement it clearly did not take on sufficient intensity to justify a separate dissent.[14]

This approach stands in stark contrast to the judgment in the appeal of Brown, where it is gradually revealed that there is a split in the Court, and one of sufficient intensity as to justify a separate and distinct dissent. The Court – and I use the collective term deliberately – begins the discussion of Brown's appeal with little indication of its internal disagreement, setting out the grounds of appeal and recognising that they raise the issue of the defence of duress 'as to which there is little direct authority and much theoretical discussion'.[15] As the judgment unfolds, from an outline of the underlying facts to a brief analysis of the directions given, the impression is given of a united Court. It is not until judgment is passed on the adequacy of the trial judge's directions, some six pages into the decision, that it becomes apparent that the initial appearance of unanimity is misplaced. The judgment suddenly shifts to the majoritarian language seen in relation to Morley ('[t]he view above expressed commands the support of the majority of us'),[16] with the possibility of duress ever being a defence to murder the subject of profound disagreement in the Court. But unlike Morley's appeal, here that disagreement is drawn into the open and made explicit, with the identity of the disputants being revealed. In disclosing that they are, 'with regret, not in accord with the learned Chief Justice',[17] Justices Bright and Mitchell become active participants in judicial discourse. Critically, they see it as 'proper' that they explain why they have adopted a contrary view. In doing so they adopt a mantle of personal responsibility that had otherwise been absent in the anonymity of the joint decision of Morley's appeal. When, six pages later, Bray CJ delivers his separate judgment on the question of the legal effect of duress as a defence to a charge of minor participation in murder, it is as an individual. From the muddle of a single (majority) judgment, a separate dissent emerges, all the stronger for emerging only as the result of deliberate choice.[18] The result is that the dissent of Bray CJ in *R v Brown and Morley* is striking, not simply for its inherent qualities of precision, judge-craft and self-awareness, nor its subsequent normative impact, but for the way it illustrates – by its very form – the value of dissent in enhancing the quality of judicial decision-making.

[14] Indeed, only with respect to the operation of the proviso did the dissenting judge feel it necessary to explain his or her reasons in the judgment.

[15] *R v Brown and Morley* [1968] SASR 467, 479. [16] Ibid 485. [17] Ibid.

[18] *Criminal Law Consolidation Act 1935* (SA) s 349(2).

The Facts of R v Brown and Morley

The relationship between Brown and Morley was nasty, brutish and short. They met on the Saturday, and spent most of the day together, along with Brown's wife. On the Sunday morning Morley came to Brown's house. In the early afternoon, Morley suggested they 'knock off' Mrs Leggett. When Brown refused, Morley threatened to harm Brown's wife before drawing a carving knife, placing it against Brown's throat (with sufficient force to draw blood) and ordering him to do what he said or suffer the same fate. The men began playing cards, with Morley decreeing that the loser had to kill Mrs Leggett. Brown lost. Morley instructed him to put Ratsac in Mrs Leggett's coffee. He complied, though put in only a quarter of a teaspoon which was, and which he knew to be, harmless. Mrs Leggett drank the coffee with no ill effects. Later that evening, Mrs Brown coincidentally became ill, and in the course of ringing around to find a doctor, Brown attempted to call the police but was stopped by Morley. Eventually, Brown and Morley took Mrs Brown to the hospital, where she received treatment following which the party returned home. Morley left, and Brown and his wife went to bed. An hour later Morley returned and woke Brown, telling him he was going to 'knock off' Mrs Leggett. When Brown protested, Morley threatened him, and told him that he would kill Brown's wife and parents if he did not cooperate. After half an hour of argument and threats, Morley, who had previously spoken of suffocating Mrs Leggett, picked up a pillow and told Brown to cough. Morley threatened Brown again, and ordered him to cough to cover the sound of Morley's movements. Brown began coughing and Morley left. Gurgling noises were heard before Morley returned, covered in blood. Having unsuccessfully attempted to suffocate Mrs Leggett, he had proceeded to stab her to death.

On Brown's evidence, at all times from the initial threat he believed Morley was armed, willing and able to attack both Brown and his wife at any point. While the majority were sceptical of the 'inherent weakness'[19] of this version of events, observing that it was 'glaringly inconsistent' with other statements of Brown,[20] they nevertheless recognised the right of the jury to be instructed as to its legal effects. The controversy was to the nature of those legal effects, and the adequacy of the directions given of them. Brown was clearly aware that Morley intended to kill, and that Morley wished to co-opt him into the enterprise. In coughing to disguise

[19] *R v Brown and Morley* [1968] SASR 467, 481.

[20] Ibid. The majority did observe of Morley that 'it is agreed on all hands [that he] is a psychopath': ibid 491.

the noise Morley might make in approaching the old lady's room, Brown lent some, albeit very minor, assistance to Morley in that murderous enterprise. If Brown was not able to rely on a valid defence, these facts would be sufficient to see him convicted for murder as (in the language of the time) a 'principal in the second degree'. Brown argued that the threats of Morley were of sufficient intensity and immediacy as to place him in genuine fear for his life if he did not comply, thereby excusing his act through a defence of duress.

The directions given by the trial judge as to the availability and scope of the defence of duress to a charge of murder are torturous and at best unclear. The majority and Bray CJ differed slightly on the construction of the directions as to an agreement to commit murder, but agreed that the judge directed that duress could not excuse any active participation in murder.[21] The heart of the matter, though, was whether duress was, in this case, or could ever be, a defence to a charge of murder.

The Decision of the Majority

The majority were unequivocal: duress could *never* 'excuse a person who performs an act which he intends to be in furtherance of a proposed murder'.[22] Justices Bright and Mitchell went to great lengths to justify their adoption of a different approach to the Chief Justice.[23] In reaching their conclusion, they relied upon two obscure Privy Council cases: *Sephakela v The Queen*,[24] and *Rossides v The Queen*.[25] As reports of both cases were not readily available the judgments were set out in full within the majority judgment.[26]

Sephakela v The Queen involved a case of ritual killing in Lesotho, and as there was no evidence that the appellant had acted under compulsion, the Privy Council merely found it 'unnecessary to express an opinion' on whether duress would be an effective defence to murder.[27] In *Rossides v The Queen*, a case out of Malta, the accused was convicted of murder on

21 Ibid 485 (Bright and Mitchell JJ), 491 (Bray CJ).

22 Ibid 485 (Bright and Mitchell JJ). 23 Ibid.

24 As reported in *The Times*, 14 July 1954; see also [1954] (September) *Criminal Law Review* 723, cited in *R v Brown and Morley* [1968] SASR 467, 486.

25 As reported in *The Times*, 3 October 1957; see also [1957] (December) *Criminal Law Review* 813, cited in *R v Brown and Morley* [1968] SASR 467, 487.

26 See *R v Brown and Morley* [1968] SASR 467, 486.

27 Ibid. The majority were dismissive of the statement in Glanville Williams, *Criminal Law: The General Part* (Stevens & Sons, 2nd ed, 1961) 753, that the Privy Council had 'assumed that duress was a defence'.

the basis of a confession that he had fired the pistol into the deceased, but only under threat of his own death if he did not. The issue of duress was raised in argument, but in dismissing the appeal the Privy Council gave no reasons at all.

Drawing on these cases, Bright and Mitchell JJ observed that it 'had never been expressly decided that duress can excuse murder' but that 'there are many cases in which a view has been expressed that it cannot, or probably cannot'.[28] They opined that it was against the public interest to allow a defence of duress for murder on the basis of difficulties of identifying the sufficiency of the immediacy and gravity of the threat, and the proximity of the act to the killing.[29] These considerations – briefly expressed, and not at all explored or justified – led the majority to hold that duress could never legally 'excuse Brown for the acts which he performed allegedly under the influence of that duress, to further the proposed murder'.[30] On that basis the appeal was dismissed.

The Dissent of Bray CJ

The decision of the majority, with its uncritical citation of two obscure, opaque, marginally relevant Privy Council decisions and little further analysis, stands in stark contrast to the principled labour of Bray CJ. The dissent begins with an explicit recognition of the restriction of s 349(2), and the need, in light of the 'misfortune' of disagreeing on the 'question of the legal effect of duress as a defence to a charge of minor participation in murder' for a separate judgment. In addressing that issue, Bray CJ not only recognised that the 'subject of duress has been discussed by the text writers for three centuries',[31] but briefly and thoughtfully outlined that history. While Hale[32] and Stephen[33] effectively denied that duress could ever be a defence to any criminal act, and East[34] and Blackstone[35] would have excluded the defence in cases of murder, more recent authors regarded

[28] *R v Brown and Morley* [1968] SASR 467, 489.
[29] Ibid 489–90. [30] Ibid 490. [31] Ibid 492.
[32] See Matthew Hale, George Wilson, Thomas Dogherty, *Hale's History of the Pleas of the Crown* (E Rider, first published 1736, 1800 ed) vol 1, 49–52, cited in *R v Brown and Morley* [1968] SASR 467, 492.
[33] James Fitzjames Stephen, *A History of the Criminal Law of England* (Macmillan, 1883) vol 2, 107, cited in *R v Brown and Morley* [1968] SASR 467, 492.
[34] Sir Edward Hyde East, *A Treatise on the Pleas of the Crown* (A Strahan, 1803) vol 1, 225, cited in *R v Brown and Morley* [1968] SASR 467, 492.
[35] Sir William Blackstone, *Commentaries on the Law of England* (19th ed) vol 4, 30, cited in *R v Brown and Morley* [1968] SASR 467, 492.

the matter 'as very much at large'.[36] In light of this uncertainty, Bray CJ sought to develop a principled position by deconstructing the cases and relying on 'general reasoning'. He began with the cases on treason ('the most serious of crimes')[37] to clearly illustrate that 'some types of duress may be a defence to some kinds of treason',[38] even if it is excluded in other cases. He then drew an analogy with murder, concluding that 'authorities which say . . . that duress is not a defence to murder generally do not necessarily prove that it is not a defence to any conceivable type of complicity in murder, however minor'.[39] In doing so, Bray CJ challenged the 'extreme absolutist views' of Hale and Stephen as not representing the law,[40] arguing that any blanket denial of duress would 'prove too much' and could not 'now be supported'.[41]

Instead, by drawing upon treason cases, Bray CJ sought to unpack the theoretical foundations of the defence of duress, and explore the rationale for its restriction in murder cases. The reasoning generally used to exclude the defence of duress for charges of murder, to quote Blackstone, is that the accused 'ought rather to die himself, than escape by the murder of an innocent'.[42] While Bray CJ was generally prepared to accept that proposition, he countered by observing:

> Its force is obviously considerably less where the act of the threatened man is not the direct act of killing but only the rendering of some minor form of assistance, particularly when it is by no means certain that if he refuses the death of the victim will be averted, or conversely when it is by no means certain that if he complies the death will be a necessary consequence.[43]

In critiquing Blackstone in this way, Bray CJ implicitly recognised that the offence of 'murder' has developed in the last 300 years to incorporate extended forms of liability for 'secondary parties' – whether assisting, encouraging or engaged in some joint enterprise – and that the old blanket prohibition may be inappropriate to these legal constructs. He illustrated this issue with well-developed examples: the passer-by seized in the street by a gang of murderous thieves, compelled at gunpoint to make misleading comments to the public; the innocent driver compelled to convey a murderer to the victim.[44] In doing so, Bray CJ effectively undermined the absolutism of Blackstone's rationale. Exclusion of any duress defence in such circumstances would seem to sever the fundamental connection between legal liability and moral wrongdoing.

[36] *R v Brown and Morley* [1968] SASR 467, 492 (Bray CJ). [37] Ibid. [38] Ibid 493.
[39] Ibid. [40] Ibid 492. [41] Ibid 494. [42] Blackstone, above n 35, 30.
[43] *R v Brown and Morley* [1968] SASR 467, 494. [44] Ibid.

Chief Justice Bray went on to explore the existence of authorities that would compel the adoption of such an approach. A Québécois case where a prisoner, at gunpoint, handed over a razor to the killer was distinguished on the basis that the relevant Code specifically excluded duress for murder.[45] In contrast to the majority, Bray CJ held that *Sephakela v The Queen* supported the availability of the defence of duress, as concerns over insufficiency of evidence implied that evidence *could* support that defence, and indeed 'may well . . . compel' that result.[46] *Rossides v The Queen* was characterised as involving an accused acting as the principal participant, and was thus 'no authority for the proposition that duress can be no defence to lesser acts of participation in murder not including any actual killing or attempted killing of the victim'.[47] The construction by Bray CJ of both of these cases is to be preferred to that of the majority, not only because the exposition and analysis is more complete, but because it more easily coheres with the (scant) reasoning of the Privy Council in each.

On this construction the authorities did not compel a denial of duress for secondary participation, and Bray CJ argued that there were 'good reasons on general grounds'[48] for rejecting such a denial. Alluding to his prior examples, Bray CJ argued that there may be circumstances 'easily conceivable' where a grave and imminent threat was directed to compelling an act only remotely connected to the death of the victim, such 'that the interests of justice were better served by allowing the defence'.[49] It followed that the defence of duress *may* be available in *some* instances of secondary or minor participation in murder, and as such the directions of the judge were erroneous.

Recognising the inherent limitations of a dissenting judgment, Bray CJ took a very restrained approach to outlining the scope of such a defence. Had the majority been in agreement with him, he would have analysed the directions of the trial judge in greater detail, and laid down an appropriate form of direction in a case such as this. However, and in light of the 'spirit' of s 349(2), he thought it improper to do the former, and dangerous to attempt the latter with any great precision as to 'do so could be of no effect at all in the present case: and it might prove an embarrassment in future cases'.[50] In adopting this approach, Bray CJ demonstrated great

[45] See *R v Faruto* (1912) 10 DLR 669, cited in *R v Brown and Morley* [1968] SASR 467, 495 (Bray CJ).

[46] *R v Brown and Morley* [1968] SASR 467, 496. [47] Ibid 497 (Bray CJ). [48] Ibid.

[49] Ibid. [50] Ibid 498.

restraint, and illustrated a deep awareness of the limitations of a dissenting judgment. Rather than fruitlessly attempt to set out a comprehensive test for this form of duress, he restricted himself to identifying five issues that would inform the future development of such a test including: (a) the requisite scope of the threat, whether personal, to a third party or to property; (b) the requisite nature of the threat, in terms of gravity and immediacy; (c) the limits necessitated by the threat; (d) restrictions upon the availability for those who place themselves in a position where they may be threatened; and (e) the need for some proportionality between the threatened harm and that which would follow from performance of the compelled act.[51] Chief Justice Bray acknowledged concerns about the recognition of duress as a murder defence, but suggested these might be addressed by drawing analogies from self-defence and provocation. He did not, however, attempt to develop a detailed and comprehensive test for when the defence would be available, expressly stating that he did 'not think these speculations should be carried further in a dissenting judgment'.[52]

In dissent, it was sufficient to recognise that the trend of cases and general reasoning 'prevent the acceptance of the simple proposition that no type of duress can ever afford a defence to any type of complicity in murder'.[53] This limited claim becomes, however, highly persuasive in light of Bray CJ's analysis and reasoning. In dissent, Bray CJ laid a firm foundation upon which a future court might recognise such a defence.

Of itself, in light of its careful reflection and engagement with difficult materials, compelling reasoning, and evident discipline and integrity, this has the hallmarks of a great dissent. There is reason to suggest that we should analyse dissents in and of themselves, without reference to the contingent issue of whether they are subsequently found to be 'correct' in later judgments. Nevertheless, the reception of a judgment does provide some indicia of its quality. In this case, that reception, occurring half a world away in the House of Lords, made plain just how sound a foundation Bray CJ established.

III The Reception of the Dissent

In *Lynch*,[54] the House of Lords heard an appeal arising from the Troubles in Northern Ireland. Like *R v Brown and Morley*, the case involved a claim of duress as a defence to murder for a principal in the second

[51] Ibid 498–9. [52] Ibid 499. [53] Ibid. [54] [1975] AC 653.

degree. Moreover, the facts of the case mirror closely those of one of the hypotheticals Bray CJ utilised to illustrate his reasoning – the innocent driver compelled to convey a murderer to the victim.

The case arose from the murder of a police officer by an IRA gunman. The appellant, Lynch, who it was accepted was not a member of the IRA, received a messenger at his house who informed him that Meehan – a 'well-known and ruthless gunman'[55] demanded his immediate presence. Lynch did not know Meehan, but knew of him and that 'what Meehan asked to be done had to be done'.[56] In fear of being shot if he did not attend, Lynch complied with the summons. After Lynch disclosed that he could drive, Meehan – who was armed and surrounded by heavily armed gunmen – told him to go with another man, named Mailey, and seize a car. Mailey held up a car, ordered the driver out, and had Lynch drive the vehicle back to the address where Meehan remained. Lynch was then permitted to return home. However, half an hour later he was summoned again to Meehan. Once there he was told to drive Meehan and his heavily armed associates to a particular address. When he asked what was going on he was told 'Bates knows a policeman'.[57] Following directions, Lynch stopped the car in front of a garage. The others ran across the road, and a number of shots were fired in quick succession. The men ran back to the car, and on their order Lynch drove them back to their starting point.

Lynch argued that everything he did was done under duress, in the genuine and reasonable belief that he would be shot if he did not comply. However, the trial judge ultimately held that duress was not available to any charge of murder, and did not allow the issue to be put to the jury. The Court of Criminal Appeal unanimously upheld the trial judge on the finding that duress cannot be accepted as a defence to murder and the issue came before the House of Lords.

Confronted with a lack of authority and a 'jurisprudential muddle of a most unfortunate kind,'[58] all five Law Lords referred to the judgment of Bray CJ, with the majority quoting from him extensively. Lord Morris described Bray CJ's dissent as a 'closely reasoned judgment the persuasive power of which appeals to me',[59] before adopting the view that duress 'can be open as a possible defence'.[60] In seeking to establish why, in principle, the defence should not be 'absolutely excluded in murder charges',[61] Lord Wilberforce turned to the 'important authority' of *R v Brown and Morley* and the 'impressive judgment of Bray CJ in dissent'[62] from which he

[55] Ibid 678. [56] Ibid 655. [57] Ibid 656. [58] Ibid 704 (Lord Edmund-Davies).
[59] Ibid 677. [60] Ibid. [61] Ibid 681. [62] Ibid 682.

quoted extensively. Building on this analysis he too held that the defence is available 'in a case of aiding and abetting murder'.[63] Lord Edmund-Davies observed that the issue had never been the subject of even obiter dicta in the House of Lords, with the result that it was 'called upon for the first time to make an unfettered decision on a point of pure common law in accordance with basic common law principles'.[64] In such a context *R v Brown and Morley* was of particular significance, and not only did Lord Edmund-Davies compliment Bray CJ's 'illuminating review of the relevant material',[65] and quote extensively from the dissent, but he expressly adopted his conclusions.[66]

Even the judges in the minority felt compelled to respond to Bray CJ's dissent. Lord Simon adopted a hard line that the law had never recognised such a defence, and that authority and 'closely cognate juridical concepts' suggest it should not be available.[67] After exploring the issues of underlying policy, he turned to discussion of authority. With contempt dripping from his pen, he states:

> Fortunately, I am absolved from reviewing them in detail, since that has been done by my noble and learned friends. My only misgiving is that such an impressive muster should be sent packing so ignominiously. Poor Hale, poor Blackstone; wretched Russell and Kenny; poor, poor Lord Denman. But at least they are in good company. There are all those famous jurists, headed by Stephen . . . like the denizens of the first circle of Hell, who, for all their wisdom and virtue, lived in such benighted times as to have forfeited salvation. So, too, these great lawyers are too eminent to go altogether unacknowledged: they are recognised with a courtly bow, but their words are lost in the gale of juristic change. For, in truth, their voices were unanimous that duress is no defence to murder. *What is to be set against them? A dissenting judgment of Bray CJ . . .* [68]

Even in his disdain, Lord Simon illustrated the significance of Bray CJ's judgment, minimising it by mockery rather than engaging with the strong substantive arguments. Lord Kilbrandon relied upon Bray CJ's conclusion that duress does not constitute a defence for one who actually kills the victim,[69] though rejected the distinction 'between the defence open to a principal in the first degree and those open to a principal in the second degree'.[70]

The majority in *Lynch*, then, effectively adopted Bray CJ's position that duress should be available as a defence to a charge of murder in the second

[63] Ibid 685. [64] Ibid 713. [65] Ibid 714. [66] Ibid 715. [67] Ibid 685.
[68] Ibid 695 (emphasis added). [69] Ibid 701.
[70] Ibid 702, expressly agreeing with the majority in *R v Brown and Morley.*

degree. Moreover, all of the Law Lords felt compelled to engage with Bray CJ, even when rejecting his conclusions; his dissent set the framework and conceptual foundations for the debate.

Subsequent Developments

The following year, in *Abbott v The Queen*, the Privy Council refused to extend the defence to a principal participant who took part in the actual killing.[71] The dissenting opinion argued that there was 'no acceptable basis of distinction' between a principal in the first and in the second degree, and on that basis would have allowed the appeal.[72] Both opinions again quoted from Bray CJ,[73] with the minority observing that 'mention must obviously be made' of *R v Brown and Morley* and the 'illuminating judgment' of Bray CJ.[74] In *R v Howe*, the House of Lords was faced with a claim for duress by accused involved in the actual killings.[75] The Law Lords adopted the minority position that the distinction between the 'actual killer' and the 'aider and abettor' was 'illogical',[76] but rather than extend the defence as previously proposed, opted to overturn its prior decision in *Lynch* and deny the defence to all charges of murder.[77]

This same difficulty in drawing the line between the 'actual killer' and the 'aider and abettor' has troubled Australian courts. In *R v McCafferty*, Glass J, of the New South Wales Supreme Court, explicitly adopted the conclusions of Bray CJ[78] in order to find that duress is a complete defence to minor participation in murder, and went further to allow it as a qualified defence for major participation.[79] This latter point was subsequently overruled in *R v McConnell* where the Court again referenced Bray CJ.[80] In *R v Harding*, the Victorian Supreme Court held that the defence was inapplicable in all murder cases, but felt compelled to spend three pages of its reasons exploring in depth the dissent of Bray CJ.[81] As in *R v*

71 [1977] AC 755, 763, 764, 767.

72 Ibid 770 (Lord Wiberforce and Lord Edmund-Davies).

73 Ibid 763–4 (Lord Salmon), delivering the majority judgment.

74 Ibid 773 (Lord Wiberforce and Lord Edmund-Davies).

75 [1987] AC 417. 76 Ibid 442 (Lord Griffith).

77 Ibid 436 (Lord Hallisham), 437–8 (Lord Bridge), 438 (Lord Brandon), 445 (Lord Griffith), 453, 456 (Lord Mackay).

78 [1974] 1 NSWLR 89, 91. 79 Ibid.

80 [1977] 1 NSWLR 714, 717, 718 (Street CJ), 723 (Taylor CJ at CL).

81 [1976] VR 129, 151–3. This compulsion was explicitly recognised as a result of strong reliance of counsel on Bray CJ's dissent: at 151.

Howe, the Court refused to find a distinction between minor and major participation in murder.[82]

The courts have continued to struggle with the difficult issue of whether or not duress should ever be a defence to any form of murder, and if so where the line is to be drawn. It does appear that those courts which excluded the defence did not feel that its denial would work any injustice on the facts of those cases. In both *Lynch* and *R v Brown and Morley*, there appears to have been a real suspicion as to the bona fides of each accused's story – on re-trial the jury rejected Lynch's defence of duress[83] and in *R v Brown and Morley* the majority clearly doubted the accused's story.[84] In *R v Howe*, Lord Griffith even went so far as to observe:

> I am not troubled by some of the extreme examples cited in favour of allowing the defence to those who are not the killer such as a woman motorist being hijacked and forced to act as a getaway driver, or a pedestrian being forced to give misleading information to the police to protect robbery and murder in a shop. The short practical answer is that it is inconceivable that such persons would be prosecuted.[85]

The denial of the defence in such circumstances leaves the 'innocent' accused deeply vulnerable to prosecutorial discretion. Moreover, on the available evidence in *Lynch*, it was a situation directly analogous to the hijacked woman, and Bray CJ properly analysed the law on the basis that Brown's version of events was accepted. It was precisely the potential for a strict approach to work profound injustice that led Bray CJ to his nuanced analysis. While different opinions as to the potential for injustice may have led courts to adopt different approaches to the defence, it remains clear that Bray CJ's dissent has had a powerful normative impact.[86] The power and persuasiveness of his opinion has dictated the terms of later discourse and profoundly influenced the development of the law, even where its conclusions have not been adopted.[87]

[82] Ibid 154.

[83] See *Abbott v The Queen* [1977] AC 755, 763; *R v Howe* [1987] AC 417, 429.

[84] *R v Brown and Morley* [1968] SASR 467, 481.

[85] *R v Howe* [1987] AC 417, 445.

[86] The dissent has also been cited with approval in cases of duress in other contexts. See *Goodard v Osborne* (1978) 18 SASR 481, 491 (Hogarth ACJ, Zelling and King JJ); *R v Gotts* [1992] 2 AC 412, 429, 436 (Lord Lowry); *R v Lorenz* (1998) 146 FLR 369, 377 (Crispin J).

[87] When the United Kingdom Law Commission proposed legislative reform to the defence of duress in 1977, the restrictions on the defence addressed each of the concerns expressly identified by Bray CJ at the end of his dissent. See Law Commission, *Report on Defences of General Application*, Law Com No 83 (27 July 1977). See also *R v Howe* [1987] AC 417, 442 (Lord Griffith). Even though the Law Commission did not explicitly cite Bray CJ, the adoption of this approach held up the inherent logic of the dissent.

IV Greatness in Dissension

It remains then only to set out explicitly why this is a great Australian dissent. The quality of 'greatness' is nearly always contested. In the context of the inherently discursive enterprise that is judicial decision-making, this contestation is compounded, and even further so for judicial dissent, defined as it is by disagreement. A dissentient may be demonised as a 'judicial activist' who selfishly undermines legal certainty, or lauded as a visionary reformer who brings responsive justice to the law. Where that line is drawn may largely depend upon whether one agrees with the conclusions reached,[88] which in turn depends upon political and social values that may vary significantly over time.

Part of the difficulty in identifying a 'great' dissent is not only the fact that there have been many different roles attributed to the judicial dissent – dissent as prophecy,[89] as embodying democratic ideal,[90] as civil disobedience,[91] as safety mechanism,[92] as spur to greater quality,[93] as clarifier,[94] as underminer,[95] or as signifier of integrity[96] – but that there has been 'little discussion'[97] and 'limited effort'[98] to systematically reflect upon and delimit the role of dissent in judicial decision-making.[99]

88 See Michael Kirby, 'Judicial Activism: Power without Responsibility? No, Appropriate Activism Conforming to Duty' (2006) 30 *Melbourne University Law Review* 576, 578, 591; Michael Kirby, *Judicial Activism: Authority, Principle and Policy in the Judicial Method* (Sweet & Maxwell, 2004).

89 See Alan Barth, *Prophets with Honor: Great Dissents and Great Dissenters on the Supreme Court* (Random House, 1974); Benjamin Cardozo, *Law and Literature and Other Essays and Addresses* (R B Rothman, 1931) 36, cited in J Louis Campbell, 'The Spirit of Dissent' (1983) 66 *Judicature* 305, 311.

90 See William O Douglas, 'The Dissent: A Safeguard on Democracy' (1948) 32 *Journal of the American Judicature Society* 104, 105; Alder, above n 6, 222.

91 See Campbell, above n 89, 306.

92 Kirby describes dissents as an 'inbuilt safety mechanism' to prevent 'the unquestioned pursuit of majoritarian opinions that may turn out to be wrong-headed, inappropriate or out of date': Kirby, above n 7, 397.

93 William J Brennan Jr, 'In Defence of Dissents' (1986) 37 *Hastings Law Journal* 427, 430; Andrew Lynch, 'Dissent: The Rewards and Risks of Judicial Disagreement in the High Court of Australia' (2003) 27 *Melbourne University Law Review* 724, 740.

94 See Matthew P Bergman, 'Dissent in the Judicial Process: Discord in Service of Harmony' (1991) 68 *Denver University Law Review* 79, 85; Roscoe Pound, 'Cacoethes Dissentiendi: The Heated Judicial Dissent' (1953) 39 *American Bar Association Journal* 794, 795.

95 Brennan, above n 93, 430.

96 Kirby, above n 7, 381; Lynch, above n 93, 725.

97 Alder, above n 6, 221.

98 Lynch, above n 93, 724.

99 Notable exceptions include Bergman, above n 94; Lynch, above n 93; Andrew Lynch, 'Is Judicial Dissent Constitutionally Protected?' (2004) 14 *Macquarie Law Journal* 81; Kirby, above n 7; Michael Kirby, 'Appellate Courts and Dissent: Diversity in the Protection of Freedom' (2004) 16(4) *Judicial Officers Bulletin* 25; Michael Kirby, 'Judicial Dissent' (2005) 12 *James Cook University Law Journal* 4; Alder, above n 6.

It is relatively easy to identify a romantic 'greatness' in soaring judgments of fiery and righteous rhetoric. This is particularly so when such judgments perform a key social and political role,[100] and take on the mantle of greatness over time as the political values they embody come to dominate.[101] This is, however, a purely contingent process,[102] with such 'greatness' determined by subsequent events, and not the inherent qualities of the judgment.

It is much more difficult to identify dissents that acquire their status of 'greatness' for their *judicial* rather than *political* quality. Chief Justice Bray's dissent in *R v Brown and Morley* is such a dissent. While written clearly and persuasively, it is not a judgment of grand rhetoric. Though literally a matter of life and death for the accused, it was not a subject to inspire marches in the streets. This dissent has largely faded from memory in Australia, no doubt partly due to the rarity of cases in which the issue is raised, and partly due to the fact that – in an age where legal research occurs in front of a computer – the case is not available online. Nevertheless, to those with an eye to judicial theory, this restrained and gentle dissent demands the mantle of greatness for it illustrates, in its form as well as its substance, not only *how* such a great dissent should be delivered, but *why*.

A dissent of the highest *judicial* quality is one that either directly or indirectly furthers the excellent performance of the judicial function. It suffices, for present purposes, to note that the judicial function has two core interrelated aspects:[103] (a) dispute-resolution[104] and (b) social (normative) governance.[105] The judicial function places the judge in an unavoidable place of tension: dispute-resolution demands finality and

[100] See Bergman, above n 94, 82–5. Justice Harlan's dissent in *Plessy v Ferguson*, 163 US 537, 552 (1896), resisting the 'separate but equal' doctrine, stands foremost among such dissents in common law judicial history. See also Holmes J in *Lochner v New York*, 198 US 45 (1905), Brandeis J in *Olmstead v United States*, 277 US 438 (1928) and Lord Atkin in *Liversidge v Anderson* [1942] AC 206, 244.

[101] As Bergman notes, the greatness of 'now-famous dissents . . . was left for future generations to determine': Bergman, above n 94, 85.

[102] See Bergman, above n 94, 85.

[103] For an extensive discussion of this topic, and its impact upon issues of judicial theory and practice, see Joe McIntyre, *The Nature and Implications of the Judicial Function* (PhD Thesis, University of Cambridge, 2013).

[104] See Martin Shapiro, *Courts: A Comparative and Political Analysis* (University of Chicago Press, 1981) 17.

[105] See Justice Brennan, 'Judging the Judges' (1979) 53 *Australian Law Journal* 767, 768; J J Spigelman, 'Judicial Accountability and Performance Indicators' (2002) 21 *Civil Justice Quarterly* 18, 26.

a focus upon the individual litigants; governance demands the pursuit of responsive correctness, focusing on broader social interests and the generalised maintenance of legal norms. The resolution of those incommensurable objectives in the particular case requires an act of judicial evaluation, upon which judges will inevitably disagree. While such inherent tensions, and the evaluations required to resolve them, makes dissent inevitable,[106] the way in which an individual judge negotiates those tensions to pursue both objectives provides some measure by which to judge the quality of a dissent. A great dissent stimulates the better performance of both aspects of the judicial function, and in doing so enhances not just the quality of the particular decision but also the broader reputation for judicial quality and integrity. Bray CJ's dissent not only performs such a role in the particular, but illustrates how dissents generally may promote such objectives.

In seriously engaging with a difficult juridical issue, Bray CJ's dissent may not have altered the outcome of the appeal, but certainly altered the conversation in a way that contributed to the deeper resolution of the underlying dispute. Knowing the Chief Justice supported his application for a re-trial may appear to have been scant comfort for Brown, but such support would have deep significance in any application for clemency. This was, after all, a man sentenced to death for acting, in fear of his life, on an order to 'cough' at a designated time. Even in dissent, the guidance of Bray CJ's decision provided a pathway for a more just resolution.

The normative consequences of the judgment were more pronounced and renowned. In his dissent Bray CJ developed a foundational understanding of the issues in play that shaped and directed the discourse on the defence of duress in murder for a generation. Chief Justice Bray provided the lens through which the House of Lords resolved *Lynch*, and even though his position was ultimately rejected in the United Kingdom, his ideas and analysis influenced judges both in Australia and abroad. Judicial law-making depends upon persuasion as well as authority, and Bray CJ's contribution to the 'marketplace of competing ideas'[107] has been deeply influential. That normative contribution extends beyond extant statements of law, and lies like a rake resting in the grass, ready to rear up

[106] That tension makes it unavoidable that there will be disagreement over the balancing of incommensurable values as it will be 'impossible that bodies of men should always be brought to think alike': *Grindley v Barker* (1798) 1 Bos & Pul 229, 238; 126 ER 875, 880 (Eyre CJ).

[107] Brennan, above n 93, 435; see also Kirby, above n 7, 393–4.

when the next judicial foot treads these uneasy grounds. The reception and demonstrable impact of the dissent illustrates the inherent quality of the decision.

This was a scholarly and comprehensive judgment that struggled – with a lack of authorities, with sweeping judgments of the great early text writers, with competing policy concerns, and with an unsympathetic defendant. Chief Justice Bray brought great discipline and integrity to his considered search for underlying principles, delivering clear and compelling legal analysis. Moreover, his legal analysis evidenced a deeply reflective awareness of the limitations of it minority status, and of the institutional costs of the dissent. Consider Bray CJ's restraint in setting out only those statements that would assist future courts, but would not embarrass nor restrict them. Further, this was all achieved in eight short pages, demonstrating that excellence does not require prolixity.

Further, the quirk provided by the operation of s 349(2), and the joinder of the two appeals, provides an almost unique illustration of how a published dissent can enhance the performance of the judicial function. It is commonly argued that dissent should be used sparingly.[108] Lord Neuberger in calling for fewer and shorter dissents, argued:

> Perhaps a judge who is considering dissenting should ask himself whether (i) he feels strongly enough, (ii) the point is important enough, (iii) it would help the development of the law, and (iv) it would help the understanding of the law, if there was a dissenting Judgment.[109]

The *fact* of the published dissent in Brown's appeal clearly evidences, in light of s 349(2), just such a deliberate consideration of not merely the existence of disagreement, but its intensity and the normative benefit of publicly developing it. Whereas Morley's appeal saw opaque reference to divergences in the Court (eg, references to 'a majority of us'), the dissent in Brown's appeal saw a clear identification of the individual judges and the position they took. Justices Bright and Mitchell became actors in the discourse, and with the strength of their position challenged by Bray CJ, they were personally called upon to justify their approach. The published dissent acted both to spur them on to a better quality of decision-making and to more effectively hold them to (external) account. This enhanced

[108] See Bergman, above n 94, 89.

[109] Lord Neuberger, 'First Annual BAILII Lecture: No Judgment – No Justice' (Speech delivered at Freshfields Bruckhaus Derringer, London, 20 November 2012) [28] http://www.bailii.org/bailii/lecture/01.html.

internal and external accountability,[110] of both the majority and the dissentient, and the greater quality of the normative statements all round, provides a graphic illustration of why we have dissent.

The unique form of this judgment, illustrating so clearly in the contrast of its two halves the positive impact a published dissent may have on judicial decision-making, makes this a most interesting dissent. The dissent itself, in light of the careful reflection and engagement with difficult materials, the compelling reasoning and evident discipline and integrity, combined with the clear awareness of the role and limitation of dissent, delivered with clarity and brevity, has strong claim to greatness. Its reception and unitisation by appellate courts, across the common law world, struggling with the issue of duress, makes such a claim irresistible.

While now largely forgotten at home, this judgment well deserves the title of 'great dissent'.

[110] The distinction between 'internal' and 'external' forms of judicial accountability reflects the difference between actual judicial integrity, quality and impartiality on one hand, and the creation and maintenance of an institutional *reputation* for such on the other. Judicial institutions depend upon both aspects. See Joe McIntyre, 'Evaluating Judicial Performance Evaluation: Theory, Purposes and Limits' (2014) 4 *Oñati Socio-Legal Series* 898; David Pimentel, 'Reframing the Independence v Accountability Debate: Defining Judicial Structure in Light of Judges' Courage and Integrity' (2009) 57 *Cleveland State Law Review* 1.

9

The 'Intelligence of a Future Day': The Vindication of Justice Stephen's Dissent in *Henry v Boehm* (1973)

MICHAEL COPER

> A dissent . . . is an appeal to the brooding spirit of the law, to the intelligence of a future day, when a later decision may possibly correct the error into which the dissenting judge believes the court to have been betrayed.[1]

I Introduction

In 1972, Victorian lawyer Edward Henry was refused admission to practice in South Australia because he did not satisfy a South Australian requirement that lawyers seeking admission in that State reside there for three months prior to admission. Henry complained to the High Court that this refusal contravened s 117 of the *Constitution*, which forbids discrimination based on state residence. In *Henry v Boehm*, the Court rejected Henry's challenge by a majority of four (Barwick CJ and McTiernan, Menzies and Gibbs JJ) to one (Stephen J dissenting).[2] In essence, the Court held that there was no discrimination because all were treated equally: residents and non-residents alike had to reside in South Australia for three months prior to admission. Non-residents could move to South Australia in order to do that.

Later developments in both the law relating to discrimination and the understanding of that concept were to sweep away this formal and artificial reasoning. Discrimination could be indirect as well as direct, and could manifest itself in the application of a law that appeared non-discriminatory on its face. Yet this was apparent to Stephen J even in 1973, only a year into his 10-year term on the Court and surrounded

[1] Charles Evan Hughes, *The Supreme Court of the United States* (Columbia University Press, 1928) 68. See also the High Court's (unacknowledged) echo of this quote in *Federation Insurance Ltd v Wasson* (1987) 163 CLR 303, 314 (Mason CJ, Wilson, Dawson and Toohey JJ).

[2] *Henry v Boehm* (1973) 128 CLR 482.

by well-established luminaries led by the always forceful Chief Justice Sir Garfield Barwick.

During his term on the Court, the mild-mannered pipe-smoking[3] Stephen J nearly always found himself in the majority. This most elegant craftsman of judgments was the archetypal centrist, on a court that was roundly conservative. On this occasion, however, Stephen J could not see the Emperor's new clothes. He had no hesitation in calling it as he saw it: here was a clear breach of s 117. Non-residents were plainly disadvantaged since, unlike the locals, they had to move to South Australia in order to satisfy the residency requirement. This was antithetical to the notion of national unity that s 117 embodied.

Sixteen years later, Stephen J was vindicated in emphatic fashion. In *Street v Queensland Bar Association* ('*Street*'), a quite differently constituted court, moving inexorably into the more robust era of the Mason Court, held unanimously that a residency requirement of this kind infringed s 117.[4] *Henry v Boehm* was overruled. In the never-ending battle between form and substance, this time it was substance that prevailed. After nearly a century of emasculation, s 117 was finally elevated to a position of significance as a pillar of national social unity in the Australian federal system.[5]

This chapter explores the role and impact of Stephen J's dissent, and some of the factors that might help to explain it, in the broader context of some pervasive and perennial issues in the interpretation of the *Constitution*: how the few 'rights' provisions are interpreted; how the mighty opposing forces of form and substance are locked in perpetual combat; and how a federal system struggles to resolve the competing demands of national unity and local autonomy.

[3] See the whimsical reminiscences by his colleagues of the hazards of this habit: Sir Gerard Brennan, 'Principle and Independence: The Guardians of Freedom' (2000) 4 *Newcastle Law Review* 1, quoted in Hilary Charlesworth, 'Stephen, Ninian Martin' in Tony Blackshield, Michael Coper and George Williams (eds), *The Oxford Companion to the High Court of Australia* (Oxford University Press, 2001) 643, 645; Sir Anthony Mason, 'Justice of the High Court' in Timothy L H McCormack and Cheryl Saunders (eds), *Sir Ninian Stephen: A Tribute* (Miegunyah Press, 2007) 3, 4.

[4] (1989) 168 CLR 461. On the Mason Court generally, see Cheryl Saunders (ed), *Courts of Final Jurisdiction: The Mason Court in Australia* (Federation Press, 1996); Jason Pierce, *Inside the Mason Court Revolution: The High Court of Australia Transformed* (Carolina Academic Press, 2006); Paul Kildea and George Williams, 'The Mason Court' in Rosalind Dixon and George Williams (eds), *The High Court, the Constitution and Australian Politics* (Cambridge University Press, 2015) 244.

[5] *Street* (1989) 168 CLR 461, 512 (Brennan J).

II Ninian Stephen: Paragon of Independence

Sir Ninian Stephen was born in England, though with Scottish heritage, in 1923, indeed on 15 June, not inappropriately the anniversary of the day on which King John signed the original Magna Carta at Runnymede in 1215. Following an eclectic education in the 1920s and 1930s in Edinburgh, London and Geneva, he came to Australia in 1940, at the age of 16. He accompanied his mother[6] and Miss Nina Mylne, the Australian woman for whom his mother worked as a companion and who, having been largely responsible for young Stephen's schooling, thought it was prudent to leave Europe on the outbreak of war. Stephen completed his secondary schooling in 1940 at Scotch College in Melbourne, embarked upon law at the University of Melbourne in 1941, and after an interruption for war service, completed his law course and his articles of clerkship with Arthur Robinson & Co in 1949. He was admitted to the Melbourne Bar in 1952, became a Queens Counsel in 1966, and was appointed to the Supreme Court of Victoria in 1970, then to the High Court in 1972. Although only a small part of his later public life, in which he served with distinction as, inter alia, Governor-General, Ambassador for the Environment, facilitator of peace talks on Northern Ireland, judge ad hoc of the International Court of Justice, judge of the International Criminal Tribunal for the Former Yugoslavia, and Chair of the United Nations Group of Experts for Cambodia, he served as a Justice of the High Court for a decade, from 1972 to 1982.

There are a number of assessments of Stephen J's work on the High Court and his contribution to its jurisprudence, of which the best, unsurprisingly, is that by Sir Anthony Mason.[7] Nevertheless, Stephen's biographer Philip Ayres offers some interesting observations on the likely impact of his education. Ms Mylne took him in 1938, aged 15, to see one of Hitler's massive Nuremburg rallies,[8] but notwithstanding this, she had provided Stephen with an education 'least likely to produce anyone attracted by regimentation and propaganda'; moreover, 'he had acquired

[6] Until 2003, Stephen believed, and official biographies noted, that his father had died when he was a baby, from the after-effects of exposure to poisonous gas in World War I: see, eg, Hilary Charlesworth, 'Stephen, Ninian Martin' in Blackshield, Coper and Williams (eds), above n 3, 643. In truth, however, his father had walked out on the family and started a new life, and a new family, in Canada. Stephen met the half-sisters he never knew he had for the first time in his eighties: see Philip Ayres, *Fortunate Voyager: The Worlds of Ninian Stephen* (Miegunyah Press, 2013) 5, 243–5.

[7] Mason, above n 3.

[8] Where he captured the immediacy of the moment in some extraordinary photos, reproduced in Ayres, above n 6, 96–7.

an interest in the complexities of history that was incompatible with political intensity'.[9] Whether as a matter of influence or merely of resonance, Stephen at Melbourne Law School is noted by Ayres to have shared many of the qualities of Professor George Paton, who was 'sceptical of dogma, eclectic in knowledge and wide in sympathies, aware of the merits of contending positions'.[10] True, Stephen later joined the Liberal Party, though, according to Ayres, more as a libertarian than as a Tory; in any event he resigned his membership in 1970 on his appointment to the Victorian Supreme Court, 'feeling that to continue a formal political allegiance might conceivably compromise his judicial independence'.[11]

Certainly, Ayres readily describes Stephen J's judicial style as 'analytical and non-political',[12] consistent with his 'fascination with language' and with interpretation.[13] Although an altogether different matter, Stephen's personality was congruent with the qualities, especially those of curiosity and detachment, which his education had fostered or revealed. Anyone who knew him, or even merely read his judgments and other writings, cannot but have been struck by his grace, warmth, elegance, charm, and lightness of touch.[14] His first High Court associate, Ross Robson, puts this into a wider context: 'It appeared as if life was a joy, not a trouble. He was not burdened by angst, worry, jealousy, ambition, envy or any other vices. He was totally relaxed and at peace, and this demeanour and bearing did not impede or detract from the diligence he applied to his judicial duties'.[15]

Mason writes of Stephen J's judicial style with the added insight of an insider. Having referred to Stephen J's elegance of literary style, lightness of touch, and indeed a certain 'elusive' quality in his writing – 'that of the essayist given to extensive use of subordinate and participial clauses' (though the judgments were nevertheless 'easy to read, a world apart from the dense, grinding judicial style which is characteristic of typical High Court judgments') – Mason makes the important observation that 'a central element in the Stephen style was the air of detached impartiality and objectivity; that of a Proustian observer seemingly disconnected from the events which he describes'.[16]

But 'aren't all judges impartial?' Mason asks on behalf of a hypothetical reader. Yes, in a general sense, he answers, but

[9] Ibid 15. [10] Ibid 26. [11] Ibid 43–4. [12] Ibid 63. [13] Ibid 58.

[14] I was privileged to have him write a delightful foreword to Michael Coper, *Encounters with the Australian Constitution* (CCH, 1987).

[15] Ayres, above n 6, 66. [16] Mason, above n 3, 5.

> they do not always convey that quality in their judgments. Some judges write judgments in a compelling, authoritative style, leaving the reader with the impression that no contrary view was arguable and no other solution was rationally open. Sir Isaac Isaacs, Sir Garfield Barwick and Viscount Simonds were exemplars of the dogmatic judicial style. They were judges who wrote to convince others, colleagues included, of the correctness of their views. Sir Ninian was not a judge of that kind.[17]

Instead, Mason writes, Stephen J 'sailed in the middle of the stream, avoiding the extremities of view expressed by his colleagues', and his judgments were 'expositions and commentaries rather than tablets handed down by a higher authority'.[18] He had a 'completely open mind, uncluttered by any preconceptions'.[19] Moreover, this 'was not simply a matter of style'; importantly in the context of this book, his 'independence of mind took the form of dissent when he considered dissent appropriate'.[20]

Justice Stephen's aversion to dogma underscored his sophisticated understanding of the nature of the judicial process. He 'recognised that the answer to many legal questions is finely balanced and open to conflicting arguments, each of which commands strong support. He did not subscribe to the view of those legalists who proclaim that every legal question admits of only one "right" answer'.[21]

A corollary of this (though not a necessary one) was the perhaps unusual fact that, unlike judges who have been known to rush their draft judgments to colleagues in order to persuade them to a particular point of view, Stephen J was quite relaxed about the ultimate outcome of a case. In an interview shortly after his retirement from the Court, he remarked that 'it's not a matter of great zeal and enthusiasm that my view should prevail . . . If it doesn't happen to be the majority view, so be it'.[22]

[17] Ibid. [18] Ibid. [19] Ibid.

[20] Ibid 5–6. Unsurprisingly, Stephen was himself the author of a number of pieces on judicial independence: see, eg, Ninian Stephen, 'Judicial Independence – A Fragile Bastion' (1982) 13 *Melbourne University Law Review* 334. He was also the obvious choice to write the relevant entry for *The Oxford Companion to the High Court of Australia*: see Ninian Stephen, 'Independence, Judicial' in Blackshield, Coper and Williams (eds), above n 3, 338.

[21] Mason, above n 3, 6.

[22] Andrew Lynch, 'Dissenting Judgments' in Blackshield, Coper and Williams (eds), above n 3, 216, 217. See also Hilary Charlesworth, 'Stephen, Ninian Martin' in Blackshield, Coper and Williams (eds), above n 3, 643, quoted in Mason, above n 3, 4. Note, however, that things may have been a little different in the international context. One of Stephen's fellow judges on the International Criminal Tribunal for the former Yugoslavia observes that Stephen:

> never took a dissenting stand for the sake of dissenting and writing his own opinion. To him, appending his opinion to a judgment was only appropriate in those extreme

Mason notes that this does not mean that Stephen J lacked a sense of justice; rather, 'he was more interested in maintaining what he saw as the correct principle than in the outcome of the case'.[23]

And so it was in *Henry v Boehm*.

III *Henry v Boehm*

As noted earlier, Victorian lawyer Henry sought to challenge South Australia's restrictive rules relating to admission to legal practice in South Australia, notably the local period of residence requirement. As also noted, s 117 of the *Constitution*, in paraphrase, forbids discrimination based on state residence. As is so often the case, however, this paraphrase does not do justice to the rather more complex wording of s 117, which in full provides:

> A subject of the Queen, resident in any State, shall not be subject in any other State to any disability or discrimination which would not be equally applicable to him if he were a subject of the Queen resident in such other State.

Early drafts of s 117 (under the influence of Andrew Inglis Clark) drew upon the privileges and immunities clause and the Fourteenth amendment of the *United States Constitution*; but in the end the ringing phrases of that document, especially 'due process' and 'equal protection', were thought to be potentially too limiting of legislative discretion, not to mention the obstacle they might create to laws based explicitly on race such as Western Australia's exclusion of Asians from its goldfields. Nevertheless, even in its more prosaic form, s 117 took a step towards a kind of common citizenship (though it preferred 'subject of the Queen') in the interests of national unity.[24]

Section 117 was litigated very early in the life of the new Commonwealth, but then not again until *Henry v Boehm* in 1973. This paucity of litigation over 70 years was probably due in part to the narrow interpretation given to s 117 from the very beginning, consistently with the High Court's approach generally to the few provisions in the *Constitution* that

> instances where the legal disagreement was so deep that there were no means to overcome it. Otherwise he preferred to be part of the majority, by actively contributing to moulding a majority view.

Professor Antonio Cassese, 'Judge of the International Criminal Tribunal for the Former Yugoslavia' in Timothy L H McCormack and Cheryl Saunders (eds), *Sir Ninian Stephen: A Tribute* (Miegunyah Press, 2007), 190, 205.

23 Mason, above n 3, 4. 24 Coper, above n 14, 338–44.

had a whiff of human rights.[25] In *Davies and Jones v Western Australia* in 1904, Western Australia had imposed death duty at half the normal rate where property passed to persons resident and domiciled in Western Australia.[26] Ironically, the Court quickly dismissed a contention that this was really a privilege rather than a discrimination, which was argued to require a double rate for persons not resident and domiciled in Western Australia. Justice Barton appropriately pointed out that this was a matter of form rather than of substance and that 'constitutional safeguards could be evaded with impunity if any other view were taken'.[27] Yet the Court declined to carry this sentiment through to a conclusion that s 117 was infringed, holding unanimously that, because of the domicile requirement, the Western Australian law did not discriminate solely on the basis of state residence.

As the plaintiff in *Davies and Jones v Western Australia* was resident and domiciled in Queensland, the Court did not have to consider whether a person domiciled in Western Australia but resident in another state would have been entitled to the protection of s 117. The decision did not therefore require, nor did it yield, any clarity on whether in applying s 117 one considers the impugned law in the abstract or rather the position of the individual asserting discrimination. One would have thought – if the reader will forgive resort to a touchstone sometimes used more as a rhetorical device than as a source of genuine guidance – that the plain meaning of the words of s 117 required a comparison between the position of the plaintiff in the legislating state and the position that he or she would have been in were he or she a resident of that state, rather than between general and hypothetical classes of residents and non-residents. While in *Henry v Boehm* Stephen J was of this view,[28] the majority preferred to take the abstract perspective, a close cousin of the preference for form over substance.

There were multiple strands to the decision of the majority in *Henry v Boehm*, so one must be careful not to reduce the contrast between form and substance to one of caricature. Thus, for example, 'resident' was interpreted as requiring a greater degree of permanence than merely being in a state temporarily or resident in some other transitory sense.[29] Yet this interpretation only accentuated the potential for an abstract

[25] Ibid 315–58.

[26] (1904) 2 CLR 29. The other major early case was *Lee Fay v Vincent* (1908) 7 CLR 389.

[27] (1904) 2 CLR 29, 45.

[28] (1973) 128 CLR 482, 502.

[29] Ibid 487 (Barwick CJ), 491 (Menzies J), 497 (Gibbs J).

comparison to exclude the operation of s 117; for example, there may have been, hypothesised the majority, residents of South Australia who were temporarily out of the state, whose compelled return to South Australia to satisfy the requirements of admission to legal practice put them in no different position from a resident of Victoria.[30] Even *Davies and Jones v Western Australia* had not taken as narrow a view as this.

In any event, Stephen J in dissent emphasised the need for a more particular comparison:

> section 117 does not concern itself with the making of any comparison between the situation of the plaintiff were he a resident of South Australia and the situation of other residents of that State. What section 117 calls for is, instead, a comparison between the plaintiff's situation as it is in fact and as it would be were he a resident of South Australia.[31]

Once that comparison was made, the plaintiff was clearly discriminated against on the basis of his out-of-state residence.

Moreover, and perhaps even more importantly, this meant that the South Australian law, which could be viewed in one light as applying equally to everyone seeking admission in South Australia – that is, they all had to reside in South Australia for three months prior to admission – had to be viewed not merely on its face but in terms of its substantive effect. Once this was done, it was apparent that a discrimination was effected against Mr Henry, and that it was a discrimination based on his residence in another state. Yet in 1973, at least in this context, only the unperturbable Stephen J could cut through the artifice of considering legislation only on its face.[32]

Of course, the elevation of substance over form does not necessarily make the resolution of disputed questions of constitutional interpretation any easier; indeed, the attraction of a formal approach is often that the elaboration of substance is perceived to be more elusive and indeed less suited to the constraints of the judicial process. In the case of s 117, the broader approach gives rise to some tricky issues: can the states properly restrict the franchise for the election of state legislatures to their own residents? Surely. Can out-of-state residents claim a share in welfare benefits provided by a state to its own residents? Surely not.[33] But articulating a

30 Ibid 489 (Barwick CJ), 492–3 Menzies J), 497–8 (Gibbs J). 31 Ibid 502.

32 The majority's view is criticised as 'pedantic' in Genevieve Ebbeck, 'Section 117: The Obscure Provision' (1991) 13 *Adelaide Law Review* 23.

33 But see Michael Mathieson, 'Section 117 of the Constitution: The Unfinished Rehabilitation' (1999) 27 *Federal Law Review* 393.

constitutionally coherent explanation of these possible 'exceptions' has been challenging. The minimal discussion of these issues in *Henry v Boehm* does not mean that they did not play a part in the attraction of the majority to the merits of form over substance.

IV *Street v Queensland Bar Association*

The short 16-year period between *Henry v Boehm* and *Street* saw some significant changes in the Australian legal system and in Australian society.[34] When *Henry v Boehm* was argued in May 1973, the Whitlam Labor Government was just months into the first year of its frenetic time in office following the long 23-year period of conservative rule, and was to introduce a raft of controversial legislative and social reforms, including anti-discrimination legislation.[35] Many of these reforms survived the demise of the short-lived Whitlam Government and indeed survived challenge in the High Court; thus, for example, the constitutional validity of the *Racial Discrimination Act 1975* (Cth) was upheld in *Koowarta v Bjelke-Petersen* in 1982.[36] Consideration of the anti-discrimination legislation in the 1980s particularly enabled the Court to develop the idea of indirect discrimination.[37]

Perhaps even more significantly, structural changes that came to a head in the 1980s enabled the High Court to grow to maturity as an apex court with final responsibility for stating, and thus inevitably shaping and developing, Australian law. First, from 1984 appeals would come to the High Court only by special leave,[38] with the consequence that a much higher proportion of cases would raise issues of endemic uncertainty that allowed, and indeed demanded, creative and often difficult choices between open-ended alternatives. Second, in 1986 all remaining appeals to the Privy Council were abolished, leaving the High Court as the sole final court of appeal in the Australian judicial system.[39]

[34] See especially Michael McHugh, 'The Constitutional Jurisprudence of the High Court 1989–2004' (2008) 30 *Sydney Law Review* 5.

[35] See Gough Whitlam, 'Whitlam Era' in Blackshield, Coper and Williams (eds), above n 3, 708.

[36] *Koowarta v Bjelke-Petersen* (1982) 153 CLR 168.

[37] See especially *Australian Iron & Steel Pty Ltd v Banovic* (1989) 168 CLR 165, argued and decided almost contemporaneously with *Street*; Katherine Lindsay, 'Discrimination' in Blackshield, Coper and Williams (eds), above n 3, 210–11.

[38] David Jackson, 'Leave to Appeal' in Blackshield, Coper and Williams (eds), above n 3, 425.

[39] Tony Blackshield, Michael Coper and John Goldring, 'Privy Council, Judicial Committee of the' in Blackshield, Coper and Williams (eds), above n 3, 560.

True, these structural changes[40] were perhaps likely to have more impact on non-constitutional than constitutional cases, which often came directly to the High Court in its original jurisdiction and important categories of which were insulated from Privy Council appeal in any event, first from 1901 under the original *Constitution*[41] and then by legislation from 1968.[42] But these changes surely encouraged a general shift in mindset and a heightened awareness of the Court's law-making role. This shift and awareness are sometimes said to have also been pushed along by the symbolism of the move of the Court to Canberra in 1980 and its consequent co-location with the other institutions of national government.[43] They are also sometimes attributed to the appointment in the 1970s and 1980s of a number of judges whose creativity is traced back to their enlightened education in jurisprudence at the University of Sydney at the hands (or perhaps the feet) of Professor Julius Stone,[44] who relentlessly exposed the 'leeways of choice' open to judges in final appellate courts.[45]

This Sydney-centric perspective has always mightily annoyed the Victorians,[46] and in truth it should not obscure or diminish recognition of the similar enlightenment of which Stephen was evidently the

40 To which may be added the creation of the Federal Court of Australia in 1976, which relieved the High Court of much of its more mundane original jurisdiction: Brian Beaumont, 'Federal Court of Australia' in Blackshield, Coper and Williams (eds), above n 3, 272.

41 Tony Blackshield, 'Inter Se Questions' in Blackshield, Coper and Williams (eds), above n 3, 350.

42 In essence, appeals from the High Court in constitutional and federal cases were abolished in 1968, remaining appeals from the High Court in 1975, and appeals direct from state courts in 1986: see Blackshield, Coper and Goldring, above n 39.

43 Peter Durack, 'Canberra, Court's Move to' in Blackshield, Coper and Williams (eds), above n 3, 80.

44 See, eg, Tony Blackshield, 'Realism' in Blackshield, Coper and Williams (eds), above n 3, 582, 583. Blackshield mentions Mason, Jacobs, Murphy, Deane and Kirby. See also Michael Kirby, 'Julius Stone and the High Court of Australia' (1997) 20 *University of New South Wales Law Journal* 239; Theunis Roux, 'Reinterpreting "The Mason Court Revolution": An Historical Institutionalist Account of Judge-Driven Constitutional Transformation in Australia' (2015) 43 *Federal Law Review* 1, 21.

45 Julius Stone, *Legal System and Lawyers' Reasonings* (Maitland, 1964). It has to be said also that the pushing of boundaries by Murphy J, whose tenure (1975–86) fell exactly mid-way between *Henry v Boehm* and *Street*, was also a catalyst for change, at the very least by enabling others to move considerably without appearing to be nearly so radical: see Michael Coper and George Williams (eds), *Justice Lionel Murphy: Influential or Merely Prescient?* (Federation Press, 1997). The appointment in 1987 of Gaudron J, the first woman on the Court, also made the Court a more diverse institution.

46 See, eg, Gavan Griffith, 'A Commonwealth Perspective' in Michael Coper and George Williams (eds), *How Many Cheers for Engineers?* (Federation Press, 1997) 118.

fortunate recipient at the University of Melbourne at the hands of George Paton and Geoffrey Sawer.[47] One should also be careful not to overstate the impact of education in one's formative years as compared with the insights one garners from a lifetime of experience. In any event, one of the alleged beneficiaries, Mason, became Chief Justice in 1987 and was thus positioned to lead the Court into a new era of law-making. The landmark decision in *Cole v Whitfield*[48] suggests that he did so with immediate effect.

The decision in *Cole v Whitfield* provides a counterpoint to the decision the following year in *Street*.[49] As I argued in diverse places in the lead-up to *Cole v Whitfield*, the High Court had over the course of the 20th century wrongly treated s 92 of the *Constitution* as a source of individual rights in the nature of personal economic liberty, yet almost perversely had emasculated any section that truly was intended to secure individual rights.[50] As the Mason Court moved into gear, it quickly embraced the challenge of correcting both errors. In *Cole v Whitfield*, a unanimous court, in a single joint judgment, returned s 92 to its intended federal purpose of preventing state protectionism. In *Street*, a unanimous court, though this time in seven separate judgments,[51] returned s 117 to its intended federal purpose of protecting individuals from discrimination based on state residence.

The bench in *Street* – Mason CJ, Brennan, Deane, Dawson, Toohey, Gaudron and McHugh JJ – was entirely different from that in *Henry v Boehm*. Though Mason had been appointed to the Court some nine months before the argument in *Henry v Boehm*; as the then most junior judge, he was probably not called upon by Barwick CJ in order to avoid having an even-numbered bench of six,[52] given that Walsh J, who died

47 See Michael Coper, 'Geoffrey Sawer and the Art of the Academic Commentator: A Preliminary Biographical Sketch' (2014) 42 *Federal Law Review* 389, 416–17.

48 (1988) 165 CLR 360. 49 (1989) 168 CLR 461. 50 See, eg, Coper, above n 14.

51 The contrasting techniques of a single joint judgment and of seven separate judgments can each in their own way be a powerful statement of the unanimity needed to persuasively effect change. On the wider issues surrounding joint versus separate opinions, of which dissenting opinions are a subset, see Michael Coper, 'Joint Judgments and Separate Judgments' in Blackshield, Coper and Williams (eds), above n 3, 367. For a provocative view in the context of the independence of the judges from each other, see Dyson Heydon, 'Threats to Judicial Independence: The Enemy Within' (2013) 129 *Law Quarterly Review* 205 (discussed in Gabrielle Appleby and Heather Roberts, 'He Who Would Not Be Muzzled: Justice Heydon's Last Dissent in *Monis v The Queen* (2013)' in ch 18 of this book); for a more moderate view, see Stephen Gageler, 'Why Write Judgments?' (2014) 36 *Sydney Law Review* 189.

52 See Michael Coper, 'Tied Vote' in Blackshield, Coper and Williams (eds), above n 3, 671.

later in 1973, had already been taken ill. *Street* involved Queensland's rules for admission to legal practice, which, in their original form, required the applicant to be a resident of Queensland and to cease practice elsewhere, and, in their amended form, to intend to practise principally in Queensland. In judgments occupying 116 pages of the *Commonwealth Law Reports* (some five times the length of the more modest 23 pages of judgments in *Henry v Boehm*), the Court held that, by virtue of s 117 of the *Constitution*, the Queensland rules were inapplicable to New South Wales barrister Sandy Street (son of former New South Wales Chief Justice Sir Laurence Street) and, in a companion case, New South Wales barrister Tim Robertson (brother of celebrated human rights lawyer Geoffrey Robertson). *Henry v Boehm* – which might have been merely distinguished on the basis of the (flawed) line it drew between temporary and permanent residence – was overruled.[53]

Although, inevitably, the seven separate judgments in *Street* varied in their approach to the question and in their modes of expression, a strong common thread runs through them. It was the impact on the individual that mattered,[54] not some general comparison between imagined categories of hypothetical cases. The relevant comparison was that outlined by Stephen J in his dissent in *Henry v Boehm*. As Mason CJ explained, a disability or discrimination would be invalid if notional residence in the legislating state effectively removed the disability or discrimination or substantially deprived it of its onerous nature.[55] Residence did not mean permanent residence, nor did it have to be the sole criterion on which the legislation operated. Discrimination could be direct or indirect. In a nutshell, it was a question of substance, not of form.

In the course of the judgments, some ringing statements were made about the importance of s 117 of the *Constitution* in securing national unity and, as Mason CJ put it, 'a national sense of identity transcending colonial and State loyalties'.[56] According to Brennan J, s 117 was

> a guarantee of equal treatment under the law . . . Sections 92 and 117 are the constitutional pillars of the legal and social unity of the Australian people

[53] Some of the Justices – most emphatically Deane J – would also have overruled *Davies and Jones v Western Australia*: *Street* (1989) 168 CLR 461, 533 (Deane J), 489 (Mason CJ), 569–70 (Gaudron J), but a majority found that to be unnecessary.

[54] But see Amelia Simpson's emphasis on the federal purpose of s 117 rather than on the position of the individual as such: Amelia Simpson, 'The (Limited) Significance of the Individual in Section 117 State Residence Discrimination' (2008) 32 *Melbourne University Law Review* 639.

[55] *Street* (1989) 168 CLR 461, 489. [56] Ibid 485.

> just as sections 90 and 92 are the constitutional pillars of national economic unity . . . The law, which today pushes open the doors of the Supreme Court of Queensland for entry by suitably qualified barristers admitted and practising in other States, opens the doors of State universities, hospitals and other institutions for entry by subjects of the Queen on the same terms as residents of the relevant State.[57]

In the words of Deane J, s 117 was 'directed to the promotion of national economic and social cohesion and the establishment of a national citizenship' and was thus 'integral to the very structure of federation'; moreover, earlier decisions represented 'a triumph of form over substance'.[58] For Dawson J, s 117 was 'designed to ensure that persons from one State are treated in another as citizens of the nation, not as foreigners'.[59] Justice Toohey opined that 'once section 117 is seen as a guarantee of equal rights for all citizens, there is little justification for giving the terms "disability" and "discrimination" some narrow or technical meaning'.[60] Justice Gaudron strongly emphasised the importance of substance over form.[61] And McHugh J described s 117 as 'a great constitutional protection'.[62]

The Justices did differ in their elaboration of the limits of s 117 and thus in their various explanations of why the familiar examples of voting rights and welfare benefits might be validly confined to state residents.[63] On one view, these were incidents of the very existence and autonomy of the states and their capacity to function,[64] and, indeed, for some, were not so much 'exceptions' as matters that in truth did not, because they were inherent in the nature of state responsibility, amount to a disability or discrimination within the meaning of s 117.[65] Justice Gaudron found the limits in the nature of discrimination itself rather than in s 117's federal purpose; there was simply no discrimination if distinctions were drawn that were appropriate to relevant differences. But these were issues for the future. And because this chapter is not a treatise on the law of s 117 as such, it can merely be noted that their resolution has not been without controversy.[66]

[57] Ibid 512, 521. [58] Ibid 522–3. [59] Ibid 541.
[60] Ibid 554. [61] Ibid 569. [62] Ibid 588.
[63] No doubt the need to maintain professional standards might in some circumstances conceivably justify a residence requirement, but there was no suggestion that the admission rules in either *Henry v Boehm* or *Street* fell into this category.
[64] See especially the judgments of Mason CJ, Brennan and McHugh JJ.
[65] See especially the judgments of Deane, Dawson and Toohey JJ.
[66] The major cases since *Street* have been *Goryl v Greyhound Australia Pty Ltd* (1994) 179 CLR 463 and *Sweedman v Transport Accident Commission* (2006) 226 CLR 362. For criticism,

V Why Did Justice Stephen Dissent in *Henry v Boehm* and Was His Dissent Influential in *Street*?

The questions posed in the sub-heading are necessarily matters of speculation, but some thoughts may be offered. An antecedent question, however, is why did the High Court prior to *Street* take a narrow view of s 117, and indeed of the other rights-conferring provisions of the *Constitution*?

Mason has found this 'not surprising', as the *Constitution* was 'framed against a background of Dicey's doctrine of parliamentary sovereignty and concerned to allocate powers of government rather than to confer individual rights'; moreover, the *Engineers Case* in 1920 'reinforced a legalist methodology, by which the Court protected itself from controversy by insisting on the importance of textualism and by being reluctant to engage in overt discussion of policy issues'.[67] Yet there are always cross-currents in constitutional interpretation that challenge too ready a generalisation.[68] The seeds for implications from the text, including implications about rights, were sown early in the Court's life.[69] And much later, Barwick CJ led the movement to take into account practical considerations – that is to say, to prefer substance over form – in the interpretation of ss 90 (the prohibition of state excise duties)[70] and 92 (the guarantee of inter-state free trade).[71] Perceived economic rights – misplaced as the perception of 'rights' may have been – were evidently open to this approach, though not civil rights.

So the short answer to why the Court took a narrow and cramped view of s 117 before and including *Henry v Boehm* may simply be 'because it did'. How, then, did Stephen J manage to break free from the dominant paradigm?

One sometimes looks first to the influence of counsel and the persuasiveness of their argument, though this is also often a matter of speculation. Counsel for the applicant in *Henry v Boehm* failed to persuade four of the five judges; but it is worth observing that counsel for Mr Henry was John Young (later Chief Justice of Victoria), who had been a mentor of

see Sarah Joseph and Melissa Castan, *Federal Constitutional Law: A Contemporary View* (Lawbook Co, 4th ed, 2014) 464–5, 550; Mathieson, above n 33.

67 Sir Anthony Mason, 'Foreword' in Rosalind Dixon and George Williams (eds), *The High Court, the Constitution and Australian Politics* (Cambridge University Press, 2015) viii.

68 See Michael Coper, 'Currents, Cross-Currents, and Undercurrents in the Turbulent Waters of Constitutional Interpretation in the High Court' (2003) 77 *Australian Law Journal* 673.

69 See, eg, *R v Smithers; Ex parte Benson* (1912) 16 CLR 99.

70 *Anderson's Pty Ltd v Victoria* (1964) 111 CLR 353.

71 *Samuels v Readers' Digest Association Pty Ltd* (1969) 120 CLR 1.

Stephen's when he was at the bar.[72] This is not for a moment to suggest any untoward influence, and indeed to do so would fly in the face of my depiction of Stephen J as the very acme of independence; moreover, newly appointed judges will frequently be confronted by counsel with whom they have had close connections at the bar. The most that can be said here is that Stephen J is likely to have viewed Mr Henry's counsel with great respect and held him in high esteem, and to have had, through familiarity, a particular access to and insight into his style of argument and ways of thinking. Equally, that is most unlikely to have made any dent in his renowned ability to exercise an extremely independent mind and to call it as he saw it.

That independence of mind is no doubt the key to Stephen J's dissent in *Henry v Boehm*. That is not to cast any aspersions on the majority judges, who undoubtedly shared the quality of independence necessary for and characteristic of any judge worthy of the High Court and who themselves had been or would be dissenters in other cases and other circumstances. Yet Stephen J's particular brand of independence enabled him to exhibit an almost Oliver Wendell Holmes-like capacity to lift himself out of the milieu and conventional wisdom of the day and to anticipate the wisdom of the future.[73]

As a person of conservative bent on a court that was broadly conservative, this was an unusual experience for Stephen J. He was not often in dissent, let alone in sole dissent.[74] Moreover, he was not a consistent advocate for substance over form – not necessarily because of any particular irregularity or failing on his part but rather because of the complexities and subtleties of the tension between form and substance in different contexts, and the impact of other considerations and other canons of construction. The year before *Henry v Boehm*, for example, Stephen J had been part of a unanimous court in *King v Jones* that declined to give a flexible meaning to the phrase 'adult person' in s 41 of the *Constitution*,

72 Ayres, above n 6, 36.

73 See Michael Coper, 'The Path of the Law' (2002) 76 *Australian Law Journal* 716.

74 Another example of Stephen J in sole dissent is *Curran v Federal Commissioner of Taxation* (1974) 131 CLR 409 (vindicated in *John v Federal Commissioner of Taxation* (1989) 166 CLR 417). Justice Stephen's dissent in *Todorovic v Waller* (1981) 150 CLR 402 received high praise in the House of Lords: see Harold Luntz, 'Damages' in Blackshield, Coper and Williams (eds), above n 3, 188–9. Although not necessarily strictly in dissent, Stephen J was sometimes an outlier with idiosyncratic views, such as in relation to standing: see for example *Victoria v Commonwealth* (1975) 134 CLR 338 ('*AAP Case*'); *Robinson v Western Australian Museum* (1977) 138 CLR 283. He also often steered a middle course, as in *Koowarta v Bjelke-Petersen* (1982) 153 CLR 168: see Hilary Charlesworth, 'Stephen, Ninian Martin' in Blackshield, Coper and Williams (eds), above n 3, 643–4.

preferring the fixed, historical meaning of 21-year-old.[75] He was also part of a court that struggled in the 1970s with the meaning of 'excise duties' in s 90 of the *Constitution*, a court that was unable to escape from the clutches of form – not so surprising considering that excise is, after all, a 'form' of tax.[76] Nevertheless, the excise cases are a perfect, if extreme, example of how constitutional interpretation is much more complex than the mere tension between substance and form; diverse views on the purpose or purposes of s 90, on legal method, and on the weight to be given to the steady accumulation of conflicting precedents, have bedevilled this area like no other[77] (except perhaps the pre-*Cole v Whitfield* law on s 92).

A further complication is that, however artificial it may seem, and however unsustainable in the long term, the choice of a formal approach has sometimes been driven not by a love of legalism for its own sake, but by a desire to achieve certain policy ends.[78] This was evident at different stages of the interpretation of both ss 90 and 92, where a narrow view based on formal considerations was seen to usefully restrain the unduly wide impact of those sections made possible by other aspects of their interpretation. And sometimes the elevation of form over substance is overtly defended on the basis of policy. A good example is provided by the prohibitions on discrimination between the states under ss 51(ii) and 99 of the *Constitution*. Significantly, these prohibitions are addressed not to the states, the more likely agents of disintegration in a federal system, but to the Commonwealth, the more likely angel of unity. In the 1980s, the Constitutional Commission's Advisory Committee on Trade and National Economic Management thought that, while these provisions may have played a useful role early in the life of the new federation, the nation had progressed to such a mature point that they were no longer needed[79] – an indirect endorsement of what others had seen as their emasculation by formalism at the hands of the High Court.

75 *King v Jones* (1972) 128 CLR 221.

76 *Gosford Meats Pty Ltd v New South Wales* (1985) 155 CLR 368, 416 (Dawson J).

77 Michael Coper, 'Excise Duties' in Blackshield, Coper and Williams (eds), above n 3, 256; Coper, above n 14, 224–42.

78 Anthony Mason, 'Form and Substance' in Blackshield, Coper and Williams (eds), above n 3, 282, 283; Leslie Zines and G J Lindell, 'Form and Substance: "Discrimination" in Modern Constitutional Law' (1992) 21 *Federal Law Review* 236. See also Richard A Posner, *Reflections on Judging* (Harvard University Press, 2013) 105–30, 351–66.

79 Advisory Committee on Trade and National Economic Management, *Report to the Constitutional Commission* (Australian Government Publishing Service, 1987) 200–4. The Commission itself preferred to make these sections subject to the supervision of the now-defunct Inter-State Commission: *Final Report of the Constitutional Commission* (Australian Government Publishing Service, 1988) 814–17.

Be that as it may, the tension between form and substance, entangled as it was with other aspects of the interpretation of s 117, was pivotal to the dissent of Stephen J in *Henry v Boehm* and to the later vindication of that dissent in *Street*. How significant was the dissent in the Court's change of direction?

Again, this is a matter of conjecture. Counsel for Mr Street, David Bennett QC, certainly submitted that the Court should adopt Stephen J's dissenting judgment in *Henry v Boehm*;[80] but he placed rather more emphasis on the proposition that *Henry v Boehm* and *Davies and Jones v Western Australia* were inconsistent with modern concepts of discrimination, which did not require precise discrimination against a whole group and no-one but that group. Indirect discrimination had also come to be recognised.[81] The seminal United States Supreme Court decision in *Griggs v Duke Power Co*[82] actually pre-dated *Henry v Boehm*, but it took some time for the message of that case to seep into the American consciousness, let alone that of Australia. These and other changes, set out earlier, left the Court poised to breathe new life into s 117.

A careful reading of the judgments in *Street* does not yield a definitive answer on the question of the influence of Stephen J's dissent. On the whole, the Court argued from first principles, referring to the dissent mainly in passing or for reinforcement. Chief Justice Mason (who may well have agreed with Stephen J had he been called upon to sit in *Henry v Boehm*) perhaps made the most of the dissent, structuring the early part of his judgment around Stephen J's exposure of the errors in the approach of the majority in *Henry v Boehm*.[83] Justice Dawson also invoked Stephen J's views to a considerable extent, as did – though to a lesser extent – McHugh J.[84] Justices Brennan, Deane, Toohey and Gaudron placed little overt reliance on Stephen J's articulation of the issues in *Henry v Boehm*, instead primarily working through those issues from first principles. In summary, two judges could be said to have put reasonably strong reliance on Stephen J's dissent (Mason CJ and Dawson J), one to have put moderate reliance on it (McHugh J), and four to have evidently not relied upon it much at all (Brennan, Deane, Toohey and Gaudron JJ).

No doubt this is all rather inconclusive, especially as it does not address what impact the dissent of Stephen J may have had below the surface. But one further point can be added. In weighing up whether it was appropriate

[80] *Street* (1989) 168 CLR 461, 466. [81] Above n 37. [82] 401 US 424 (1971).
[83] *Street* (1989) 168 CLR 461, 483–8.
[84] Ibid 543–9 (Dawson J), 582, 587–9 (McHugh J).

to overrule an earlier decision of the Court[85] – far from a rare occurrence but something never taken lightly – two judges (Dawson and McHugh JJ) noted among the list of factors to be taken into account the fact that there had been a dissenting opinion in the earlier case.[86] At the very least, in this sense the dissent prised open the door for a future consideration of the conventional wisdom.

VI Conclusion

In 2006, I had the privilege of interviewing Stephen for the High Court Oral History Project.[87] His memory of the cases had faded, but I asked him whether the highly unusual experience (for him) of finding himself in a minority of one in *Henry v Boehm* had made him feel awkward or self-conscious. Consistently with his comments on retirement, he said: 'No, I never felt any problem at all about not being in a majority'.[88] Indeed, 'it was stimulating'. Referring to his later vindication, he quipped: 'It was good to know that you alone were right and all the others were wrong!'[89]

Stephen's tongue-in-cheek comment belied his thoughtful sensitivity to the complexities of constitutional adjudication and his careful avoidance, in more serious moments, of the language of right and wrong in favour of the more nuanced language of which was the better or more preferable view.[90] Moreover, despite the air of inevitability things have once they have come to pass, there was no certainty that his view on s 117 would be vindicated – dissenting views characteristically are not, despite the romanticising of those that are – nor that the High Court would consistently maintain the Mason Court's preference for substance over form.[91] Yet the story of Stephen J's dissent in *Henry v Boehm* and

[85] See David Bennett, 'Overruling' in Blackshield, Coper and Williams (eds), above n 3, 516.

[86] *Street* (1989) 168 CLR 461, 549 (Dawson J), 588 (McHugh J). *Contra* Brennan J in *John v Federal Commissioner of Taxation* (1989) 166 CLR 417, 451.

[87] See Research Data Australia, *Judicially Speaking: An Oral History of the High Court of Australia [2006–2010]* TRC 5744 National Library of Australia <https://researchdata.ands.org.au/judicially-speaking-an-court-australia/69078>. The High Court Oral History Project was conducted in conjunction with Fiona Wheeler and John Williams.

[88] But see Cassese, above n 22.

[89] See Fiona Wheeler and Michael Coper, Interview with Sir Ninian Stephen (Sound Recording, 14 December 2006, TRC 5744 National Library of Australia) <http://trove.nla.gov.au/version/201468175>; transcript of interview lines 1232–5.

[90] Mason, above n 3. See especially *Queensland v Commonwealth* (1977) 139 CLR 585, 603 (Stephen J), 606 (Mason J).

[91] See, eg, Rosalind Dixon and Sean Lau, 'The Gleeson Court' in Rosalind Dixon and George Williams (eds), *The High Court, the Constitution and Australian Politics* (Cambridge University Press, 2015) 284.

its vindication in *Street* illustrates the role that a dissenting opinion can potentially play.[92]

Ironically, the power of that story lies in the excessive ordinariness of its telling in the law reports. The dissent exhibits no histrionics, no passionate appeal to the intelligence of a future day, no bitter regrets at being unable to agree. The independent-minded Stephen J simply takes a different view, states his reasons dispassionately and with respect, and, perhaps atypically for judges generally but consistently with his own stated philosophy, lets the outcome of the case take care of itself. In a multi-member court in which outcomes are determined by the accidental aggregation of individual views to form a majority,[93] could there be a better model for judicial decision-making?

92 The wider issues around the role and value of judicial dissent are dealt with elsewhere in this book. However, two general works worth perusing are Cass R Sunstein, *Why Societies Need Dissent* (Harvard University Press, 2003) and Amartya Sen, *The Argumentative Indian: Writings on Indian Culture, History and Identity* (Penguin Books, 2006).

93 The multiple membership of the Court itself being a safeguard against idiosyncrasy. For an interesting comment on the aggregation of views and the problem of inconsistency, see Stephen Gageler and Brendan Lim, 'Collective Irrationality and the Doctrine of Precedent' (2014) 38 *Melbourne University Law Review* 525.

10

Justice Mason in the *Australian Assistance Plan Case* (1975): Nationhood, Federalism and Commonwealth Executive Power

PETA STEPHENSON

I Introduction

Justice Anthony Mason's judgment in *Victoria v Commonwealth* ('*AAP Case*')[1] has proven to be one of the most influential dissents in Australian constitutional law. The *AAP Case* concerned a challenge to the Whitlam Government's Australian Assistance Plan ('AAP'). Under the AAP, the Commonwealth made direct grants to Regional Councils for Social Development ('Regional Councils') which facilitated the provision of social welfare services in regional communities. The Commonwealth bypassed the states in making these direct grants, and Victoria subsequently challenged the validity of the AAP. The action was ultimately dismissed by a bare majority of the High Court, consisting of Justices McTiernan, Stephen, Jacobs and Murphy. Justice Mason, alongside Barwick CJ and Gibbs J, was in the minority.

As no uniform line of reasoning emerged from either the majority or minority in the *AAP Case*, some may query whether it is especially meaningful to classify Mason J's judgment as, in fact, a dissent. Justice Mason was, however, alone in concluding that the AAP fell outside the scope of the Commonwealth's executive power. On this particular question, Mason J adopted an approach which represented a clear departure from that of the other members of the Court, but which has since been endorsed in the decades following the *AAP Case*. Indeed, when the decision was handed down in 1975, it would have been difficult to predict that Mason J's dissent would emerge so spectacularly from the inconclusive assortment of opinion in the *AAP Case*, to influence and define the Court's

[1] (1975) 134 CLR 338.

later jurisprudence on the executive power of the Commonwealth. This destiny for a minority opinion, in what was ultimately a fragmented and somewhat confusing case, was an unexpected one.

The constitutional significance of Mason J's dissent in the *AAP Case* stems largely from the way in which it reconceptualised our understanding of the Commonwealth's executive power. First, Mason J took the unprecedented step of finding that the Commonwealth had 'a capacity to engage in enterprises and activities peculiarly adapted to the government of a nation and which cannot otherwise be carried on for the benefit of the nation'.[2] Justice Mason sourced this 'nationhood power' in ss 51(xxxix) and 61 of the *Constitution* and the 'existence and character of the Commonwealth as a national government'.[3] Second, Mason J derived limits on the nationhood power and executive power more broadly from the federal character of the Australian polity established by the *Constitution.* Both aspects of Mason J's dissent in the *AAP Case* have had a profound and enduring influence on the High Court, and have earned it the title of a 'great Australian dissent'.

II The Australian Assistance Plan in Political Context

Gough Whitlam's historic general election victory on 2 December 1972 marked the end of 23 years in opposition for the Australian Labor Party. It brought to office a government with an agenda for widespread social reform, aimed at promoting equality, increasing public participation in decision-making and 'liberat[ing] the talents and uplift[ing] the horizons of the Australian people'.[4]

The Whitlam Government identified community participation through local government as being integral to its reform agenda. Accordingly, local governments were afforded a greater participatory role in areas such as social welfare, health, education and urban planning.[5] Whitlam referred to this widening of the role of local government as 'a new federalism'.[6] This approach was certainly 'new' – it represented

[2] Ibid 397. [3] Ibid.

[4] E G Whitlam, 'People and Power – Community Participation in Federal Government' (1975) 47(2) *Australian Quarterly* 36, 36; E G Whitlam, *The Whitlam Government 1972–1975* (Penguin, 1985) 12.

[5] E G Whitlam, 'A New Federalism' (1971) 43(3) *Australian Quarterly* 6, 11, 17; E G Whitlam, 'The Labor Government and the Constitution' in Gareth Evans (ed), *Labor and the Constitution 1972–1975* (Heinemann, 1977) 305, 306–8.

[6] Whitlam, 'New Federalism', above n 5, 6–17.

nothing short of a radical departure from the traditional federal system, which divided and distributed responsibilities between the Commonwealth and the states. Whitlam was of the view that the existing federal system was inefficient, dysfunctional, and 'wholly inadequate to the needs of a modern federal state'.[7]

Whitlam's 'new federalism' required new funding arrangements. Accordingly, the Whitlam Government utilised 'direct funding', that is, 'funding provided directly to the ultimate non-State recipient'[8] to secure the participation of local government in the implementation of its policy initiatives. Traditionally, the Commonwealth would have provided the states with a conditional grant made under s 96 of the *Constitution*. However, as Whitlam himself stated, '[g]overnment activities are most responsibly planned and executed if the government which pays for them also shares the responsibility and the glory for them'.[9] The Whitlam Government's reliance on direct funding correspondingly increased its involvement in areas which had traditionally been the responsibility of the states.[10]

The Whitlam Government introduced the AAP in 1973 as part of its 'pioneering experiment' in community involvement under the 'new federalism'.[11] The programme's primary purpose was to facilitate the provision of improved social welfare services across Australia. Under the AAP, the Regional Councils were tasked with stimulating increased public participation in the identification of core areas of need in regional communities. The Regional Councils were also responsible for co-ordinating the activities already being undertaken by other organisations, such as voluntary agencies, local community groups and each level of government.[12]

The Commonwealth government could make four types of direct grants to the Regional Councils under the AAP. These included: initiating grants for the establishment of new regional councils; administrative grants for staff salaries and other related costs; capitation grants for community welfare activities of $2 per head of population per annum; and annual

[7] Whitlam, 'Labor Government', above n 5, 305.

[8] Gabrielle Appleby, 'There Must be Limits: The Commonwealth Spending Power' (2009) 37 *Federal Law Review* 93, 104.

[9] Whitlam, 'New Federalism', above n 5, 11.

[10] See Jenny Hocking, *Gough Whitlam: His Time* (Miegunyah Press, 2012) 87–8.

[11] Whitlam, 'People and Power', above n 4, 39.

[12] Ibid. See also Melanie Oppenheimer, 'Voluntary Action, Social Welfare and the Australian Assistance Plan in the 1970s' (2008) 39 *Australian Historical Studies* 167.

grants to employ Community Development Officers.[13] The grants were to be directed at social welfare programmes to assist children, families and adolescents and to provide aged care, accommodation, financial assistance and information services as well as the establishment of Community Health and Welfare Centres.

In order to fund the AAP, the Commonwealth government appropriated $5 970 000 from the Consolidated Revenue Fund ('CRF') consisting of $5 620 000 for the direct grants to the Regional Councils and $350 000 for 'development and evaluation expenses'. The appropriation for the AAP was not authorised by legislation, save for a brief description of it in item 4 div 530 of sch 2 of the *Appropriation Act (No 1) 1974–1975* (Cth). The details of the AAP were contained in two discussion papers and a document entitled 'Guidelines for Pilot Programme – Australian Assistance Plan'. Although it was intended that the AAP would be subsequently enshrined in legislation, this never eventuated. For the duration of its lifetime, the AAP was administered by the executive free of any underpinning legislative foundation. The AAP also operated independently of the states. In keeping with Whitlam's 'new federalism', it was never intended that the Commonwealth government would administer the AAP through the state governments.[14]

III The High Court Challenge

The State of Victoria and its Attorney-General challenged the AAP in the High Court and sought a declaration that the appropriation for the AAP was invalid, insofar as it exceeded the limited social welfare which the Commonwealth was authorised to carry out pursuant to ss 51(xxiii) and 51(xxiiiA) of the *Constitution*. The plaintiffs also sought an injunction restraining the defendants, the Commonwealth and the Minister for Social Security, Bill Hayden, from expending any funds for the purposes of the AAP. The defendants asserted the validity of the AAP and the associated appropriation.

Argument began on 6 May 1975 and concluded two days later. The High Court handed down its decision on 17 October 1975. In a narrow 4:3 result, the Court dismissed the plaintiffs' action. Justices McTiernan, Jacobs and Murphy were members of the majority which upheld the AAP.

[13] Whitlam, 'People and Power', above n 4, 39.

[14] See also Cheryl Saunders, 'The Development of the Commonwealth Spending Power' (1978) 11 *Melbourne University Law Review* 369, 402.

Chief Justice Barwick, Gibbs and Mason JJ, in dissent, struck down the AAP as being beyond Commonwealth power. Justice Stephen did not decide the issue, having concluded that Victoria and its Attorney-General lacked standing to institute the proceedings.

Validity of Appropriation

One issue which arose for determination concerned the scope of the Commonwealth's power to appropriate funds from the CRF. The Court was required to consider whether the appropriation for the AAP in the Act was for the 'purposes of the Commonwealth' in s 81 of the *Constitution.* Chief Justice Barwick and Gibbs J, in dissent, favoured a narrow interpretation of this provision,[15] holding that it was limited to those purposes for which the Commonwealth had power to make laws, including those set out in ss 51 and 52 of the *Constitution* and the powers inherent in the Commonwealth's existence and international personality.[16] As the AAP was not supported by these powers, the appropriation of funds was invalid.

On this particular question, McTiernan and Murphy JJ were joined by Mason J in finding that the impugned appropriation was for the 'purposes of the Commonwealth'. In reaching this conclusion, McTiernan J relied extensively on Latham CJ's judgment in the *Pharmaceutical Benefits Case* and held that s 81 was essentially unlimited in scope.[17] Justices Mason and Murphy also afforded s 81 a wide operation and concluded that it extended to 'such purposes as the Parliament may determine'.[18] Accordingly, the appropriation of funds for the AAP was valid.

However, Mason J observed that an appropriation had a limited effect. Sections 81 and 83 enabled the Commonwealth to withdraw money from the CRF, but it did not supply legal authority for the Commonwealth's engagement in the relevant activities which called for the expenditure of the funds.[19] Justice Jacobs similarly remarked that the appropriation Act merely 'earmark[ed]' the money.[20] For Mason and Jacobs JJ, then, ss 81 and 83 did not confer any substantive power on the Commonwealth to implement the AAP. That power needed to be found elsewhere in the *Constitution.* As the AAP operated as an administrative scheme which

[15] This view was adopted by the majority in *A-G (Vic) ex rel Dale v Commonwealth* (1945) 71 CLR 237 ('*Pharmaceutical Benefits Case*').

[16] *AAP Case* (1975) 134 CLR 338, 361–2 (Barwick CJ), 373–4 (Gibbs J).

[17] Ibid 367–9. [18] Ibid 396 (Mason J), 419 (Murphy J).

[19] Ibid 396. [20] Ibid 411.

was not supported by legislation, Mason and Jacobs JJ were required to consider whether it was supported by the Commonwealth's executive power in s 61 of the *Constitution.*

Scope of Executive Power

In his judgment, Jacobs J held that the AAP was a valid exercise of the Commonwealth's executive power. Justice Jacobs construed the words 'maintenance of this *Constitution*' in s 61 as importing the 'idea of Australia as a nation' into the *Constitution.*[21] The Commonwealth could, therefore, carry out activities with an 'Australian rather than a local flavour' and formulate and co-ordinate national programmes such as the AAP.[22]

Justice Mason similarly observed that the Commonwealth Executive had a capacity to engage in activities 'peculiarly adapted' to a national government by virtue of its 'existence and character' as a polity.[23] However, in Mason J's view, the AAP amounted to a new social welfare scheme, which could have been administered by the states instead of the Regional Councils, had the Commonwealth made a grant to them under s 96. The activities associated with the AAP went beyond the limited social welfare services the Commonwealth was authorised to carry out under ss 51(xxiii) and 51(xxiiiA) of the *Constitution.*[24] Justice Mason held that the Commonwealth's executive power did not support it engaging in these activities and joined the other two dissentients, Barwick CJ and Gibbs J, in declaring the AAP to be invalid.[25]

IV The Significance of Mason J's Dissent

Justice Mason's understanding of the nature and effect of an appropriation Act in the *AAP Case* has been influential, as evinced by the more recent decisions of *Pape v Commissioner of Taxation* ('*Pape*')[26] and *Williams v Commonwealth* ('*Williams*').[27] In the former, the Court unanimously confirmed that Mason J was correct in finding that ss 81 and 83 do not confer the power to spend on the Commonwealth.[28] This finding was

[21] Ibid 405–6. See also Anne Twomey, 'Pushing the Boundaries of Commonwealth Executive Power – Pape, the Prerogative and Nationhood Powers' (2010) 34 *Melbourne University Law Review* 313, 331–2.

[22] *AAP Case* (1975) 134 CLR 338, 412–13. [23] Ibid 397.

[24] Ibid 400. [25] Ibid 400–1. [26] (2009) 238 CLR 1. [27] (2012) 248 CLR 156.

[28] *Pape* (2009) 238 CLR 1, 23, 50, 55 (French CJ), 73, 80 (Gummow, Crennan and Bell JJ), 105, 113 (Hayne and Kiefel JJ); 210–11 (Heydon J). For confirmation, see *Williams* (2012)

significant because it directed attention to the scope of the Commonwealth's executive power in s 61 of the *Constitution*, and it is this particular aspect of Mason J's dissent in the *AAP Case* which is the focus of this chapter.

The High Court has been careful to refrain from providing a detailed account of the Commonwealth's executive power, which is identified, but not defined, in s 61 of the *Constitution*. Section 61 provides:

> The executive power of the Commonwealth is vested in the Queen and is exercisable by the Governor-General as the Queen's representative, and extends to the execution and maintenance of this *Constitution*, and of the laws of the Commonwealth.

Prior to the *AAP Case*, it was generally accepted that the Commonwealth's executive power in s 61 extended to powers conferred by the *Constitution* and statute; powers necessary for the execution and maintenance of Commonwealth laws and constitutional provisions; powers defined by reference to the common law prerogatives; and powers defined by the legal capacities of the Commonwealth.[29] In the *AAP Case*, Mason J held that the Commonwealth's executive power included an implied nationhood power.[30]

The significance of this dissent cannot be attributed solely to Mason J's finding that the *Constitution* contains an implied nationhood power. Another important aspect of the judgment concerns the scope of the power.[31] Mason J emphasised, in this regard, that it was subject to limitations derived from the federal character of the polity established by the *Constitution*.[32] In an area of constitutional law where there is a paucity of decided cases, both aspects of Mason J's dissent in the *AAP Case* – namely, the creation of the nationhood power and the use of federalism to limit the scope of it – have been able to influence the High Court's interpretation of the Commonwealth's executive power. The extent of this influence is evident in the High Court's reasoning in the contemporary

248 CLR 156, 193 (French CJ), 230–1 (Gummow and Bell JJ), 305 (Heydon J), 373–4 (Kiefel J).

29 *Williams* (2012) 248 CLR 156, 184–5 (French CJ). For a useful overview of the sources of executive power, see Twomey, above n 21, 324–7; Gabrielle Appleby and Stephen McDonald, 'Looking at the Executive Power through the High Court's New Spectacles' (2013) 35 *Sydney Law Review* 253.

30 *AAP Case* (1975) 134 CLR 338, 397.

31 Ibid 397–8.

32 Ibid. See also James Stellios (ed), *Zines's The High Court and the Constitution* (Federation Press, 6th ed, 2015) 455.

cases concerning executive power, and lends support to the classification of this judgment as a 'great Australian dissent'.

The Nationhood Power

In the *AAP Case*, Mason J reasoned that the Commonwealth Executive needed to be conferred with powers 'appropriate' to its position as the national government.[33] In this regard, he held that

> there is to be deduced from the existence and character of the Commonwealth as a national government and from the presence of ss 51(xxxix) and 61 a capacity to engage in enterprises and activities peculiarly adapted to the government of a nation and which cannot otherwise be carried on for the benefit of the nation.[34]

In addition to responding to national emergencies, it has been suggested that the nationhood power provides the constitutional basis for a range of Commonwealth activities, including inquiries, investigations and advocacy.[35] Exploration and scientific research, including the establishment of the CSIRO, as well as national cultural initiatives and the arts are also examples of activities which could be characterised as being 'peculiarly adapted' to the national government.[36] In light of the potentially wide range of Commonwealth activities which might be supported by this power, it is perhaps unsurprising that it has attracted considerable criticism from scholars.

The nationhood power has been described as 'vague',[37] 'amorphous'[38] and 'elusive'.[39] Furthermore, the difficulties surrounding its application have prompted some commentators to express concern that it

[33] *AAP Case* (1975) 134 CLR 338, 397–8. [34] Ibid 397.

[35] Ibid 397 (Mason J), 412–13 (Jacobs J).

[36] Ibid 362 (Barwick CJ); *Davis v Commonwealth* (1988) 166 CLR 79, 111 (Brennan J) ('*Davis*'). See also Leslie Zines, *The High Court and the Constitution* (Federation Press, 5th ed, 2008) 414–15; Stellios, above n 32, 450–2.

[37] Zines, above n 36, 417.

[38] A R Blackshield, 'The Siege of Bowral – The Legal Issues' (1978) 4(9) *Pacific Defence Reporter* 6, 7.

[39] Peter Gerangelos, 'The Executive Power of the Commonwealth of Australia: Section 61 of the Commonwealth Constitution, "Nationhood" and the Future of the Prerogative' (2012) 12 *Oxford University Commonwealth Law Journal* 97, 99.

is 'politically-charged',[40] potentially 'dangerous'[41] and 'ill-defined and ill-confined'.[42] Justice Mason's judgment in the *AAP Case* deserves the title of a 'great Australian dissent' despite these criticisms. As the remainder of this chapter demonstrates, the High Court has endorsed the nationhood power as an accepted 'dimension'[43] of executive power.

Justice Mason was not, however, the first judge to interpret the *Constitution* having regard to the Commonwealth's character and status as the national government. After the landmark decision of *Amalgamated Society of Engineers v Adelaide Steamship Co Ltd* ('*Engineers' Case*'),[44] for example, the Court read the *Constitution* in

> a new light, a light reflected from events that had, over twenty years, led to a growing realization that Australians were now one people and Australia one country and that national laws might meet national needs.[45]

Australia had, since Federation, taken important steps towards the attainment of sovereignty and international personality.[46] The enactment of the *Statute of Westminster 1931* (UK) and its subsequent adoption by the Commonwealth were particularly important in this regard.[47] In this

40 George Winterton, 'The Relationship between Commonwealth Legislative and Executive Power' (2004) 25 *Adelaide Law Review* 21, 33.

41 George Winterton, *Parliament, the Executive and the Governor-General: A Constitutional Analysis* (Melbourne University Press, 1983) 44.

42 Twomey, above n 21, 313. 43 Appleby and McDonald, above n 29, 255.

44 (1920) 28 CLR 129.

45 *Victoria v Commonwealth* (1971) 122 CLR 353, 396 (Windeyer J) ('*Payroll Tax Case*').

46 In 1919 Australian representatives attended the Peace Conference. Australia also became a signatory to the Treaty of Versailles and a member of the League of Nations. The Balfour Declaration of 1926 declared the United Kingdom and its dominions, including Australia, to be equal in status. The *Statute of Westminster 1931* (UK) granted legislative independence to Australia and the other dominions. The *Statute of Westminster Adoption Act 1942* (Cth) declared that the *Statute of Westminster 1931* (UK) had retrospective effect in Australia from 3 September 1939. See further Zines, above n 36, 376; Leslie Zines, 'The Growth of Australian Nationhood and its Effect on the Powers of the Commonwealth' in Leslie Zines (ed), *Commentaries on the Australian Constitution: A Tribute to Geoffrey Sawer* (Butterworths, 1977) 1, 27–30; Anne Twomey, 'Sue v Hill – The Evolution of Australian Independence' in Adrienne Stone and George Williams (eds), *The High Court at the Crossroads: Essays in Constitutional Law* (Federation Press, 2000) 82–4, 94–6; George Winterton, 'The Acquisition of Independence' in Robert French, Geoffrey Lindell and Cheryl Saunders (eds), *Reflections on the Australian Constitution* (Federation Press, 2003), 36, 41–3.

47 See, eg, *Bonser v La Macchia* (1969) 122 CLR 177, 189 (Barwick CJ), 223–4 (Windeyer J); *Barton v Commonwealth* (1974) 131 CLR 477, 498 (Mason J); *New South Wales v Commonwealth* (1975) 135 CLR 337, 373 (Barwick CJ) ('*Seas and Submerged Lands Case*'); *China Ocean Shipping Co v South Australia* (1979) 145 CLR 172, 183 (Barwick CJ), 195

context, Dixon J had reasoned in *Australian Communist Party v Commonwealth* ('*Communist Party Case*') that the Commonwealth possessed certain legislative powers which were inherent in the 'establishment' and 'character' of the Commonwealth as a sovereign nation.[48] These powers were limited in scope, supporting only those activities which were 'necessary'[49] to protect the Commonwealth's existence, functions and operations.[50]

As already noted, in the *AAP Case*, Mason J also derived an implied power from the 'existence and character' of the Commonwealth as the national government.[51] This nationhood power was, however, an executive power. It was also wider than Dixon J's inherent powers of self-protection, as it supported activities 'appropriate'[52] and 'peculiarly adapted'[53] to a national government, rather than those 'necessary' for the protection of the Commonwealth.[54] The context surrounding the *AAP Case* is also important and helps explain this shift. While the enactment of the *Statute of Westminster 1931* (UK) may have removed 'all vestiges of colonialism',[55] the strong historical and cultural links which existed between Australia and the United Kingdom undeniably continued. Indeed, it has been argued that it was not until the early 1970s, which coincided with Sir Anthony Mason's service on the High Court, that Australia witnessed 'an imperceptible but distinct growth in the *Australian* sense of nationhood and independence'.[56]

Whitlam shared these broad community attitudes, and during his time in office made some important changes to Australia's national symbols which reflected this growing sense of independence and national identity.[57] On Australia Day 1973, Whitlam publicly announced his intention to replace *God Save the Queen* with an Australian national anthem.[58] *Advance Australia Fair* was selected by the people through a

(Gibbs J), 211 (Stephen J); *Southern Centre of Theosophy Inc v South Australia* (1979) 145 CLR 246, 257 (Gibbs J). See also Zines, above n 36, 376; Anne Twomey, 'Sue v Hill – The Evolution of Australian Independence' in Stone and Williams (eds), above n 46, 94–6, 108; George Winterton, 'The Acquisition of Independence' in French, Lindell and Saunders (eds), above n 46, 41–3.

[48] (1951) 83 CLR 1, 188. [49] Ibid. [50] Ibid 188, 192.

[51] *AAP Case* (1975) 134 CLR 338, 397. [52] Ibid 397–8. [53] Ibid 397.

[54] See also Twomey, above n 21, 333–4.

[55] George Winterton, 'The Acquisition of Independence' in French, Lindell and Saunders (eds), above n 46, 42.

[56] Michael Kirby, 'Sir Anthony Mason Lecture 1996: A F Mason – From Trigwell to Teoh' (1996) 20 *Melbourne University Law Review* 1087, 1096 (emphasis added).

[57] See also Hocking, above n 10, 72–6.

[58] Whitlam, *Whitlam Government*, above n 4, 144.

public opinion poll in early 1974.[59] On 19 October 1973, Her Royal Highness Queen Elizabeth II assented to the Whitlam Government's *Royal Style and Titles Act 1973* (Cth), which designated Her Majesty the 'Queen of Australia', and removed references to the 'United Kingdom' and 'Defender of the Faith' from Her Majesty's Australian title.[60] On Australia Day 1975, the Whitlam Government successfully established an Australian system of honours, the Order of Australia, to replace the Imperial honours system.[61]

One event which held particular significance during this period was the abolition of Privy Council appeals from the High Court.[62] In Whitlam's view, the retention of these appeals was 'not consonant with Australia's nationhood'.[63] If Australia was to become truly independent, it was imperative that appeals to 'a court sitting in another country, to a court comprising judges appointed by the Government of that other country' be removed.[64] The *Privy Council (Appeals from the High Court) Act 1975* (Cth) vested the High Court with final jurisdiction in all non-constitutional matters decided by it, and together with the *Privy Council (Limitations of Appeals) Act 1968* (Cth), which had already precluded appeals to the Privy Council on issues concerning constitutional law and federal laws, ensured that 'Australia's sovereignty was fully exercised in all judicial matters'.[65] The *AAP Case* was decided against this backdrop.

Several members of the Court attributed some constitutional significance to events leading up to Australia's attainment of national status.[66] However, in the opinion of Sir Gerard Brennan, Mason J articulated in the *AAP Case*, 'a vision of Australia as an independent nation fully equipped to take its place as a member of the international community'.[67] The

[59] Ibid 145–6. *Advance Australia Fair* was proclaimed Australia's national anthem on 19 April 1984.

[60] Ibid 131–2; Anne Twomey, *The Constitution of New South Wales* (Federation Press, 2004) 594–5; Stellios, above n 32, 469–74.

[61] Whitlam, *Whitlam Government*, above n 4, 142.

[62] See also Kirby, above n 56, 1095–6; Jason Pierce, *Inside the Mason Court Revolution: The High Court of Australia Transformed* (Carolina Academic Press, 2006) 226–31.

[63] Whitlam, *Whitlam Government*, above n 4, 602. [64] Ibid 602.

[65] See further Michael Kirby AC CMG, 'Whitlam as Law Reformer' (1979) 10 *Federal Law Review* 53, 58; Michael Kirby AC CMG, 'Whitlam as Internationalist' (Speech delivered at the University of Western Sydney Whitlam Lecture, Sydney, 25 February 2010) 34; Anne Twomey, 'Sue v Hill – The Evolution of Australian Independence' in Stone and Williams (eds), above n 46, 106–7. Appeals to the Privy Council from the states were finally abolished by the *Australia Act 1986* (Cth).

[66] *AAP Case* (1975) 135 CLR 338, 362 (Barwick CJ), 378 (Gibbs J), 412–13 (Jacobs J).

[67] Sir Gerard Brennan, 'A Tribute to The Hon Sir Anthony Mason' in Cheryl Saunders, *Courts of Final Jurisdiction – The Mason Court in Australia* (Federation Press, 1996) 10, 10–11. References were also made to *Koowarta v Bjelke-Petersen* (1982) 153 CLR 168, 229

starting point, then, for Mason J in ascertaining the scope of the Commonwealth's executive power, was not the common law of the United Kingdom regarding the power of the British Executive, but the areas of responsibility allocated to the Commonwealth by the *Constitution*, and in particular, by ss 51 and 52. Justice Mason also had regard to the 'character and status' of the Commonwealth as the national, and federal, government.[68]

In Mason J's opinion, the Commonwealth's executive power needed to be appropriate to its status as a sovereign nation in the international community, and, importantly, to its position as the central government in the Australian federation. Consistent with the unique, federal character of the Commonwealth established by the *Constitution*, Mason J reasoned that the nationhood power could only support activities 'peculiarly adapted' to a national government and which could not otherwise be carried on for the national benefit, including by the states.[69] Therefore, in his dissent in the *AAP Case*, Mason J managed to formulate a category of executive power which struck a balance between ensuring that the Commonwealth Executive had the flexibility to function effectively as the national government, while maintaining the federal distribution of powers and responsibilities effected by the *Constitution*.

Thirteen years later, Mason J's formulation of the nationhood power in the *AAP Case* was endorsed in *Davis v Commonwealth* ('*Davis*').[70] By the time *Davis* was decided in 1988, Mason had been appointed Chief Justice of the High Court. During his tenure as Chief Justice, Mason's judgments would continue to be influenced by what McHugh J described as a particular 'attitude of mind' which was characterised by

> the belief that Australia was now an independent nation whose political, legal and economic underpinnings had recently and essentially changed. These developments outside the pages of the *Commonwealth Law Reports* required a different approach to the interpretation of the *Constitution* and a different approach to judging, generally.[71]

(Mason J) ('*Koowarta*'); *Commonwealth v Tasmania* (1983) 158 CLR 1, 124, 127 (Mason J) ('*Tasmanian Dam Case*'); *Davis* (1988) 166 CLR 79, 94–5 (Mason CJ, Deane and Gaudron JJ).

68 *AAP Case* (1975) 134 CLR 338, 396.

69 Ibid 397.

70 (1988) 166 CLR 79.

71 Justice Michael McHugh AC, 'The Constitutional Jurisprudence of the High Court: 1989–2004' (Speech delivered at the Inaugural Sir Anthony Mason Lecture in Constitutional Law, Sydney, 26 November 2004).

The enactment of the *Australia Acts* in 1986 by the Commonwealth and United Kingdom Parliaments just two years prior to *Davis*, formally severed Australia's remaining constitutional links with the United Kingdom,[72] which had 'been weakening for decades'.[73] Accordingly, when *Davis* was decided, Australia's status as a sovereign, independent nation continued to be a relevant factor in ascertaining the scope of the Commonwealth's executive power in its domestic application.[74] As Chief Justice of the Court, Mason was also able to command the support of other members of the bench who shared his 'attitude of mind'.

In *Davis*, Deane and Gaudron JJ joined with Mason CJ in finding that activities associated with the organisation and commemoration of the Australian Bicentenary fell within the 'peculiar province of the Commonwealth in its capacity as the national and federal government'.[75] These activities, which included the establishment of the Australian Bicentennial Corporation, were therefore supported by the nationhood power. In a separate judgment, Brennan J similarly found that Mason J's 'peculiarly adapted' test was an 'appropriate formulation of a criterion to determine whether an enterprise or activity lies within the executive power of the Commonwealth'.[76] Justice Brennan was of the view that a narrow construction of it would 'deny to the Australian people many of the symbols of nationhood – a flag or anthem . . . or the benefit of many national initiatives in science, literature and the arts'[77] and concluded that the Commonwealth's executive power extended to the commemoration of the Bicentenary.

The nationhood power was subsequently considered in the decision of *Pape*. This case concerned the validity of the one-off tax bonus payments made to individual taxpayers and the *Tax Bonus for Working Australians Act (No 2) 2009* (Cth), which comprised part of the Rudd Labor Government's response to the 'global financial crisis'. In his judgment, French CJ applied Mason J's test in the *AAP Case*, and confirmed that the Commonwealth's executive power extended to 'short-term fiscal measures to meet adverse economic conditions affecting the nation as a whole, where such measures are on their face *peculiarly* within the capacity and resources of the Commonwealth Government'.[78] In reaching this conclusion, French

72 *Sue v Hill* (1999) 199 CLR 462, 528 (Gaudron J); *Pape* (2009) 238 CLR 1, 84 (Gummow, Crennan and Bell JJ).

73 McHugh, above n 71.

74 *Davis* (1988) 166 CLR 79, 94 (Mason CJ, Deane and Gaudron JJ).

75 Ibid. 76 Ibid 111. 77 Ibid.

78 *Pape* (2009) 238 CLR 1, 63 (emphasis added).

CJ echoed the observations made by Mason J in the *AAP Case* that the executive power 'has to be capable of serving the proper purposes of a national government'[79] and accepted that s 61 included an area of inherent authority derived, at least in part, from 'the necessities of a modern national government'.[80] Expenditure of public funds aimed at 'avoiding or mitigating the large scale adverse effects' of a global financial crisis on the Australian economy was, in French CJ's opinion, a 'proper purpose' of national government.[81] However, the Chief Justice cautioned that this did not amount to a 'general power to manage the national economy'.[82]

Justices Gummow, Crennan and Bell similarly remarked that the Commonwealth Executive did not have power to engage in anything it regarded as being of 'national interest and concern'[83] but also accepted Mason J's formulation of the nationhood power in the *AAP Case*.[84] Their Honours likened the global financial crisis to a national emergency and concluded that the tax bonus payments were examples of activities 'peculiarly adapted to the government of a country and which otherwise could not be carried on for the public benefit'.[85]

The existence of the nationhood power as a dimension of executive power was approved by a majority of the High Court in *Williams*. *Williams* concerned a challenge to Commonwealth funding pursuant to the National School Chaplaincy Program ('NSCP'). Under this programme, which was not established or regulated by legislation, the Commonwealth entered into a funding agreement with Scripture Union Queensland for the provision of chaplaincy services to the Darling Heights State School in Queensland ('Funding Agreement'). While it did not fall directly for consideration, the Court held that the Funding Agreement and associated expenditure could not be supported by the nationhood power. It was not an activity which was 'peculiarly adapted' to the national government, as the states had the capacity to provide chaplaincy programmes in state schools. Furthermore, there was no crisis or emergency which, in this instance, justified the Commonwealth bypassing the states.[86]

In reaching this conclusion, the majority quoted with approval Mason J's formulation of the nationhood power in the *AAP Case*. Chief Justice French listed 'the inherent authority derived from the character and status of the Commonwealth as a national government' as one of five

[79] Ibid 60. [80] Ibid 60–1. [81] Ibid 63. [82] Ibid.
[83] Ibid 87–8. [84] Ibid. [85] Ibid 91–2.
[86] *Williams* (2012) 248 CLR 156, 235 (Gummow and Bell JJ), 240 (Hayne J), 346–7 (Crennan J), 362 (Kiefel J).

'accepted' categories of Commonwealth executive power.[87] The remainder, consisting of Gummow and Bell JJ, Crennan J and Kiefel J regarded it as settled that the executive power of the Commonwealth extends to activities 'peculiarly adapted' to the national government, which cannot otherwise be carried on for the public benefit.[88]

Justice Mason's dissent in the *AAP Case* is significant not only because the nationhood power has endured over time, but it continues to influence the High Court in the contemporary constitutional context. This was evident in *Williams v Commonwealth [No 2]* ('*Williams [No 2]*'),[89] where French CJ, Hayne, Kiefel, Bell and Keane JJ confirmed the existence of

> those aspects of executive power which might be referred to loosely as the Executive's power to deal with or respond to a national emergency (considered in *Pape*) or other matters of the kind commonly grouped under the heading 'nationhood'.[90]

Federalism

In the *AAP Case*, Mason J ultimately concluded that the AAP was not supported by the Commonwealth's executive power, including the nationhood aspect of it. The activities in question needed to be 'peculiarly adapted' to the national government *and* of such a character that they '[could not] otherwise be carried on for the benefit of the nation'. This second limb of Mason J's test required a consideration of whether the establishment and direct financing of the Regional Councils was the only way in which the Commonwealth could have implemented the AAP. Justice Mason answered this in the negative. In his view, it was a scheme which could have been effectively administered by the states.

Justice Mason's willingness to use federalism as a constraint on the scope of the Commonwealth's executive power contrasted with his wide interpretation of the Commonwealth's legislative powers.[91] However, this more cautious approach to executive power was consistent with what Sir Gerard Brennan described as a concern 'to diminish the possibility of

87 Ibid 184–5.

88 Ibid 250–1 (Gummow and Bell JJ), 342, 346, 348 (Crennan J), 370, 373 (Kiefel J).

89 (2014) 252 CLR 416.

90 Ibid 454.

91 See, eg, *Koowarta* (1982) 153 CLR 168; *Tasmanian Dam Case* (1983) 158 CLR 1. A similar point was made by Leslie Zines, 'Sir Anthony Mason' (2008) 28 *Federal Law Review* 171, 171.

abuse of power',[92] which could be traced back to Mason's appointment as Commonwealth Solicitor-General from 1964 until 1969.[93]

A reluctance to confer unbounded power on the Commonwealth was evident in Mason J's dissent, where he remarked that the Commonwealth's executive power 'is not unlimited'[94] and that its 'content'

> does not reach beyond the area of responsibilities allocated to the Commonwealth by the *Constitution*, responsibilities which are ascertainable from the distribution of powers, more particularly the distribution of legislative powers, effected by the *Constitution* itself and the character and status of the Commonwealth as a national government.[95]

This dictum has been influential in defining the outer limits of the Commonwealth's executive power, as evinced by its subsequent approval in the decisions of *R v Duncan; Ex parte Australian Iron and Steel Pty Ltd*,[96] *Davis*,[97] *R v Hughes*,[98] *Pape*[99] and *Williams*.[100]

Justice Mason went on to observe that the scope of the nationhood power, as an aspect of executive power, also needed to be consistent with the federal character of the polity from which it was derived. Justice Mason elaborated:

> It would be inconsistent with the broad division of responsibilities between the Commonwealth and the States achieved by the distribution of legislative powers to concede to this [nationhood] aspect of the executive power a wide operation effecting a radical transformation in what has hitherto been thought to be the Commonwealth's area of responsibility under the *Constitution*, thereby enabling the Commonwealth to carry out within Australia programmes standing outside the acknowledged heads of legislative power merely because these programmes can be conveniently formulated and administered by the national government.[101]

92 Brennan, above n 67. 93 Ibid. See also Zines, above n 91, 171–2.
94 (1975) 134 CLR 338, 396. 95 Ibid.
96 (1983) 158 CLR 535, 560 (Mason J).
97 (1988) 166 CLR 79, 93–4 (Mason CJ, Deane and Gaudron JJ).
98 (2000) 202 CLR 535, 554–5 (Gleeson CJ, Gaudron, McHugh, Gummow, Hayne and Callinan JJ).
99 (2009) 238 CLR 1, 63 (French CJ), 114, 115–16, 124 (Hayne and Kiefel JJ), 188–9 (Heydon J).
100 (2012) 248 CLR 156, 188 (French CJ), 156 (Gummow and Bell JJ), 251 (Hayne J), 303 (Heydon J), 356–7 (Crennan J), 371 (Kiefel J).
101 *AAP Case* (1975) 134 CLR 338, 398, quoted with approval in *Davis* (1988) 166 CLR 79, 103 (Wilson and Dawson JJ); *Pape* (2009) 238 CLR 1, 50 (French CJ), 117, 124 (Hayne and Kiefel JJ), 181, 187 (Heydon J); *Williams* (2012) 248 CLR 156, 303–4 (Heydon J), 348 (Crennan J), 371, 372 (Kiefel J).

As these passages reveal, the second limb of Mason J's test incorporates federalism as a constraint on the scope of the nationhood power. It confines the Commonwealth Executive to the areas of responsibility allocated to it by the *Constitution* and which are appropriate to its status as the national, and federal, government. The test requires the Court to consider whether, apart from the Commonwealth exercising its nationhood power, the activities could have been carried on for the national benefit. In answering this question, the High Court has consistently had regard to the capacity of the states to effectively engage in the activities in question.

In *Davis*, for example, Mason CJ, Deane and Gaudron JJ considered whether the states could have effectively organised and commemorated the Australian Bicentenary. They noted that while the states had a 'part to play, whether as part of an exercise in co-operative federalism or otherwise',[102] the 'interest of the States in the commemoration of the Bicentenary is of a more limited character'.[103] Indeed, they confirmed that the exercise of the Commonwealth's nationhood power would be clearest where it 'involves no real competition with State executive or legislative competence'.[104]

Similarly, Brennan J endorsed Mason J's formulation of the nationhood power, because it 'invites consideration of the sufficiency of the powers of the States to engage effectively in the enterprise or activity in question and of the need for national action (whether unilateral or in co-operation with the States) to secure the contemplated benefit'.[105] Although Brennan J thought it was 'arguable' that the commemoration was a 'State affair', as European settlement had first occurred in New South Wales, it had had 'undoubted significance for the whole of Australia'.[106] In Brennan J's view, it was more appropriate for the Commonwealth, as the national government, to celebrate an event of national significance such as the Bicentenary.

The influence of the federalism aspect of Mason J's dissent in the *AAP Case* is also evident in each of the judgments in *Pape*, even if the majority seemingly did not honour the second limb of Mason J's test in application. Four members of the Court in *Pape* found that the nationhood power supported the tax bonus payments. However, it has been argued by scholars[107] and members of the judiciary[108] alike that the Commonwealth could have stimulated the economy through other

102 *Davis* (1988) 166 CLR 79, 94. 103 Ibid. 104 Ibid.
105 Ibid 111. 106 Ibid 114. 107 See especially Twomey, above n 21, 330.
108 *Pape* (2009) 238 CLR 1, 123–4 (Hayne and Kiefel JJ); 178–9 (Heydon J).

means, namely, by enacting legislation under the taxation power in s 51(ii) or by increasing welfare payments under s 51(xxiiiA). Alternatively, the Commonwealth could have made conditional grants to the states under s 96 of the *Constitution*.[109]

A critical feature of the judgments of French CJ and Gummow, Crennan and Bell JJ, which relied on the nationhood power to support the payments, was the acceptance that the global financial crisis posed a threat to Australia's economic security, and that a swift response was necessary to prevent a national economic recession. Chief Justice French quoted with approval Mason J's remarks in the *AAP Case* about the need to confine the Commonwealth Executive to those areas of responsibility allocated to it by the *Constitution*, but took the view that the direct payments to taxpayers, as a short-term measure to respond to an urgent national economic problem, was not an interference with the federal distribution of powers.[110] In their joint judgment, Gummow, Crennan and Bell JJ considered whether the states could have responded effectively to the global financial crisis, but concluded that only the Commonwealth had the resources to respond expediently to the emergency before it.[111]

The influence of Mason J's dissent in the *AAP Case* is, therefore, still evident in *Pape*. It is significant that the majority felt compelled to explain why the states were not capable of addressing the immediate threat to the national economy posed by the global financial crisis. Furthermore, those members of the Court in *Pape* who did not rely on the nationhood power to support the Commonwealth's expenditure still referred approvingly to Mason J's dictum, which marked the outer limits of the Commonwealth's executive power.[112]

Justice Mason's dissent in the *AAP Case* has, however, found its fullest expression in *Williams*. A majority of the Court considered in that case whether the services covered by the NSCP fell within an area of responsibility allocated to the Commonwealth by the *Constitution*.[113] Justices Gummow and Bell referred approvingly to the observations made by Mason J on this point in the *AAP Case* and concluded that the states had the 'legal and practical capacity to provide for a scheme such as the

[109] Ibid 178–9; Twomey, above n 21, 330.

[110] *Pape* (2009) 238 CLR 1, 60. [111] Ibid 91.

[112] Ibid 114, 115–16, 124 (Hayne and Kiefel JJ), 181, 188–9 (Heydon J).

[113] For further discussions on federalism and Commonwealth executive power, see David Hume, Andrew Lynch and George Williams, 'Heresy in the High Court? Federalism as a Constraint on Commonwealth Power' (2013) 41 *Federal Law Review* 71; Appleby and McDonald, above n 29.

NSCP'.[114] Furthermore, their Honours were of the view that the conduct of the public school system in Queensland was the 'responsibility' of that state.[115]

Similar observations were made by Crennan J and Kiefel J in their respective judgments. They were of the view that the states were capable of providing the services covered by the NSCP, as underscored by Queensland's own funding scheme for school chaplaincy services. Furthermore, like the AAP, the NSCP could have been made the subject of a conditional grant to the states under s 96 of the *Constitution*.[116] Justice Crennan noted that there was no evidence to suggest that the Commonwealth was the level of government 'exclusively, best, or uniquely authorised'[117] to engage in this particular activity and was of the view that there was nothing to 'explain or justify . . . the bypassing of s 96'.[118] Justice Kiefel similarly observed that the funding for the NSCP could have been 'accommodated by grant on condition under s 96'.[119] She was satisfied that the NSCP fell within the 'province of the States'.[120] Accordingly, there was no justification for Commonwealth incursion into an area of state competence by executive action alone.

In *Williams [No 2]*, the majority joint judgment described the federal distribution of powers and functions between the Commonwealth and the states as being a 'basal consideration'.[121] It was acknowledged that the Commonwealth must 'possess all the powers that it needs in order to function as a polity'.[122] However, in a manner reminiscent of Mason J in the *AAP Case*, the joint judgment remarked that the Commonwealth has the character of a 'central polity of a federation in which independent governments exist in the one area and exercise powers in different fields of action carefully defined by law'.[123] Thus the vision of the Australian nation articulated by Mason J in 1975 was strongly endorsed by the Court almost 40 years later in *Williams [No 2]*.

Justice Mason was not prepared to embrace Whitlam's 'new federalism' in the *AAP Case*. Instead, he preferred to uphold the version of federalism provided for in the *Constitution* as an important check on the scope of the Commonwealth's executive power. Justice Mason's dissent reiterates the important role that the states play as active participants in a federation. For

114 *Williams* (2012) 248 CLR 156, 235. 115 Ibid.
116 Ibid 348 (Crennan J), 373 (Kiefel J). See also 270–1 (Hayne J). 117 Ibid 348.
118 Ibid. 119 Ibid 373. 120 Ibid.
121 (2014) 252 CLR 416, 469 (French CJ, Hayne, Kiefel, Bell and Keane JJ).
122 Ibid 467–8.
123 Ibid 469. See also *AAP Case* (1975) 134 CLR 338, 396–7 (Mason J).

him, the federal character of the Australian polity was not just a source of the nationhood power, but also an important constraint on it. This aspect of Mason J's dissent in the *AAP Case* continues to speak to the present-day High Court in its interpretation of the scope of Commonwealth executive power.

V Conclusion

A dissent which has not only endured for over 40 years, but been elevated to represent the majority position of the High Court is worthy of the title of a 'great Australian dissent'. Justice Mason's judgment in the *AAP Case* reconceptualised our understanding of Commonwealth executive power. It is now generally accepted that the Commonwealth is conferred with a nationhood power and that its scope needs to be ascertained having regard to the federal character of the Australian polity established by the *Constitution.*

However, the significance of the dissent cannot be measured solely by reference to its subsequent adoption by the High Court. In the *AAP Case*, Mason J drew on Australia's national status and federal character to aid his interpretation of the *Constitution.* Therefore, while this dissent has certainly made a substantial and enduring contribution to this complex area of constitutional law, it also occupies an important place within Australia's broader independence movement. As such, it is not merely a 'great dissent' – but truly a great *Australian* dissent.

11

Justice Murphy's Dissent in *Australian Conservation Foundation v Commonwealth* (1980): The Birth of Public Interest Standing in Australia?

MATTHEW GROVES

I Introduction

Justice Murphy once labelled standing 'a judicial invention'.[1] He was right. Standing is a malleable concept that allows judges to regulate and restrict public access to the courts.[2] Standing principles in administrative law reflect decades of collective judicial thinking that make it difficult to discern the views of particular judges but every so often a case presents the opportunity for significant change. Whether judges adopt or reject any change to the rules of standing, their very consideration of the issue reveals much about their personal attitudes to the nature of public law litigation. The best modern example in the High Court is *Australian Conservation Foundation v Commonwealth* ('*ACF*').[3] A majority of the court flatly rejected submissions to relax common law standing rules. The majority doubted the interest claimed by the conservation group and its underlying arguments that public interest groups should play a greater role in ensuring governments act lawfully. Justice Murphy dissented in typically crisp terms, holding that the Australian Conservation Fund ('ACF') had a sufficient interest to commence judicial review proceedings and a legitimate role to play in public governance. He rejected suggestions the ACF was a mere 'busybody', a fearsome but rarely seen creature of administrative law that makes even stoic judges tremble. Justice Murphy proceeded on the (then) far-sighted assumption that public interest groups could

1 *Onus v Alcoa of Australia Ltd* (1981) 149 CLR 27, 44.

2 Carol Harlow and Richard Rawlings describe standing as a 'rationing device': Carol Harlow and Richard Rawlings, *Law and Administration* (Cambridge University Press, 3rd ed, 2009) 694.

3 (1980) 146 CLR 493.

play a constructive role in public life and public law, which should not be frustrated by restrictive standing rules.

Thirty-five years later, *ACF* remains good law. Conservation and other public interest groups still struggle to establish standing. They must prove they are not busybodies and that their activities are legitimate in the eyes of the courts. Those requirements are not easy to meet. But on closer inspection, *ACF* remains good law in name only. The approach of Murphy J has clearly won the day. Public interest groups can establish standing if they satisfy a court that they perform the goals Murphy J envisaged for them. What makes the triumph of Murphy J so remarkable is that it occurred in the lower courts. Before examining *ACF* and its consequences, however, it is useful to examine notions of dissent and the evolution of standing.

II Some Thoughts on Dissent

There are many theories on dissent but none seem wholly honest. In my view, judges, lawyers and legal academics like dissent because of our training in the adversarial common law technique. The common law is grounded in evolutionary and incremental reasoning. For that reason, its very life depends on dissent. Unless new principles are plucked out of the air, there must be different strands of reasoning within existing principles and cases to fuel the organic growth of the common law.[4] Dissenting judgments offer an important source from which judges can adopt new principles or amend existing ones.[5] Academics are equally dependent on dissenting judgments because disagreement and diversity of opinion within and between courts provides raw material to satisfy the intellectual curiosity at the heart of academic life.

I am not greatly attached to academic writing about dissents and judgment writing except, perhaps, my own. Professor Russell Smyth and I examined High Court judgments over a century and found the only clear

[4] Dissenting opinions can also inform Parliament. See, eg, Lord Robert Walker, 'Developing the Common Law: How Far is Too Far?' (2013) 37 *Melbourne University Law Review* 232, 249–50, where Lord Walker notes that the dissent of Lord Rodger in *Barker v Corus UK Ltd* [2006] 2 AC 572, 606–8, was essentially adopted within a few weeks of publication of the judgment by insertion of s 3 of the *Compensation Act 2006* (UK) c 29.

[5] Andrew Lynch notes that separate concurring opinions perform a similar function by providing an 'acceptable face' of disagreement and hints of possible change: Andrew Lynch, 'Dissent: The Rewards and Risks of Judicial Disagreement in the High Court of Australia' (2003) 27 *Melbourne University Law Review* 724, 749–52.

trend was their increased length over time.[6] We also found the level of joint, concurring and dissenting opinions varied considerably over time. Those variations were, surprisingly, not clearly linked to the increasing length of judgments. In related research, my co-author found dissent rates in the High Court varied greatly over time. Smyth attributed that to the combined effect of several factors, particularly: the style and influence of each Chief Justice; the perceived acceptability of dissent at any time; the caseload of the High Court; and the enactment of the *Australian Act 1986* (Cth) and *Australia Act 1986* (UK).[7] These findings suggest the level of dissents within the High Court depends on the combined effect of all such factors at any time. In fact, further research reveals the level of dissents in courts is due to more subtle processes.

Competing bodies of American literature on dissenting judgment writing are often divided into two schools. The 'attitudinal model' seeks to explain why judges dissent by reference to their personal background, such as their socio-economic class and political and other ideology.[8] The 'institutional model' seeks to explain why judges dissent by reference to institutional factors and other external (ie, non-personal) factors. Institutional factors that have been studied include the caseload of a court, the leadership (or lack of it) within the court,[9] and whether the court is intermediate or one of final appeal. The external factors examined under this institutional rubric include government spending, and the levels of industrialisation and urbanisation at the time.[10] As many American jurisdictions elect their judicial officers, several studies have examined electoral issues as a possible motivation in judicial behaviour.[11] When Smyth examined if these approaches explained dissent rates in the High Court of Australia, he concluded that neither appeared decisive but both

6 Matthew Groves and Russell Smyth, 'A Century of Judicial Style: Changing Patterns in Judgment Writing on the High Court 1903–2004' (2004) 32 *Federal Law Review* 255.

7 Russell Smyth, 'What Explains Variations in Dissent Rates? Time Series Evidence from the High Court' (2004) 26 *Sydney Law Review* 221.

8 Orley Ashenfelter, Theodore Eisenberg and Stewart Schwab, 'Politics and the Judiciary: The Influence of Judicial Backgrounds on Case Outcomes' (1995) 24 *Journal of Legal Studies* 257.

9 American research shows this issue is particularly influential in decision-making in the United States Supreme Court. See, eg, Stacia Haynie, 'Leadership and Consensus on the US Supreme Court' (1992) 54 *Journal of Politics* 1158.

10 Roger Handberg, 'Leadership in State Courts of Last Resort: The Interaction of Environment and Procedure' (1978) 19 *Jurimetrics* 178; Paul Brace and Melinda Hall, 'Neo-Institutionalism and Dissent in State Supreme Courts' (1990) 52 *Journal of Politics* 54.

11 Melinda Hall, 'Electoral Politics and Strategic Voting in State Supreme Courts' Order in the Courts: A Neo-In' (1992) 54 *Journal of Politics* 427.

seemed influential.[12] His study did, however, suggest that caseloads and real GDP per capita both clearly influenced dissent rates. The obvious reason for the former was that judges become less willing and able to write separate opinions as their court becomes busier. The latter reason is explicable by a correlation between rising income and litigation, which increases the caseload of most courts.

Smyth then considered whether a 'consensual norm' operated within the High Court. A consensual norm is a long run (or long term) outcome that underpins the interaction between individuals and reflects their common understanding of acceptable behaviour in particular circumstances. There is a difference between consensus and a consensual norm. The existence of a consensual norm does not mean there is agreement within an institution such as a court, and therefore a low level of dissent, only that there is a norm.[13] A consensual norm can be one of actual consensus, such as the trends apparent by the strikingly high level of unanimity in decisions of the Supreme Court of Canada.[14] But it may just as equally explain high levels of dissent. When Smyth examined this concept, he initially found no 'consensual norm' existed within the High Court during the 20th century. One did not exist because one had never emerged.[15] Smyth revised that finding with a more subtle investigation which found a long tradition of individualism within the High Court, at least when compared to an institution such as its American counterpart. That meant there was long a consensual norm in the High Court which tolerated, arguably even encouraged, judges writing separate concurring or dissenting opinions.[16]

Two standing cases neatly illustrate that principle. In *ACF*, the four majority judges each delivered separate opinions rather than a single joint judgment. In *Argos Pty Ltd v Corball* ('*Argos*') in 2014,[17] five judges delivered three opinions, all holding that the key applicants had standing.

[12] Paresh Narayan and Russell Smyth, 'What Explains Dissent on the High Court of Australia? An Empirical Assessment Using a Cointegration and Error Correction Approach' (2007) 4 *Journal of Empirical Legal Studies* 401.

[13] An influential American study is Gregory Caldeira and Christopher Zorn, 'On Time and Consensual Norms in the Supreme Court' (1998) 42 *American Journal of Political Science* 874.

[14] Canadian research is examined in Emmett Macfarlane, 'Consensus and Unanimity at the Supreme Court of Canada' (2010) 52 *Supreme Court Law Review* 379.

[15] Russell Smyth, 'Historical Consensual Norms in the High Court' (2002) 37 *Australian Journal of Political Science* 255.

[16] Paresh Narayan and Russell Smyth, 'The Consensual Norm of the High Court of Australia 1904–2001' (2005) 26 *International Political Science Review* 147.

[17] (2014) 254 CLR 394.

Only Gageler J would have issued slightly different orders because his acceptance of the standing of one applicant was rejected by all other members of the Court. That small difference meant *Argos*, like *ACF*, could have been disposed by two judgments – one of the four-member majority and separate reasons by Gageler J. If we ask why the Court delivered three or five different sets of reasons rather than two, Smyth's findings suggest the answer is not simply that the absence of a consensual norm signals a tradition within the High Court against fewer rather than more separate judgments. It is also that the fragmented reasons in these and other cases *is* the norm in the High Court. Once it is understood that the High Court has traditionally had a consensual norm for a lack of consensus, one can question whether the presence of dissenting judgments has the same significance it does in otherwise comparable courts.[18] The widely held view of the dissenting judge as the one who stands apart is true in the literal sense, but wider trends in the High Court suggest such judges are not unusual. The consensual norm in the High Court may, ironically, suggest that an individualist judge is more likely to participate in joint opinions rather than write separate or dissenting ones.

III The Functions of Standing

The value of standing is typically assumed rather than explained. Douglas has noted the judicial reasons for standing are 'rarely persuasive'.[19] Even so, there are clear arguments for standing. A functional one has long held sway. As one member of the Federal Court explained, standing rules

> ensure that applicants only litigate their own business. For an applicant to have standing demands a connection between the applicant's interests and the relief sought. As a general rule the Court will not recognise busybodies who interfere in things that do not concern them.[20]

Such statements reflect the purpose of standing rules and the courts' role in their enforcement. Standing rules ensure applicants mind their own business and stay out of the business of others. The courts are cast in the role of gatekeeper and maintain the boundaries demarcated by standing rules. This conception of standing says nothing about the legality of decisions. An unlawful decision may stand if no-one has standing to

[18] Such arguments are considered by Lynch, above n 5, 756–9.

[19] Roger Douglas, 'Use of Standing Rules 1980–2006' (2006) 14 *Australian Journal of Administrative Law* 22, 23.

[20] *Hussein v Secretary of the Department of Immigration and Multicultural and Indigenous Affairs* [2006] FCA 286, [46] (Graham J).

challenge it. This possibility does not sit well with the rule of law but that doctrine can be deployed in different ways. The rule of law could require relaxed standing rules, even none at all, to maximise the ability of the courts to strike down unlawful decisions. But the rule of law may also justify standing principles, even strict ones, because cases where standing presents problems may also not involve a real controversy between the parties.[21]

Casting aside rule of law considerations, the filtering function of standing weakens on closer inspection. That filtering function is typically justified by the spectre of the busybody. This superficially attractive concept can be traced to Lord Denning, but his use of the term was just one paradox about the man himself.[22] After all, Lord Denning was a judicial busybody who invented new principles or remedies to assist parties with whom he sympathised.[23] His phobia of busybodies sat uneasily with his quixotic attempts to radically alter standing rules, by allowing parties who lacked standing to seek review of the Attorney-General's refusal to grant a fiat to commence proceedings.[24] All this while he stood guard against busybodies who might sneak into the courts.[25]

A better justification of standing rules is their potential to improve the quality of litigation. Justice Murphy conceded that in *Attorney-General (Cth) ex rel McKinlay v Commonwealth*.[26] The underlying assumption is the value of self-interest. Those with a personal stake in a case will provide the best evidence to a court. But in *Ogle v Strickland* Wilcox J suggested that to accept

> competitive instincts are aroused only by concern for material wealth would be to ignore history. Much of the progress of mankind has been

[21] A point Hayne J conceded in *Re McBain; Ex parte Catholic Bishops Conference* (2002) 209 CLR 372, 459.

[22] Lord Denning used the phrase in *A-G of the Gambia v N'Jai* [1961] AC 617, 634.

[23] An example is the 'legitimate expectation', which described interests falling short of a clear right. In *Minister for Immigration and Ethnic Affairs v Teoh* (1995) 183 CLR 273, 310–1, McHugh J suggested this was 'invented' by Lord Denning in *Schmidt v Secretary of State for Home Affairs* [1969] 2 Ch 149, 170–1. The doctrine actually has a long European heritage. Lord Denning imported rather than invented it, though he deserves much blame for subsequent problems caused by the inexact nature of legitimate expectations in public law.

[24] *A-G ex rel McWhirter v Independent Broadcasting Authority* [1973] QB 629. That novel finding was rejected in *Gouriet v Union of Postal Workers* [1978] AC 435.

[25] Other judges are also mindful of busybodies. See *Byron Environment Centre Inc v Arakwal People* (1997) 78 FCR 1, 45 (Merkel J).

[26] (1975) 135 CLR 1, 76, citing *Baker v Carr*, 369 US 186, 204 (1962).

> achieved by people who have sacrificed their own material interests in order to champion ideals against fierce resistance. The recent Australian experience is that, in cases where ideologues have been able to gain access to the courts, cases have been hard fought and professionally conducted.[27]

Justice Murphy acknowledged that possibility in *ACF* when he reasoned that claims brought by representative groups in public interest proceedings in the United States had made a 'real contribution' to the level of environmental protection in that country.[28]

IV The Evolution and Reform of Standing before *ACF*

Standing has a chequered history in public law. For many centuries the prerogative and equitable remedies at the heart of supervisory review had different standing tests.[29] For a long time only the Attorney-General could seek remedies to enforce public duties but the rapidly expanding nature and number of those duties during the 19th century led to changes. The common law slowly allowed other people to enforce public duties.[30] A useful modern starting point is the influential decision of *Boyce v Paddington Borough Council* ('*Boyce*'), where Buckley J held private individuals could sue in relation to the performance (or non-performance) of public duties in two instances.[31] These were:

> first, where the interference with the public right is such as that some private right of his is at the same time interfered with... and, secondly, where no private right is interfered with, but the plaintiff, in respect of his public right, suffers special damage peculiar to himself from the interference with the public right.[32]

This reasoning places private rights in a privileged position by accepting that the decisions of public officials affecting those rights will invariably provide standing to the disaffected right holder. Indeed, the very

27 *Ogle v Strickland* (1987) 71 ALR 41, 58.

28 (1980) 146 CLR 493, 558.

29 Except habeas corpus, which has no standing requirement: Mark Aronson and Matthew Groves, *Judicial Review of Administrative Action* (Thomson Reuters, 5th ed, 2013) 761.

30 That meant aspects of standing were uncertain when the *Constitution* was drafted: *Truth About Motorways Pty Ltd v Macquarie Infrastructure Investment Management Ltd* (2000) 200 CLR 591, 627–8 (Gummow J).

31 [1903] 1 Ch 109. The decision at first instance was influential because the appellate decisions of the Court of Appeal and House of Lords did not disturb its basic reasoning. See *Boyce v Paddington Borough Council* [1903] 2 Ch 556; *Boyce v Paddington Borough Council* [1906] AC 1.

32 *Boyce* [1903] 1 Ch 109 114.

description of such actions as ones that 'interfere' with private rights separates and prioritises them over public rights. It accepts public rights as a possible foundation for standing but in a narrow sense only. The public right must be affected differently to, or must be greater than, that held by other members of the public. A public right that must be different to one held by the public has caused much conceptual trouble. Additionally, the approach of Buckley J gives no clear guidance on how, or how much more affected, a person must be compared to others to suffer 'special damage'. The vital issue is perhaps then not 'special damage' but whether there is 'sufficient damage' or affectation to satisfy the test.

This special damage test was confirmed before the great expansion in the scope and depth of supervisory review in the middle of the 20th century. As that century unfolded, old restrictions on the duty to observe the rules of natural justice fell away and fairness extended to a vast range of public decisions.[33] The courts' reluctance to restrict the scope of review became even clearer as they accepted the important question was not the status of decision makers but the source of their power.[34] Standing rules remained almost unchanged. The key requirement of *Boyce* – some sort of special or different damage on the part of an applicant – remained.

Although the common law hardly moved in Australia before *ACF*, Parliament had been active. Just before *ACF* commenced, standing rules were reformed at the federal level by the *Administrative Decisions (Judicial Review) Act 1977* (Cth) ('*ADJR Act*'). That Act was part of the (then) new administrative law package that saw the introduction of a federal Ombudsman and the Administrative Appeals Tribunal ('AAT') and then freedom of information legislation. The Federal Court of Australia was created to exercise original jurisdiction over the new judicial review scheme and appellate jurisdiction from the AAT. Murphy championed these reforms during his tenure as Attorney-General, though most had bi-partisan support.[35] Standing rules were also greatly reformed in these changes.

[33] The widening scope of natural justice is explained in Aronson and Groves, above n 29, 405–12.

[34] Such reasoning allowed judicial review of decisions made under exercise of prerogative powers: *R v Toohey; Ex parte Northern Land v Council* (1981) 151 CLR 170; *FAI Insurances Ltd v Winneke* (1982) 151 CLR 342.

[35] The ALP Government enacted the *Administrative Appeals Tribunal Act 1975* (Cth). The subsequent conservative government enacted the *Ombudsman Act 1976* (Cth), the *ADJR Act*, the *Federal Court of Australia Act 1976* (Cth) and the *Freedom of Information Act 1982* (Cth).

Murphy oversaw the *Administrative Appeals Tribunal Act 1975* (Cth) ('*AAT Act*'), which introduced a simple standing test. Section 27(1) of that Act allows any person whose 'interests are affected' by a decision to seek review of it in the AAT.[36] That unremarkable requirement largely codified existing standing rules but a further clause provided that representative groups would be 'taken to have interests that are affected by a decision if the decision relates to a matter included in the objects or purposes of the organization or association'.[37] This simple standing rule for representative bodies was radical because it equated the objects or purposes of a relevant body with the notion of 'affected' or 'aggrieved'. The test is broad because it applies to bodies 'whether incorporated or not'.[38] This test aligned standing requirements for associations and individuals by providing that both had standing if their interests were 'affected'. Importantly, the connection drawn between the purposes of an association's objects and its being affected swept aside the historical, technical problems those groups faced in establishing standing. The new AAT standing test included protection against misuse, which could occur if those who lacked standing established a body with purposes or objects relating to a decision they wished to challenge, by providing that the relaxed standing test did not apply to bodies formed after the decision was made or ones that existed but relevantly altered their purposes or objects after the decision.[39]

The quite different standing test in the *ADJR Act* allowed review of decisions by people who 'are aggrieved'.[40] The *ADJR Act* made no special provision for representative bodies. It is not clear why two statutes arising from the same programme of institutional reform to public administration, and enacted only two years apart, contained such different standing rules. The most likely reason is that no-one noticed at the time. Another might be that the new administrative law package was driven by imperatives of greater 'public accountability of government and administrative justice for the individual'.[41] If this new regime was focused on greater administrative accountability and justice for individuals,[42] the neglected

[36] Administrative Appeals Tribunal Act 1975 (Cth) s 27(1).

[37] Ibid s 27(2). [38] Ibid. [39] Ibid s 27(3).

[40] The phrase 'a person aggrieved' is adopted in ss 5, 6 and 7 of the *ADJR Act* and defined in s 3(4).

[41] Robin Creyke and John McMillian, 'Administrative Law Assumptions' in Robin Creyke and John McMillan (eds), *The Kerr Vision of Australian Administrative Law – At the Twenty-Five Year Mark* (Centre for International and Public Law, 1998) 2.

[42] It has been suggested the new administrative law changed 'the balance of authority between *the citizen* and the state in a way the common law never recognised': J J Spigelman,

position of groups was unsurprising. In any case, the newly minted *ADJR Act* and its standing test did not commence operation until 1 October 1980, which was several months after *ACF* was heard in early 1979, so the High Court proceeded without any reference to the statutory judicial review scheme about to recast federal judicial review.

The Administrative Review Council recently recognised the benefits the simpler standing test of the AAT could provide to representative and public interest groups and recommended its adoption in the *ADJR Act*.[43] The Council found the AAT provision had operated without difficulty for over two decades and might therefore provide a useful model to overcome the persistent standing problems that public interest groups faced in statutory judicial review. That suggestion has not been adopted by the Commonwealth or any of several other states and territories which have enacted judicial review statutes modelled on the federal one. The very different tests for the standing of public interest and other representative groups, and the clear refusal of Australian governments to extend the broader test of the AAT provision to judicial review, explains why the difficulties environmental and other public interest groups face in establishing standing in judicial review have never arisen in federal merits review.[44]

V The Decision in *ACF*

ACF arose from technical challenges to a development proposed for Farnborough in central Queensland. The developer was a Japanese company, Iwasaki Sangyo, which required approvals under environmental and banking legislation. Iwasaki Sangyo prepared a draft environmental impact statement, about which ACF submitted detailed comments. Six days after the time for public comment ended, the Minister announced the required approvals would be granted. Iwasaki Sangyo then prepared what it termed a 'final' environmental impact statement, though by then the key approvals had clearly been made. ACF argued the draft statement failed to comply with mandatory legislative requirements and these flaws were not cured by the final statement. It commenced judicial review

'Foundations of Administrative Law: Toward General Principles of Institutional Law' (1999) 58 *Australian Journal of Public Administration* 3, 8 (emphasis added).

43 Administrative Review Council, *Federal Judicial Review in Australia* (Report No 50, 2012) 146–51.

44 Notably, none of the state merits review tribunals have a standing test for groups similar to the AAT legislation.

proceedings, claiming these flaws made the subsequent approvals invalid and a nullity.

The High Court's Aickin J held the ACF lacked standing and dismissed its claim without considering the substantive issues. The case proceeded to the Full Court solely on the question of ACF's standing.[45] The ACF claimed standing on two separate arguments, both of which failed. First, the ACF argued that the High Court should 'disregard the existing authorities' and sanction open standing.[46] That would enable 'any private citizen to enforce public duties unless the court considers it inadvisable that the action should be allowed to proceed'.[47] A majority of the High Court held that such a radical step was one for Parliament to take.[48] That may at first seem odd, but not when one considers the radical reforms to administrative law explained above, which were made not long before *ACF* was heard. Justices Stephen and Mason noted those reforms may not have ended, at least in the area of standing, because the Australian Law Reform Commission was investigating standing at that very time.[49]

The second basis of the ACF's claim to standing rested on a modified version of the special interest test but this was also rejected by a majority of the High Court.[50] The majority modified the second limb of the *Boyce* test so that standing could be granted to people with a special interest in the subject matter of the case rather than the special damage.[51] The difficulty for ACF lay in the finer details of what might support such an interest. The influential judgment of Gibbs J declared the special interest test required an applicant to demonstrate more than a 'mere intellectual or emotional concern'.[52] A person could not establish a special interest

> unless he is likely to gain some advantage, other than the satisfaction of righting a wrong, upholding a principle or winning a contest, if his action

45 Justice Gibbs examined the legislation governing the Reserve Bank's approval of foreign exchange transactions and held it did not create private rights or public duties that were enforceable per se: *ACF* (1980) 146 CLR 493, 520–5.

46 Ibid 528.

47 Ibid.

48 Ibid 529 (Gibbs J), 540 (Stephen J), 552 (Mason J). The High Court has confirmed legislation granting open standing is constitutionally permissible: *Truth About Motorways Pty Ltd v Macquarie Infrastructure Investment Management Ltd* (2000) 200 CLR 591.

49 *ACF* (1980) 146 CLR 540 (Stephen J), 552 (Mason J).

50 Ibid 527 (Gibbs J), 547 (Mason J).

51 In *Onus v Alcoa of Australia Ltd* (1981) 149 CLR 27, 69–70, Brennan J noted that the special interest requirement in *ACF* was wider than the special damage one of *Boyce*.

52 *ACF* (1980) 146 CLR 493, 530. Justice Mason similarly remarked that 'a mere belief or concern, however genuine, does not in itself constitute a sufficient locus standi': at 548. See also at 539 (Stephen J).

Table 11.1 *Popular Concern about the Environment 1978–1993 (per cent)*

Year	1978	1980	1982	1983	1985	1986	1988	1989	1990	1992	1993
Most important issue	4	4	4	4	2	4	5	26	27	20	21

> succeeds or to suffer some disadvantage, other than a sense of grievance or a debt for costs, if his action fails. A belief, however strongly felt, that the law generally, or a particular law, should be observed, or that conduct of a particular kind should be prevented, does not suffice to give its possessor locus standi.[53]

According to this view, the role of the ACF as the leading national conservation body, its dedication to environmental issues as evidenced in its objects of association and its participation in the consultation process were not sufficient to provide standing.[54] That was because the crucial issues was not who or what the ACF was, but whether and how it might be adversely affected by the decision.

The reasoning of the majority in *ACF* implicitly downplays the strength of environmental concerns. Whatever one may think of that implication, it clearly aligned with public opinion of that time. Crook and Pakulski examined polling data relating to the level of concern about conservation issues among Australian voters from the late 1970s to the mid-1990s and found that environmental concerns were very low until the very end of the 1980s.[55] At that point, environmental concerns became much stronger and seemed to persist, though vary, from then on. Crook and Pakulski rated popular concern about the environment in percentage terms as shown in Table 11.1[56]

The data in Table 11.1 suggest environmental concerns did not rate highly among Australian voters until the very end of the 1980s. Later parts of this chapter show that the late 1980s was when courts became much more receptive to the standing claims of environmental groups. These cases eschewed the statistical evidence collated by Crook and Pakulski and instead placed weight on vague notions about the perceived public

[53] Ibid 530 (Gibbs J). [54] Ibid 531–2.

[55] Stephen Crook and Jan Pakulski, 'Shades of Green: Public Opinion on Environmental Issues in Australia' (1995) 30 *Australian Journal of Political Science* 39.

[56] Ibid 43.

acceptance of the role of environmental groups in public interest litigation. A good example occurred in another case involving the ACF, decided in 1989, the very year Crook and Pakulski detected a sudden jump in the perceived public importance of environmental concerns. Justice Davies reasoned:

> the community at the present time expect that there will be a body such as the ACF to concern itself with this particular issue and expects the ACF to act in the public interest to put forward a conservation viewpoint as a counter to the viewpoint of economic exploitation.[57]

This passage presumes what we now know to be true – the public values environmental concerns – but whether the public expects or wants a public interest group such as the ACF to protect those interests is more speculative. How a judge might know that is even more mysterious. The difference in the approach of Davies J and that of Murphy J, explained below, is that the latter was comfortable in making clear that he favoured an expansive standing test because *he* thought that was appropriate. Justice Davies instead rested on the time-honoured tactic of common law judges, explaining his decision to refine the law by reference to the attitudes of others rather than his own.

VI The Absence of Chief Justice Barwick – The Second Possible Dissent in *ACF*?

Before considering Murphy J's dissent, it is worth reflecting that there could easily have been a second dissent in *ACF*. Chief Justice Barwick did not preside in that case. The possibility that Barwick CJ might have dissented would surprise many observers because it is fair to say that Barwick CJ and Murphy J seemed polar opposites. Murphy was a radical reformer during his time as Attorney-General and his policies regularly enraged Barwick. One example was Murphy's comprehensive programme of federally funded legal aid, which Barwick thought posed 'a serious threat to the administration of law'.[58] But the two had superficial similarities.

[57] *Australian Conservation Foundation v Minister for Resources* (1989) 19 ALD 70, 74. That more receptive approach to the role of the ACF and comparable groups led Davies J to accept ACF's standing. However, in the same case he denied standing to a landowner whose property adjoined the site where a disputed development would occur, even though the amenity of that landowner would be diminished by the decision under challenge.

[58] United Kingdom, *Royal Commission on Legal Services*, Cmnd 7648 (1979) 13 (evidence of Sir Garfield Barwick). Ferocious conservative attacks on the establishment of Legal Aid in the 1970s are recounted in Keith Scott, *Gareth Evans* (Allen & Unwin, 1999) 88–9.

Both had served as Attorney-General for the Commonwealth (though on different sides of politics). Both were distinguished former barristers (though Barwick much more so). The similarities seemed to end there but, like Murphy, Barwick was something of a renegade. In keeping with that trait, Barwick had assumed an unexpected role: for many years, he was President of the ACF.[59] Barwick cherished the role because he opposed large scale and ugly developments. He also felt that areas of great natural beauty such as the Great Barrier Reef had an inherent value that should be preserved for future generations. That stance would have been unusual for any leading figure in Australian life in the 1960s. For a leading conservative, it was astonishing. Barwick remained President of the ACF until the early 1970s, when the organisation moved into open political activism. At that point, both the organisation and Barwick attracted increasingly harsh criticism from conservatives.

Barwick affirmed his own conservatism with aplomb when he resigned the position. He fended off many eminent Australians who craved the role and persuaded the Duke of Edinburgh to succeed him, despite the objections of the conservative cabinet.[60] At the time of *ACF*,[61] the rule against bias would not have caused the automatic disqualification of Barwick CJ but would instead have required a messy argument about whether his past association with the ACF made him a 'judge in his own cause'.[62] Although Barwick CJ had relinquished his ACF role, his long and ardent leadership would have allowed only one answer if he had tried to sit in *ACF*. We can only wonder how Barwick CJ might have balanced his inherent conservatism and passion for conservation if the bias rule had not clearly forced his hand.

VII The Dissent of Justice Murphy

Justice Murphy delivered a short dissent, holding that the ACF had standing. He also questioned the need for standing in all cases and even the very basis of the special interest test. At a superficial level, his Honour's dissent was notable for two qualities – it was short and made several references to

[59] David Marr, *Barwick* (Allen & Unwin, 1980) 235.

[60] Marr concludes the Duke of Edinburgh's acceptance of the role stroked Barwick's ego by implying that no mere Australian could replace him: ibid 237.

[61] At this time, automatic disqualification for bias was required only when judges held a pecuniary interest in the case: *Dimes v Grant Junction Canal* (1852) 3 HLC 759. The automatic disqualification rule was discarded in *Ebner v Official Trustee* (2000) 205 CLR 337.

[62] *Dickason v Edwards* (1910) 10 CLR 243, 259.

scholarly articles about American law. These aspects of Murphy J's reasons are entirely consistent with his wider style of writing judgments. He frequently made much more use of academic and comparative sources than other High Court judges.[63] His Honour's decisions were also consistently among the shortest in the Court's history.[64]

The more substantive elements of Murphy J's dissent included his dismissal of the 'floodgates' argument that liberal standing would see the courts 'overwhelmed with litigants'.[65] Justice Murphy accepted the submissions of the ACF based on the American experience, which suggested that people were not anxious to rush into the courts particularly over trivial matters. The American experience demonstrated that public interest litigants were likely to make a real and significant contribution to environmental protection and that many of their cases would be brought to trial quicker than others.[66] The floodgates argument is closely associated with the 'mere busybody' explained above because it is typically deployed in caution against the horde of busybodies who will swamp the courts with frivolous claims. Justice Murphy's doubts about that possibility were vindicated by the analysis by Douglas of standing cases over 27 years, beginning with the year *ACF* was decided. Douglas found no evidence to support the existence of busybodies.[67]

Another substantive suggestion of Murphy J was that parties to whom a decision-maker had a duty to provide natural justice should have standing.[68] Justice Murphy reasoned that, if legislation provided people with a right to be heard, or to make submissions or comments, it was 'not sensible to deny standing to members of the public to enforce rules under the Act by which Parliament has provided they shall be consulted'.[69] This statement foreshadowed the expansion of the duty to observe the requirements of natural justice, which began shortly after *ACF*. Justice Murphy was right to stress the relevance of legislation on this issue because it is clear that applicants in many public interest cases may not have a right to be heard but may still have standing.[70] Nonetheless, the connection between standing and the duty to observe the rules of natural justice both

[63] Russell Smyth, 'Other Than "Accepted Sources of Law?" A Quantitative Study of Secondary Source Citation in the High Court' (1999) 22 *University of New South Wales Law Journal* 19.

[64] Groves and Smyth, above n 6, 277.

[65] *ACF* (1980) 146 CLR 493, 557.

[66] Ibid 557–8.

[67] Douglas, above n 19.

[68] *ACF* (1980) 146 CLR 493, 556–7.

[69] Ibid 557.

[70] See, eg, the statement to this effect of Lehane J in *Botany Bay City Council v Minister of State for Transport and Regional Development* (1996) 66 FCR 537, 568, quoted in *Griffith University v Tang* (2005) 221 CLR 99, 118 (Gummow, Callinan and Heydon JJ).

came to be explained by reference to notions of affectation of the party seeking the benefit of the doctrine.[71] In the landmark case of *Kioa v West*, Brennan J accepted that 'it is right to equate the interest which tends to attract the protection of the principles of natural justice with the interest which, if affected, gives standing at common law to seek a public law remedy'.[72]

The most important part of Justice Murphy's dissent is the most neglected. This was his holistic assessment of the reasons for which he concluded the ACF had standing. His Honour listed the many features the ACF offered in support of claim for standing. These were that: it was long-standing and well known before the decision it sought to challenge had been made; it had 6500 members; it regularly made submissions to governments and public agencies about environmental issues; it often received funding from governments to further its work; and the comments and submissions of the ACF were regularly included in environmental impact statements made pursuant to the legislation under which the challenged decision was made. Justice Murphy also made reference to the objects of the ACF organisation, as if to suggest that its objects of seeking to protect the environment were clearly relevant to its standing.[73]

The list of factors considered by Murphy J are almost identical to those devised by Sackville J 14 years later in the landmark case of *North Coast Environmental Council Inc v Minister for Resources* ('*North Coast*') in the Federal Court of Australia.[74] That case adopted what is often described as a multifactorial approach to determine standing, particularly in environmental cases. Justice Murphy devised all but the name of that test which eventually came to reshape and recognise the standing of public interest groups in Australia. *North Coast* marked the adoption of the approach of Murphy J, though Sackville J was careful to make clear that a dutiful lower court was bound by the reasoning of the majority in *ACF*. His Honour instead accepted the suggestion of counsel that the wider reasoning in *ACF* must be understood as a response by the High Court to the breadth of the arguments put by the ACF.[75] In other words, the wider reasoning in *ACF* was actually a rejection of calls for wholesale

[71] *Kioa v West* (1985) 159 CLR 550, 621 (Brennan J). See also at 584 (Mason J), 632 (Deane J). Their Honours each explained the threshold test of natural justice as requiring a level of direct affectation. This has clear parallels with the special interest requirement in standing after *ACF*.

[72] Ibid 621. [73] (1980) 146 CLR 493, 556–7. [74] (1994) 55 FCR 492.

[75] Ibid 504. An astute submission from John Basten QC, now Basten JA of the New South Wales Court of Appeal.

changes to standing law and did not necessarily preclude incremental change. By implication, the majority of the High Court may not have been uncomfortable with the latter. Justice Sackville was certainly not.

Justice Sackville relied upon the overall effect of the following factors to find the environmental group in that case had standing: the group was a peak one that represented many other groups; it had long been recognised by the Commonwealth as an important conservation organisation, as evidenced by public grants to assist its work; the group's work had also been recognised by the relevant state government by its inclusion in many consultation processes; the group managed or participated in many conferences and projects about the environment; the group had long conducted research about, and made submissions in relation to, wilderness areas like the one at the centre of the present case.[76] Justice Sackville concluded the group had standing because of the combined effect of these factors. This approach enables public interest groups to acquire standing in their own right by reason of the activities which, typically, can only be conducted by a group rather than an individual. It is also strikingly similar to the one used by Murphy J. The list is longer and more polished but otherwise unchanged.

The importance of *North Coast* was partly its acceptance that the sum total of the activities of a pressure or public interest group can be greater than its individual parts, but also its implication that the relevance and overall effect of these activities on standing will vary in each case. That implication arises because Sackville J provided no clear guidance on how he weighed the many relevant activities of the group before him or how, more generally, that exercise should be conducted. This flexibility can take many forms. One is the cases recognising the standing of bodies which are not peak ones.[77] Those decisions confirm that whether a group has no effective rival is relevant but clearly not decisive. Thus a public interest group need not have the best possible claim to speak on an issue, only a good claim. Another example are the cases which question the relevance of government funding or recognition of a group.[78] Aronson and Groves note that flexibility on this issue means governments cannot effectively

[76] Ibid 513–14.

[77] *Hobsons Bay City Council v Viking Group Holdings Pty Ltd* [2010] VSC 386; *Environmental East Gippsland Inc v VicForests* (2010) 30 VR 1.

[78] *Right to Life Association (NSW) Inc v Secretary, Department of Human Services and Health* (1995) 128 ALR 238, 253; *Bridgetown/Greenbushes Friends of the Forest Inc v Department of Conservation* (1997) 18 WAR 126, 134.

control the judicial recognition of the standing of public interest groups.[79] Many decisions of the state courts have stressed the local nature of bodies and their members,[80] which suggests that bodies that work closely within the area affected by a decision they wish to challenge, or whose members live within or close to the relevant area, may be better able to claim standing.

A possible criticism of this approach was signalled during the emergence of a similar, less sophisticated, approach to the standing of public interest groups in the United Kingdom. Harlow concluded that the growing number of cases there which allowed claims raising quite broad questions of public interest, under the guise that the group in question was sufficiently representative of a sector of the public for it to have standing, concealed a worrying and unprincipled judicial discretion.[81] She was concerned that this discretion allowed courts to very selectively choose which executive decisions should go through the wringer of judicial review. That concern appears to have been both vindicated, and perhaps responded to, by subsequent United Kingdom cases which have greatly relaxed standing principles. In the first key case, *AXA General Insurance Ltd v HM Advocate*,[82] the Supreme Court adopted a much wider notion than *ACF* of the type of 'rights' that could support standing in public law. The Court made clear that notions of rights were too narrow a basis to accommodate the role the courts played in fostering the rule of law in judicial review proceedings.[83] Lord Reed, with whom Lords Kerr, Clarke and Dyson agreed, essentially jettisoned the special interest requirement altogether:

> A requirement that the applicant demonstrate an interest in the matter complained of will not however operate satisfactorily if it is applied in the same way in all contexts. In some contexts, it is appropriate to require an applicant for judicial review to demonstrate that he has a particular interest in the matter complained of: the type of interest which is relevant, and therefore required in order to have standing, will depend upon the particular context . . . What is to be regarded as sufficient interest to justify a particular applicant's bringing a particular application before the court,

[79] Aronson and Groves, above n 29, 749.

[80] *Bridgetown/Greenbushes Friends of the Forest Inc v Department of Conservation* (1997) 18 WAR 126; *Tipler v A-G (Vic)* (1998) 104 LGERA 230; *North Queensland Conservation Council Inc v Executive Director, Queensland Parks and Wildlife Service* [2000] QSC 172; *Save Bell Park Group v Kennedy* [2002] QSC 174; *Alliance to Save Hinchinbrook Inc v Cook* [2007] 1 Qd R 102.

[81] Carol Harlow, 'Public Law and Popular Justice' (2002) 65 *Modern Law Review* 1.

[82] [2012] 1 AC 868. [83] Ibid 951.

> and thus as conferring standing, depends therefore upon the context, and in particular upon what will best serve the purposes of judicial review in that context.[84]

This reasoning reveals a flaw arguably present in the dissent of Murphy J in *ACF*, which did not clarify whether this more relaxed approach to standing is limited to environmental proceedings. Lord Reed also declined to adopt the list or multifactorial approach devised by Murphy J. The key benefit of the multifactorial approach is to provide structure to an otherwise overly discretionary assessment of the reasons why a public interest group might have standing. The absence of such structure amplifies the discretionary nature of the United Kingdom approach.

The Supreme Court refined its approach a year later in *Walton v Scottish Ministers*,[85] where it carved out special rules for environmental cases. The Court held that a special standing rule was appropriate for such cases 'because the very nature of environmental law proceeds on the basis that the quality of the natural environment is of legitimate concern to everyone'.[86] Lord Hope cautioned that this new approach was not an open invitation to busybodies because individuals who wished to challenge public decisions

> on environmental grounds will have to demonstrate that they have a genuine interest in the aspects of the environment that they seek to protect, and that they have sufficient knowledge of the subject to qualify them to act in the public interest in what is, in essence, a representative capacity. There is, after all, no shortage of well-informed bodies that are equipped to raise issues of this kind . . . It would normally be to bodies of that kind that one would look if there were good grounds for objection. But it is well-known they do not have the resources to object to every development that might have adverse consequences for the environment. So there has to be some room for individuals who are sufficiently concerned, and sufficiently well-informed, to do this too. It will be for the court to judge in each case whether these requirements are satisfied.[87]

With this reasoning, the Supreme Court of the United Kingdom has taken the step that appears to be the next logical one in standing for Australian courts. That is to recognise, as a general rule, that public interest groups are the most appropriate parties to maintain public interest claims about environmental matters. The novel element of the United Kingdom approach is its presumption that representative groups will fulfil this function, though individuals may very occasionally step into the breach.

[84] Ibid 952. [85] [2012] UKSC 44. [86] Ibid [152]. [87] Ibid [153].

In the *ACF* and subsequent cases, Australian courts have struggled to come to terms with the reverse – when and why representative groups might assume the role traditionally assumed by individuals. Justice Murphy presumed the legitimacy of the ACF so easily that his Honour seemed willing to take that step 35 years ago. His Australian successors still seem hesitant to do so.

VIII Conclusion

Like most significant decisions of a final court of appeal, *ACF* is a creature of its time. The reasoning in *ACF* and later environmental cases suggests judges have struggled to come to terms with the changing role of public interest groups in modern society, though they also signal that judges are increasingly accepting the legitimate role such groups may play in the legal process. Perhaps that change mirrors the trend Arthurs detected in 19th century English public law, during which pluralism expanded and ultimately became embedded in English law.[88] Arthurs concluded that administrative law was both a cause and effect of this pluralism because it began to mature as a separate body of doctrine. That change was partly in response to the raft of legislation enacted in the wake of the industrial revolution but also because the unfolding of administrative law laid the path for more of that legislation. Changing judicial attitudes were central to that change. The judges who had never ventured into a factory or a mill understood the need for legal regulation of those new places and, in turn, judicial responses to that legislation.

The modern standing cases reveal a similar change in miniature because they show judicial acceptance of the evolving role of public interest groups in judicial review. However, those changing judicial attitudes have clearly sparked more of the very litigation from public interest groups that courts have struggled to accommodate. Conservation and other public interest groups continue to push the outer edges on standing in environmental proceedings and will surely keep doing so until their legitimacy in modern society is fully accepted by the courts.

[88] Harry Arthurs, *'Without the Law' – Administrative Justice and Legal Pluralism in Nineteenth-Century England* (Toronto, 1985) 132–66.

12

The Essence of a Fiduciary Relationship: Justice Mason's Dissent in *Hospital Products Ltd v United States Surgical Corporation* (1984)

SIMONE DEGELING AND GREG WEEKS

I Introduction

Hospital Products Ltd v United States Surgical Corporation ('*Hospital Products*')[1] concerned a dispute between a distributor and manufacturer. The High Court was asked to decide whether the distributor was the manufacturer's fiduciary and thus whether equity's profit-stripping remedies were available to the manufacturer. Justice Mason alone characterised the relationship as fiduciary, undeterred by the contractual paradigm which governed the parties' relationship. His dissent has eclipsed the majority judgments in the years since *Hospital Products* was decided without those judgments being formally disapproved.

That a fiduciary owes a core obligation of loyalty to his or her principal is uncontroversial. Within the scope of the fiduciary relationship,[2] the fiduciary must not obtain any unauthorised profit from the relationship and must not put himself or herself into a position of conflict or serious possibility of conflict.[3] Breach may arise on an actual or serious possibility of conflict of duty owed to the principal and self-interest, or as between the duty owed to one principal and a second or other principal(s). Equity is devastating in its prophylaxis: the fiduciary may not keep a profit made in breach of a fiduciary duty, even if the principal could not have pursued

[1] (1984) 156 CLR 41.

[2] *Howard v Federal Commissioner of Taxation* (2014) 253 CLR 83, 100 (French CJ and Keane J).

[3] *Commonwealth Bank of Australia v Smith* (1991) 42 FCR 390, 392; *Breen v Williams* (1996) 186 CLR 71, 135 (Gummow J); *Birtchnell v Equity Trustees and Agency Co Ltd* (1929) 42 CLR 384, 408 (Dixon J); *Boardman v Phipps* [1967] 2 AC 46, 124 (Lord Upjohn); *Hospital Products* (1984) 156 CLR 41, 103 (Mason J); *Pilmer v Duke Group Ltd (in liq)* (2001) 207 CLR 165 (McHugh, Gummow, Hayne and Callinan JJ) ('*Pilmer*').

that same opportunity.[4] Similarly, breach will be made out not only where the fiduciary acts in the absence of bad faith, but where he or she acts in good faith. The only defence to conduct which would otherwise amount to breach is the principal's fully informed consent.[5] What amounts to sufficient disclosure 'can depend on the sophistication and intelligence of the persons to whom disclosure must be made'.[6]

Breach of fiduciary duty activates equity's remedial arsenal, whose options include a constructive trust,[7] an account of profits[8] and equitable compensation for loss, possibly secured by a lien.[9] Where the fiduciary relationship is custodial (for example, because assets are held on trust or there is care and control of property), compensation may in addition be in the so-called substitutive or performance measure,[10] pursuant to which the object of any money award is to put the fund in the position before breach. In such a case, there is minimal or no causation inquiry. The defaulting fiduciary must simply restore the fund to the position before breach and, in awarding compensation, the court does not engage in a counterfactual inquiry about the causes of the loss.[11]

Against this apparent bedrock of principle, it may come as something of a shock to realise that '[t]here are few legal concepts more frequently invoked but less conceptually certain than that of the fiduciary relationship'.[12] Indeed, after *Hospital Products*, Mason J wrote extracurially that '[t]he fiduciary relationship is a concept in search of a principle',[13] further noting that one of the motivations for the expansion of the fiduciary concept has been because of the equitable remedies

[4] *Furs v Tomkies* (1936) 54 CLR 583; *Boardman v Phipps* [1967] 2 AC 46.

[5] *Boardman v Phipps* [1967] 2 AC 46, 104 (Lord Cohen), 105, 112 (Lord Hodson), 117 (Lord Guest); *New Zealand Netherlands Society 'Oranje' Inc v Kuys* [1973] 1 WLR 1126, 1131–2; *Maguire v Makaronis* (1997) 188 CLR 449, 466–7 (Brennan CJ, Gaudron, McHugh and Gummow JJ); *Hasler v Singtel Optus Pty Ltd* [2014] NSWCA 266, [3] (Barrett JA), [133]–[135] (Leeming JA).

[6] *Farah Constructions Pty Ltd v Say-Dee Pty Ltd* (2007) 230 CLR 89, 139.

[7] *Furs v Tomkies* (1936) 54 CLR 583.

[8] The court retains a discretion to award an allowance for the fiduciary's care and skill in earning the profit: *Warman International Ltd v Dwyer* (1995) 182 CLR 544.

[9] *Giumelli v Giumelli* (1999) 196 CLR 101.

[10] *Agricultural Land Management v Jackson [No 2]* (2014) 285 FLR 121, 186 (Edelman J).

[11] *Re Dawson* [1966] 2 NSWR 211; *Youyang Pty Ltd v Minter Ellison Morris Fletcher* (2003) 56 NSWLR 298.

[12] *Lac Minerals Ltd v International Corona Resources Ltd* [1989] 2 SCR 574, 643–4 (La Forest J).

[13] A F Mason, 'Themes and Prospects' in P D Finn (ed), *Essays in Equity* (Law Book Co, 1985) 242, 246.

thereby 'unleashed'.[14] Professor Laura Hoyano graphically describes the 'flight to fiduciary haven' and lists various motivations which include the remedial advantages noted above, but also various procedural and evidential advantages.[15] The law has a long and disreputable history of identifying relationships as fiduciary merely to secure these benefits without necessary attention to the prior question of whether in substance the relationship is, or ought to be classified as, fiduciary. Appellate courts are now alive to this risk[16] and modern authority is gradually stripping out the instrumental or 'convenient' fiduciary cases.[17]

A discussion about heretical or instrumental fiduciary relationships, and, by implication, 'reputable' fiduciary relationships, presupposes some agreement or understanding about when fiduciary duties should be imposed and to what relevant legal phenomenon their recognition responds. It is not our purpose to interrogate the policies lying behind equity's recognition of fiduciary duties or the precise events giving rise to those duties.[18] However, an understanding of these debates assists in

[14] Ibid.

[15] Laura Hoyano, 'The Flight to Fiduciary Haven' in Peter Birks (ed), *Privacy and Loyalty* (Clarendon Press, Oxford, 1997) 168, 174–5.

[16] See, eg, the warnings given in *Howard v Federal Commissioner of Taxation* (2014) 253 CLR 83, 100–1 (French CJ and Keane J); *Maguire v Makaronis* (1997) 188 CLR 449, 463–4 (Brennan CJ, Gaudron, McHugh and Gummow JJ).

[17] See, eg, *Chase Manhattan Bank NA v Israel-British Bank (London) Ltd* [1981] 1 Ch 105, 119 (Goulding J). Modern dicta now suggest doing away with this heresy: *Foskett v McKeown* [2001] 1 AC 102, 108 (Lord Millett); J D Heydon, M J Leeming and P G Turner, *Meagher Gummow and Lehane's Equity Doctrines & Remedies* (LexisNexis, 5th ed, 2015) 154 [5–045].

[18] There is an abundant literature. See, eg, Matthew Conaglen, *Fiduciary Loyalty: Protecting the Due Performance of Non-Fiduciary Duties* (Hart Publishing, 2010); Matthew Conaglen, 'Fiduciary Duties and Voluntary Undertakings' (2013) 7 *Journal of Equity* 105; James Edelman, 'When Do Fiduciary Duties Arise?' (2010) 126 *Law Quarterly Review* 302; James Edelman, 'The Importance of the Fiduciary Undertaking' (2013) 7 *Journal of Equity* 128; P D Finn, *Fiduciary Obligations* (Law Book Co, 1977); P D Finn, 'The Fiduciary Principle' in T G Youdan (ed), *Equity, Fiduciaries and Trusts* (Carswell, 1989) 1; Tamar Frankel, *Fiduciary Law* (Oxford University Press, 2011); Andrew S Gold and Paul B Miller (eds), *Philosophical Foundations of Fiduciary Law* (Oxford University Press, 2014); Joshua Getzler, 'Rumford Market and the Genesis of Fiduciary Obligations' in Andrew Burrows and Lord Rodger of Earlsferry (eds), *Mapping the Law: Essays in Memory of Peter Birks* (Oxford University Press, 2006) 577; Joshua Getzler, '"As If". Accountability and the Counterfactual Trust' (2011) 91 *Boston University Law Review* 973; Matthew Harding, 'Trust and Fiduciary Law' (2013) 33 *Oxford Journal of Legal Studies* 81; Paul B Miller, 'Justifying Fiduciary Duties' (2013) 58 *McGill Law Journal* 969; Lionel Smith, 'Deterrence, Prophylaxis and Punishment in Fiduciary Obligation' (2013) 7 *Journal of Equity* 87; Lionel Smith, 'The Motive, Not the Deed' in Joshua Getzler (ed), *Rationalizing Property, Equity and Trusts: Essays in Honour of Edward Burn* (LexisNexis, 2003) 53; Lionel Smith,

appreciating the contribution of Mason J's dictum in *Hospital Products*. Among other accounts of the fiduciary principle[19] are those which seek an explanation in either the fiduciary's undertaking to act in some way as the representative of the principal,[20] the presence of consent,[21] or the principal's reasonable expectations.[22] The facts of *Hospital Products* and parts of Mason J's decision have resonance with these latter three accounts.

Professor Lionel Smith argues that fiduciary relationships are those in which one person holds the authority to make discretionary decisions on behalf of another person, where these decisions will affect the other person's situation and where the authority was given to manage the affairs of that person.[23] The power to make decisions may be given voluntarily, by statute or non-statute law.[24] In all of these instances, Smith says the 'fundamental question is whether a person holds powers in the role or capacity of a manager or an administrator, rather than as a form of personal wealth'.[25] In this sense, there is a representative quality to the relationship. A narrower consent-based explanation is that fiduciary obligations arise in response to the fiduciary's consent or undertaking to act for the benefit of the principal, in which an undertaking appears to be necessary but not sufficient for a fiduciary relationship. Justice Edelman extra-judicially extends the undertaking thesis to relationships which are frequently cited as fiduciary in virtue of status, such as trusteeship.[26] Pointing to the fact that some constructive trustees do not owe fiduciary

'Fiduciary Relationships: Ensuring the Loyal Exercise of Judgment on Behalf of Another' (2014) 130 *Law Quarterly Review* 608.

19 See, eg, Dawson J in *Hospital Products* who in part identifies disadvantage, vulnerability and dependence of the principal on the putative fiduciary as factors important to the existence of a fiduciary relationship and whose absence on the facts justified his conclusion *against* a fiduciary relationship: *Hospital Products* (1984) 156 CLR 1, 142.

20 See, eg, Smith, 'The Motive, Not the Deed', above n 18; Smith, 'Fiduciary Relationships', above n 18; Lionel Smith, 'Can We Be Obliged To Be Selfless?' in Andrew S Gold and Paul B Miller (eds), *Philosophical Foundations of Fiduciary Law* (Oxford University Press, 2014) 141.

21 Edelman, 'When Do Fiduciary Duties Arise?', above n 18; Edelman, 'The Importance of the Fiduciary Undertaking', above n 18; James Edelman, 'The Role of Status in the Law of Obligations' in Andrew S Gold and Paul B Miller (eds), *Philosophical Foundations of Fiduciary Law* (Oxford University Press, 2014) 21. See also *Bristol & West Building Society v Mothew* [1998] 1 Ch 18, 1 (Millett LJ). It is important to notice that the normative basis for this argument is consent which may be *voluntarily* given, rather than as necessarily arising pursuant to a contract.

22 Paul Finn, 'Fiduciary Reflections' (2014) 88 *Australian Law Journal* 127.

23 Smith, 'Fiduciary Relationships', above n 18, 633. 24 Ibid 616. 25 Ibid.

26 Edelman, 'The Role of Status in the Law of Obligations', above n 21.

duties,[27] or may by the trust instrument be relieved of such duties, he argues that while the status or office of the putative fiduciary 'is an important and relevant matter in construing the scope of the undertaking and the duties which arise from it, it is only part of the inquiry concerning the undertaking'.[28] Contrary to a view which sees fiduciary obligations arising from the trustee's status as such, on the undertaking thesis the *fact* of trusteeship is relevant to interpreting and construing the context and content of the undertaking and thus the existence and scope of fiduciary obligation.

Another account identifies the reasonable expectations of the principal as diagnostic of a fiduciary relationship. Professor Paul Finn explains:

> One can only describe, but not define, when a relationship will be a fiduciary one in whole or in part. The description I have proposed is this: 'A person will be in a fiduciary relationship with another when that other is reasonably entitled to expect that he or she will act in that other's interests (or in their joint interest) to the exclusion of his or her own several interests, for a purpose, or some or all purposes, of their relationship'.[29]

Thus, Finn considers a relationship to be fiduciary when the principal is entitled to expect that the fiduciary will act in his or her interests, which may arise when the one party entrusts property to another or entrusts the other with a task or confidence.[30]

II The Decision

United States Surgical Corporation ('USSC') was a United States manufacturer of surgical stapling products. USSC entered into an oral contract with Blackman, who later became the distributor of USSC's products in Australia. USSC's products were not patented in Australia. Blackman's Australian company was Hospital Products International Ltd ('HPI'). In competition with USSC, HPI repackaged USSC's products and sold them under the HPI brand. In addition, HPI and Blackman reverse-engineered USSC's surgical stapling devices, thus enabling competing products to be

27 See, eg, *Giumelli v Giumelli* (1999) 196 CLR 101, 112 (Gleeson CJ, McHugh, Gummow and Callinan JJ).

28 Edelman, 'The Role of Status in the Law of Obligations', above n 21, 37.

29 Finn, above n 22, 137.

30 Ibid 137–40. A similar approach was taken in *Grimaldi v Chameleon Mining NL [No 2]* (2012) 200 FCR 296, 345 (Finn, Stone and Perram JJ). See also *ASIC v Citigroup* [2007] FCA 963, [273]–[274] (Jacobson J); *News Ltd v Australian Rugby Football League Ltd* (1996) 64 FCR 410, 541.

developed and sold into other markets including the United States. HPI thus competed with USSC in the United States and Australian markets. USSC terminated its distributorship contract with Blackman and sued him and HPI for breach of contract and breach of fiduciary duty. Justice Mason was the only judge to find a fiduciary relationship between the two companies, albeit one limited in scope.[31] Importantly, Mason J attempted to describe an architecture whose columns and buttresses would potentially encompass all fiduciary relationships but did not attempt to *define* the fiduciary relationship. This distinction is crucial to understanding the impact of his judgment.

The other members of the Court differed in their approach when considering whether a fiduciary relationship existed. Justice Dawson opined that there is 'no satisfactory, single test . . . which will serve to identify a relationship which is fiduciary'[32] although he noted:

> There is, however, the notion underlying all the cases of fiduciary obligation that inherent in the nature of the relationship itself is a position of disadvantage or vulnerability on the part of one of the parties which causes him to place reliance upon the other and requires the protection of equity acting upon the conscience of that other . . . [33]

Justice Dawson held that it is from these elements that fiduciary obligations arise but that none arose on the facts. Nothing beyond a contractual 'best efforts' obligation to act for the common benefit of both USSC and HPI required Blackman to have any regard to USSC's interests to the exclusion of his own or those of HPI.

Chief Justice Gibbs similarly doubted the productivity of attempting 'a general statement of the circumstances in which a fiduciary relationship will be found to exist'.[34] After reciting various fiduciary categories including status-based examples[35] and tests founded in confidence[36] and entrustment,[37] he held that the commercial context and fact that HPI was entitled to make a profit from the arrangement under an arm's-length contract presented an 'insuperable obstacle'[38] to finding a fiduciary

[31] The fiduciary relationship found by Mason J covered only USSC's 'product goodwill': *Hospital Products* (1984) 156 CLR 41, 101. In contrast, the New South Wales Court of Appeal had held that a more general fiduciary relationship existed, covering the 'entire distributorship business': at 97 (Mason J). Justice Mason found that since HPI was at 'liberty to make some business decisions by reference to its own interests' this was an 'overwhelming obstacle' to the existence of a general fiduciary relationship: at 97–8.

[32] Ibid 141. [33] Ibid 142. [34] Ibid 69. [35] Ibid. [36] Ibid. [37] Ibid 70.

[38] Ibid 72.

relationship. Although Gibbs CJ and Dawson J adopted differing positions as to the practicality of a general test, Wilson J stated himself to be 'substantially in accord' with both.[39]

Justice Deane held that, subject to the possibility of a more limited fiduciary relationship, the arrangement was not fiduciary,[40] noting that the distributorship did not establish a partnership, joint venture or agency (which might have led to a conclusion that the relationship between the parties was in any event fiduciary through status). Speaking of the possibility of a narrower fiduciary relationship, Deane J pointed out that his finding against the alleged fiduciary character of the USSC–HPI relationship overall did not 'preclude the possibility that, within or arising from that relationship, a more restricted fiduciary relationship might exist' and that, indeed, their continuing relationship might make it 'easier to imply an undertaking by one party to act as a fiduciary in relation to a particular matter than would be the case if that relationship did not exist', although on the facts, this more limited fiduciary relationship had not been established.[41] HPI was by contract given the exclusive opportunity of exploiting and developing the local goodwill of USSC's products, subject only to the contractual 'best efforts' obligation.

In determining whether HPI was a fiduciary to USSC, Mason J delivered the following oft-quoted dictum, reproduced here in full:

> Because distributor-manufacturer is not an established fiduciary relationship, it is important in the first instance to ascertain the characteristics which, according to tradition, identify a fiduciary relationship. As the courts have declined to define the concept, preferring instead to develop the law in a case by case approach, we have to distil the essence or the characteristics of the relationship from the illustrations which the judicial decisions provide. In so doing we must recognize that the categories of fiduciary relationships are not closed: *Tufton v Sperni*; *English v Dedham Vale Properties Ltd*.
>
> The accepted fiduciary relationships are sometimes referred to as relationships of trust and confidence or confidential relations (cf *Phipps v Boardman*), viz, trustee and beneficiary, agent and principal, solicitor and client, employee and employer, director and company, and partners. The critical feature of these relationships is that the fiduciary undertakes or agrees to act for or on behalf of or in the interests of another person in

[39] Ibid 116.

[40] Ibid 124. Justice Deane referred to the 'one possible qualification' of a restricted or limited fiduciary relationship: at 123.

[41] Ibid.

> the exercise of a power or discretion which will affect the interests of that other person in a legal or practical sense. The relationship between the parties is therefore one which gives the fiduciary a special opportunity to exercise the power or discretion to the detriment of that other person who is accordingly vulnerable to abuse by the fiduciary of his position. The expressions 'for', 'on behalf of', and 'in the interests of' signify that the fiduciary acts in a 'representative' character in the exercise of his responsibility, to adopt an expression used by the Court of Appeal.
>
> It is partly because the fiduciary's exercise of the power or discretion can adversely affect the interests of the person to whom the duty is owed and because the latter is at the mercy of the former that the fiduciary comes under a duty to exercise his power or discretion in the interests of the person to whom it is owed: see generally Weinrib, 'The Fiduciary Obligation', *University of Toronto Law Journal*, vol 25 (1975), pp 4–8. Thus a mere subcontractor is not a fiduciary. Although his work may be described loosely as work which is to be carried out in the interests of the head contractor, the sub-contractor cannot in any meaningful sense be said to exercise a power or discretion which places the head contractor in a position of vulnerability.
>
> That contractual and fiduciary relationships may coexist between the same parties has never been doubted. Indeed, the existence of a basic contractual relationship has in many situations provided a foundation for the erection of a fiduciary relationship. In these situations it is the contractual foundation which is all important because it is the contract that regulates the basic rights and liabilities of the parties. The fiduciary relationship, if it is to exist at all, must accommodate itself to the terms of the contract so that it is consistent with, and conforms to, them. The fiduciary relationship cannot be superimposed upon the contract in such a way as to alter the operation which the contract was intended to have according to its true construction.[42]

Justice Mason construed the contract as obligating HPI to exercise its 'best efforts' to promote USSC's surgical stapling product in the Australian market. Importantly, he held that HPI's discretion in discharging that responsibility was subject to its obligations as USSC's fiduciary.[43]

III The Nature of Justice Mason's Dissent

The various chapters of this book highlight the different ways in which a dissent may earn a reputation for 'greatness'. These include the opinion as a *cri de coeur* from a judge who sees an injustice being done; a catalogue

[42] Ibid 96–7 (case citations omitted). [43] Ibid 98–101.

(expressed with either rancour or regret) of the perceived 'mistakes' being made by the majority; or a vision for the future development of the law which is at odds with today's orthodoxy. Some dissents represent more than one of the entries in this taxonomy; a good example is one of the most famous dissents ever given, Lord Atkin's furious and divisive declaration of principle in *Liversidge v Anderson*.[44]

It is notable that most characterisations of dissent place the dissentient actively in disagreement with the balance of the court.[45] Put another way, 'dissent' is a verb that characteristically comes with an object: judges dissent *from* a conclusion or line of reasoning followed by their colleagues. This explains why it might not always be readily apparent that a judgment has been given in dissent. What might popularly be assumed to be a dissenting judgment, based either upon the differences between the reasoning it employs and that of the majority judges, or because it has been written in a style more frequently associated with dissenting judgments, is sometimes in fact a concurrence as to the result of a case.[46] Justice Mason's dissent in *Hospital Products* presents us with a converse example. He was undoubtedly in dissent in finding a 'limited fiduciary relationship' between HPI and USSC, because he differed with his colleagues on the disposition of the case. The fact that nevertheless the dissent reads in many respects like a concurring judgment does not, we argue, diminish its claim to greatness.

The dissent's greatness owes much to its impact. The two points which Mason J developed independently from the rest of the Court were his essence account of fiduciary relationships and also his vision of the relationship between contract and fiduciary law. These statements of law were of limited or doubtful precedential value. They have nonetheless subsequently been treated as significant and are the only points for which any judgment in *Hospital Products* is now regularly cited. Accordingly, Mason J's dissent in *Hospital Products* is noteworthy because it has been treated effectively as law even though it lacks any formal power to bind.

44 [1942] AC 206, 225–47.

45 See, eg, Michael Kirby, 'Judicial Dissent: Common Law and Civil Law Traditions' (2007) 123 *Law Quarterly Review* 379, 380; John Alder, 'Dissents in Courts of Last Resort: Tragic Choices?' (2000) 20 *Oxford Journal of Legal Studies* 221, 227; cf Andrew Lynch, 'Dissent: The Rewards and Risks of Judicial Disagreement in the High Court of Australia' (2003) 27 *Melbourne University Law Review* 724, 749.

46 Andrew Lynch, 'Dissent: Towards a Methodology for Measuring Judicial Disagreement in the High Court of Australia' (2002) 24 *Sydney Law Review* 470, 476.

The discussion below separates subsequent High Court treatment of the case from that of intermediate appellate courts.[47] It should also be emphasised that this is not empirical research. We have not located every case, in part because of the enormous volume of cases which refer to Mason's dictum, itself testimony to the significance of the statement. However, from the evidence gathered, it seems that a general pattern is observable. In evaluating Mason J's judgment, two elements are separated for the purposes of analysis: the identification of the essence of a fiduciary relationship, and the relationship between contract and equity as sources of rights and obligations.

Essence of the Relationship

Justice Mason referred to his account as a distillation of 'the essence'[48] of a fiduciary relationship rather than a definition or precise statement of the limits of the fiduciary principle. As has been pointed out, Mason J provided a statement of the true nature of the fiduciary relationship which 'offers a general description, not an exhaustive definition'.[49] Analysis of the elements of Mason J's 'essence' shows that they are not sensibly to be understood as a cumulative list.[50]

Turning first to subsequent treatment by the High Court, Mason J's essence account has been referred to in several judgments, in each instance in a neutral tone, generally with respect and even affection, but never adopted or disapproved in deciding a case. In *Mabo v Queensland [No 2]*, Toohey J cited with approval Mason J's critical features of fiduciary relationships in support of his reasoning that extinguishment of native title would involve a breach of the Crown's fiduciary obligation to native title holders,[51] an approach which was not taken by the other members of the Court.

Not until the subsequent decision of *Breen v Williams*, shortly following the retirement of Sir Anthony Mason from the High Court, did the

[47] We have also excluded those many cases that cite Mason J in support of other well-established fiduciary principles; eg, relationships which are fiduciary per se, the conflict principle or the remedies which are triggered on breach.

[48] *Hospital Products* (1984) 156 CLR 41, 96.

[49] Heydon, Leeming and Turner, above n 17, 142 [5–005].

[50] J C Campbell, 'Fiduciary Relationships in a Commercial Context' (Sydney Law School Research Paper No 14/26, 3 March 2014) 18 ff. See also Heydon, Leeming and Turner, above n 17, 142–3 [5–005].

[51] (1992) 175 CLR 1, 200.

Court engage more directly with his dictum. This in itself is important. After *Hospital Products*, there had been other prominent fiduciary cases,[52] but none of these considered Mason J's dictum. *Breen v Williams* concerned a plaintiff who wished to access her medical records in New South Wales for the purpose of participating in a class action in the United States against Dow Corning, the manufacturer of her breast implants. She asserted, inter alia, a fiduciary duty owed by her New South Wales doctor in order to obtain access to her records. A majority of the High Court declined to find a fiduciary relationship.[53] Although the plaintiff did not succeed, the case is important because it sets out a parallel narrative describing when fiduciary relationships exist. Justices Gaudron and McHugh quoted Gibbs CJ in *Hospital Products*,[54] pointing out that 'Australian courts have consciously refrained from attempting to provide a general test for determining when persons or classes of persons stand in a fiduciary relationship with one another'.[55] They then continued by identifying certain factors which might 'point towards' a fiduciary relationship without being determinative,[56] including:

> the existence of a relation of confidence; inequality of bargaining power; an undertaking by one party to perform or fulfil a duty in the interests of another party; the scope for one party unilaterally to exercise a discretion or power which may affect the rights or interests of another; and a dependency or vulnerability on the part of one party that causes that party to rely on another.[57]

In identifying these factors, *Hospital Products* was not cited. However, the judges remarked that 'the categories of fiduciary relationships are not closed'[58] as a preface to the list of 'factors' and, in the list of status relationships (such as agent and principal, solicitor and client), noted that the fiduciary acts 'in a representative character in the exercise of his responsibility'.[59] Although these comments are referenced to Mason J's

[52] See, eg, *United Dominions Corporation Ltd v Brian Pty Ltd* (1985) 157 CLR 1 (a case involving a fiduciary relationship between joint venture partners in which Mason J sat but which made no reference to Mason J's dictum, or indeed to the case at all, apart from Gibbs CJ citing himself); *Daly v Sydney Stock Exchange* (1986) 160 CLR 371 (a case involving an alleged fiduciary relationship by a financial adviser in the absence of a pre-existing agency which made no reference to Mason J's dictum. Reference was made by Gibbs CJ to the judgments of himself and Dawson J).

[53] *Breen v Williams* (1996) 186 CLR 71, 82–3 (Brennan CJ), 98 (Dawson and Toohey JJ), 109 (Gaudron and McHugh JJ), *contra* 134 (Gummow J).

[54] (1984) 156 CLR 41, 69. [55] *Breen v Williams* (1996) 186 CLR 71, 106.

[56] Ibid 107. [57] Ibid. [58] Ibid. [59] Ibid.

dictum in *Hospital Products*, they are not in any sense an adoption of it. It is clear that Gaudron and McHugh JJ intended to present an opposing account. Justices Dawson and Toohey quoted the essence dictum, citing the 'critical features' of the fiduciary relationship.[60] However, they immediately qualified this by stating that 'Mason J did not intend to suggest that this description of a fiduciary relationship isolated those features from other relationships of trust and confidence which do not impose fiduciary obligations'.[61]

Studied neutrality towards Mason J's dictum followed in *Pilmer v Duke Group Ltd (in liq)* ('*Pilmer*'), in which the plurality referred in passing to the essence account in discussing the trial judge's reasoning.[62] However, in the subsequent case of *Howard v Federal Commissioner of Taxation*, French CJ and Keane J cited this passage in *Pilmer* as having '*quoted with approval*'[63] the 'protective rationale for the proscriptive duties attaching to a fiduciary's powers . . . explained by Mason J in [*Hospital Products*]'.[64] Finally, in *John Alexander's Clubs Pty Ltd v White City Tennis Club* ('*John Alexander's Clubs*'), the *parties* 'accepted that the relevant principles regarding the existence of a fiduciary relationship which does not fall within an established category . . . are those stated by Mason J'.[65] However, those principles were not necessarily accepted by the Court, which notably characterised the parties' acceptance of Mason J's principles as being 'notwithstanding that Mason J was in dissent'.[66] Although *Hospital Products* was referenced, Mason J's opinion was not cited when the Court in *Commissioner of Taxation (SA) v Cyril Henschke Pty Ltd* appeared tacitly to accept his formulation.[67] Intermediate courts of appeal, and also in some instances the Federal Court, have treated the essence account either as binding or quasi-binding. A prominent example in the Federal

[60] Ibid 92–3. [61] Ibid 93.

[62] (2001) 207 CLR 165, 196 (McHugh, Gummow, Hayne and Callinan JJ). See also the Court's citation of this passage from *Pilmer* in *ABN Amro Bank NV v Bathurst Regional Council* (2014) 224 FCR 1, 210–11 (Jacobson, Gilmour and Gordon JJ). Shortly after *Pilmer*, Callinan J in his dissenting judgment in *Australian Broadcasting Corporation v Lenah Game Meats Pty Ltd* (2001) 208 CLR 199, 313–14, 315–16, applied Mason J's essence account to find the parties' 'relationship of a fiduciary kind and of confidence'.

[63] (2014) 253 CLR 83, 99 (emphasis added). [64] Ibid (citations omitted).

[65] (2010) 241 CLR 1, 34 (French CJ, Gummow, Hayne, Heydon and Kiefel JJ).

[66] Ibid. Admittedly, the lack of vulnerability of the principal to the putative fiduciary was a reason no fiduciary duty was found, and this was in the Court's reasoning linked back to Mason J's concept of vulnerability. However, the Court did not import the essence account: at 34, 36–7.

[67] (2010) 242 CLR 508, 516 (French CJ, Gummow, Hayne, Heydon and Kiefel JJ).

Court is *Grimaldi v Chameleon Mining NL [No 2]*, in which the Court referred to the pages on which Mason J's essence account was set out to establish 'who is a fiduciary'.[68] The essence account was similarly applied by Rares J in *Wingecarribee Shire Council v Lehman Brothers Australia Ltd (in liq)*.[69]

Fiduciaries and Contract

That contracting parties might be fiduciaries is not legally surprising but is sometimes commercially contentious because it may be assumed that contracting parties wish to have the freedom to act self-interestedly whereas, if a fiduciary for the other, a contracting party is duty-bound to act within the scope of fiduciary obligation in the interests of the other. As sources of rights and obligations, fiduciary law and contract law have interesting intersections and interactions. Contract may be the context and course of dealing in which a fiduciary relationship arises. Equally, a putative fiduciary may attempt to limit the existence or scope of any fiduciary obligation via a contractual device.[70]

As earlier noted, HPI reverse-engineered the auto-suture technology of USSC and sold the rival product into the Australian and later the United States markets. Paramount in the majority's reasoning in declining to find a fiduciary relationship was the commercial, contractual and self-interested nature of the relationship between the two companies.[71] Equity's gain-based remedies were denied[72] on the ground that it was sufficient that the 'ordinary remedies for damages for fraud and breach of contract were available to USSC although it did not choose to pursue the former'.[73] By contrast, Mason J declared a vision of fiduciary law which allowed for the coexistence of fiduciary and contractual paradigms, in which a contract may lay the foundation for the finding of a fiduciary relationship. However, the juridical source of the resulting rights and obligations remains distinct. The nature of the contractual obligation will

[68] (2012) 200 FCR 296, 345. [69] [2012] FCA 1028, [743] (Rares J).

[70] See generally Mark Leeming, 'The Scope of Fiduciary Obligations: How Contract Informs, but Does Not Determine, the Scope of Fiduciary Obligations' (2009) 3 *Journal of Equity* 181; Joshua Getzler, '*ASIC v Citigroup*: Bankers' Conflict of Interest and the Contractual Exclusion of Fiduciary Duties' (2007) 2 *Journal of Equity* 62.

[71] *Hospital Products* (1984) 156 CLR 41, 72 (Gibbs CJ), 147 (Dawson J).

[72] Cf Deane J, who would have required HPI to 'account as a constructive trustee for the profits' made in breach of contract but did not link the availability of this remedy to a breach of fiduciary duty: ibid 125.

[73] Ibid 73–4 (Gibbs CJ).

assist the court in determining the existence, scope and 'intensity'[74] of any fiduciary relationship. Thus, rather than being kept out of equity by the presence of a contractual paradigm, Mason J highlighted that contract is the very foundation of some fiduciary relationships. However, the fiduciary relationship is not superimposed over the contract and cannot alter its operation.

This part of Mason J's dictum has been well received in intermediate courts of appeal in Australia[75] and in appellate courts across the common law world.[76] It has also been applied by the High Court in cases involving the allegation of a fiduciary relationship between contracting parties. In *John Alexander's Clubs*, the Court used the dictum to find that the terms of a series of contracts prohibited any fiduciary obligations between the parties.[77] Professor Joshua Getzler has pointed out that 'lower-court judges and commentators have not found the ratio of *John Alexander's Clubs* easy to frame or follow',[78] but the Court made clear that finding a fiduciary relationship contrary to terms of contractual arrangements was prohibited by Mason J's principle.[79] The part of his dictum holding that the scope of any fiduciary relationship found must accommodate itself to the 'particulars of the underlying relationship which give rise to the duty so that it is consistent with and conforms to the relationship and facts of the case' has been more widely applied by the High Court.[80]

The paragraphs above describe contracts which themselves form the foundation of a fiduciary relationship. However, the parties may already have a pattern of interaction which equity characterises as fiduciary before they contract with each other. A term of that contract may in fact seek to limit or nullify the existence of any pre-existing fiduciary relationship. Such an attempt is itself an exercise of fiduciary power, caught by the

[74] Joshua Getzler, 'Ascribing and Limiting Fiduciary Obligations' in Andrew S Gold and Paul B Miller (eds), *Philosophical Foundations of Fiduciary Law* (Oxford University Press, 2014) 39, 47.

[75] See, eg, *Streetscape Projects (Australia) Pty Ltd v City of Sydney* (2013) 85 NSWLR 196, 215 (Barrett JA). See also *Blackmagic Design Pty Ltd v Overliese* [2011] FCAFC 24.

[76] *Kelly v Cooper* [1993] AC 205, 215; *Hilton v Barker Booth & Eastwood* [2005] 1 WLR 567, 575; *Strother v Canada Inc* [2007] 2 SCR 177, 253 (McLachlin CJC dissenting).

[77] (2010) 241 CLR 1, 34–8. [78] Getzler, above n 74, 54.

[79] *John Alexander's Clubs* (2010) 241 CLR 1, 36–7.

[80] *Howard v Federal Commissioner of Taxation* (2014) 253 CLR 83, 100 (French CJ and Keane J), citing *Hospital Products* (1984) 156 CLR 41, 102 (Mason J). See also *Clay v Clay* (2001) 202 CLR 410, 432–3 (Gleeson CJ, McHugh, Gummow, Hayne and Callinan JJ). By parity of reasoning, these cases considered Mason J's approach in determining scope of fiduciary duty.

fiduciary's obligation to act with loyalty to the principal. Cases like these fall outside Mason J's explanation of the relationship of equity and contract since, properly understood, the fiduciary relationship pre-exists and overarches any attempt to contract.[81] Where such a fiduciary relationship exists, the only method of escaping liability is for the fiduciary properly to disclose the conflict and obtain the client's informed consent to the change.[82]

Justice Mason's statement about the coexistence of equity and contract must be sited within his dissent as a whole. He did not purport to set out a hierarchy pursuant to which contract would always exclude or shape fiduciary obligations; but intended merely to delineate the fiduciary relationship arising from the contractual paradigm. This difficulty is illustrated by the decision in *Streetscape Projects (Australia) Pty Ltd v City of Sydney*, in which Barrett JA referred to Mason J's dictum to hold that a 'fiduciary duty may exist in a contractual setting'[83] before saying:

> The contractual terms are paramount. A fiduciary duty cannot detract from or contradict them. The two types of obligation – contractual and fiduciary – will, in general, coexist only if and to the extent that the sanctions available for breach of contract (including any implied terms) are insufficient to deal with some possibility of unconscionable conduct to which one party is exposed.[84]

With respect, this extends the impact of Mason J's statement too far and shows how easily the relationship between the categories may be muddled. As has been pointed out by Finn, equity independently will decide if there is a fiduciary relationship which, if arising between contractual parties, cannot impose a fiduciary obligation contrary to the express or implied terms of the contract.[85] It is not the inadequacy of contractual remedies which attracts the attention of fiduciary law in this configuration.

[81] *ASIC v Citigroup* [2007] FCA 963, in which Jacobson J controversially held that the contractual exclusion of a fiduciary relationship in a standard mandate letter between an investment bank and a commercial client *was* valid. As this was an arm's-length commercial transaction between seasoned commercial parties with access to independent advice, there was no fiduciary relationship founded on the pre-contractual course of dealing between the parties which would otherwise have made execution of the mandate a breach of duty. See Getzler, above n 74; Finn, above n 22. See further Simone Degeling and Jessica Hudson, 'Fiduciary Obligations, Financial Advisers and FOFA' (2014) 32 *Company & Securities Law Journal* 527.

[82] *Maguire v Makaronis* (1997) 188 CLR 449, 466–7 (Brennan CJ, Gaudron, McHugh and Gummow JJ).

[83] (2013) 85 NSWLR 196, 215.

[84] Ibid 215 (Meagher and Ward JJA agreeing).

[85] Finn, above n 22, 143–4.

IV Understanding the Contribution of Justice Mason's Dissent

Justice Mason's dictum in *Hospital Products* has had an undoubted impact and influence not just in Australia but across the common law world.[86] Put simply, it is great (rather than merely influential) because it has been heavily cited and extensively followed. The High Court is not bound by its own previous decisions, and there are occasions when it has overruled or simply ignored an earlier authority of apparent relevance.[87] Yet conversely, despite the fact that it was not a majority judgment, and might just have been ignored, Mason J's dictum has been followed.[88] Why?

Perhaps one answer lies in the vision of private law that it offers. Justice Mason approached his task as an architect designing a gracious and hopefully enduring public building. To the extent that this approach is conducive to a broad understanding of private law, on which fundamental distinctions may be drawn between wrongs and not wrongs, unjust enrichments, and those responsibilities which are assumed via the parties' consent,[89] Mason J's technique lends itself to a rational understanding and model of private law liabilities. Whilst not purporting to define the relationship or give the set of necessary or sufficient criteria by which the law might identify fiduciary relationships, the account nonetheless attempted unity via their 'essence'. Although the essence model has internal inconsistencies,[90] it pursues a bold vision in a search for doctrinal synthesis.

In holding that the fiduciary relationship arose out of the contractual relationship, Mason J reinforced the independence of the fiduciary relationship from contract. In fact, the majority of the Court held that no fiduciary duties arose, despite the distributorship agreement between the two companies being construed as expressly prohibiting HPI from competing with USSC and in which HPI was the exclusive distributor

[86] See, eg, *Kelly v Cooper* [1993] AC 205, 215; *Hilton v Barker Booth & Eastwood* [2005] 1 WLR 567, 575; *Strother v Canada Inc* [2007] 2 SCR 177, 253 (McLachlin CJC dissenting).

[87] See, eg, the fate of *Minister for Immigration and Ethnic Affairs v Teoh* (1995) 183 CLR 273 after *Re Minister for Immigration and Multicultural Affairs; Ex parte Lam* (2003) 214 CLR 1; Michael Taggart, '"Australian Exceptionalism" in Judicial Review' (2008) 36 *Federal Law Review* 1, 17.

[88] In his extra-curial writing, Mason J himself cited the majority judgments in *Hospital Products* without mentioning – or seeking to justify – his own dissent: Sir Anthony Mason, 'The Place of Equity and Equitable Remedies in the Contemporary Common Law World' (1994) 110 *Law Quarterly Review* 238, 245–8.

[89] See generally Peter Birks, 'Definition and Division: A Meditation on Institutes 3.13' in Peter Birks (ed), *The Classification of Obligations* (Clarendon Press, 1997) 1.

[90] See Campbell, above n 50, 18.

for USSC. Within the terms of this contract as he interpreted them,[91] Mason J nonetheless held that a fiduciary relationship *could* exist conformably with contractual duties, thus exposing HPI to equity's weaponry in the face of the distributor's profit-taking activity. Rather than limiting USSC to any contractual remedy, Mason J thereby opened the door to gain-based responses such as an account of profits. In doing so, the genius of his judgment is that it reinforced breach of fiduciary duty as an equitable wrong, the existence of which stands independently of contact. This has obvious ramifications in confirming equity's capacity to make its presence felt regardless of the relative power of the parties. The reach of equity is sufficiently long to bring to account those who have contractual or economic power, particularly when an attempt to contract out of a pre-existing fiduciary relationship will be caught by that relationship. However, the deeper significance is conceptual: the juridical basis of liability in contract and for breach of fiduciary duty is distinct. That the course of dealing was between contracting and self-interested parties did not prevent a fiduciary relationship.

Justice Mason delivered his judgment at a time when appellate courts had little considered the nature of fiduciary relationships, or at least an overarching theory of fiduciary relationships,[92] and academic writing on the subject was only just beginning. Against that backdrop, Mason J offered a reasoned account of the characteristics of the relationship and did so drawing on the work of legal scholars. It is not the purpose of this chapter to write a genealogy of the ideas expressed in Mason J's judgment. However, within the text he acknowledged the work of Professor Ernest Weinrib and it is perhaps noteworthy that Finn's *Fiduciary Obligations* was published just a few years before.[93] Debates about the normative and

91 *Hospital Products* (1984) 156 CLR 41, 97.

92 *Chan v Zacharia* (1984) 154 CLR 178 pre-dated *Hospital Products* but was largely confined to the fiduciary obligations of partners and the relationship between the profit and conflict principle. *Queensland Mines Ltd v Hudson* (1978) 18 ALR 1 was a case about a company director who was alleged to have made a profit in breach of duty. *Consul Developments Pty Ltd v DPC Estates Pty Ltd* (1975) 132 CLR 323 was principally about third-party liability and in *New Zealand Netherlands Society 'Oranje' Inc v Kuys* [1973] 1 WLR 1126, Lord Wilberforce was able to conclude that the secretary of the society was not a fiduciary without propounding an overarching theory of fiduciary duties. None of these cases was a vehicle for a general discussion of this nature.

93 There are also resonances with the work of Austin W Scott, 'The Fiduciary Principle' (1949) 37 *California Law Review* 539. Michael Bryan, 'Unifying Estoppel Doctrine: The Argument for Heresy' (2013) 7 *Journal of Equity* 209, 213, points out that Mason J's description 'was a synthesis of earlier characterisations of fiduciary status'.

juridical foundations of fiduciary law continue and it is perhaps too early to appreciate the significance of any single contribution. Nonetheless, accounts of private law and fiduciary law within that landscape which place central importance on a party's decision-making power held for another person,[94] on undertakings made,[95] or, in the language of Finn, 'entitlement to expect' the fiduciary standard,[96] have perhaps already appreciated the significance of Mason J's dictum.

Another reason why dissents are later followed may lie in the identity of the author. Sir Anthony Mason himself has remarked that the persuasiveness of any proposition lacking majority support 'depends to some extent on the reputation and standing of the author'.[97] Some judges achieve a higher standing among their judicial peers than others due to their possession of outstanding 'legal skill, [a] logical prose style and [a] quick mind'.[98] As a result, judges with such capabilities might better be able to lead and foster unanimity in a multimember court. Michael Kirby noted this capacity in Chief Justices Marshall and Griffith during the early years of the United States Supreme Court and High Court of Australia respectively.[99] Other judges demonstrate superior skills as 'judicial politicians' and are frequently able to assemble a coalition of their colleagues to participate in joint judgments.[100]

However, it is not to this kind of 'persuasiveness' that Mason J was referring. Rather, he was pointing out that sometimes a judge who writes alone, including in dissent, may possess such personal characteristics that his or her judgment attracts a level of attention and enjoys a longevity that would not otherwise be the case. For example, dicta and sole judgments written by Sir Owen Dixon have regularly assumed an eminence that is seldom bestowed on judgments of other individual High Court judges.[101] The significance of Dixon's reputation in understanding the resilience of his minority opinions is discussed in the two earlier chapters of this book that consider his dissents.[102] Although Mason did not seek to say so in

[94] Smith, 'Fiduciary Relationships', above n 18.
[95] See Edelman generally, above nn 18 and 21.
[96] Finn, 'The Fiduciary Principle', above n 18; Finn, above n 22.
[97] Sir Anthony Mason, 'The Use and Abuse of Precedent' (1988) 4 *Australian Bar Review* 93, 109.
[98] Kirby, above n 45, 387. [99] Ibid. See Lynch, above n 45, 726.
[100] Michael Pelly, *Murray Gleeson: The Smiler* (Federation Press, 2014) 196.
[101] See, eg, *R v Hickman; Ex parte Fox and Clinton* (1945) 70 CLR 598; *Briginshaw v Briginshaw* (1938) 60 CLR 336.
[102] See Andrew Lynch, 'Unrequited but Still Great – The Dissent of Justices Dixon and Evatt in *R v Federal Court of Bankruptcy; Ex parte Lowenstein* (1938)' in ch 3 of this book; Stephen

his article, a similar status has since frequently been accorded to his own judgments. Arguably, the fact that Mason J wrote the dissent in *Hospital Products* is an integral aspect to understanding the appeal it has held for later courts.

A judge's identity may not invest his or her opinions with any greater lustre while that individual is on the bench. In the case of Mason J and, specifically, his *Hospital Products* dissent, the particular appreciation of the rest of the judiciary was a circumstance that only really gathered pace after Mason J had retired from the High Court. As discussed above, the dissent was not immediately influential in cases about fiduciary relationships. It is quite possible that, had it been written by another member of the Court, Mason J's *Hospital Products* dissent might never have achieved the influence that it has. It has force that belies its lack of precedential value.

Notwithstanding the above, we do not discount the strategic impact of Mason J's decision- making. For example, his judgment on the perennially contentious s 92 of the *Constitution* in *Miller v TCN Channel Nine Pty Ltd*,[103] given alone (albeit not in dissent), became the orthodox position within two years when the entire Court joined in a single joint judgment in *Cole v Whitfield*.[104] When he dissented, he did so effectively; his views remained likely to attract attention in future cases. Justice Mason's suggestions were not always adopted and some would ultimately be rejected.[105] However, he gave current and future judges seriously considered views with which to contend in reaching their own views. Whether due to his stature or his style, Mason J's dissents invite engagement with his views in later cases.

V Conclusion

The dissenting judgment of Sir Anthony Mason in *Hospital Products* has been both important and influential but is in many respects an odd choice for inclusion in a book on 'great' dissents. It neither thunders against injustice, nor predicts and plans for its ultimate vindication in more enlightened times. To the extent that it refers at all to the judgments of the other judges deciding the appeal, it does not decry or denounce them as

McDonald and Anne Carter, '*Uther's Case* (1947): Justice Dixon and the Troubled Legacy of the Commonwealth Immunity Doctrine' in ch 5 of this book.

103 (1986) 161 CLR 556. 104 (1988) 165 CLR 360.

105 See, eg, *Council of the Shire of Sutherland v Heyman* (1985) 157 CLR 424. Justice Mason's theory of 'general reliance' was later rejected by a majority of the High Court in *Pyrenees Shire Council v Day* (1998) 192 CLR 330.

misguided or mistaken. This is ultimately a *quiet* dissent; so much so, that it often does not feel like a dissent at all. However, it contributed two major concepts to subsequent judicial consideration of fiduciary relationships – the 'essence' account and clarity on the interaction between fiduciary law and contract. It has achieved prominence in every Australian court and elsewhere without ever having been adopted as a binding statement of precedent by the High Court. It is in all these senses a remarkable dissent. It is in keeping with the slow-burning recognition of Mason J's judgment that, after more than three decades, it might still be too early to describe it unequivocally as a 'great' dissent.

13

The *Chamberlain* Dissents (1984)

JEREMY GANS

I Introduction: Gun Alley

> I deeply regret there should be any division in this 'remarkable case,'... I am fully conscious of the weight of judicial opinion opposed to my own, all of which I unfeignedly respect and value. But as the conclusion I have formed is clear and distinct, and affects not merely the present appellant but also the general administration of the criminal law, I take the liberty of stating my reasons explicitly.[1]

These words open Isaacs J's lone dissent from the High Court's ruling in *Ross v The King* ('*Ross*') – the *Chamberlain* case of its day. According to an early newspaper report on the matter, '[t]he history of crime in Victoria contains no more horrible murder' than that of 12-year-old Alma Tirtschke, whose strangled and 'outraged' body was found on New Year's Eve of 1921 in Gun Alley (off Little Collins Street), 18 hours after the dux of Hawthorn West Primary School vanished while running a city errand.[2] After a fortnight of gawkers thronging the alley and daily front-page coverage of the investigation's every (non-)development, the police arrested the proprietor of the nearby Australian Wine Bar. Justice was swift. Three months later, the High Court dismissed Colin Ross' final appeal against his murder conviction and, three weeks after, Ross became the first High Court litigant to hang.[3]

History's judgment on *Ross* was slower. Three of the majority's most commonly cited pronouncements – a definition of felony murder; a bar on overturning jury verdicts 'if there be evidence on which reasonable men could find a verdict of guilty'; and the absence of any 'rule of law or

[1] *Ross v The King* (1922) 30 CLR 246, 256 (Isaacs J) ('*Ross*').

[2] 'Murder of Girl', *The Argus* (Melbourne), 2 January 1922, 7.

[3] Justice Michael Kirby, 'The High Court and the Death Penalty: Looking Forward, Looking Back' (2003) 27 *Australian Law Journal* 811, 812. However, as Kirby notes, records of executions may be inaccurate and identifying High Court capital matters is not straightforward. For an instance of a capital matter Kirby missed, see *Shaw v The Queen* (1952) 85 CLR 365.

of practice which requires the Judge to caution the jury' about disputed confessions – were respectively abandoned in 1949, 1958 and 1991.[4] More dramatically, in 2007 the Supreme Court of Victoria advised the Attorney-General to pardon Ross, relying on fresh expert evidence rejecting a trial witness' claim that hairs found on a blanket at his house were similar to Tirtschke's.[5]

These events no more prove the High Court's error in Ross' appeal than Lindy and Michael Chamberlain's eventual pardoning and acquittal for the murder of their baby daughter Azaria prove the majority's error in *Chamberlain v The Queen [No 2]* ('*Chamberlain*').[6] Nor does Australia's only officially wrong death sentence vindicate Isaacs J's dissent 19 days before its administration. Justice Isaacs agreed with the majority on each of the above pronouncements, as well as its dismissal of Ross' complaints against his trial judge's direction on the hairs. Rather, his sole ground for dissent was that one of Ross' alleged confessions (where he supposedly told a fellow prisoner that he fatally covered the 12-year-old's mouth to stop her moaning after he raped her) was consistent with manslaughter. The majority's view that a murder trial cannot miscarry merely because the option of a manslaughter verdict was not left to the jury was their fourth pronouncement to be eventually overruled, this time in 2000.[7] However, Isaacs J's strident stance that Ross was denied a fair chance to be labelled a negligent rapist rather than a murderer, based exclusively on the evidence of a serial perjurer (a fact known at the trial and confirmed by copious further evidence in 2007), is a parody of the more potent lessons the case teaches.

This, then, is one of the many burdens that fall on judges who hear criminal appeals in cases of potential miscarriage of justice. If the judgment of the High Court's first 'great dissenter' in *Ross* were examined in the seven years after 2000 (when his legal analysis was vindicated), it would be an excellent example of a 'great dissent', gelling with modern notions that death penalty cases need extra care. However, from around 2007 onwards, Isaacs J's judgment would be tainted by his lack of prescience on the facts, although it took 85 years for his failure to be demonstrated.

It took only a handful of years for the joint judgment of Gibbs CJ and Mason J in *Chamberlain* to be similarly diminished. Few would

4 *R v Brown* [1949] VLR 177, 182; *Raspor v The Queen* (1958) 99 CLR 346; *McKinney v The Queen* (1991) 171 CLR 468.

5 *Re Ross* [2007] VSC 572.

6 (1984) 153 CLR 521.

7 *Gilbert v The Queen* (2000) 201 CLR 414.

read it for any reason other than to determine where two fine judges went so wrong. However, the same cannot be said for the other three judgments in the case, which each contrast in different ways with the joint judgment. In this chapter, I consider whether that case's three dissents by, respectively, a former Attorney-General, a future Chief Justice and a future Governor-General achieve the greatness in a cause célèbre that, on an earlier occasion, eluded the only High Court judge to combine all three of those distinctions – Sir Isaac Isaacs.

The chapter will address each of the three dissents in the order they appear in the law reports (reflecting the seniority of each judge). Justice Murphy's judgment, a direct rejoinder to Gibbs CJ and Mason J, reads the best to current eyes but (as will be argued below) fell well short in addressing the intense contemporaneous public interest in the case in 1984. Justice Brennan's judgment, technically a concurrence, but in substance both a dissent and a rejoinder to Murphy J's dissent, failed to predict the dramatic developments in the Chamberlain case, but best engages with the then mood. Justice Deane's judgment, in substance a rejoinder to Brennan J's, is an intensely personal statement that is neither ahead nor of its time. Rather, it achieves greatness through its timelessness.

II Justice Murphy's Dissent: 'the hinge of the Crown's theory'

> Even in the course of this appeal the presumption of innocence often seemed to have been forgotten. Instead, in examining the evidence, there was a tendency to apply a presumption of guilt, as if Mr and Mrs Chamberlain were required to prove their innocence.[8]

These words were published on 22 February 1984, one day after a Liberal MP breached the New South Wales Parliament's *sub judice* convention to cryptically identify Lionel Murphy as the judge named in covert tapes of allegedly corrupt phone conversations *The Age* published earlier that month.[9] The 'Murphy Affair' that ensued, with its rumour-mongering, pair of inquiries, trial, appeal and subsequent acquittal, contained numerous overlaps in time, personage and themes with the Chamberlain case, despite their different subject matter.[10] A day after Murphy's death on

[8] *Chamberlain* (1984) 153 CLR 521, 570 (Murphy J).

[9] New South Wales, *Parliamentary Debates*, 21 February 1984, 4401 (Jim Cameron).

[10] See Jenny Hocking, *Lionel Murphy – A Political Biography* (Cambridge University Press, 1997) 282–314.

21 October 1986, another Liberal MP braved *sub judice* to remind the Commonwealth Parliament of Murphy J's dissent in *Chamberlain*, praising it as 'a masterpiece of insight and brevity' and correctly predicting its vindication in the then pending royal commission into the Chamberlains' convictions by Morling J.[11]

That Murphy J's dissent is by far the shortest of all the judicial pronouncements on the Chamberlains up to that time reflects not just his hallmark style but also the narrowness of his difference with the joint judgment of Gibbs CJ and Mason J. The High Court appeal was from a Federal Court decision that unanimously dismissed the Chamberlains' appeal but split on two issues. The first was whether territory appeal courts, like state ones, can overturn a jury verdict on the ground that it is 'unsafe and unsatisfactory'. The second was whether the jury could safely find that a spray pattern of alleged blood in the Chamberlains' Torana car was foetal blood, in light of trial evidence from two biology professors that the test applied by state forensic biologist Joy Kuhl was not specific to such blood.[12] The Chief Justice and Mason J sided with the minority view of Jenkinson J in the Federal Court in favour of the Chamberlains on both issues, but also agreed with Jenkinson J that 'the jury were entitled safely to convict' the Chamberlains on the remaining evidence.[13] Justice Murphy tersely agreed with all of the joint judgment's reasoning, except for the last point.

Unlike Isaacs J in *Ross*, Murphy J's point of difference from the majority puts him firmly on the right side of history. Having observed that Gibbs CJ and Mason J's comprehensive discussion of the evidence meant that 'there is no need to go over it at any length',[14] the bulk of his judgment outlined all of the now-recognised flaws of the case against the Chamberlains. In four short paragraphs, Murphy J identified the two most important weaknesses in the Crown's theory. The first was the unlikelihood that Lindy Chamberlain would commit murder 'in a most gruesome manner, within an extremely limited time and in difficult circumstances where the chances of discovery were high'.[15] The second weakness was the evidence that 'three people, none of whom on the Crown's hypothesis was yet a party to the alleged crime, and one of whom was an entirely independent witness who had only met the Chamberlains that night,

[11] Commonwealth, *Parliamentary Debates*, House of Representatives, 22 October 1986, 2506 (Harry Edwards).

[12] *Chamberlain v The Queen* (1983) 72 FLR 1.

[13] *Chamberlain* (1984) 153 CLR 521, 568.

[14] *Chamberlain* (1984) 153 CLR 521, 572.

[15] Ibid 570.

heard the baby cry after it is said to have been dead'.[16] Justice Murphy then listed a string of deficiencies in the prosecution evidence, ranging from the case's signature features (no body, no weapon, no admissions, no motive and no evidence of bad character) to specifics that have since loomed large: the trial evidence supporting the dingo hypothesis, the state's failure to preserve the blood samples from the car for testing by the defence, and the 'imaginative',[17] inconsistent and fallible opinions of British forensic pathologist James Cameron about the blood on Azaria's jumpsuit. His judgment's final paragraph – noting that, even if Lindy Chamberlain killed her daughter, there was nothing beyond presumption to implicate her husband – speaks not to history's eventual reckoning but rather to the overarching 'presumption of guilt' with which he opened his dissent.

But Murphy J's tour de force had a significant flaw of its own: his discussion simply ignored all of the prosecution case's strengths, such as they were. In the case of the myriad strange (and arguably suspicious) things the Chamberlains allegedly said and did in the aftermath of Azaria's disappearance, Murphy J's omission may signify wisdom ahead of his time; most today dismiss such matters as the ineffable correlates of grief in the public gaze. However, the same cannot be said of the trial evidence of human intervention in the disposal of Azaria's jumpsuit (and, by implication, her body), which was seriously questioned only after the Chamberlains lost their High Court appeal (specifically through a fresh examination of Azaria's jumpsuit in the Court's own basement, and the chance discovery of her matinee jacket that prompted the Northern Territory government to remit the remainder of Lindy Chamberlain's prison sentence). Even the Chamberlains' supporters interpreted Murphy J's omission of evidence that the jumpsuit had been cut by scissors as 'tacitly admitt[ing] that it was difficult to account for the evidence concerning the damage to the baby's garments on the basis of the hypothesis of innocence'.[18]

Any defence of Murphy J's selective presentation of the evidence rests on the final part of his judgment, where he focused on the majority's endorsement of Jenkinson J's dissenting view in the Federal Court that the jury could not safely find that alleged blood stains found in the Chamberlains' car were 'foetal' (and hence Azaria's). Justice Murphy wrote:

16 Ibid 571. 17 Ibid 575.

18 Norman Young, *Innocence Regained: The Fight to Free Lindy Chamberlain* (Federation Press, 1989) 76.

> The Crown contends that the jury were entitled to take a view of the whole of the evidence which would justify a conviction, even if the blood were not accepted as foetal. As I understand it, the Chief Justice and Mason J. accept that contention and as a result would disallow the appeal. In my opinion that is not the correct test. The real question is whether the jury might have arrived at its verdict against the accused because they accepted the evidence that the blood was foetal, and whether had they been directed otherwise the result may well have been different.[19]

This passage sets an incredibly low threshold for overturning a jury verdict, obliging an appeal court to quash any conviction if a single piece of prosecution evidence that 'might' have influenced the verdict is judged unsafe on appeal.

It is likely, though, that Murphy J's stance was contingent on his evocative characterisation of the foetal blood evidence as the 'hinge of the Crown case'.[20] This (otherwise unexplained) description gains support from the joint judgment's analysis, which portrayed the foetal blood evidence as falling within the general proposition about circumstantial evidence put by the majority: 'the jury cannot view a fact as a basis for an inference of guilt unless at the end of the day they are satisfied of the existence of that fact beyond reasonable doubt'.[21]

However, Gibbs CJ and Mason J's analysis is very problematic.[22] The majority's general proposition is clearly wrong as written, because an inference of guilt beyond reasonable doubt can be readily drawn from the combination of less certain facts; as Mason CJ acknowledged six years later, the sentence 'would have been more accurate to refer to "an intermediate fact as an indispensable basis for an inference of guilt"'.[23] But this raises a further problem. Although there are several 'indispensable' facts in the Chamberlain case – the non-involvement of a dingo in Azaria's death, the absence of a baby's cry moments before Lindy Chamberlain announced that Azaria was missing – the foetal blood evidence does not fit the bill. While the presence of foetal blood in the Chamberlains' car might well have sustained a guilty verdict on its own, its absence contradicts neither the prosecution's theory nor its remaining evidence, which hence required comprehensive examination on appeal.

[19] *Chamberlain* (1984) 153 CLR 521, 576. [20] Ibid.

[21] Ibid 536 (Gibbs CJ and Mason J).

[22] For a full critique, see David Hamer, 'The Continuing Saga of the Chamberlain Direction: Untangling the Cables and Chains of Criminal Proof' (1997) 23 *Monash University Law Review* 43.

[23] *Shepherd v The Queen* (1990) 170 CLR 573, 576.

Justice Murphy's approach is better supported by a further legal argument that was unique to his dissent:

> Muirhead ACJ's summing up to the jury was undoubtedly on the whole favourable to the accused. However the above view that a majority of this Court has formed concerning the blood in the car raises a further central issue concerning the summing up. Muirhead ACJ told the jury that it was entirely for them to decide which of the expert opinions they should accept, on the presence of the foetal blood. He directed them that they could act 'completely on her (Mrs Kuhl's) evidence, if the other evidence leaves you to have no reasonable doubt as to its validity'. In the circumstances of this case that was a misdirection. Eminent experts had raised serious and not satisfactorily answered objections to Mrs Kuhl's evidence on foetal blood. The judge's directions invited the jury to undertake an unsafe and dangerous assessment.[24]

As usual, Murphy J's brevity is to a fault. He neither addressed the Chamberlains' failure to object to the direction at the trial nor explained why a misdirection would justify his order of their acquittal, rather than their retrial.

His proposition that trial judges must dissuade jurors from (or at least refrain from permitting) reliance on unsafe evidence is a classic instance of Murphy J's 'merely prescient'[25] legal analysis. Two years later (a month before Murphy J's death, and without any reference to his dissent in *Chamberlain*), the High Court for the first time required that trial judges tell jurors that it is dangerous to rely on certain categories of potentially unreliable evidence to conclude that an accused is guilty.[26] This was the start of a lengthy (and increasingly strident) chain of such decisions that became a signature of the Mason, Brennan and Gleeson courts and is now partly embodied in the uniform evidence law.[27] However, three decades later, the High Court is yet to reach Murphy J's position that mere contradiction by qualified defence experts is ground enough to require such a direction. Moreover, the last decade has seen a backlash from outside the Court against this line of jurisprudence, which has been skewered as overly intrusive, biased against sexual assault complainants,

24 *Chamberlain* (1984) 153 CLR 521, 575.

25 See Michael Coper and George Williams (eds), *Justice Lionel Murphy: Influential or Merely Prescient?* (Federation Press, 1997).

26 *Bromley v The Queen* (1986) 161 CLR 315.

27 See *Longman v The Queen* (1989) 168 CLR 79; *Pollitt v The Queen* (1992) 174 CLR 558; *Crampton v The Queen* (2000) 206 CLR 161; *Doggett v The Queen* (2001) 208 CLR 343. See also *Evidence (National Uniform Legislation) Act 2011* (NT) s 165.

and productive of both overlong directions and technical appeals; much of the Court's work has been reversed by statute.[28] In short, from this vantage point, Murphy J's legal prescience in *Chamberlain* is both steadfastly ahead of its time and quaintly dated.

III Justice Brennan's Dissent: 'the jury's critical judgment of men and affairs'

> To grant bail in such a case is to whittle away the finality of the jury's finding and to treat the verdict merely as a step in the process of appeal. The central feature in the administration of criminal justice is the jury, and it is a mistake to regard the effect of its verdict as contingent upon confirmation by an appellate court.[29]

Justice Brennan was the only judge to rule twice on the Chamberlains. In *Chamberlain v The Queen [No 1]*, he set out an oft-cited analysis of the High Court's power and criteria for ordering bail for a prospective appellant. Dismissing such an application by Lindy Chamberlain, he predicted (presciently, in the short term) that '[i]t cannot be said that the [jury's] verdict is likely to be set aside'.[30] His ruling caused Lindy Chamberlain (who had spent only three weeks in custody at that point) to spend 10 months in prison and her daughter Kahlia to spend that time in foster care. His crucial third vote in *Chamberlain* added two years to both of those tallies.

Despite his shared willingness with Gibbs CJ and Mason J to reject the Chamberlains' appeal, Brennan J's concurrence in *Chamberlain* was firmly in dissent in two respects. First, he was alone in the High Court in preferring to refuse the Chamberlains special leave to appeal (although he put aside that preference to ensure there was a majority supporting the order to dismiss their appeal). Second, although (like all except Murphy J) he did not refer to the other opinions handed down, he largely disagreed with the legal and factual analysis of both the joint judgment and Murphy J.

On the law, Brennan J sided with the majority in the Federal Court below on the safety of the foetal blood evidence and the absence of any power in territory matters for courts to allow an appeal on the basis

[28] See Jeremy Gans and Andrew Palmer, 'Evidence' in Ian Freckelton and Hugh Selby (eds), *Appealing to the Future: Michael Kirby and His Legacy* (Thomson Reuters, 2009). See also *Jury Directions Act 2015* (Vic).

[29] *Chamberlain v The Queen [No 1]* (1983) 153 CLR 514, 520 (Brennan J).

[30] Ibid.

that the jury's verdict was unsafe and unsatisfactory. His latter stance is no surprise, as the majority below had itself followed an earlier unanimous ruling Brennan J co-authored when he was on the Federal Court.[31] Justice Brennan did agree with the joint judgment on one legal issue, their analysis of circumstantial evidence, stating that 'the primary facts from which the inference of guilt is to be drawn must be proved beyond reasonable doubt'.[32] That agreement (together with Murphy J's brief similar remark in dissent) provided a clear majority in support of Gibbs CJ and Mason J's analysis. This prompted a string of lower court decisions quashing convictions (including Murphy J's own subsequent conviction for attempting to pervert the course of justice) in part because of the trial judge's failure to give jurors a so-called '*Chamberlain* direction'.[33] When the High Court intervened in 1990 to narrow its earlier pronouncement, Brennan J's unique application of the criminal standard to 'primary' facts was especially difficult to explain away.[34]

On the facts, Brennan J's analysis is the opposite of Murphy J's in every way. Commencing his factual discussion with a two-page section titled 'The Dingo Hypothesis', Brennan J fairly set out the (then) evidence about dingoes, concluding that '[t]here was much to support' the hypothesis, 'at least on first appearances'.[35] However, after observing that the defence did not have to prove the hypothesis but that its falsehood would give Lindy Chamberlain's assertion that a dingo took Azaria 'a sinister significance',[36] the remaining 30 pages of his reasons are titled 'Grounds for Rejecting the Dingo Hypothesis'. His discussion details all the matters Murphy J omitted: the expert opinions of human intervention in Azaria's disposal and (with lengthy verbatim extracts) the Chamberlains' words and deeds after Azaria's disappearance. Justice Brennan concluded that the jury may have regarded Lindy Chamberlain as 'deliberately prevaricating'[37] in her cross-examination, rendering the dingo hypothesis untenable and her conviction inevitable. Likewise, the jury could have regarded evidence of Michael Chamberlain's speedy acceptance of Azaria's death as 'indicating knowledge of the baby's fate',[38] observing that '[t]he prosecution did not have to prove that Mr Chamberlain was privy to his

31 *Duff v The Queen* (1979) 39 FLR 315.

32 *Chamberlain* (1984) 153 CLR 521, 599.

33 See Hamer, above n 22; *R v Murphy* (1985) 4 NSWLR 42, 55–60.

34 See *Shepherd v The Queen* (1990) 170 CLR 573, 584, 591. Three years later, Brennan J attributed 'whatever misunderstanding there may be' about the majority's reasons to 'an absence of a uniform nomenclature': *Edwards v The Queen* (1993) 178 CLR 193, 202, 203.

35 *Chamberlain* (1984) 153 CLR 521, 581.

36 Ibid.

37 Ibid 590.

38 Ibid 597.

wife's plan to kill Azaria, but neither did the prosecution allege that he was ignorant of it'.[39]

Justice Brennan, again unlike Murphy J, then expressly addressed the relevant evidence marshalled against his position, albeit at times in a dismissive manner. The jury may have seen Lindy and Michael Chamberlain's reported 'apparent distress' as 'a diversionary tactic'[40] that deceived those who rushed to their aid. Evidence that an uninvolved camper told several others that she heard a baby cry out (after the prosecution said that Azaria had been murdered) could be dismissed beyond reasonable doubt in light of conflicts on other details about the evening between that witness's later account and those of others who were there. Ten minutes was 'time enough to kill Azaria'[41] in the privacy of the Torana. Although 'they would have had to watch for the opportunity',[42] the chaos of the search provided cover for the couple to clean the car and bury their child. As for the uncontradicted evidence that Lindy Chamberlain 'had been an apparently loving mother':[43] 'If Azaria had been murdered, it was unlikely that the murderer's motive – whoever the murderer was – would have been easily discoverable; nor is it likely that the motive for her murder was a familiar motive in cases of child murder'.[44] Norman Young, a supporter of the Chamberlains and fellow Seventh Day Adventist, singled out this passage in Brennan J's reasons as 'add[ing] respectability and judicial prose to the sensational diction of the tabloids', which had openly speculated that Azaria was killed in a religious ritual.[45]

None of this means that Brennan J shared the then common view of the strength of the case against the Chamberlains. His judgment provides an alternative explanation of why he was willing to reprise the case's now notorious public tropes in dismissing the Chamberlains' appeal. From the opening of his bail judgment through to his concurrence's closing paragraph, Brennan J highlighted one undisputed fact against the Chamberlains: the jury's verdict against them, a fact from which he drew several related consequences.

The verdict is exclusively the province of the jury: 'The drawing of the inference [of guilt] is not a matter of evidence: it is solely a function of the jury's critical judgment of men and affairs, their experience and their reason'.[46] It largely excludes legal analysis: 'Whether the jury has too readily rejected innocent inferences is not demonstrable in a case where a jury, impartially applying its critical judgment of men and affairs, could

[39] Ibid 596. [40] Ibid 592–3. [41] Ibid 594. [42] Ibid 595. [43] Ibid. [44] Ibid.
[45] Young, above n 18, 20. [46] *Chamberlain* (1984) 153 CLR 521, 599.

have drawn the guilty inference'.[47] And it fundamentally limits the role of judges:

> If a jury could reasonably draw that inference from the primary facts as they are entitled to find them and, exercising their critical judgment of men and affairs, could conclude that no other hypothesis was reasonably open on those facts (that is, if the verdict could not be said to be unreasonable or not supportable having regard to the evidence) it would be an exceptional case where the court would hold that it was unsafe to draw and act upon the inference.[48]

While many High Court judges (including, indeed especially, Murphy J and Deane J) have feted the jury system, Brennan J's concurrence in *Chamberlain* is by far the strongest endorsement of that system by any judge in the one case that, more than any other in Australia, exposes its frailties.

Part of Brennan J's stance on jurors has since been wholly rejected by his colleagues. In addition to arguing that territory courts are more restricted than state ones when it comes to criminal appeals (a position conclusively rejected 4:1 in *Chamberlain*), he argued the liberal approach to state criminal appeals stated by Barwick CJ a decade earlier in *Ratten v The Queen* ('*Ratten*')[49] should be rejected in favour of the restrained approach first stated by the High Court in *Ross* five decades before:

> If Ratten were to be taken as requiring a Court of Criminal Appeal to set aside a conviction whenever the evidence given at the trial leaves that court with a reasonable doubt about the appellant's guilt, the function of returning the effective verdict would be transferred from the jury to the court – a course which would at once erode public confidence in the administration of criminal justice and impose upon the court the impossible burden of retrying every appeal case on the papers.[50]

When Brennan J wrote these words, Colin Ross' pardon was 23 years in the future. However, when a seven-judge bench of the High Court was eventually formed to resolve the issue in 1994, the Chamberlains' own pardon was seven years in the past. Five judges of the Court endorsed *Ratten*, with only Brennan J continuing to support the *Ross* approach.[51]

However, the Court's practice is another matter. In *Chamberlain*, Brennan J proposed a criterion for determining whether a court can deem a jury verdict unsafe even though the verdict is supported by the evidence:

[47] Ibid 607. [48] Ibid 606. [49] (1974) 131 CLR 510, 516.
[50] *Chamberlain* (1984) 153 CLR 521, 603. [51] *M v The Queen* (1994) 181 CLR 487.

> Long curial experience has satisfied Courts of Criminal Appeal that some categories of evidence which a reasonable jury might act upon in returning a guilty verdict are frequently unsafe, and should be acted on (if at all) only after the jury has been warned of the danger of acting on them. Those categories of evidence, as the court's experience shows, have a special character: apparently safe to act upon, but frequently unsafe in fact. Acting under the extraordinary power in the common form statute, the court has given effect to its superior experience of these categories of evidence and has set aside verdicts which would otherwise have been allowed to stand.[52]

Although the High Court formally rejected this categorical approach to criminal appeals in 1994, it nevertheless allowed the appeal in that case, which fell within one of the two categories Brennan J specified: 'where a prosecutrix alleged that a sexual offence had been committed on her'.[53] In the following two decades, nearly every appeal the Court upheld on this ground fell within this category or the other he listed ('[e]vidence of identification').[54] The two exceptions (including a case last year that rested on a single piece of DNA evidence)[55] fell within another, narrow criterion Brennan J proposed in *Chamberlain*, that '[a]n appellate court will give more anxious consideration to a verdict of guilty where the basis of primary fact is thin and the room for inference is large'.[56]

Since *Chamberlain*, the Court has invariably dismissed arguments that murder convictions based on a mass of circumstantial evidence are unsafe and even overturned such a finding by the Australian Capital Territory Court of Appeal.[57] In one case, a majority of the Court rejected (or confined) the view of the joint judgment and Murphy J in *Chamberlain* that a conflict in expert evidence provided an occasion when an appellate court could deem such evidence unsafe, consistent with Brennan J's detailed critique of that approach in *Chamberlain*.[58]

More broadly, Brennan J's juxtaposing of jurors as 'the central feature in the administration of criminal justice' with the 'whittl[ing] away' of that role by appeal courts[59] has generally gained favour in the three decades since *Chamberlain*. For example, in 1992, Brennan J declared that courts

[52] *Chamberlain* (1984) 153 CLR 521, 604. [53] Ibid 605.

[54] Ibid. See *Pitkin v The Queen* (1995) 69 ALJR 612; *Jones v The Queen* (1997) 191 CLR 439; *Palmer v The Queen* (1998) 193 CLR 1; *SKA v The Queen* (2011) 243 CLR 400; *Douglass v The Queen* (2012) 86 ALJR 1086.

[55] *Cutter v The Queen* (1997) 143 ALR 498; *Fitzgerald v The Queen* (2014) 88 ALJR 779.

[56] *Chamberlain* (1984) 153 CLR 521, 600.

[57] See, eg, *Meyers v The Queen* (1997) 147 ALR 440; *Velevski v The Queen* (2002) 187 ALR 233; *De Gruchy v The Queen* (2002) 211 CLR 85; *R v Hillier* (2007) 228 CLR 618.

[58] *Velevski v The Queen* (2002) 187 ALR 233, [37], [180].

[59] *Chamberlain v The Queen [No 1]* (1983) 153 CLR 514, 520 (Brennan J).

can never permanently stay a trial due to adverse publicity, even if the court lacks the means to ensure a fair trial: 'Our system of protecting jurors from external influences may not be perfect, but a trial conducted with all the safeguards that the court can provide is a trial according to law and there is no miscarriage of justice in a conviction after such a trial'.[60]

At the time, only Dawson J agreed, while Mason CJ and Toohey J were content to permit such stays in exceptional cases and Deane, Gaudron and McHugh JJ would have ordered a stay in the case before the Court. Eighteen years later, the French Court unanimously endorsed Brennan J's stance.[61]

The 1992 case is one of 27 occasions where Brennan J would have dismissed a criminal appeal that Deane J would have allowed;[62] in their 13 shared years on the High Court, the opposite occurred only four times.[63] That pattern had its beginning in *Chamberlain*, the first occasion when the two judges took opposing sides in a criminal appeal.

IV Justice Deane's Dissent: 'the best that I can'

> Nor is the cause of the continued acceptance of trial by jury likely to be served by treating a jury's verdict of guilty as unchallengeable or unexaminable. To the contrary, so to treat a jury's verdict of guilty could sap and undermine the institution of trial by jury in that it would, in the context of modern views of what is desirable in the administration of criminal justice, be liable to be seen as a potential instrument of entrenched injustice.[64]

60 *R v Glennon* (1992) 173 CLR 592, 615.

61 *Dupas v The Queen* (2010) 241 CLR 237, 247–9 [25]–[30]. See also *R v Dupas [No 3]* [2009] VSCA 202, [62]–[63].

62 See also *Gerakiteys v The Queen* (1984) 153 CLR 317; *Davern v Messel* (1984) 155 CLR 21; *Phillips v The Queen* (1985) 159 CLR 45; *Rohde v DPP (Cth)* (1986) 161 CLR 119; *King v The Queen* (1986) 161 CLR 423; *Bennett v The Queen* (1986) 68 ALR 584; *John L Pty Ltd v A-G (NSW)* (1987) 163 CLR 508; *Coulter v The Queen* (1988) 164 CLR 350; *Wilde v The Queen* (1988) 164 CLR 365; *Veen v The Queen [No 2]* (1988) 164 CLR 465; *Duke v The Queen* (1994) 180 CLR 508; *Re Tracey; Ex parte Ryan* (1989) 166 CLR 518; *Murphy v The Queen* (1989) 167 CLR 94; *Mickelberg v The Queen* (1989) 167 CLR 259; *Grassby v The Queen* (1989) 168 CLR 1; *R v Falconer* (1990) 171 CLR 30; *McKinney v The Queen* (1991) 171 CLR 468; *R v Shrestha* (1991) 173 CLR 48; *Brott v The Queen* (1992) 173 CLR 426; *R v Glennon* (1992) 173 CLR 592; *Dietrich v The Queen* (1992) 177 CLR 292; *Anderson v The Queen* (1993) 177 CLR 520; *Edwards v The Queen* (1993) 178 CLR 193; *R v Van Den Bemd* (1994) 179 CLR 137; *M v The Queen* (1994) 181 CLR 487; *McGhee v The Queen* (1995) 130 ALR 142.

63 *Halliday v Nevill* (1984) 155 CLR 1; *Boughey v The Queen* (1986) 161 CLR 10; *De Jesus v The Queen* (1986) 61 ALJR 1; *Petty v The Queen* (1991) 173 CLR 95.

64 *Chamberlain* (1984) 153 CLR 521, 617–18 (Deane J).

It is easy to miss this paragraph of Deane J's dissent in *Chamberlain*. Many would not reach his dissent at all, overshadowed as it is by both the lengthy analyses of the evidence in the two majority judgments and the stridency of Murphy J's dissent. Those that start to read the case's final judgment may be put off by its first half, which makes no reference to the Chamberlains and instead works through what Deane J terms 'two questions of some general importance' that lie '[a]t the threshold of these applications'.[65] He sided with the joint judgment and Murphy J (and the Chamberlains) on territory criminal appeals and expressly preferred *Ratten* over *Ross* as the correct test for finding that a conviction is unsafe and unsatisfactory.

In the middle of this dense analysis of judicial and statutory precedents, there is a single paragraph that is bare of any legal references. It commences:

> The principle that no person should be convicted of a serious crime except by a jury on the evidence has no corollary requiring that every person who is found guilty by a jury's verdict should remain so convicted. The safeguard provided by trial by jury is not dependent upon any assumption of the infallibility of the verdict of a jury. It would be foolish to deny that a jury may be prejudiced, perverse or wrong.[66]

Then follows Deane J's evocative statement that the assumption of jury system's infallibility would leave it 'liable to be seen as a potential instrument of entrenched injustice',[67] a direct (if not express) response to Brennan J's stance on how best to protect the jury system. This paragraph, although not mentioned in subsequent Australian judgments, was cited by the New Zealand Court of Appeal 23 years later in its landmark analysis of that nation's approach to criminal appeals, expressly relying on it to reject a prosecution submission that appellate review 'could undermine confidence in the jury system'.[68]

How could an assumption of jury *infallibility* 'sap and undermine the institution of trial by jury'? In 2007, the New Zealand Court of Appeal understood Deane J as referring to how 'letting unreasonable verdicts stand' would reduce 'public confidence in the jury system',[69] a phenomenon the *Chamberlain* case has come to epitomise. However, there is an alternative interpretation that does not require so much prescience: that Deane J was speaking of the burden an unreviewable verdict places on jurors themselves. No one would find it hard to imagine the enormous

[65] Ibid 611. [66] Ibid 617. [67] Ibid 618. [68] *R v Munro* [2007] NZCA 510, [52].
[69] Ibid [57].

stress borne by the *Chamberlain* jury, not only during the trial, but in its continuing aftermath. Moreover, in this unusual case, unsourced (but also uncontradicted) media reports that the jury was initially evenly split three ways between guilt, uncertainty and innocence meant that anyone could readily picture four (or eight) jurors, eventually worn down by the remainder, for whom the case would be a continuing nightmare.[70] On this approach, robust appellate review (labelled 'the impossible burden' by Brennan J)[71] would actually *ease* jurors' burden by sharing with them the risk of injustice.[72]

Justice Deane's stance on reviewing jury verdicts played out in three ways in his judgment's second half, where he analysed the evidence at the Chamberlains' trial. First was the language of his analysis. Compare how each of the four High Court judgments discusses Lindy Chamberlain's credibility:

> Although the mere disbelief of her statements that she saw the dingo emerge from the tent would not in itself provide proof that she did not see the dingo, the inconsistencies in her statements *would have justified the jury in concluding* that they were false and that she made the false statements because she had something to hide.
>
> (Gibbs CJ and Mason J)

> If in accordance with the directions, the jury accepted the evidence that the blood was foetal, it was irresistible that *they should then disbelieve* Mrs Chamberlain and the other evidence pointing to her innocence.
>
> (Murphy J)

> Juries are likely to put great store by the way in which a witness deals with propositions put in cross-examination. If the jury formed an adverse view about Mrs Chamberlain's truthfulness, *they were entitled to find* that she did not see a dingo at the tent and had no reason to believe that Azaria had been taken by a dingo.
>
> (Brennan J)

70 Malcolm Brown, 'How the Azaria Jury Was Swayed', *The Sydney Morning Herald* (Sydney), 2 November 1982.

71 Cf the majority in *Ross* (1922) 30 CLR 246, 256 (Knox CJ, Gavan Duffy and Starke JJ): 'If there be evidence on which reasonable men could find a verdict of guilty, the determination of the guilt or innocence of the prisoner is a matter for the jury and for them alone'.

72 Cf ABC Radio National, *Encounter*, 12 May 2002, which includes Sir William Deane reciting the following passage from Matthew 11:30 at a service for the Port Arthur massacre: 'Come to me all you that are weary, and are carrying heavy burdens, and I will give you rest. Take my yoke upon you and learn from me, for I am gentle, and humble in heart and you will find rest for your souls. For my yoke is easy and my burden is light'.

> Mrs Chamberlain's own evidence of her observations in the moment or moments before, without having reached the tent, she cried out that 'That dog has got my baby' *reads unconvincingly and contains what seem to me to* be elements of striking improbability. (Deane J)[73]

Consistently with his view of appellate review, and his endorsement of *Ratten*, Deane J's dissent repeatedly voiced his *own* view of the evidence, in place of asserting how the jury should, were entitled, or would have been justified to view it.

Second, Deane J rejected the other four judges' view that the criminal standard of proof justifies discarding parts of the prosecution case. His view that any requirement of proof beyond reasonable doubt is limited to facts that 'an individual juryman sees' as 'essential' to 'reach his conclusion on the ultimate question of guilt or innocence'[74] (ie, links in a chain of reasoning), was adopted by the Supreme Court of Canada in 1988 and the High Court itself in 1990.[75] Justice Deane's impeccable logic requires that jurors and appeal judges weigh the effect of multiple pieces of individually doubtful evidence (ie, strands in a cable), a task that is pregnant with risk. In *Chamberlain*, Deane J, like Brennan J, held that in assessing the Chamberlains' guilt it was necessary to consider Joy Kuhl's opinion that stains in the Chamberlains' car (subsequently identified as industrial chemicals) were foetal blood, even though, like Gibbs CJ and Mason J and also Murphy J, he accepted that those tests were 'open to reasonable doubt'.[76] In Canada, the Supreme Court's similar stance led it to quash a man's acquittal of murder by a jury who had been directed in accordance with the views of the *Chamberlain* majority; Guy Paul Morin's subsequent conviction has since become one of that nation's most bemoaned miscarriages of justice.[77]

The final way that Deane J shared the *Chamberlain* jurors' burden is evident in the opening of his dissenting judgment's 'Conclusion': 'I have found the question whether the evidence failed to establish beyond reasonable doubt that Mrs Chamberlain murdered Azaria a difficult one'.[78]

[73] *Chamberlain* (1984) 153 CLR 521, 564 (Gibbs CJ and Mason J) (emphasis added), 576 (Murphy J) (emphasis added), 592 (Brennan J) (emphasis added), 623–4 (Deane J) (emphasis added).

[74] Ibid 627.

[75] *R v Morin* [1988] 2 SCR 345, [32]–[40]; *Shepherd v The Queen* (1990) 170 CLR 573, 585.

[76] *Chamberlain* (1984) 153 CLR 521, 623.

[77] See Fred Kaufman, *Report of the Kaufman Commission on Proceedings Involving Guy Paul Morin* (Toronto, 1998).

[78] *Chamberlain* (1984) 153 CLR 521, 627.

This admission is unique among the 16 judges, commissioners and coroners who have ruled on the Chamberlain case over the past three decades. The remaining 15 rendered their judgments or opinions (for or against the Chamberlains) without any express reluctance, hesitation or doubt. While Gibbs CJ and Mason J acknowledged 'mysteries' in the case when dismissing the appeal and Nader J later addressed the absence of certainty of the Chamberlains' innocence when entering their acquittal, both insisted that these were beside the point.[79] By contrast, Deane J proceeded to perform the very task as he admitted to struggling with it.[80]

In 2012, a Northern Territory Coroner held (as did an initial inquest in 1981) that Azaria Chamberlain's 'death was as the result of being attacked and taken by a dingo', observing that 'the evidence is sufficiently adequate, clear, cogent and exact, and that the evidence excludes all other reasonable possibilities'.[81] Justice Deane's conclusion 28 years earlier was much more hesitant. He observed that '[t]here is much about the defence story of a dingo that strikes me as far-fetched'[82] and accepted expert evidence (not even mentioned in the 2012 coronial report) of human intervention in Azaria's clothing:

> In this case of the bizarre however, I am unpersuaded that it is plain beyond reasonable doubt that that damage was not caused by some such unexplained intervention. The unlikeliness of such intervention is a factor, and an important cumulative factor, to be taken into account in deciding whether the evidence established Mrs Chamberlain's guilt beyond reasonable doubt. It is not, in my view, decisive of that question.[83]

What was decisive was set out in the most quoted passage from his dissent:

> the Crown case (that, within the five to ten minutes while she and Aiden were together absent from the barbecue area, Mrs Chamberlain put on tracksuit pants in preparation for her crime; took her baby to the front seat of the family car; there cut the baby's throat; and afterwards hid the

[79] Ibid 568; *Reference under s 433A of the Criminal Code by the Attorney-General for the Northern Territory of Australia of Convictions of Alice Lynne Chamberlain and Michael Lee Chamberlain* [1988] NTSC 64 (15 September 1988) 26–8.

[80] Consider Sir William Deane's later statement: 'There are a lot of things that I'd like to be certain about, that currently I simply believe. Perhaps it may be that the inability to be uncertain protects you from the disappointment of finding out that something you believed in wasn't right': ABC National Radio, *Encounter*, 12 May 2002.

[81] *Inquest into the Death of Azaria Chantel Loren Chamberlain* [2012] NTMC 20 (12 June 2012) [23].

[82] *Chamberlain* (1984) 153 CLR 521, 627. [83] Ibid 629.

> body) strikes me as being, in its own less spectacular way, almost as unlikely as is the story of the dingo. And there remains the clear evidence that the baby was heard to cry after, according to the Crown case, she was dead.[84]

Notably, this passage expressly acknowledged Deane J's belief that the Chamberlains' guilt remains the most likely of the two scenarios.

Today, armed with not only new knowledge about dingoes' willingness to attack children but also decades of observing the normalcy and dignity of the Chamberlains, it is easy to dismiss the Crown's case as not merely (much) less plausible than the dingo hypothesis, but inherently implausible. That makes it straightforward to accept not only the Chamberlains' innocence but also the guilt of myriad police, prosecutors, experts, reporters, judges and jurors in perpetrating their victimisation. Without doubting either of those conclusions, my view is that Deane J's expressed personal views in 1984 provided him with an opportunity to teach a far more important lesson about how to ensure the carriage of justice. It is an opportunity he took:

> Doing the best that I can, I have finally come to a firm view that, notwithstanding the jury's verdict of guilty, the evidence did not establish beyond reasonable doubt that Mrs Chamberlain killed Azaria. That being so, the verdict that she was guilty of murdering her child is unsafe and unsatisfactory and constituted a miscarriage of justice.[85]

V Conclusion: Into the Æther

> [W]e are sitting as an Appellate Court of Criminal Appeal constituted by the will of the Australian people, not only for Federal matters, but as truly representative of each State as its own Supreme Court to guard and maintain its laws, to protect the weak and to punish aggressors, but at the same time to see that no person is called on to suffer punishment except in substantial accordance with law. It follows that an Australian citizen does not approach this Court, in either civil or criminal matters, as a suppliant asking for intervention by way of grace – as in the Privy Council. He comes with a right to ask for justice, and I hold, as I have fully stated on a former occasion, that our sole duty in such a case is to see whether justice to him requires an appeal to be allowed.[86]

Justice Isaacs saw no need to name the 'former occasion' on which he first put these views. That is most likely because the earlier judgment to which he refers has a fair claim to being one of the greatest dissents of all time, anywhere.

[84] Ibid 629–30. [85] Ibid. [86] *Ross* (1922) 30 CLR 246, 259 (Isaacs J).

In 1914's *Eather v The King* (a criminal appeal whose facts are best forgotten),[87] five High Court judges jointly declared that 'in granting special leave to appeal in criminal cases this Court should follow the practice of the [Privy Council]',[88] namely that

> it is not a court of criminal appeal . . . It is not guided by its own doubts of the appellant's innocence or suspicions of his guilt. It will not interfere with the course of the criminal law unless there has been such an interference with the elementary rights of the accused as has placed him outside of the pale of the regular law . . . [89]

In response to Isaacs J's strident dissent both rejecting the Court's rescission of special leave and allowing the appeal, Griffith CJ added (in presumably *ex tempore* remarks) that 'at least a statutory majority of the Court' took a different view of both the facts and the law.[90] However, exactly six months later, four of those five judges joined Isaacs J and Higgins J to make a 'statement from the Bench' (reported as *Re Eather v The King*),[91] observing that the case can no longer 'be regarded as authority' because the rule of practice 'is interpreted by the members of the Court in different senses'.[92] The judges then declared that 'the Court has an unfettered discretion to grant or refuse special leave in every case' so long as there is a 'prima facie case showing special circumstances'. As Fullagar J later observed, 'the dissenting judgment of Isaacs J in that case may be said to have prevailed almost from the outset'.[93]

However, speedy acceptance does not ensure longevity. Seven years later, the *Ross* majority held that, in applying *Re Eather v The King*, 'we must never lose sight of the fact that in regulating our practice the interests of the community as well as those of the prisoner are to be considered'.[94] They added (three weeks ahead of Ross' wrongful execution):

> If throughout Australia it were supposed that the course and execution of justice could suffer serious impediment, which in many cases might amount to practical obstruction, by an appeal to this Court, then it

[87] (1914) 19 CLR 409. The question was whether a child's complaint that the accused wiped her genitals with a towel could be corroborated by evidence that both the child and the accused had the same venereal disease. I did warn you.

[88] Ibid 412. [89] *Arnold v King Emperor* [1914] AC 644, 646.

[90] *Eather v The King* (1914) 19 CLR 409, 429. [91] (1915) 20 CLR 147.

[92] This may be a reference to an intervening case, *Corbet v Lovekin* (1915) 19 CLR 562 (the Court rescinded special leave granted to a prosecutor in a case involving a publication alleged to have aided the enemy, a month ahead of the battle at Gallipoli), where Griffith CJ and Isaacs J disputed the meaning of *Eather v The King*.

[93] *Shaw v The Queen* (1952) 85 CLR 365, 382. [94] *Ross* (1922) 30 CLR 246, 251.

> becomes plain that a severe blow would have been dealt to the ordered administration of law within the several States.[95]

A year after *Chamberlain* (and the adoption of a new statutory test for special leave), *Re Eather v The King* was entirely forgotten[96] when a majority of the Court declared:

> It has been repeatedly affirmed by this Court that it is not a court of criminal appeal and that it will not grant special leave to appeal in criminal cases unless some point of general importance is involved, which, if wrongly decided, might seriously interfere with the administration of criminal justice.[97]

In that case, Brennan J and Deane J separately dissented as, in the words of the latter, 'the merits have been fully argued'.[98] However, a decade later, after the High Court established a new practice of hearing applications for special leave separately from the merits of the appeal (a practice that leaves little or no room for reasoned dissent), both judges joined in one of their last judgments together to hold that '[t]his Court cannot and should not wish to undertake a general supervisory role of courts of criminal appeal on questions of fact'.[99] So (in what King CJ, in dissent below, had declared 'a troubling case'),[100] the Court held that 'cases where the ground relied on is in substance that the verdict is unsafe or unsatisfactory are not likely to succeed'.[101]

Today, defendants convicted on the basis of complex and controversial circumstantial evidence who have failed in their first appeal must frame their application for special leave around the law, rather than the facts. If Lindy Chamberlain had brought her appeal to the High Court today, she might have been tempted to argue, as Robert Farquharson and Keli Lane (two other infamous convicted killers of their children) recently did, that her murder conviction was unsafe because of the possibility that she merely killed her child with gross negligence.[102] While such an argument (the very one Isaacs J raised in *Ross*) has technical merit, it also largely

95 Ibid.

96 But see *Mickelberg v The Queen* (1989) 167 CLR 259, 276 (Deane J), citing Isaacs J's dissent in *Ross* to the same effect as *Eather v The King*.

97 *Liberato v The Queen* (1985) 159 CLR 507, 509.

98 Ibid 521 (Deane J).

99 *Warner v The Queen* (1995) 69 ALJR 557.

100 *Warner v The Queen* (1994) 62 SASR 403, 404.

101 *Warner v The Queen* (1995) 69 ALJR 557.

102 Transcript of Proceedings, *Farquharson v The Queen* [2013] HCATrans 182 (16 August 2013); Transcript of Proceedings, *Lane v The Queen* [2014] HCATrans 171 (15 August 2014).

forecloses the kind of public campaign that eventually exonerated the Chamberlains. By contrast, although Lindy Chamberlain lost her appeal in 1984, it seems plausible that the reasoned dissents of Murphy J and Deane J about the guilt of the Chamberlains (of any crime) contributed to the seeds of public doubt that later grew about their case.

It is interesting to consider how other hypothetical High Court outcomes may have played out. For example, if Brennan J's dissent had carried the day unanimously in 1984, what the Chamberlains lost in two reasoned judgments explaining why their convictions should not stand may well have been balanced by an unequivocal ruling that Australian defendants in general (and territory ones in particular) have less recourse on appeal than English defendants. On the other hand, the (unlikely) hypothetical of Murphy J's dissent gaining the unanimous support of the Court may well not have been positive for the Chamberlains. Although it would have freed Lindy Chamberlain two years early, it would also have robbed the public campaign against her treatment of much of its momentum. Consider the case of Raymond Carroll, who was convicted by a jury of the murder of three-year-old Deidre Kennedy, but acquitted by the Queensland Court of Criminal Appeal in 1985, relying on the (later overruled) *Chamberlain* direction jurisprudence, the (later overruled) common law rule on similar fact evidence and doubts about forensic bite mark evidence.[103] That acquittal prompted a public backlash that continues to this day, resulting in a perjury conviction, overturned on appeal as a breach of the rule against double jeopardy, and then that rule's partial repeal throughout Australia, followed by a campaign for Carroll's retrial.[104] Rather than his vindication, Carroll's appeals guaranteed the destruction of his reputation, even though several courts (rightly) judged the evidence against him too weak to support a conviction.

In my view, the most beguiling hypothetical is Deane J's dissent gaining the Court's unanimous support in 1984. What if the Australian public was told that its top judges, despite finding the dingo hypothesis 'far-fetched',[105] nevertheless declared the Crown's more plausible theory of what happened at Uluru to be still too doubtful to support the Chamberlains' conviction? Perhaps the result may have been a backlash against

[103] *R v Carroll* (1985) 19 A Crim R 410.

[104] See *R v Carroll* (2002) 213 CLR 635; David Murray, '"Deidre's Law", Sparked by Murdered Toddler, May See Three Other Cases Revisited', *The Courier Mail* (Brisbane), 2 May 2014; *Criminal Law Amendment Act 2014* (Qld) s 35.

[105] *Chamberlain* (1984) 153 CLR 521, 628 (Deane J).

criminal appeals in general and the High Court in particular. Or perhaps it might have brought forward the collective national shrug and eventual relief that occurred in the actual case, minus the shameful recognition that the Chamberlains owed their freedom to charity, perseverance, public relations and luck. And perhaps the High Court, rather than being a mere footnote in a painful national lesson in justice, might have instead held a 'mirror to the nation',[106] the very quality that Deane J would later bring, in his 'own less spectacular way',[107] to the office of the Governor-General.

[106] Sir William Deane, *Directions: A Vision for Australia* (St Pauls Publications, 2002) 79, cited in Heather Roberts, 'A Mirror to the Man Reflecting on Justice William Deane: A Private Man in Public Office' (2011) 32 *Adelaide Law Review* 17, 18.

[107] *Chamberlain* (1984) 153 CLR 521, 628.

14

Treachery or Heroism? The Judgment of Justices Deane and Toohey in *Leeth v Commonwealth* (1992)

AMELIA SIMPSON

I Introduction

The dissenting reasons of Deane and Toohey JJ in *Leeth v Commonwealth* ('*Leeth*')[1] won little praise in the months and years following the decision. Rather, many critics – including leading figures within the constitutional law academy – reacted with disbelief and contempt to both the methodology that Deane and Toohey JJ adopted and their apparent vision of a more potent kind of judicial review. This chapter examines those criticisms and considers to what extent they were deserved. Rather than setting out to vindicate Deane and Toohey JJ, however, my goal is simply to illuminate the way in which this particular dissent was received, illustrating thereby Professor Mark Tushnet's thesis that 'dissents have their meaning defined, in part, by those interpreting them'.[2] In addition, I will look beyond strictly legal evaluative criteria and, from a broader vantage point, advance some reasons for seeing value in Deane and Toohey JJ's dissent.

II *Leeth v Commonwealth*: The Context

Background

Richard Leeth pleaded guilty in the Supreme Court of Queensland to offences under s 233B of the *Customs Act 1901* (Cth), concerning the importation of a commercial quantity of illicit drugs. On appeal, and in conformity with s 4 of the *Commonwealth Prisoners Act 1967* (Cth),

[1] (1992) 174 CLR 455.

[2] Mark Tushnet (ed), *I Dissent: Great Opposing Opinions in Landmark Supreme Court Cases* (Beacon Press, 2008) xxiii.

his sentence was adjusted to 25 years' imprisonment with a non-parole period of 12-and-a-half years. Section 4 obliged judges dealing with federal offenders to fix non-parole periods according to applicable rules in the place of sentencing; that is, by reference to state or territory law. This rule aimed to ensure that parole expectations were consistent for all prisoners in a single prison, whether convicted under federal, state or territory law.

By the time Leeth's appeal reached the High Court the *Commonwealth Prisoners Act 1967* (Cth) had been repealed and the non-parole fixing rules for federal prisoners had migrated to div 4 of pt 1B of the *Crimes Act 1914* (Cth). Non-parole periods fixed under the repealed provision, including Leeth's, were preserved by the new provision.

Leeth asserted in the High Court that these provisions, dictating the alignment of non-parole periods with local state or territory law, infringed constitutional principles requiring equality of treatment. This argument stemmed from the fact that two offenders convicted of an identical federal offence, in relevantly identical circumstances, could receive starkly differing non-parole periods depending upon their places of conviction.

The High Court dismissed the appeal 4:3. The plurality judgment of Mason CJ, Dawson and McHugh JJ rejected all of the appellant's arguments for a general constitutional principle of equality.[3] Justice Brennan seemed to endorse a limited principle requiring equality of treatment on the basis of one's location within Australia.[4] However, he upheld s 4(1) of the *Commonwealth Prisoners Act 1967* (Cth), on the basis that the chosen comparator for fixing minimum non-parole periods – state prisoners alongside whom a federal prisoner would be housed – was rational and appropriate.[5]

Justice Gaudron, in dissent, based her reasons on implications drawn from Chapter III of the *Constitution*. She found that the impugned Commonwealth provision infringed a requirement, grounded in s 71 of the *Constitution*, of equal justice before the courts. Justice Gaudron explicitly sidestepped the appellant's arguments for a broader doctrine of legal equality, confining her analysis carefully to the requirements of the judicial process.[6]

[3] *Leeth* (1992) 174 CLR 455, 467–8. [4] Ibid 475. [5] Ibid 479.
[6] Ibid 501–2; cf Haig Patapan, *Judging Democracy* (Cambridge University Press, 2000) 29, 162.

Justices Deane and Toohey's Reasons

Justices Deane and Toohey, in a joint dissent, readily grasped the opportunity to innovate that this case presented. However, they recast the appellant's argument in terms considerably more ambitious; in particular, they declined the invitation to build a non-discrimination rule linked to incidental power and its purposive nature. Rather, they elected to formulate a principle that would reach discriminatory treatment in exercises of Commonwealth power more generally.[7]

Justice Deane had, years before, shown some enthusiasm for this idea in *Queensland Electricity Commission v Commonwealth*.[8] In that case, he pondered whether the established principle protecting state polities from discrimination under Commonwealth law may, in fact, be a subset of a broader limitation upon discriminatory exercises of Commonwealth power.[9]

Leeth provided the occasion to grapple with that proposition. Such was Deane and Toohey JJ's enthusiasm for this broader principle of equality that they chose not to engage at all with the appellant's lengthy – and more clearly pedigreed – arguments from Chapter III.[10] Instead, their attention was focused solely on the idea of a generalised constitutional requirement of equality.[11]

Derivation

In a nod to Deane J's earlier musings in *Queensland Electricity Commission v Commonwealth*, Deane and Toohey JJ's judgment in *Leeth* first articulated their 'doctrine of legal equality'[12] by analogy with the implication-based doctrine of state immunity. Aligning themselves unequivocally with the notion of popular sovereignty, they insisted it is logical and fitting that the *Constitution* protect individuals from discrimination – just as, via state immunity principles, it protects polities.[13] The equality of the people as parties to the constitutional compact carries, they reasoned, a necessary implication of their equal treatment under that compact.[14]

Justices Deane and Toohey found further support for their equality principle both within and beyond the *Constitution*'s terms. They identified several provisions and some structural arrangements in the

[7] *Leeth* (1992) 174 CLR 455, 483. [8] (1985) 159 CLR 192.
[9] Ibid 247–8. [10] *Leeth* (1992) 174 CLR 455, 493.
[11] Ibid 483. [12] Ibid 488. [13] Ibid 484. [14] Ibid.

Constitution as suggesting that 'equality' was among the meta-principles undergirding the Australian federation.[15] Anticipating objections here based in *expressio unius* logic, they rejected the idea that these discrete provisions amounted to proof that a more general equality principle was not intended. Rather, they insisted, the sprinkling of non-discrimination references in the *Constitution* is more appropriately regarded as evidence in support of equality's foundational status.[16]

The traditions of the common law, Deane and Toohey JJ contended, also corroborate a meta-principle of equality. They found in AV Dicey's writings confirmation of that principle's deep roots in common law constitutionalism.[17] In considering whether this claimed common law constitutional doctrine informs Australia's *Constitution*, Deane and Toohey JJ again focused on the latter's 'conceptual basis', understood in terms of popular sovereignty.[18] They also emphasised the explicit conferral, and separation, of judicial power, which necessarily incorporates a requirement to extend 'equal justice' and 'refrain from discrimination'.[19]

Content

What, then, was the suggested content of this claimed doctrine of legal equality? Justices Deane and Toohey framed it as a two-part doctrine, involving (a) 'the subjection of all persons to the [same] law', and (b) the 'inherent theoretical equality of all persons under the law and before the courts'.[20] Yet they readily acknowledged that, in those terms, the doctrine's reach could be excessive. To address this – and consistently with the High Court's growing standardisation of its discrimination jurisprudence in other contexts[21] – they adopted an exculpatory proviso, saying: '[t]he doctrine of legal equality is not infringed by a law which discriminates between people on grounds which are reasonably capable of being seen as providing a rational and relevant basis for the discriminatory treatment'.[22]

Justices Deane and Toohey also conceded that the *Constitution*'s express terms are, in places, inhospitable to the notion of equality and that any implied guarantee of legal equality must cede in those instances. In particular, they noted that several of the specific powers conferred

[15] Ibid 484–5. [16] Ibid 488. [17] Ibid 485–6.
[18] Ibid 486. [19] Ibid 486–7. [20] Ibid 485.
[21] Amelia Simpson, 'The High Court's Conception of Discrimination: Origins, Applications and Implications' (2007) 29 *Sydney Law Review*, 263, 267–8.
[22] *Leeth* (1992) 174 CLR 455, 488.

by the *Constitution* are framed in terms that clearly contemplate discriminatory distinctions, including the races power, aliens power and the power to acquire property on just terms.[23] Likewise, they observed, aspects of the states' involvement in administering federal justice invite unequal – and arguably discriminatory – treatment of some accused or convicted persons.[24] These express provisions were said to demand 'adjustment' of the implied principle.

Application

Nevertheless, Deane and Toohey JJ were not prepared, via this logic of 'adjustment', to subordinate their doctrine of legal equality to the parole fixing provisions of s 4(1) of the *Commonwealth Prisoners Act 1967* (Cth). The latter could not be justified as a 'necessary incident' of either the vesting of federal judicial power in state courts or the reliance on state prisons to house federal prisoners. Rather, s 4(1) 'require[d] an extraordinary degree of disproportionality' in the fixing of non-parole periods which have become, they insisted, the most significant element of a prison sentence.[25] Importantly, for Deane and Toohey JJ, the place of conviction could not be assumed to be the place of imprisonment. The latter may have been a rational basis for fixing the minimum non-parole periods of federal prisoners but the former, they insisted, was not.[26]

Nor did Deane and Toohey JJ find the suggested logic of uniform parole expectations as between state or territory and federal prisoners especially compelling. Rather, they saw the parallel operation of separate parole systems, administered by different people, as pointing away from any need for or expectation of uniformity as to parole entitlements. When considering the parole arrangements for a federal prisoner the more compelling comparator, they reasoned, was actually the treatment of other federal prisoners convicted of the same offence(s) in similar circumstances. That this was indeed the preferable comparison was, they reasoned, confirmed by the Commonwealth's abandonment in 1990 of the scheme implicating s 4(1).[27]

III A Torrent of Criticism

The judgment of Deane and Toohey JJ in *Leeth* prompted a chorus of condemnation that extended over several years. A cast of Australian

[23] Ibid 489. [24] Ibid 490. [25] Ibid 490–1. [26] Ibid 491–2. [27] Ibid 492–3.

constitutional luminaries lined up to lambast their reasoning and admonish their audacity. Those on the attack included Professors Geoffrey Lindell,[28] George Winterton[29] and Leslie Zines,[30] along with some very senior practitioners.[31] Many others added their voices. With varying levels of diplomacy, they all took much the same view: Deane and Toohey JJ's methodology, and vision, was deeply flawed and a threat to the very foundations of Australia's constitutional system. Cumulatively, this strong critique suggested almost that Deane and Toohey JJ were guilty of treachery; that is, fundamental disloyalty to the accepted institutional rules.

The Methodology

There was a shrill tone to much of the published commentary on Deane and Toohey JJ's dissenting reasons.[32] Some critics did concede that their methodology might credibly have supported a guarantee of procedural equality, closer to the positions adopted by Gaudron J and Brennan J in *Leeth*.[33] However, few thought that Deane and Toohey JJ's methodology offered adequate grounds for their more ambitious and radical position on equality.[34]

In particular, critics decried Deane and Toohey JJ's position that the common law had solid credentials in safeguarding equality. Many observed that women had suffered a great deal of discrimination under the common law, doubtless implying that Deane and Toohey JJ had been

[28] Geoffrey Lindell, 'Recent Developments in the Judicial Interpretation of the Australian Constitution' in Geoffrey Lindell (ed), *Future Directions in Australian Constitutional Law* (Federation Press, 1994) 1.

[29] George Winterton, 'The Separation of Judicial Power as an Implied Bill of Rights' in Lindell (ed), above n 28, 185; George Winterton, 'Popular Sovereignty and Constitutional Continuity' (1998) 26 *Federal Law Review* 1.

[30] Leslie Zines, *The High Court and the Constitution* (Federation Press, 4th ed, 1997) ch 16.

[31] Dennis Rose, 'Reasonings and Responsibilities in Constitutional Cases' (1994) 20 *Monash University Law Review* 195; John Doyle, 'Courts Unmaking the Laws' in Australian Institute of Judicial Administration (ed), *Courts in a Representative Democracy* (Australian Institute of Judicial Administration, 1995) 148.

[32] See, eg, the accusation of 'methodological free-fall' made by Geoffrey Kennett, 'Individual Rights, the High Court and the Constitution' (1994) 19 *Melbourne University Law Review* 581, 613.

[33] See, eg, Rose, above n 31, 208.

[34] But see M J Detmold 'The New Constitutional Law' (1994) 16 *Sydney Law Review* 228; A R Blackshield, 'The Implied Freedom of Communication' in Lindell (ed), above n 28, 232; and perhaps also Cheryl Saunders, 'Concepts of Equality in the Constitution' in Lindell (ed), above n 28, 209, 228–31.

insensitive to cast this as an 'anomal[y]'.[35] Some critics did resist such easy emotive shots to take a more measured, scholarly approach. Jeremy Kirk, for instance, emphasised that Deane and Toohey JJ's reasons did not, in declaring equality a fundamental principle of the common law, refer to any case law at all; rather, they cited only two secondary sources, being Dicey and another heavily derivative of Dicey.[36] But this understated tone was certainly atypical among critics, perhaps reflecting Kirk's greater temporal distance from the *Leeth* decision.

Jeffrey Goldsworthy's critique took an entirely different approach to questioning Deane and Toohey JJ's use of the common law.[37] In his view, even if one were prepared to concede the point that the common law valued and promoted equality, Deane and Toohey JJ had still been unjustifiably selective, drawing on only one common law theme among many of relevance to the case. Goldsworthy suggested that if one were looking, even-handedly, for fundamental common law principles that might be incorporated into the *Constitution* by implication, the principle of parliamentary supremacy would have to be high on the list. Yet that would, obviously, stand in abject tension with an implied principle permitting broad judicial review against an implicit equality standard.[38]

Another common refrain was that Deane and Toohey JJ had misconstrued or misrepresented the Convention Debates. Several prominent critics saw no evidence that the framers envisaged, for the courts, anything more than narrowly circumscribed and occasional roles in adjudging questions of equal treatment.[39] On the contrary, some noted, the debates around Andrew Inglis Clark's proposed 'Equal Protection' clause confirmed that most framers were hostile to the idea of a judicially maintained equality principle.[40]

Lindell advanced a variant argument based on the Convention Debates. He focused on whether the Convention Debates substantiate Deane and Toohey JJ's claim that fundamental rights at common law were implicitly incorporated in the *Constitution*'s framework. In Lindell's view, the

35 Rose, above n 31, 212.

36 Jeremy Kirk, 'Constitutional Implications (II): Doctrines of Equality and Democracy' (2001) 25 *Melbourne University Law Review* 24, 38.

37 Jeffrey Goldsworthy, 'Implications in Language, Law and the Constitution' in Lindell (ed), above n 28, 150.

38 Ibid 174–8.

39 Winterton, 'The Separation of Judicial Power as an Implied Bill of Rights', above n 29, 205; Kennett above n 32, 603.

40 Leslie Zines, *The High Court and the Constitution* (Federation Press, 5th ed, 2008) 594.

Convention Debates suggest nothing of the sort. Rather, they make clear that the decision not to include an explicit equality guarantee reflected absolute trust that parliaments would refrain from interfering with individual rights.[41]

The lack of a clear textual hook for an equality guarantee was a stumbling point for most critics. As Zines put it, the equality guarantee framed by Deane and Toohey JJ was instead rooted in the opaque 'assumptions' of the people at Federation. Those assumptions, Zines observed, are both hard to verify and have the potential to flow in many unpredictable and undesirable directions.[42]

Some critics faulted Deane and Toohey JJ's attempts to reason by analogy in building their case for an equality guarantee. In relation to their invocation of popular sovereignty, for example, critics pointed out that a commitment to equality in one domain (ie, sharing sovereign power) in no way implies a need for equality in all other corners of constitutional law.[43] Similarly, Deane and Toohey JJ's attempted analogy between the established doctrine of intergovernmental immunity and their implied equality guarantee was rejected by those commentators who considered it. Critics could not accept that a commitment to equality among individuals follows self-evidently from a commitment to equal treatment of polities with the federation, given the very different motivations underpinning each principle.[44]

The Vision

While those methodological quibbles varied in their emphases, critics spoke almost in unison regarding the constitutional vision underpinning Deane and Toohey JJ's proposed equality guarantee. In tones ranging from measured unease to palpable outrage, they emphasised the radical shift in power between the political branches and the judiciary that would ensue if the suggested equality guarantee ever won majority acceptance.

Some critics elected to view any constitutionalisation of the concept of equality as a kind of judicial *coup d'état* – a judge-led, dramatic shift in power away from parliaments and towards the High Court. Several variations on this imagery were developed in the commentary on *Leeth*. Some foresaw that an equality guarantee of the kind proposed by Deane and Toohey JJ would provide a kind of portal through which a range

[41] Geoffrey Lindell, 'Recent Developments in the Judicial Interpretation of the Australian Constitution' in Lindell (ed), above n 28, 34 n 129.

[42] Zines, above n 40, 594. [43] Kirk, above n 36, 38. [44] Ibid 39.

of other interests and statuses could achieve constitutional protection – generating an 'implied bill of rights'.[45] On this logic, judges administering an equality guarantee could be expected consistently to privilege certain types of interest over others, solidifying protection around those interests almost as though they were freestanding rights. For example, if privacy were considered by the High Court to be an important interest, then a right to equal treatment with respect to privacy might be given specific protection under the umbrella of a general equality guarantee.

Zines, developing this theme, observed that the power to impugn legislative provisions based on a bare criterion of equal treatment would leave judges with little by way of discernible criteria and force them, ultimately, to adjudge enactments against their own values or their perception of society's values.[46] As Kirk put it, the vast reach of an implied equality guarantee (because all legislation treats people differently in some respect) coupled with the inherently unconfined nature of the inquiry (subjective determination of what is 'fair' or 'reasonable') risked casting the judiciary in the role of a third house of Parliament, with a broad remit to disallow any legislation it considered unfair.[47]

Another line of criticism was that Deane and Toohey JJ's vision of a constitutional protection for equality was at odds with the expressed will of a majority of Australians, not just historically but also in modern times. Kennett noted that four years prior to *Leeth* the Australian people had, at referendum, rejected resoundingly a proposal to strengthen constitutional protection for individual rights.[48] Likewise, parliamentary efforts to encode comprehensive rights protections had faltered. On that basis, Kennett wondered 'what business it is of judges to effect that entrenchment by forging new constitutional rules[?]'[49] Within the context of a recent failed referendum, he suggested, the judicial manufacture of a sweeping protection for individual rights would be in defiance not just of parliamentary sovereignty but also of popular sovereignty – a principle that Deane and Toohey JJ had claimed to honour.[50]

Some commentators linked Deane and Toohey JJ's reasoning in *Leeth* with a candid and provocative conference paper delivered by Toohey J in Darwin soon after. Justice Toohey there outlined his vision for developing constitutional law towards a greater focus on rights protection. In particular, he proposed a rule of constitutional construction, deriving

[45] Zines, above n 40, 594; Rose, above n 31, 207.
[46] Zines, above n 40, 594; Rose, above n 31, 209; Kennett, above n 32, 604.
[47] Kirk, above n 36, 35. [48] Kennett, above n 32, 609.
[49] Ibid. [50] Ibid 611.

from popular sovereignty, by which Commonwealth heads of power would be construed consistently with 'fundamental common law liberties' in the absence of clear contrary intent.[51] Rose's searing comment on this was to say the methodology was 'difficult to distinguish from the behaviour of Justice Benjamin Boothby', a colonial-era judge notorious for his supposed disregard of colonial parliamentary supremacy.[52]

Why Such Intense Hostility?

The especially hostile reaction to the *Leeth* dissent, in contrast to other instances of bold implication-based reasoning from the High Court, provides fertile ground for contemplating the treatment of dissent within Australia's constitutional law discourse. While I cannot do justice here to that broader topic, there is one recent decision, in particular, that makes for such an interesting contrast that I will address it briefly.

In the 2010 case of *Kirk v Industrial Court of New South Wales* ('*Kirk*'), a unanimous High Court showed a willingness to make daring leaps in constitutional principle via an implication-based mode of reasoning.[53] The *Constitution* was there found to preclude state parliaments from ousting the jurisdiction of superior courts to provide judicial review of administrative decisions.[54] The joint judgment in *Kirk* arrived at that result by reference to policy considerations but also by invoking assumptions – arguably rather bold assumptions – said to underlie the *Constitution*'s provision for federal jurisdiction.[55] Specifically, it held that, around the time of Federation, it was a 'defining characteristic' of a 'Supreme Court' that it have an irrevocable jurisdiction to examine the decisions of lesser judicial and administrative bodies for jurisdictional error.[56] Commentators have since pointed out that the available support for this claim, in case law and secondary literature, is slim.[57]

51 Justice John Toohey AC, 'A Government of Laws, and Not of Men' (1993) 4 *Public Law Review* 158, 170.

52 Rose, above n 31, 210–11; see also Goldsworthy, above n 37, 175.

53 (2010) 239 CLR 531; Jeffrey Goldsworthy, 'Kable, Kirk and Judicial Statesmanship' (2014) 40 *Monash University Law Review* 75, 93 ff.

54 *Kirk* (2010) 2139 CLR 531.

55 Ibid 566–7, 580–1 (French CJ, Gummow, Hayne, Crennan, Kiefel and Bell JJ).

56 Ibid 566 (French CJ, Gummow, Hayne, Crennan, Kiefel and Bell JJ).

57 Goldsworthy, above n 37, 93–9; Oscar Roos, 'Accepted Doctrine at the Time of Federation and *Kirk v Industrial Court of New South Wales*' (2013) 35 *Sydney Law Review* 781; Luke Beck, 'What Is a "Supreme Court of a State?"' (2012) 34 *Sydney Law Review* 295.

The sweeping and yet thinly referenced nature of the reasoning in *Kirk* might bring to mind Deane and Toohey JJ's dissenting reasons in *Leeth*. Curiously, though, despite the obvious parallels, the reasoning in *Kirk* was received quite differently. While there has certainly been criticism of the reasoning in *Kirk*,[58] it has in sum been not nearly so shrill and castigating as that directed at Deane and Toohey JJ's position in *Leeth*. In any case, the criticism of *Kirk* seems to have been outweighed by a greater volume of commentary in praise. Many factors might help to explain the very different reception given to these two similarly reasoned points of view. Most obviously, it could be that the academy and profession has greater sympathy for the policy objectives underlying the *Kirk* decision than for those underlying the *Leeth* dissent. But perhaps also, the very fact that the latter represented a *minority* position emboldened critics who might have shied away from strong criticism of any position taken by a unanimous High Court. Indeed, the formal principles, and the attendant culture, of the common law tradition typically offer little incentive for celebrating or defending dissenting reasons.

IV Weaknesses in the Critique

In this Part I point to some flaws in the logic underpinning the standard critiques of Deane and Toohey JJ's dissent. My purpose is not so ambitious as to change the views of sceptics and critics, but to suggest that Deane and Toohey JJ's position was closer to the orthodoxy than many critics implied, and accordingly should not have inspired the shrill indignation described in the previous Part.

It is worth noting, at the outset, that not all commentators on Deane and Toohey JJ's reasoning in *Leeth* found it to be irresponsible or absurd. From within the senior ranks of the constitutional law academy there were some voices of approval, though they were drowned out by the louder critics at the time.[59] Kirk, writing several years after *Leeth* was decided, considered the idea of an implied equality guarantee to have sufficient plausibility to be taken seriously. He carefully unpicked and examined Deane and Toohey JJ's reasoning and found that, at least from the vantage point of an evolutionary interpretative theory, the idea and the

58 Ibid.

59 See above n 34. Interestingly, only one woman of this standing – Professor Cheryl Saunders – entered the debate and she seemed cautiously accepting of Deane and Toohey JJ's position: Saunders, above n 34, 228–31.

methodology both made enough sense to warrant a considered response, rather than an outcry.[60]

In considering the potential weaknesses in critics' positions, I will once again focus first on methodology and then deal separately with questions of vision. While this explicit division is not a feature of the critiques explored above, it helps to illuminate the issues.

Weaknesses in the Critique around Methodology

Though expressed with unwavering conviction, the standard criticisms of Deane and Toohey JJ's methodology in *Leeth* were certainly not flawless in their logic. Several points of weakness emerge on close examination. Kirk catalogued a number of them in his careful and even-handed examination of that methodology. In particular, he discussed the difficulty in gleaning anything conclusive from the Convention Debates, the problems with an *expressio unius* argument against an implied equality principle, and the fact that some evidence of distrust of legislatures can indeed be found in Australia's *Constitution*.[61] I cannot improve on Kirk's treatment of those points, which I commend to the reader. But I wish to develop an additional idea that might show Deane and Toohey JJ's reasoning to be, if not correct, then at least undeserving of the taint of illegitimacy.

As already noted, critics of Deane and Toohey JJ's dissent made much of its assertion that legal equality has long been a fundamental value of the common law. Indeed, many seemed to regard the exclusion of women from various rights and entitlements at common law as proof positive that the common law has never valued equality as a principle.[62] This particular criticism is, however, built on a penurious logic. Few would assert that the contemporary Australian politico-legal system is ignorant of, or completely misunderstands, the concept of equality because it denies voting rights to teenagers, certain prisoners and many resident non-citizens. Likewise, few would contend that the 18th century's French revolutionaries, or the American anti-slavery movement of the 19th century, were not really committed to equality because they neglected issues of gender-, disability- or sexuality-based discrimination. A society's conception of worthy beneficiaries for the dignity of 'equal treatment' evolves over time; earlier, narrower, iterations cannot sensibly be understood to

[60] Kirk, above n 36, 25. [61] Ibid 27–30.

[62] Zines, above n 40, 593; Kennett, above n 32, 603–4; Rose, above n 31, 207–8.

evidence a repudiation of the very idea of equality. A commitment to equal treatment in the abstract says nothing about who will, or should, be the beneficiaries of such protection.[63]

In their joint reasons in *Leeth*, Deane and Toohey JJ were, on my reading, only attempting to claim that the idea of equality – rather than a particular stage in its evolution – was evident in the common law historically. On that basis, if the common law did indeed display any track record of weighing competing claims with the familiar conceptual apparatus of equality norms – ie, treating likes alike, rejecting inappropriate comparators, and so on – then that record is surely relevant to the appropriateness of a wider principle today.

The real mistake made by Toohey and Deane JJ, here, was to inadequately explain and support their assertion that equality was an idea with deep roots in the common law tradition. They provided just two, secondary, references on this point – to Dicey and another source derivative of Dicey.[64] Equality was indeed an important part of Dicey's theory of the rule of law, making that theory a legitimate source of inspiration here. However, the brevity of Deane and Toohey JJ's reference proved to be problematic. Critics, perhaps inevitably, emphasised the better known aspect of Dicey's theory, being the centrality of parliamentary sovereignty, permitting an inference that Deane and Toohey JJ's reliance had been misplaced.

Aside from the underdeveloped treatment of Dicey, there were other opportunities lost to Deane and Toohey JJ's case for the central place of equality within the common law. One might imagine that the idea of equality could, even if only in a procedural sense, be credibly located in the very bones of the common law legal system. For instance, the analogical reasoning that lies at the heart of common law methodology presumably reflects the perceived importance of treating likes alike.[65] Politically, notions of equality have been the oxygen of democracy, as successive generations have demanded, and achieved, greater political

[63] This was a key factor leading Professor Peter Westen famously to declare 'equality' a purely rhetorical, or 'empty', concept: Peter Westen, 'The Empty Idea of Equality' (1982) 95 *Harvard Law Review* 537.

[64] *Leeth* (1992) 174 CLR 455, 490 nn 61–2 (Deane and Toohey JJ), citing A V Dicey, *Introduction to the Study of the Law of the Constitution* (Macmillan, 10th ed, 1959) 193; W S Holdsworth, *A History of English Law* (Methuen, 1938) vol 10, 649. See also Kirk, above n 36, 38.

[65] See, eg, Karl N Llewellyn, 'Case Law' in Edwin Seligman (ed), *Encyclopaedia of the Social Sciences* (Macmillan, 1930) vol 3, 249.

inclusion. The failure to bring any of these larger considerations to bear, in asserting the common law roots of equality, seems regrettable.

In any case, the widespread seizing upon the unequal position of women at common law is perhaps instructive as to the motivations of Deane and Toohey JJ's critics. These critics may have taken a few liberties of their own, and cut a few corners in reasoning out their objections, in their eagerness to slay the idea of a judicially created bill of rights.

Weaknesses in the Critique around Vision

Justices Deane and Toohey's reasons were perhaps also unfairly maligned as to the presumed substance of their vision. This claim is complicated by the fact that their proposed equality principle was embryonic, rough-edged and stated from a position of conscious dissent. Key specifics – including just how much policy intervention it would permit judges – were absent. Clearly, Deane and Toohey JJ's vision involved something beyond a purely formal conception of equal treatment, in which Parliament and the executive would determine appropriate comparators and judges could only question their application. Their findings on the facts of *Leeth* indicate that they envisaged, at the very least, a judicial capacity to second-guess a poorly chosen comparator.

However, this still falls well short of a fully substantive constitutional equality principle – as can be seen today in the constitutional jurisprudence of South Africa and Canada – empowering courts to direct positive action (and, crucially, the allocation of resources) to further the inclusion of disadvantaged groups. There is scant evidence that Deane and Toohey JJ imagined anything like the latter in *Leeth*.[66] More probably, they had in mind a generalised version of the kind of equal treatment that the Court had recently established in the specific context of s 117 of the *Constitution*, requiring that any differential treatment be sufficiently 'rational and relevant'.[67]

Any thorough evaluation of Deane and Toohey JJ's vision would have to consider whether there are persuasive value-based reasons to believe that an implied equality guarantee is necessary or appropriate in the Australian constitutional context. That question, needless to say, runs headlong into eternally contested deontological and political questions that I will not wrestle with here. An alternative way to evaluate their vision would be to

[66] Cf, in a different context, *Dietrich v The Queen* (1992) 177 CLR 292.

[67] *Street v Queensland Bar Association* (1989) 168 CLR 461; Simpson, above n 21, 267–8.

concentrate on questions of its workability; that is, whether the proposed principle could be slotted into the pre-existing constitutional framework without too much collateral damage. I will here consider that question, invoking a comparative perspective to suggest that criticisms of Deane and Toohey JJ's vision were exaggerated in their depiction of its likely ramifications.

With the notable exception of Kirk, critics of Deane and Toohey JJ's *Leeth* reasoning were casually dismissive as to whether an implied equality principle might be an acceptable 'fit' with the broader Australian constitutional system. Possible comparative insights were widely overlooked. In particular, while some critics noted the Australian framers' explicit rejection of a United States-inspired 'equal protection' clause, few stopped to dwell on the United States experience of over 100 years of cautious, and often quite deferential, refinement of a general, constitutionalised, equality guarantee.

The so-called 'Equal Protection Clause' forms part of the Fourteenth amendment to the *United States Constitution*, added in 1868 in the context of post-Civil War reconstruction. The clause was clearly intended, first and foremost, to protect the newly freed slaves from racial discrimination. Even within those narrow parameters, however, the United States Supreme Court construed the clause so as to minimise its reach. It was not until well into the 20th century that the Court extended the reach of 'equal protection' to discriminatory treatment in other contexts.[68]

Today, the Equal Protection Clause is administered by reference to a set of Court-engineered 'tiers of scrutiny', which command different degrees of deference to legislatures in different circumstances. So, statutes making 'suspect' classifications – eg, drawn along racial lines or by reference to national origin – or impeding fundamental rights are given 'strict scrutiny' with minimal deference to legislators' opinions and objectives. Few provisions survive this strict scrutiny.[69] A second category of 'intermediate' or 'heightened' scrutiny is reserved for laws drawing distinctions that may be based on irrelevant stereotypes, chiefly gender.[70] This is, as the name suggests, more deferential than the strict scrutiny reserved for suspect classifications; to survive intermediate scrutiny a classification

68 Donald E Lively, *Foreshadows of the Law* (Praeger, 1992) 48–9.

69 *City of Cleburne v Cleburne Living Center Inc*, 473 US 432, 440 (1985); Richard H Fallon Jr, 'Strict Judicial Scrutiny' (2007) 54 *UCLA Law Review* 1267; most recently, see *Obergefell v Hodges* (USSC, No 14–566, 26 June 2015) slip op 22–3.

70 *United States v Virginia*, 518 US 515 (1996).

must 'serve important governmental objectives and must be substantially related to the achievement of those objectives'.[71] Finally, laws drawing no suspect or quasi-suspect distinction, and affecting no fundamental right, are approached with 'minimal scrutiny'. A provision will survive this scrutiny if a court accepts that it is rationally related to a legitimate government purpose, a standard that is most often met in practice.[72]

In short, the United States Supreme Court has taken a clause that provides scant textual guidance and, with care and time, has worked up a sophisticated – perhaps elaborate – self-imposed structure to confine and channel judicial discretion in predictable ways. That is not to say that the Equal Protection Clause, and the Court's application of it, has avoided controversy. Some of the cases decided in this area have given rise to fierce, ongoing disagreement; this is especially true of those presenting questions of affirmative action and its location within the doctrinal structure.[73] Nevertheless, the United States experience provides a prominent example of the capacity of a constitutional court to take the slippery concept of 'equality' and, over a series of cases, ground it in a way that provides enough stability – and demonstrates sufficient restraint – to dissolve fears of a judicial dictatorship. The diverse, yet generally measured and cautious, refinement of broad equality principles in many other constitutional traditions ought to provide further comfort to the anxious.[74] The fact that each of those provisions has emerged from a completely different textual and contextual milieu – when compared with the Australian framework on which Deane and Toohey JJ were building – does not diminish and perhaps even reinforces the point that judges can readily recognise, and effectively confine, a power of review that might strain their own legitimacy.[75]

71 *Craig v Boren*, 429 US 190, 197 (1976).

72 *Romer v Evans*, 517 US 620, 631 (1996).

73 *Washington v Davis*, 426 US 229 (1976); Owen M Fiss, 'Groups and the Equal Protection Clause' (1976) 5 *Philosophy & Public Affairs* 107; Catharine A MacKinnon, *Feminism Unmodified: Discourses on Life and Law* (Harvard University Press, 1987) ch 2; Derrick Bell, *And We Are Not Saved: The Elusive Quest for Racial Justice* (Basic Books, 1987) ch 7.

74 Louise Parrott, 'Considering Canadian Models of Equality in the Context of Constitutional Recognition of Aboriginal and Torres Strait Islander Peoples' (2013) 41 *Federal Law Review* 160; Henk Botha, 'Human Dignity: Lodestar for Equality in South Africa' [2014] *Journal of South African Law* 914; Ivana Radacic, 'Gender Equality Jurisprudence of the European Court of Human Rights' (2008) 19 *European Journal of International Law* 841.

75 This claim has been made in the United States context by Jack M Balkin, 'Framework Originalism and the Living Constitution' (2009) 103 *Northwestern University Law Review* 549, 565–6.

With this in mind, one might consider that the vehement critics of Deane and Toohey JJ's proposal, who implied that its wider adoption would herald a seismic shift in power, were getting ahead of themselves. Some were perhaps even revealing an ungenerous view of the professionalism and far-sightedness of our highest judges – a potentially counterproductive stance if these critics were hoping to influence judicial opinion.

V Finding Value in This Dissent

Do the reasons of Deane and Toohey JJ in *Leeth* have value that transcends debates about their methodology and vision? Whatever praise they received at the time was drowned out resoundingly by their critics. Nevertheless, there are ways of viewing their judgment sympathetically, or even with appreciation.

Scholarly discussions of judicial dissent often contend that dissenting judgments, or at least the scope for them, are crucial to the vitality of common law courts' dialectical and transparent approach to decision-making – a model said to produce, over time, the best possible reconciliation of different points of view.[76] If one accepts this theory of dissent – whether in the limited context of judging or as to the broader marketplace of ideas – then Deane and Toohey JJ's judgment should be viewed as making an important contribution.

Even the most ardent critics of Deane and Toohey JJ's reasoning would have to concede that Australia is better off for having had the debate that it prompted. The dissent was a significant factor in an explosion of interest in and scholarly discussion of the respective roles of Parliament and the judiciary. The looming spectre of a judicially created bill of rights forced judges, lawyers, academics, law students and perhaps broader communities of interest to form a view. As a new law student in 1992 I found it hard to avoid this controversy – not just in the classroom but in social situations too. It was doubtless a difficult and bruising debate to have, within a small scholarly community more accustomed to broad agreement. Yet that community survived and became stronger, its scholarship undoubtedly gaining in maturity and insight.

[76] On the place of dissent within a dialectical, or deliberative, conception of judging, see Kevin Stack, 'The Practice of Dissent in the Supreme Court' (1996) 105 *Yale Law Journal* 2235; Michael Kirby, 'Judicial Dissent – Common Law and Civil Law Traditions' (2007) 123 *Law Quarterly Review* 379; Andrew Lynch, 'Dissent: The Rewards and Risks of Judicial Disagreement in the High Court of Australia' (2003) 27 *Melbourne University Law Review* 724.

Looking through a differently positioned socio-legal lens, the fact that Deane and Toohey JJ were able to propose a doctrine that seemed so radical to so many, yet without suffering any evident ridicule from or ostracism by their judicial peers, holds an important lesson. Leaving aside the scholarly criticism, the fairly civilised aftermath of *Leeth* in the pages of the *Commonwealth Law Reports* demonstrates how well our highest court can accommodate dissent. Hopefully other judges, present and future, will remain mindful of this demonstration that comity can survive under significant pressure.

As a teacher of constitutional law, I have long found that Deane and Toohey JJ's reasons have an important educative role. Their judgment can underpin a kind of grand counterfactual – a peek into a parallel universe in which rigorous and extensive judicial protection of rights might take flight. To the extent that this kind of thought experiment needs a plausible doorway back to existing constitutional jurisprudence, Deane and Toohey JJ provide one in *Leeth*. One can imagine future generations of law students still being required to read this judgment and asked, 'Where would we have ended up if . . . ?' Relatedly, Deane and Toohey JJ's reasoning, and the publicity it attracted, contributed to wider public education on models of rights protection, their differences and merits.

It is, I think, also possible to consider Deane and Toohey JJ's dissent in terms of courage. In his examination of the phenomenon of dissent within and outside the law, Professor Cass Sunstein contends that dissenters are generally providing an important public service; they deepen the pool of information available to everyone, so that better decisions – public and private – might be made. Sunstein suggests that dissenters often possess a valuable combination of clarity and strength of character, rather than being, as so often cast, self-indulgent or undisciplined.[77]

This is, of course, not an analysis with which everyone would agree, especially when it comes to judicial reasoning. Chief Justice Gleeson memorably told an audience of barristers that 'only someone given to mock heroics or lacking a sense of the ridiculous, could characterise differences of judicial opinion in terms of bravery'.[78] While this possibly came from a place of frustration – Gleeson CJ was, at the time, presiding over some very persistent dissenting voices – it nevertheless reflects the viewpoint of many within the legal community.

[77] Cass R Sunstein, *Why Societies Need Dissent* (Harvard University Press, 2003) 6–7.

[78] Murray Gleeson, 'Judicial Legitimacy' (Speech delivered at the Australian Bar Association Conference, New York, 2 July 2000).

It is hard to talk meaningfully about courage without implicating one's values – one person's courage will, as Gleeson CJ implied, probably always be another's stupidity or vanity. Nonetheless, if one takes courage simply to mean persevering despite personal risk, and especially when advancing unpopular views, then there are good grounds for viewing Deane and Toohey JJ's position in *Leeth* as courageous. They submitted to the potential disapproval of judicial peers, and the wider legal community, to ensure that a divisive, but important, idea was put forward and debated thoroughly. With the benefit of the literature on dissent – a literature that views judicial dissent as supporting effective dialectical decision-making – Deane and Toohey JJ's opinion can, I think, be viewed more sympathetically than many of their critics seem prepared to countenance.

VI Reflections and Conclusions

Who knows how long Deane and Toohey JJ had been waiting to work their equality idea into a judgment. I suspect they had been waiting a while, with dwindling patience, because they chose to unfurl their implied equality principle in a case that was far from ideal for that purpose. As Brennan J rightly insisted, the Commonwealth provision impugned in *Leeth* was not self-evidently unfair.[79] Rather, it could be viewed as making a perfectly rational – perhaps superior – selection of a comparator against which to peg the non-parole periods of federal prisoners. Parliament had evidently decided that the more important comparison, from a fairness perspective, was with prisoners housed in the same prison. With that in mind, *Leeth* was probably a case where deference to Parliament was appropriate; there were two alternate and plausible 'baselines' for measuring equal treatment. Yet, in their haste to get their equality principle cast and unmoulded, Deane and Toohey JJ neglected to discuss the role of deference. This unfortunate oversight probably made their idea seem more radical and threatening than was necessary.

It is also worth remembering that Deane and Toohey JJ passed up an opportunity to solidify a majority (with Brennan and Gaudron JJ) around a narrower principle of 'procedural' equality grounded in Chapter III. We will likely never know how seriously they considered this lowest common denominator path. Given the significant shifts in the High Court's constitutional jurisprudence in the few years prior to *Leeth*, Deane and Toohey JJ might well have perceived some momentum for broader rights-protective

[79] *Leeth* (1992) 174 CLR 455, 479.

implications and made a strategic choice to feed that momentum with a bold dissent. However, if so, that gamble has paid no dividends in terms of influencing the course of doctrine to date.

In fact, the boldness of the judgment may have been counterproductive, perhaps hardening the opposition to free-standing implications that was building in other corners of the Court. Conventional wisdom holds that, five years after *Leeth*, the idea of an implied equality guarantee was explicitly rejected by a six-member High Court majority in *Kruger v Commonwealth*.[80] Just three weeks earlier the Court had unanimously declared, in *Lange v Australian Broadcasting Corporation* ('*Lange*'), that implied principles were legitimate only if anchored in the *Constitution*'s text and structure.[81] Those two decisions were widely assumed to mark the end for Deane and Toohey JJ's equality principle.

Yet a future revival cannot be ruled out. According to Kirk, Deane and Toohey JJ's methodology was closer to the Australian constitutional orthodoxy than other critics had let on, making revival a real possibility.[82] Robert Woods rightly contends, from a broader perspective, that the only thing inhibiting a more comprehensive High Court move into implication-based rights protections are the political and cultural constraints to which the Court submits itself.[83] Those constraints can shift, as can the Court's willingness to go along with them. Arguably, the High Court's institutional capital was spread especially thin in 1992 – with innovation underway on many fronts, including political communication and native title – such that opening up a further front on which to defend its legitimacy would have seemed untenable. However, since *Leeth* was decided these waters have calmed considerably. Meanwhile, the practice of government in Australia has become an ever more intensely poll-driven, reactionary undertaking. Vulnerable minorities can expect to fare particularly poorly under those conditions and an awareness of this could yet revive judicial interest in some sort of self-dealt corrective role.

I, for one, would not lose too much sleep over that kind of development. I would assume that – at least in the case of an equality guarantee – the Court would gradually work its way towards some inbuilt mechanism of significant deference in most cases, in parallel with the United States experience. Thanks to Deane and Toohey JJ, most public lawyers in

[80] (1997) 190 CLR 1. [81] (1997) 189 CLR 520. [82] Kirk, above n 36, 25.

[83] Robert Woods, 'Rights Review in the High Court and the Cultural Limits of Judicial Power' (2013) 41 *Federal Law Review* 585.

Australia – and doubtless many in the wider community – have already pondered the arguments and evolved an opinion on implication-based rights reasoning. Whenever these matters reappear on the High Court's radar, then, critics and commentators can hit the ground running.

Finally, it is interesting to consider how Deane and Toohey JJ reacted to the realisation that their vision was not gaining wider traction. Justice Deane, of course, left the Court late in 1995 – five years earlier than his mandated retirement age – to become Governor-General. Rumours abounded, at the time, as to why and how that appointment came to pass. It is easy, though, to imagine Deane J feeling deeply conflicted about his duty to uphold the law in a form he considered gravely inadequate, on an issue so dear to his heart.[84] In stark contrast, Toohey J took the pragmatic course and joined the majority in *Lange*, renouncing his *Leeth* views and never returning to them. Given the apparently strong motivation for change evident in his controversial Darwin paper, the quietness with which he retreated was surprising.

These two very different courses taken, in attempting to reconcile principle and pragmatism in the aftermath of such a significant dissent, underline that dissent is as much a human story as it is a legal phenomenon. And through that wider lens, I think, Deane and Toohey JJ's reasons in *Leeth* can be viewed more sympathetically and with a greater sense of appreciation than was forthcoming from many leading scholars and commentators of the day.

[84] On Deane's passion for protecting the rights of vulnerable minorities, see Heather Roberts, 'A Mirror to the Man: Reflecting on Justice William Deane: A Private Man in Public Office' (2011) 32 *Adelaide Law Review* 17.

15

Justice Dawson's Steadfast Defence of the 'Very Essence of Political Discussion' in *Langer v Commonwealth* (1996)

ADRIENNE STONE AND KRISTEN WALKER QC

I Introduction

Justice Dawson could reasonably lay claim to be a 'great dissenter' or even *the* great dissenter of the era of the 'Mason Court'.[1] His was certainly a very distinctive voice.[2] His dissenting judgments – such as those in *Mabo v Queensland [No 2]*[3] and in *Australian Capital Television v Commonwealth* ('*ACTV*')[4] – frequently exhibited a conservative approach to precedent and to constitutional interpretation. Equally, and at their best, his dissents provide a comprehensively argued alternative approach to that of the majority. In this vein, Dawson J's dissent (jointly with Gaudron and Toohey JJ) in *Ha v New South Wales*[5] is especially notable for the 'distinct vision[] of the economic and federal structure of federation'[6] that it offers.

In comparison with those just mentioned, his dissent in *Langer v Commonwealth* ('*Langer*')[7] is quite different. It neither offered an alternative substantive interpretation of the core issue, nor did it offer an alternative method. Nonetheless, it demonstrated compelling legal reasoning and it avoided a result that was widely derided[8] and that exposed Australia to

[1] See Michael Kirby, 'Address Given by the Honourable Justice Michael Kirby' [2005] 12 *James Cook Law Review* 4.

[2] Although, as Cheryl Saunders notes, Dawson J's dissents were more notable for their prominence than their number: Cheryl Saunders, 'Oration: Sir Daryl Dawson' (1998) 20 *Adelaide Law Review* 1, 5.

[3] (1992) 175 CLR 1. [4] (1992) 177 CLR 106. [5] (1997) 189 CLR 465.

[6] Saunders, above n 2, 2. [7] (1996) 186 CLR 302.

[8] For critical analyses see, Kristen Walker and Kristie Dunn, 'Mr Langer is Not Entitled to be an Agitator: *Albert Langer v The Commonwealth*' (1996) 20 *Melbourne University Law Review* 909; Graeme Orr 'The Choice Not to Choose: Commonwealth Electoral Law and

international criticism for basic human rights violations.[9] On these criteria Dawson J's dissent in *Langer* is a great dissent, even though its central finding is yet to be taken up by a majority in a later case (and may never be so taken up, given the particular nature of the regime in issue).

Further, Dawson J's dissent rested on a more tenable reading of the challenged statute and was more consistent with the High Court's previous decisions, including the Court's decisions on the freedom of political communication. His dissent is also, we argue, more consistent with later cases in which the Court has applied the implied freedom in the electoral context. Indeed, we contend that the majority's decision in *Langer* marks a low point in the Court's implied freedom jurisprudence.

Lastly, we suggest that Dawson J's judgment is all the more remarkable because he had previously rejected the existence of an implied freedom of political communication, yet in his reasons in *Langer* Dawson J demonstrated that the law in question should be found invalid without reference to the implied freedom previously developed by the High Court.

II Background

Albert Langer, a well-known political activist,[10] was jailed in 1996 for 10 weeks for contempt of court.[11] More specifically, he was jailed for breaching an injunction that directed him not to distribute publications during an election campaign with the intention of encouraging voters to vote in the election other than by numbering every square on the ballot-paper (which he referred to as 'optional preferential voting').[12] Langer had sought to encourage voters to give preference to smaller political parties

the Withholding of Preferences' (1997) 23 *Monash University Law Review* 285, 299–304; Kate Eastman, '*Langer v The Commonwealth of Australia*: The High Court's Retreat on the Implied Guarantee on Freedom of Communication' (1996) 3 *Australian Journal of Human Rights* 152; Anne Twomey, 'Free to Choose or Compelled to Lie? The Rights of Voters after *Langer v The Commonwealth*' (1996) 24 *Federal Law Review* 201.

9 See, eg, Amnesty International News Service, 'Australia: Political Activist Becomes First Prisoner of Conscience for over 20 Years' (Media Release, ASA 12/05/96, 23 February 1996) <http://www.amnesty.org/download/Documents/168000/asa120051996en.pdf>; Laksiri Fernando, 'Albert Langer: Australia's First Political Prisoner' (1996) 5(1) *Human Rights Defender* 11.

10 See *R v Langer* [1972] VR 973.

11 The Full Court of the Federal Court allowed Langer's appeal against the severity of his sentence and ordered Langer's release after he had served over three weeks of his term: *Langer v Australian Electoral Commission* [1996] FCA 1295.

12 Chris Field, '"Tweedledum and Tweedledee 1,2,3,3" – The Albert Langer Story' (Current Issues Brief No 14, Parliamentary Library, Parliament of Australia, 1995–96)

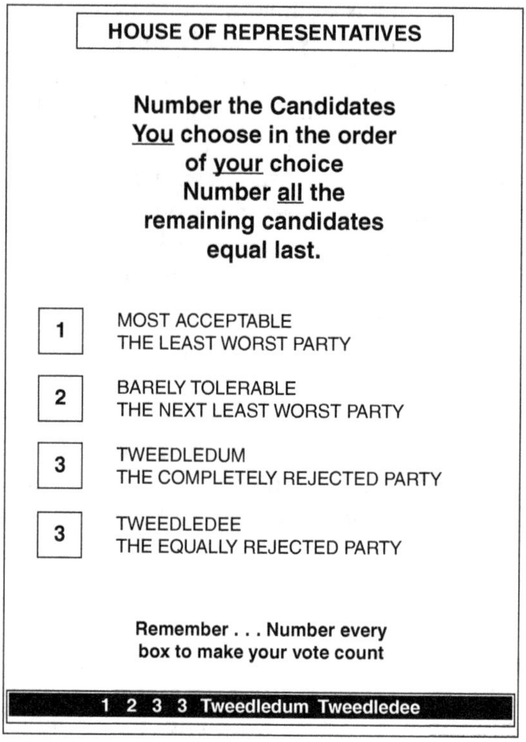

Figure 15.1 'How to Vote' Card distributed by Mr Albert Langer

at the expense of the Labor and Liberal parties.[13] This became known as a 'Langer vote'.[14]

Langer had taken out an advertisement in a newspaper headed 'How to Vote for Neither!' The advertisement displayed photographs of the then Prime Minister and Leader of the Opposition, labelling them 'Tweedledum' and 'Tweedledee' respectively, followed by a how to vote card.[15] The how to vote card looked something like Figure 15.1:[16]

<http://www.aph.gov.au/About_Parliament/Parliamentary_Departments/Parliamentary_Library/Publications_Archive/CIB/cib9596/96CIB14>.

[13] Fernando, above n 9.

[14] *Langer Vote* (12 September 2015) Wikipedia <https://en.wikipedia.org/wiki/Langer_vote>.

[15] The advertisement is described in *Australian Electoral Commission v Langer* (1996) 126 FLR 346, 348–9.

[16] The image is taken from Field, above n 12, 2. See also the examples set out in *Langer* (1996) 186 CLR 302, 321 (Dawson J).

In order to understand the *Langer* case it is necessary first to explain the operation of certain provisions of the *Commonwealth Electoral Act 1918* (Cth) ('the Act'), as in force in 1996, that established a preferential voting scheme for elections of members to the House of Representatives.

The provisions central to the operation of the preferential voting scheme, and considered by the Court, were ss 240, 268 and 270 of the Act. The most important provision was s 240, which provided:

In a House of Representatives election a person shall mark his or her vote on the ballot-paper by:

(a) writing the number 1 in the square opposite the name of the candidate for whom the person votes as his or her first preference; and
(b) writing the numbers 2, 3, 4 (and so on, as the case requires) in the squares opposite the names of all the remaining candidates so as to indicate the order of the person's preference for them.

Section 240 thus prescribed a method of voting referred to as 'full preferential voting'.[17]

If a voter failed to indicate an order of preference for all candidates listed on the ballot-paper in accordance with s 240, a related provision, s 268, came into operation. Section 268 outlined the circumstances in which a ballot-paper was rendered an 'informal' vote, constituting less than a 'full preferential vote'. Relevantly, s 268(1)(c) provided, subject to s 270(2), that a vote made in a House of Representatives election was informal if the ballot-paper had no vote indicated on it, or if it did not indicate the voter's first preference for one candidate and the sequential numbering of preferences for the other candidates.

Section 268(1) also included two relevant exceptions to the creation of an informal vote, namely:

(a) when a voter indicated a first preference for one candidate and an order of preference for other candidates, yet leaves one square blank; or
(b) when there were only two candidates and the voter had indicated a preference for only one of those candidates.

However, s 270 of the Act operated to ensure that certain votes made otherwise than in accordance with s 240 – and that would be informal under s 268(1) – still counted as formal (full preferential) votes. These were referred to as 'saving provisions'. Significantly, s 270(2) allowed

[17] *Langer* (1996) 186 CLR 302, 313 (Brennan CJ).

a ballot-paper that was not completed in accordance with s 240 to be treated as a formal ballot-paper provided that the voter had at least marked the number 1 in the square opposite a candidate's name, and had marked numbers in all other squares opposite candidates' names, or all others squares except one that was left blank. In these circumstances, the number 1 was taken as an expression of the voter's first preference, and any other consecutive numbers following this first preference were taken to express the voter's other preferences. Further, pursuant to s 270(3), any repeated numbers included in the sequence of consecutive numbers on a ballot-paper were to be disregarded.

The combined effect of the various parts of s 270 was that a voter could express a preference for one candidate, and no other, by nominating their first choice and then numbering other candidates equally or otherwise non-sequentially (for example: 1–2–3–3 or 1–2–2–2–2). It was this that Langer had sought to encourage.

The High Court's decision in *Langer* focused on the validity of s 329A of the Act, which made it an offence to distribute material that encouraged persons to vote otherwise than in accordance with s 240. Section 329A(1) provided:

> A person must not, during the relevant period [defined by s 322] in relation to a House of Representatives election under this Act, print, publish or distribute, or cause, permit or authorise to be printed, published or distributed, any matter or thing with the intention of encouraging persons voting at the election to fill in a ballot paper otherwise than in accordance with section 240.
>
> Penalty: Imprisonment for 6 months.

As noted above, Langer sought to encourage voters to vote in a way rendered formal by reason of s 270. He commenced this campaign in 1993, prior to the enactment of s 329A. He continued his campaign during the 1993 and 1996 elections, by which time the offence in s 329A had been inserted into the Act by the *Electoral and Referendum Amendment Act 1992* (Cth). In 1995 he commenced proceedings in the High Court for a declaration that s 329A of the Act was invalid. Justice Deane reserved a question for consideration by the Full Court, namely: 'Is s 329A of the *Commonwealth Electoral Act 1918* a valid enactment of the Parliament of the Commonwealth?'[18]

Langer, who appeared in person, challenged the validity of s 329A of the Act on the ground that the combined operation of ss 240 and 329A

[18] Ibid 303–4, 313.

of the Act contravened the constitutional requirement that members of the House of Representatives are 'directly chosen by the people',[19] and therefore that s 329A was beyond power.[20] A second submission, concerning whether s 329A was invalid due to infringement of the implied freedom of political communication,[21] was not pressed by Langer. However, that argument was nevertheless considered by the Court.[22] Ultimately a majority of the High Court upheld the validity of s 329A.

III Reasoning of the Majority in *Langer*

The majority in *Langer* consisted of Brennan CJ, Toohey, Gaudron, McHugh and Gummow JJ, writing in four separate judgments.

Each of the majority judges held that s 240 of the Act was valid and within power, having been enacted by Parliament pursuant to ss 24 and 51(xxxvi) of the *Constitution.*[23] In particular, the majority noted that s 24 of the *Constitution*, prescribing the requirement that the members of the House of Representatives be 'directly chosen by the people',[24] does not place an obligation upon the Parliament to adopt any particular electoral system, nor does it require that the adopted electoral system will provide the voter with the 'best' way of expressing that choice (a conclusion with which Dawson J agreed). As a result, no inconsistency or limitation arose by virtue of the operation of s 240 of the Act in relation to the requirements of s 24 of the *Constitution.*[25]

This point was further illustrated in the judgment of Brennan CJ:

> [T]he Parliament is empowered to prescribe a method of voting in an election for the House of Representatives that requires a voter to fill in a ballot paper in accordance with s 240, although that method requires a voter to choose by allocating preferences among candidates for whom the

19 *Constitution* s 24. 20 *Langer* (1996) 186 CLR 302, 315.

21 The *Langer* case was preceded by a significant development within Australian constitutional law, namely, the High Court's recognition of the implied freedom of political communication in the *ACTV* (1992) 177 CLR 106 and *Nationwide News v Wills* (1992) 177 CLR 1 cases. Shortly after the decision in *Langer*, the Court in *Lange* unanimously affirmed the existence of the implied freedom, adopting a two-limbed test for use to determine the validity of legislation that purports to burden the implied freedom.

22 *Langer* (1996) 186 CLR 302, 315 (Brennan CJ), 333 (Toohey and Gaudron JJ), 324 (Dawson J), 340 (McHugh J).

23 Ibid 315 (Brennan CJ), 331–2 (Toohey and Gaudron JJ), 341–2 (McHugh J), 349 (Gummow J).

24 *Constitution* s 24.

25 *Langer* (1996) 186 CLR 302, 317 (Brennan CJ), 333 (Toohey and Gaudron JJ), 341–2 (McHugh J), 349 (Gummow J).

> voter does not wish to vote. It is not to the point that, if a ballot paper were filled in otherwise than in accordance with s 240, the vote would better express the voter's political opinion.[26]

Justices McHugh and Gummow each took a similar approach, holding that the phrase 'directly chosen by the people' does not confer rights on individual voters to vote for the candidate of their choice or, conversely, to refuse to vote for candidates whom they dislike.[27] Rather, s 24 is a general power of 'inexact application'.[28] Justices Toohey and Gaudron, on the other hand, stated that the phrase 'must be taken as primarily mandating a democratic electoral system'.[29]

Having dealt with, and confirmed, the validity of s 240 under s 24 of the *Constitution*, the majority turned to the consequential validity of s 329A. Considering the plenary nature of the power granted by ss 31 and 51(xxxvi) and the validity of s 240, Brennan CJ and Gummow J had no hesitation in declaring s 329A to be a valid provision on the basis that it protected the method of voting laid down by s 240.[30] Justice McHugh agreed, stating that the power of the Parliament to enact laws 'relating to elections' extends to laws preventing persons from interfering with or undermining the electoral system. According to McHugh J, the object of s 329A was to protect the preference system set out in s 240 from being undermined. Therefore s 329A was a valid law with respect to elections for the purposes of ss 31 and 51(xxxvi) of the *Constitution.*[31] Justices Toohey and Gaudron were content to state that, having established the validity of s 240, the plaintiff's argument with respect to s 329A must fail.[32]

For similar reasons the majority also held that any separate challenge to s 329A based on the implied freedom of political communication must also fail, because the burden placed on political communication by operation of the provision was 'reasonably appropriate and adapted' to the object of preventing any subversion or circumvention of the method of full preferential voting prescribed by s 240.[33] As Brennan CJ put it:

> Section 329A does not prohibit discussion about the operation or desirability of the method of voting prescribed by s 240 nor does it prohibit advocacy of its amendment or repeal. Section 329A operates in the context of the method of voting prescribed by s 240 and prohibits intentional

[26] Ibid 317. [27] Ibid 342–3 (McHugh J), 349 (Gummow J).
[28] Ibid 342–3 (McHugh J). [29] Ibid 333.
[30] Ibid 317 (Brennan CJ), 349 (Gummow J).
[31] Ibid 339–40 (McHugh J). [32] Ibid 333.
[33] Ibid 318 (Brennan CJ), 334 (Toohey and Gaudron JJ), 340 (McHugh J), 350–1 (Gummow J).

> encouragement of the filling in of ballot papers in a way which, if not within the saving provisions, will result in the exclusion of the ballot paper from the scrutiny and which, if within the saving provisions of s 270(2), will result in a diminished expression of the elector's preferences. The prohibition contained in s 329A is thus a means of protecting the method which Parliament has selected for the choosing of members of the House of Representatives. The restriction on freedom of speech imposed by s 329A is not imposed with a view to repressing freedom of political discussion; it is imposed as an incident to the protection of the s 240 method of voting.[34]

He also took the view that the saving provisions did not prescribe an alternative method of voting; rather, they saved from invalidity certain ballot-papers not filled in in accordance with the Act.[35]

Justices Toohey and Gaudron approached the relationship between the savings provisions and s 329A in a similar way:

> Although the provisos operate to give effect to a ballot paper which might otherwise be informal, the democratic process is enhanced if a voter's actual intention is capable of ascertainment from the ballot-paper and effect is given to that intention rather than an intention which he or she is deemed to have expressed. In relation to ballot-papers which fall within the provisos to s 268(1)(c), s 329A operates to proscribe conduct which might encourage voters to fill in their ballot-papers in a way that does not make their intentions manifest. Because it operates in this way, it is reasonably capable of being viewed as appropriate and adapted to the enhancement of the democratic process.[36]

And Gummow J said this:

> It is one thing to advocate the abrogation or modification of the particular system by which the legislature provides for the exercise of the franchise. It is another intentionally to seek to undermine the effective franchise by encouraging a course of action which may lead to the casting by electors of informal votes in an election for the House of Representatives, thereby denying the effective exercise by those electors of their right to participate in the activity whereby representative government is constituted and renewed. . . .
>
> It cannot be inimical to representative government to forbid intentional conduct comprising advocacy of the casting of a vote in such a way as may be an ineffective exercise of the franchise. I use the term 'may be' to allow for the savings provisions which give effect to the franchise in some cases despite failure by the elector to mark the vote of that person on the ballot-paper as stated in s 240. The primary objective of the

[34] Ibid 318. [35] Ibid. See also at 337–8 (McHugh J). [36] Ibid 334–5.

> system established by the legislation involves observance by electors of s 240.[37]

Justice McHugh took a somewhat different approach to the question. He was of the view that if Parliament could validly enact s 240, it was no breach of the implied freedom to punish those who sought to undermine the system of compulsory voting laid down by the Act.[38] He considered that the matter might have been different if the Parliament were not able to compel people to vote. Without a challenge to the system of compulsory voting, however, it was not inconsistent with the implied freedom for Parliament to prohibit a person from encouraging voters to disregard a system of voting validly set up under the *Constitution*.[39]

IV Justice Dawson's Dissent

Justice Dawson delivered the sole dissenting judgment in *Langer*. First, Dawson J reiterated his dissenting position in relation to the implied freedom of political communication accepted in earlier cases (most notably *ACTV*):

> I was unable to accept the line of reasoning adopted by the majority of the Court in finding a constitutionally guaranteed freedom of communication because that guarantee was derived, in my view, from a notion of representative government which does not appear from any requirement contained in the *Constitution* itself. The freedom of communication which I thought to be required by the *Constitution* was confined to what is necessary for the conduct of elections by direct popular vote as envisaged by 7 and 24 and related sections.[40]

We note as an aside that there is some question as to whether there is a difference in substance in the position adopted by Dawson J and that adopted by the majority in *ACTV*. On one analysis all judges in that case derived a form of constitutional guarantee in a substantially similar way.[41] Certainly, the Court later explicitly rejected the idea that the freedom of political communication was derived from a 'free standing notion of representative government' in *Lange v Australian Broadcasting Corporation* ('*Lange*').[42]

[37] Ibid 350–1. [38] Ibid 340. [39] Ibid.

[40] (1996) 186 CLR 302, 324 (citations omitted).

[41] For an argument along these lines, see Leslie Zines 'The Present State of Constitutional Interpretation' in Adrienne Stone and George Williams (eds), *The High Court at the Crossroads: Essays in Constitutional Law* (Federation Press, 2000) 224, 226–8.

[42] (1997) 189 CLR 520.

Returning to *Langer*, notwithstanding his reiterated disagreement with the majority in *ACTV* and related cases, Dawson J concluded that s 329A of the Act was invalid. He held that 'the choice which is required by s 24 [of the *Constitution*] must be a genuine choice' and thus the voters 'must have available to them the information necessary to exercise such a choice'.[43] Section 329A was designed to deny voters such information.

This finding rested, in part, on his approach to the construction of the relevant provisions of the Act that established the preferential voting scheme. On his view, s 240 of the Act should be read together with the related provisions of ss 268, 270 and 274.[44] Construed in this way, he concluded that the effect of ss 268 and 270 was to make available a method of voting – optional or selective preferential voting – in addition to the full preferential method prescribed by s 240 of the Act.

Justice Dawson then held that the restriction of voters' access to information about a lawful voting method effected by s 329A was beyond power and inconsistent with the requirements of s 24 of the *Constitution* because it placed a restriction on access to information 'essential to the formation of the choice required by s 24 of the *Constitution*'.[45] Justice Dawson observed, however, that had s 240 been a stand-alone provision, without the saving provision in s 270, then s 329A would have been valid.[46]

When considering whether s 329A adversely affected the implied freedom of political communication (or what he referred to as a constitutional guarantee of 'freedom of political discussion'),[47] Dawson J concluded that s 329A constituted an unreasonable burden on voters' freedom of political expression:

> The effect of s 329A in any practical sense must, in my view, be to discourage, if not prevent, persons from imparting to eligible voters knowledge that the electoral system permits optional or selective preferential voting. It cannot, therefore, be a law which is reasonably and appropriately adapted to the achievement of an end which lies within the ambit of the relevant legislative power.[48]

As a result, Dawson J held that s 329A was invalid because it prevented Langer from encouraging voters to vote in a method that was lawful, formal and permissible under the Act, thereby unlawfully inhibiting freedom of political communication.[49]

[43] *Langer* (1996) 186 CLR 302, 325. [44] Ibid. [45] Ibid 325–6. [46] Ibid.
[47] Ibid 326. [48] Ibid. [49] Ibid 326–7.

In a final, and telling, passage Dawson J gently[50] took the majority to task for their failure to apply the implied freedom in this case:

> I have been able to reach my conclusion without reliance upon the reasoning of the majority with regard to freedom of communication in the previous cases. With the greatest of respect, that reasoning does not, as I have indicated, commend itself to me. But upon that reasoning, the *Constitution* guarantees freedom of political discussion. I must confess that I am unable to see how political discussion can be confined to the mere imparting of information and why it should not extend to the furnishing of information with the intention that it should be used. Indeed, exhortation or encouragement of electors to adopt a particular course in an election is of the very essence of political discussion and *it would seem to me that upon the view adopted by the majority in the earlier cases, s 329A must infringe the guarantee which they discern.* It is true that the encouragement of voters to adopt a course which is inconsistent with the casting of a formal vote may not infringe that guarantee because the casting of a formal, and therefore, effective, vote is in the interests of representative government, as are the various other controls which may impede freedom of discussion but which are required to ensure that an electoral system works properly. But s 329A goes beyond matters of that kind. It seeks to prevent the encouragement of voters to cast their votes in a form which is open to them. It must inevitably inhibit freedom of political discussion in a manner which does nothing to aid the proper conduct of elections in accordance with the Act.[51]

Justice Dawson's Judgment as a 'Great Dissent'

As we set out above, Dawson J's dissent qualifies as a 'great dissent' for several reasons: its reasoning; its result; and its relationship to the High Court's jurisprudence on the implied freedom of political communication both before and after *Langer.*

The Reasoning

In assessing Dawson J's dissent against the majority position, it must first be conceded that neither the statutory language nor the content of limits

[50] This civility and moderation is characteristic of Dawson J. It stands in marked contrast to the other freedom of political communication dissent featured in this collection: the dissent of Heydon J in *Monis v The Queen* (2013) 249 CLR 92, 178–84. See Gabrielle Appleby and Heather Roberts, 'He Who Would Not Be Muzzled: Justice Heydon's Last Dissent in *Monis v The Queen* (2013)' in ch 18 of this book.

[51] (1996) 186 CLR 302, 326–7 (emphasis added).

on constitutional power[52] are sufficiently precise to dictate one conclusion or the other. Nonetheless, accepting that both views are open, Dawson J's approach is, in our view, clearly preferable.

Turning first to the question of statutory interpretation, Dawson J's characterisation of s 329A, read in context, as a prohibition on encouraging the use of a legal and formal method of voting has the virtue of paying attention to the real, practical effect of the law. Likewise, his insistence that the prohibition on 'encouraging' extends to informing is attentive to practical effects. The line between 'encouraging' and 'informing' is a difficult one to draw, and, given that the law creates a criminal offence, it seems likely that the existence of the section would produce a degree of self-censorship. Individuals may well avoid any activity that could potentially be classed as 'encouragement', and in doing so, abstain from informing others of the voting method permitted by s 270.

Our principal focus, however, is in his treatment of constitutional principle. The principles governing the freedom of political communication were most clearly articulated by the High Court in its decision in *Lange* in which it articulated a two-stage test for determining whether the freedom has been infringed:

> First, does the law effectively burden freedom of communication about government or political matters either in its terms, operation or effect? Second, if the law effectively burdens that freedom, is the law reasonably appropriate and adapted to serve a legitimate end in a manner which is compatible with the maintenance of the constitutionally prescribed system of representative government?[53]

Because *Langer* preceded the decision in *Lange*, the reasoning is not explicitly organised along these lines. Nonetheless, a reading of the judgments in *Langer* makes clear that all judges were, in effect, applying the second step in this analysis. That is, both the majority and the dissent assumed (correctly, we argue) that the challenged law *burdens* political communication and therefore considered, in substance, whether it was 'reasonably appropriate and adapted to serve a legitimate end'.

52 As one of us has argued elsewhere, the 'text and structure' of the *Constitution* provides little determinate content to the freedom of political communication: Adrienne Stone, 'The Limits of Constitutional Text and Structure' (1999) 23 *Melbourne University Law Review* 668.

53 (1997) 189 CLR 520, 567–8, as reformulated in *Coleman v Power* (2004) 220 CLR 1, 51–2 (McHugh J); 77 (Gummow and Hayne JJ); 82 (Kirby J).

In answering this question the majority emphasised that, while the Parliament must be 'directly chosen by the people', the Parliament has considerable scope to determine the circumstances in which that choice is made. This scope for legislative choice informs the 'legitimate end' to which the general scheme of provisions is directed – namely, the choice of full preferential voting as the mode of voting for federal elections. Building upon this analysis, the majority concluded that it was permissible for the Parliament to provide for full preferential voting in s 240, and also in s 270 to allow (or save) certain other votes.

Up to this point the majority and Dawson J are in agreement. The fault in the majority's reasoning lies, we argue, in proceeding too quickly from identifying that the general legislative scheme pursues a valid end to a conclusion of that s 329A was valid. The question that we consider received too little attention was whether *this particular provision* was 'reasonably appropriate and adapted' to that end.

There are several matters that strongly militated against concluding that s 329A was 'reasonably appropriate and adapted' to a legitimate end. First, the political communication affected by the law – advocacy of a lawful voting method – is undoubtedly at the core of the constitutional freedom. While the freedom clearly covers a broader category of expression,[54] the communication restricted by s 329A was explicitly concerned with the very election process that the freedom protects. Moreover, the restriction at issue in this case was in a form that was notably severe both in its reach and its consequences. It was a blanket ban on all 'encouragement' of this form of voting and it created a criminal offence punishable with imprisonment. These factors ought, we argue, to have weighed heavily in the determining of the constitutionality of the provision.

The Result

The severity of the restriction imposed by s 329A was vividly illustrated by Langer's eventual fate under the legislation. Prior to the High Court's decision the Australian Electoral Commission, in separate proceedings, had sought an injunction against Langer to prevent him from continuing to distribute material in contravention of s 329A. The day after

[54] Consider the protection afforded to 'street preaching' in *A-G (SA) v Corporation of the City of Adelaide* (2013) 249 CLR 1. On political communication generally, See Adrienne Stone, 'Rights, Personal Rights and Freedoms' (2002) 25 *Melbourne University Law Review* 274; Daniel Meagher, 'What Is "Political" Communication? The Rationale of the Implied Freedom of Political Communication' (2004) 28 *Melbourne University Law Review* 438.

the High Court's decision,[55] the Supreme Court of Victoria granted the injunction.[56] As explained above, Langer persisted with his campaign and was then imprisoned for contempt of court[57] and lost a further appeal in the Federal Court.[58]

The jailing of Langer for his political speech[59] was regarded by Amnesty International as a violation of international human rights law and Amnesty International issued a statement to the effect that Langer was a prisoner of conscience.[60] His imprisonment brought the effect of the majority's decision into vivid relief.[61] The consequence was that a modern democracy with an explicit constitutional commitment to free elections nonetheless imprisoned a person for advocacy of a legal and formal voting method. It is not surprising that s 329A was subsequently repealed (in 1998); indeed, embarrassment created by the case may have contributed to the decision to do so.[62]

55 The High Court pronounced its orders on 7 February 1996, with reasons following on 20 February 1996.

56 *Australian Electoral Commission v Langer* (1996) 126 FLR 346.

57 *Commonwealth Electoral Commission v Langer* (Unreported, Supreme Court of Victoria, Beach J, 14 February 1996).

58 *Langer v Australian Electoral Commission [No 1]* (1996) 59 FCR 450.

59 Although, technically, he was jailed for contempt of court, there would have been no contempt had freedom of political communication been properly protected. See Orr, above n 8, 306–8; Twomey, above n 8, 203–4; Karin Derkley, 'Go Directly to Jail: The Langer Affair and Contempt of Court' (1996) 70(5) *Law Institute Journal* 12. See also the judgment of Black CJ, Lockhart and Beaumont JJ in *Langer v Australian Electoral Commission [No 2]* (1996) 59 FCR 463, 469:

> In exercising our discretion, we take into account the attitude of Mr Langer in his rejection of the authority of the judicial system to grant the present injunction which, however, stems from a belief he holds that the laws sought to be enforced against him are not valid and are destructive of true freedom of electoral choice. We have concluded that, in all the circumstances, a term of imprisonment is the appropriate sentence. This would, we think, reflect the gravity of the contempt, given the public importance of compliance with the laws made by the Parliament for the conduct of elections. The imposition of a fine would not adequately reflect this. The question remains of the term of that imprisonment.

60 Amnesty International News Service, above n 9. Amnesty International 'uses the term "prisoner of conscience" to describe those imprisoned for their political, religious or other conscientiously held beliefs, or by reason of their ethnic origin, sex, colour, language, national or social origin, economic status, birth or other status who have not used or advocated violence'.

61 See above n 59.

62 Section 329A was repealed by the *Electoral and Referendum Amendment Act 1998* (Cth). In the second reading speech s 329A was described as 'infamous' and Langer's circumstances were referred to in the course of the parliamentary debates. The Joint Standing Committee on Electoral Matters also drew attention to Langer's circumstances, described s 329A as

The Relationship of Langer *to the Court's Implied Freedom Jurisprudence*

This brings us to the defining difference between the majority and Dawson J, which lies in the degree of deference accorded to the Parliament. All judges accepted that the Parliament has considerable scope to determine the circumstances under which the people choose their representatives. But extending that scope to allow the Parliament to enact the criminal offence provided for by s 329A involved a level of deference that seems at odds, at the very least, with the High Court's previous decision in *ACTV*.

The law at issue in *ACTV* provided for bans on paid political advertising during election periods, coupled with the provision of 'free time' for political advertising. The Commonwealth sought to justify the law in a somewhat similar way to the justification of s 329A – as a protection for the electoral system. Section 329A was justified as protecting the electoral system from 'ineffective' voting;[63] the law challenged in *ACTV* was also aimed at protecting the electoral system, in this by reducing the influence of donors to political parties and candidates by reducing such parties' and candidates' reliance on the funding needed for electronic advertising.

Notwithstanding this legitimate end, the majority in *ACTV* was concerned that the law would produce an adverse consequence inimical to the justification, because the provisions that provided for the allocation of 'free time' were drafted in such a way as to disadvantage smaller parties and independents.[64] Far from ensuring that the Parliament was 'directly chosen by the people', the regime could assist in entrenching the status quo. The law in *Langer* similarly brought adverse consequences inimical to the law's objective. Although ostensibly directed to protecting the expression of the franchise through preferential voting, s 329A actually served to *prevent* voters fully understanding how they might validly exercise their vote.

'ineffective', 'heavy-handed' and 'highly objectionable', and called for repeal of the section: Joint Standing Committee on Electoral Matters, Parliament of Australia, *Report of Inquiry into All Aspects of the 1996 Federal Election and Matters Related Thereto* (1997) 30.

[63] See above nn 37–8 and accompanying text.

[64] The *Political Broadcasts and Disclosures Act 1991* (Cth) required broadcasters to provide some broadcast time to political parties free of charge. That time was distributed largely on the basis of representation in the Parliament (ss 95H, 95K, 95L, 95M). For a critique of the lack of deference in this case, see Gerald N Rosenberg and John Williams, 'Do Not Go Gently into that Good Right: The First Amendment in the High Court of Australia' [1997] *Supreme Court Review* 43.

The deference shown by the majority in upholding s 329A is not logically inconsistent with the freedom of political communication, but it is not required and has not been evident in later cases. Indeed, it is indicative of a vindication of Dawson J's dissent that *Langer* has turned out to be a low point in the protection of political communication. When, in the year following *Langer*, the High Court consolidated its approach to the freedom in its unanimous decision in *Lange*, that case was widely, though mistakenly,[65] seen as limiting the freedom of political communication by taking a more restrictive view of the source of the implication of representative and responsible government. However, in the cases since *Lange* the High Court has developed an approach to the implied freedom of political communication that, in some respects, confers a surprisingly high level of protection on a wide range of political communication.[66]

Significantly, we note that it is in the area of electoral regulation that the Court has been especially active. In *Roach v Electoral Commissioner* the Court held a 'blanket ban' on prisoner voting to be invalid;[67] and in *Rowe v Electoral Commissioner* the Court held a law that restricted the time for enrolment on the electoral role to be invalid.[68] In these cases the Court held that a 'substantial reason' is required to justify an exclusion from the franchise, a reason that was found wanting in both cases.

In another closely analogous case, *Unions NSW v New South Wales*,[69] the Court ruled invalid two sections of the *Election Funding, Expenditure and Disclosures Act 1981* (NSW) ('*EFED Act*'). The first of these (s 96D) prohibited 'political donations' from persons or entities not on the electoral roll. The second (s 95G(b)) operated in the context of other provisions limiting campaign spending by political parties. It provided for the campaign spending of a party to be aggregated with an affiliated organisation, a term that was defined so that, as a practical matter, it would apply principally to aggregate expenditure by trade unions with the Australian Labor Party. Its effect was thus to limit campaign spending by the Labor Party. In relation to both sections, the Court identified ways in which the provisions had adverse consequences on the political

[65] Adrienne Stone, '"Insult and Emotion, Calumny and Invective': Twenty Years of Freedom of Political Communication' (2011) 30 *University of Queensland Law Journal* 79, 81; and Zines, above n 41.

[66] Adrienne Stone and Simon Evans, 'Free Speech and Insult in the Australian High Court' (2006) 4 *International Journal of Constitutional Law* 677.

[67] (2007) 233 CLR 162. [68] (2010) 243 CLR 1. [69] (2013) 252 CLR 530.

system. At the time of writing, the Court is currently reserved on a further case challenging further provisions of the *EFED Act*, concerning caps on campaign contributions and a prohibition on any donations by property developers.[70]

The reasoning in these cases reflects the structure given to the doctrine of freedom of political communication one year after *Langer*, in *Lange*. As discussed above, there the High Court held that a law burdening political communication must be 'reasonably appropriate and adapted to serve a legitimate end'. In *Unions NSW v New South Wales* the Court concluded that neither of the two sections was directed to a legitimate end. The problem with the s 96D law was a combination of over-inclusiveness and under-inclusiveness.[71] While the Court accepted that political donations from some non-electors (such as, perhaps, corporations) could be limited in some circumstances, the Court was not convinced that there was any reason to apply the prohibitions to such a large group of persons. In addition, the reasons contemplated that political donations might be prohibited altogether. However, the Court did not accept that the category of non-electors could, as a general matter, be singled out in this way.

Section 95G(6) was found to be invalid for similar reasons. Although the Court accepted that New South Wales was entitled to address the risk of corruption in the political system, its narrow application to industrial organisations could not be connected with the wider anti-corruption purpose of the Act.

It is clear from the electoral cases that the identification of a legitimate end, while important, is insufficient to justify the challenged law. On the contrary, it is merely the starting point for a careful analysis of whether the challenged law serves that end and whether it does so in a manner that is reasonably appropriate and adapted to the end. That analysis ought, in *Langer*, to have provided the basis for the invalidation of the law, a position reached only by Dawson J, in sole – but persuasive – dissent.

[70] *McCloy v New South Wales* [2015] HCA 34. For catchwords, short particulars, submissions and transcript, see <http://www.hcourt.gov.au/cases/case_s211-2014>. The prohibition on donations by property developers was also applied to other 'prohibited donors' (operators of tobacco, gambling and liquor businesses) but these other categories of donors were not in issue in the proceedings.

[71] See Adrienne Stone, 'The High Court Strikes Down a Campaign Finance Law (Again): *Unions NSW v New South Wales*' on *Opinions on High* (14 May 2014) <http://blogs.unimelb.edu.au/opinionsonhigh/2014/05/14/stone-unions-nsw>.

V Conclusion

On one view it might be said that the judgments in *Langer* are not marked by great methodological or substantive differences. On the contrary, Dawson J and the majority agree on some basic propositions: that s 24 of the *Constitution* places some limits on the power to make laws that govern the exercise of the voters' choice and that the requirement for full preferential voting imposed by s 240 is within power.

Justice Dawson's dissent is not characterised by a bold or visionary departure from an established method of reasoning or line of authority, nor is it ultimately vindicated by later adoption. Rather, the virtue of his dissent lies in his careful construction of the statute and his steadfast attention to underlying principle, his scrupulous examination of the reasonableness of the law, and his insistent but civil chiding of the majority for their position.[72] And it lies in its just outcome, both for Langer directly and also more generally as a result that is protective of political communication in the core area of such communication: how one is to vote.

[72] Contrast Heydon J's far less gentle chiding of those who accept the implied freedom of political communication in *Monis v The Queen* (2013) 249 CLR 92, 179–82.

16

Certainty, Co-existence and the Legacy of *Mabo*: Justice North in the Miriuwung-Gajerrong Native Title Case (2000)

SEAN BRENNAN

I Introduction

Aboriginal and Torres Strait Islander groups face two main obstacles in seeking legal recognition as native title holders. They must prove that they are the right people for the country, with the requisite continuing connection, and they must avert the conclusion that their native title rights have been extinguished by legislative or executive action at some point in the period since the Crown asserted sovereignty.

There is a hierarchy here between the anthropological question and the technical legal one, and a consequent potential for harsh and arbitrary operation. Even if the group can satisfy the first requirement, according to the high standard of continuity set in *Members of the Yorta Yorta Aboriginal Community v Victoria,*[1] that may count for nothing. The conclusion that native title is extinguished has an overriding legal effect. Extinguishment doctrine is blind – avowedly so[2] – to the fact of continued Aboriginal connection to land through the observance of traditional law and custom. Extinguishment, at common law,[3] is also permanent – there can be no revival of native title once the stroke of a pen or some other official act, often thousands of kilometres from the scene, is deemed on these technical legal grounds to have terminated native title.

These and many other features of extinguishment law have emerged in the years since 1992. The High Court's decision in *Mabo v Queensland*

[1] (2002) 214 CLR 422.

[2] *Western Australia v Ward* (2002) 213 CLR 1, 67 (Gleeson CJ, Gaudron, Gummow and Hayne JJ).

[3] There are some statutory exceptions in the *Native Title Act 1993* (Cth) ('*NTA*') which allow extinguishment to be disregarded if the native title group can satisfy certain conditions.

[No 2] ('*Mabo No 2*')[4] created a new imperative in Australian law: to develop doctrine that explained how the friction between legislative or executive action on the one hand and native title on the other should be appropriately characterised in legal terms. It was a task shared with the legislature, but which the courts have dominated. Although Commonwealth, state and territory native title statutes are replete with extinguishment provisions, most of the critical choices in extinguishment doctrine have been made by the High Court.

The spate of extinguishment cases in the High Court[5] in the period 2013–15 cast those choices in the austere and technocratic language of statutory construction, precedent and 'inconsistency of incidents' analysis. However, large value-laden questions lurk close by this technical discourse. Fresh legal questions have involved significant judicial choice. Those choices are part of the belated working out of the relationship between prior owners and incoming dispossessors, some of the most fundamental questions to confront the High Court.

In its earliest and rudimentary form, the High Court's extinguishment doctrine showed some consciousness of the serious and existential nature of the question.[6] But it is surprising how little could be said with confidence about extinguishment law a decade after *Mabo No 2*, beyond the terminal effect of an unqualified grant of fee simple and of certain tenures listed in the *Native Title Act 1993* (Cth) ('*NTA*').

There was thus a point in the late 1990s when the most important questions in extinguishment law hung in the balance. As the first native title claims moved from mediation into litigation and began to grind their way through the courts, there was speculation about which cases would resolve the most pressing and fundamental questions. It turned out that the decisive test case on the nature of the property interest known as native title and on the rules for its extinguishment was the Miriuwung-Gajerrong claim, also known as the *Ward* litigation, after the lead representative applicant Ben Ward.

[4] (1992) 175 CLR 1.

[5] *Queensland v Congoo* (2015) 320 ALR 1 ('*Congoo*'); *Western Australia v Brown* (2014) 253 CLR 507; *Karpany v Dietman* (2013) 252 CLR 507; *Akiba v Commonwealth* (2013) 250 CLR 209.

[6] *Mabo v Queensland* (1988) 166 CLR 186, 213 (Brennan, Toohey and Gaudron JJ) ('*Mabo No 1*'). In response to the State's contention that its legislation extinguished traditional land rights without compensation, they said that '[s]o draconian an effect can be attributed to the 1985 Act only if its terms do not reasonably admit of another'.

The *Ward* litigation involved a trial before Lee J, an intermediate level appeal in the Full Federal Court decided by a 2:1 majority, and a High Court appeal. The focus of this chapter is the dissent of North J in the Full Federal Court. In substance, he upheld the results reached by Lee J on questions of extinguishment, adding important intellectual support for this more benign approach to the survival of native title. That more benign approach was repudiated to a significant extent by the majority joint judgment in the subsequent High Court appeal. An initial analysis of Lee J's judgment thus provides a platform for describing North J's approach and its contrast with that of the Full Federal Court and High Court majority judgments.

II Factual and Procedural Setting

Western Australia is conspicuous among Australian states in not having Aboriginal land rights legislation to address past dispossession, and the Miriuwung and Gajerrong peoples of the East Kimberley were fast out of the blocks with their application for native title recognition in April 1994, shortly after the enactment of the *NTA*. The trial judgment of Lee J in *Ward v Western Australia* arrived in November 1998,[7] just weeks after key provisions of the Howard Government's 10 Point Plan took effect, amending the *NTA* in substantial ways.[8] It was the first litigated outcome in a mainland claimant application under the Act.

Justice Lee conducted 83 days of hearings, many of them 'on country' within the 7900 square kilometres of the tropical and semi-tropical claim area.[9] The geography of Miriuwung-Gajerrong country varies from coastal mangroves and deep sandstone gorges to semi-desert savannah. The land tenure arrangements in 1994 were also mixed, including vacant Crown land, Crown reserves vested mainly in statutory authorities or the Shire council, some small freehold parcels, an Aboriginal pastoral lease, and intertidal waters.

The area first saw European settlers in the 1880s, after early pastoralists from the eastern colonies claimed one million hectares of unsurveyed holdings by marking out lines on a map. Due to its marginal character and limited carrying capacity, much of the original pastoral lease land was quickly forfeited or abandoned (though leaving an extinguishment footprint). Plans for irrigated agriculture emerged in the mid-20th century

[7] (1998) 159 ALR 483. [8] *Native Title Amendment Act 1998* (Cth).

[9] The transcript ran to more than 9000 pages: *Western Australia v Ward* (2000) 99 FCR 316, 337 (Beaumont and von Doussa JJ).

and, in the 1960s and 1970s, pastoral land was resumed and inundated by two dams, the larger of which (Lake Argyle) can spread at full flood over 2000 square kilometres.[10] This first stage of the Ord River Project was done without reference to the traditional owners. The unresolved grievance associated with that comprehensive, uncompensated and relatively recent dispossession informed some of the sentiment and strategy behind the native title claims, and the subsequent Ord Final Agreement that cleared the way for the second stage of the Project. As well as pastoralism and limited agriculture, the local economy of the East Kimberley also features tourism and the world's largest single diamond producer, the Argyle Diamond Mine operated by Rio Tinto.

III Justice Lee at Trial: A Holistic Right to the Land and a Focus on Regulation

Justice Lee found the Miriuwung and Gajerrong peoples of the East Kimberley region in Western Australia to be a 'composite community with shared interests' who have 'maintained a connection with the ancestral communities which held the native title at sovereignty and . . . with the land to which to the native title applied'.[11] Drawing on statements in *Mabo No 2* and leading Canadian Aboriginal rights and Aboriginal title cases such as *Delgamuukw v British Columbia* ('*Delgamuukw*'),[12] Lee J posited 'native title' as a central unifying concept and rights to engage in various activities and uses of the land as merely derivative incidents of that underlying title. It was, to use the Canadian phrase, 'the right to the land itself'.[13] He rejected the idea of native title as a mere bundle of severable rights.

While acknowledging that extinguishment will occur where the Crown has displayed a clear and plain intention to that effect, this holistic 'title' view meant that, for Lee J, there was no such thing as partial extinguishment of one or more components of a native title bundle of rights. The 'rights parasitic upon native title' may be regulated in quite forceful ways, resulting in 'suspension, suppression, curtailment or control of those rights by legislation or by acts of the Crown'.[14] But such regulation impaired the *exercise* of such rights and did not extinguish the native

[10] *Ward v Western Australia* (1998) 159 ALR 483, 489–91. A small part of the claim area sat on the other side of the state border in the Northern Territory, mainly inside the Keep River National Park purportedly declared in 1981 (as it turns out, invalidly so).

[11] Ibid 541, 544. [12] (1997) 153 DLR (4th) 193. [13] Ibid 252 (Lamer CJ).

[14] *Ward v Western Australia* (1998) 159 ALR 483, 508.

title itself. Extinguishment depended on demonstrating a clear and plain intention that was express, or was impliedly demonstrated by fundamental inconsistency or incompatibility between native title and rights created by the Crown. Justice Lee continued:

> Coexistence of competing interests in land, whether recognized at common law or derived from statute, is accommodated under common law and in Australia land law . . . It is not contrary to legal principle for two interests in land to coexist in respect of the one area of land and it is not a requirement of law in such circumstance that a concept of 'extinguishment' or 'partial extinguishment' be applied to defeat one of those interests despite the fact that there may be some inconsistency between incidents of the respective rights as exercised.[15]

The damage, if any, done to native title by the grant of rights to graze cattle for a defined purpose and a finite duration – that is by the grant of a pastoral lease – was at the centre of the *Ward* litigation. Nearly the entirety of this massive 7900 square kilometre area had once been covered by pastoral leases first granted in the 1890s, though at the time of claim it had reverted to 'vacant Crown land' or Crown reserves.[16] The pastoral estate in the East Kimberley, which had rapidly retreated from the most marginal cattle country through forfeiture and abandonment in the wake of over-ambitious land grabbing in the 1890s, shrank further when the Crown later resumed land for the Ord River Scheme. As a consequence, the *Ward* litigation was overwhelmingly concerned with 'ghost' or 'historical' pastoral leases, not present day ones.

Over time, land grants and other official action had proved to be transitory, especially when measured against the deep longevity of Aboriginal occupation of the area. Yet the legal shadow left behind by now obsolete land tenure decisions had a potentially fatal effect on ancient Aboriginal property rights. Everything depended on the choices made by judges in developing the common law rules of extinguishment.

There were three options for determining the effect of such ghost leases where traditional Aboriginal connection had been maintained. The grant of a pastoral lease for a period up to 48 years could be equated to a grant of exclusive possession and have the same overriding and comprehensive extinguishing effect as freehold ('total extinguishment'). Alternatively, the grant of a pastoral lease could permanently extinguish some aspects of native title (the right to exclude others) but leave others (such as the rights to camp, hunt, gather and conduct ceremonies) to survive ('partial

[15] Ibid 510. [16] Ibid 553.

extinguishment'). Finally – and more like the consequences of action short of compulsory acquisition taken on non-Aboriginal land – the pastoral lease could subordinate native title rights for the duration of the grant and to the extent necessary to give effect to the rights conferred by the Crown or Parliament, but in such a way that the full exercise of native title could revive if and when the grant expired ('suppression' or 'regulation').

Justice Lee chose to characterise the friction caused for native title by the grant of a pastoral lease as 'regulation' for several reasons. The existence of a statutory reservation in favour of Aboriginal access to the land for traditional purposes, together with the qualified nature of the interest conferred by statute and lease instrument on the pastoral lease holder, negated any clear and plain intention that native title in the area would be extinguished. He also cited a third factor: the background awareness that pastoralists' rights subordinated native title rights and interests anyway.[17] This priority for interests granted by the Crown was perhaps the most powerful but least clearly enunciated principle of native title law from its inception in *Mabo No 2*.[18] This third point was one that North J would elaborate on, in the appeal from Lee J's judgment.

That appeal to a Full Federal Court bench (Beaumont, von Doussa and North JJ) would have to deal with more than the pastoral lease issue, because the trial before Lee J involved the allegedly extinguishing consequences of many other grants and official actions on land in the claim area over a period of 100 years.[19] Justice Lee did accept some State submissions asserting total extinguishment, for certain freehold grants, roads and other public works,[20] but he rejected many others, favouring regulation or suppression. In other words, he mostly concluded that the full and free exercise of native title rights and interests was suppressed for the time, and to the extent, necessary to give legal effect to the rights, powers and obligations created by the legislature or the executive. Beyond

[17] Ibid 557. It appeared as a single sentence: 'Section 106(2) [of the *Land Act 1933* (WA)] is to be read with the knowledge that rights granted to a pastoral lessee by the Crown under a pastoral lease may subordinate rights of Aboriginal people under native title if the exercise of those rights conflicts with the exercise of rights granted by the Crown under a pastoral lease'.

[18] See, eg, the postscript in Toohey J's judgment in *Wik Peoples v Queensland* (1996) 187 CLR 1.

[19] *Western Australia v Ward* (2000) 99 FCR 316. Beyond extinguishment (and the associated issue of conceptualising native title as a property interest), the appeal also dealt with a range of other issues, about which North J almost entirely agreed with Beaumont and von Doussa JJ.

[20] *Ward v Western Australia* (1998) 159 ALR 483, 567–8, 572, 609.

pastoral leases, he applied the same conclusion to leases over a national park granted to the government body responsible for park management, the vesting of reserves in public authorities so as to give them powers of control and management, and the grant of a mining lease for a fixed term.[21]

Justice Lee contemplated that official action could interfere extensively with the free exercise of native title rights without resulting in extinguishment because, he said, there is a distinction between native title itself and the outward manifestations of that title:

> That an aboriginal right is controlled stringently or in great detail does not mean that right and title is intended to be extinguished . . . Even the imposition of stringent regulation does not deny the continuation of native title and the exercise of the Crown's power of regulation is not to be confused with the exercise of a power to extinguish native title.[22]

Apart from characterising the underlying native title as relatively robust in this way, Lee J cited other factors in support of a regulatory conclusion: the lack of permanence exhibited by time-limited grants or official action (duration), and the limited purpose for which particular rights, powers and obligations were conferred on non-native title entities (purpose).[23]

IV The Full Federal Court Majority Decision

The State and the Northern Territory appealed against Lee J's judgment, as did the Argyle mining company, a cattle company with a special purpose grazing lease and various private persons and entities. The State's appeal listed 96 grounds asserting errors of law and fact and asked the Full Court to set aside Lee J's determination and entirely dismiss the Miriuwung and Gajerrong peoples' claim for native title recognition.[24] In their majority joint judgment, Beaumont and von Doussa JJ allowed the appeals in part.

[21] Ibid 562–3, 576, 579. This is an illustrative not an exhaustive list of tenures addressed in the *Ward* litigation.

[22] Ibid 557, 583–4. As Lee J put it in the final determination, 'by operation of legislation or by reason of the nature and extent of the "other interests" created by the Crown, the exercise of some of those concurrent rights, including "native title rights and interests", may be regulated, controlled, curtailed, restricted, suspended or postponed': at 640.

[23] Ibid 604, 622, 629.

[24] *Western Australia v Ward* (2000) 99 FCR 316, 336 (Beaumont and von Doussa JJ). A cross-appeal by an Aboriginal party was dismissed.

The presently relevant aspect of their judgment was the rejection of Lee J's approach to the question of extinguishment and the associated question of how to conceptualise native title as a legal interest relating to land.

The majority said that by looking to Canadian case law Lee J had strayed from the proper application of the Australian inconsistency of incidents test. At the level of doctrine the majority found three main errors in Lee J's approach to extinguishment. He had sought to give undue prominence to the question of '*clear and plain intention*' as a threshold for finding extinguishment. Second, he had indicated that the *duration* of a grant or other official action had a direct bearing on whether inconsistency (or 'permanent adverse dominion' over the land by the Crown) was demonstrated. Third, he had said that facts about the actual use to which land was put *after* the grant was made were relevant to determining extinguishment. I will take up the first two points here.[25]

Clear and Plain Intention

At face value, the majority joint judgment accepted that demonstration of a clear and plain intention to extinguish was needed, that being a rule of statutory interpretation which a six-member judgment of the High Court had endorsed in 1995 (and essentially an example of the principle of legality).[26] The Full Court majority in *Ward* said that intention was to be objectively ascertained from statutory language, in the service of identifying *inconsistency* – that is, whether the continued existence of native title was possible or not in the face of the rights, powers or obligations clearly created by statute. Justice Lee had said the same thing in his trial judgment: if there was no express intention to extinguish then it would be implied if comparing the two sets of rights revealed inconsistency.

The difference between Lee J and the Full Federal Court majority was one of nuance. The majority essentially said inconsistency entirely

25 The complicated issues raised by this third point are beyond the scope of this chapter. The essential point is that while the Federal Court majority accepted the State's contention that Lee J erred in this respect, North J argued that the State had misconceived and exaggerated the significance attached by Lee J to use of the land subsequent to grant in determining extinguishment questions: ibid 535–8.

26 *Western Australia v Commonwealth* (1995) 183 CLR 373, 422–3. The principle of legality is a rights-protective common law presumption in the law of statutory interpretation. It says that in giving meaning to a statute, the courts will presume, absent contrary material, that Parliament intends not to infringe upon fundamental rights traditionally protected by the common law, such as free speech and property rights.

displaced any notion of 'intention', while Lee J retained intention as a tool of analysis in assessing the question of inconsistency. When Lee J asked 'did parliament have a clear and plain intention to extinguish native title in creating third party rights' the majority said that he had followed Canadian thinking and wrongly strayed from a focus on inconsistency.

While the distinction at a doctrinal level is subtle, in practical terms it was very substantial. Behind the distinction are two very different mind-sets on the question of how vulnerable native title is to extinguishment, or to put it another way, how high the legal threshold must be for a finding of inconsistency and hence extinguishment. Again, at face value, the majority said the threshold for a finding of extinguishment is high. It is a test of necessity or necessary implication: 'The question is whether the respective incidents are such that the native title rights cannot be exercised without abrogating rights created by the statutory grant. If they cannot, then by necessary implication the native title rights are extinguished'.[27]

But at the end of the day, large swathes of land over which native title had been recognised by Lee J were found by the Full Court majority to be devoid of native title because of extinguishment. Their respective views of inconsistency were dramatically different, and likewise their views on the normative power of the clear and plain intention principle that, ostensibly at least, was meant to inform inconsistency analysis.

Duration

On the second question of *duration*, the doctrinal difference was sharper. If official action lacked permanence, for example because it granted a right to graze cattle for a fixed term or created a one-year permit to occupy land, then that was relevant for Lee J. He looked for 'permanent adverse dominion' being exercised over the land by the Crown before drawing a conclusion of extinguishment – the classic example being the grant of a fee simple to someone else. The Full Court majority said he was wrong to suggest inconsistency must be permanent. Inconsistency is about comparing rights and powers, not their duration. Likewise, Lee J was wrong to suggest that judges should look for '*fundamental* inconsistency'[28] before finding extinguishment.

The Full Court majority said that Lee J was also wrong to conceptualise native title as 'an abstract form of title from which pendant rights

[27] *Western Australia v Ward* (2000) 99 FCR 316, 341.

[28] *Ward v Western Australia* (1998) 159 ALR 483, 510 (emphasis added).

are derived'.[29] Instead, it is a bundle of rights, capable of being disaggregated and separately extinguished in a piecemeal way. This idea of partial extinguishment radically differentiates native title from the way in which other property rights are treated, when subjected to land use decisions by the legislature or executive. The rule of non-derogation in property law means that common law tenures are not permanently abridged unless the state engages in a process of compulsory acquisition (to which a presumption of compensation applies). The belated recognition of native title in Australia had forced pragmatism on the High Court in *Mabo No 2*. The Court relaxed that rule, to the extent of permitting total extinguishment of native title without consent or a prior process of compulsory acquisition. The recognition in *Ward* of a doctrine of partial extinguishment (as an alternative to regulation or suppression) was a massive extension of that departure from the ordinary common law treatment of property rights.

By treating *duration* as essentially irrelevant to inconsistency, by rejecting the 'question of degree' approach to extinguishment implicit in the search for *fundamental* inconsistency, and by affirming a doctrine of partial extinguishment, the Full Court majority revealed a very different mindset to that of Lee J, with huge practical consequences. Instead of being a legal conclusion of last resort, extinguishment became commonplace across Miriuwung-Gajerrong country.

When this case went on appeal to the High Court, the majority joint judgment of Gleeson CJ, Gaudron, Gummow and Hayne JJ varied some of the extinguishment findings made by the majority, hardening them in certain areas and softening them in others. But they largely shared the mindset of the Federal Court majority, with many of the practical consequences that followed. Native title is not a title but a bundle of rights. It should be radically differentiated from other property rights. It can be partially extinguished. The notion of clear and plain intention should be looked at warily – it is apt to mislead in the application of an inconsistency analysis. Duration is irrelevant – a one-year grant can wipe out a native title right that goes back thousands of years. And there are no questions of degree – something is inconsistent or it is not.[30]

So when North J dissented in 2000 against the findings of Beaumont and von Doussa JJ about extinguishment and the character of the property right called 'native title', it turns out he also starkly differentiated himself

[29] *Western Australia v Ward* (2000) 99 FCR 316, 349.

[30] *Western Australia v Ward* (2002) 213 CLR 1, 95, 91–2, 131, 89, 90, 91.

from what would become the dominant legal mindset on extinguishment. At least, that is, until a more recent High Court bench began to drag doctrine and mindset back in the direction established in *Ward* by Lee J and by North J in his Full Court dissent. The sharp divisions within the High Court on native title extinguishment evident in May 2015[31] strongly resembled those that emerged among federal judges in the *Ward* litigation more than a decade earlier.

V The Dissent of Justice North

With the terms of disagreement in the *Ward* litigation now established, it is possible to summarise the elements of North J's dissent in reasonably brief terms:

- native title was a *right to the land* itself;
- extinguishment requires a demonstration of a *clear and plain intention* to extinguish;[32]
- the test for extinguishment is one of *inconsistency* between native title and the rights and interests created by the law or executive act;
- extinguish means to *permanently and totally abrogate* the right of Aboriginal people to the land itself;[33] and
- *duration* (that is, the permanence or otherwise of a grant or other official action) is relevant to the assessment of inconsistency.

There was one more proposition from North J, implicit in these findings, which illustrates the fork in the road between his approach and the one that the High Court took in the subsequent further appeal in *Ward.* Justice North said there are *degrees of inconsistency*; it is not an all or nothing matter:

> There are degrees of inconsistency between rights and interests created by a law or act and native title. It is only where the inconsistency is of such a high degree that the necessary intention to extinguish native title is revealed. Such inconsistency may usefully be described as fundamental,

[31] *Congoo* (2015) 320 ALR 1.

[32] 'This requirement recognises the serious consequences akin to expropriation which flow to the aboriginal people from extinguishment of their native title': *Western Australia v Ward* (2002) 213 CLR 1, 496.

[33] Justice North referred to an 'impossibility of coexistence' approach: ibid 499.

> total or absolute inconsistency. It must reflect the intention of the Crown to remove all connection of the aboriginal people from the land in question.[34]

One of the most interesting things about North J's judgment is that, after itemising a 10-point summary of his general approach to extinguishment, he did something that I am not aware any other Australian judge has done. He addressed the 'purpose of the concept of extinguishment'.[35]

He did so by drawing attention to a pertinent reality beyond the courtroom. In a practical way, in a human way, the word extinguishment is inaccurate. Extinguishment is a technical finding that native title ceases for the purposes of the common law, without reference to its potential existence 'as an operative force among aboriginal people'.[36] It is the stroke of a pen, often far away, that can leave untouched the customary law that binds a people to their territory.

The seriousness of the consequence called for a focus on proportionality, North J said, and clarity about the purpose that extinguishment law is designed to serve. He posited that the purpose is certainty for holders of rights derived from the Crown:

> The purpose of the concept of extinguishment is to ensure that inconsistent rights or interests have priority over native title and override native title. It is aimed at ensuring that the rights or interests created by a law or act can be enjoyed without interference from the claims of native title holders.[37]

Embedded in this is an axiom of native title law in Australia, what might be called a subordinating principle or priority principle. If there is a conflict between native title and rights derived from the legislature or the executive, then the latter rights prevail and the native title must yield.[38] The distinctive intellectual contribution North J made here at the heart of extinguishment doctrine was to go further and say that (a) this is *the* purpose of extinguishment law and (b) the development and application of this body of law should be proportionate to that purpose. If the recipient of an unqualified fee simple has a permanent set of the widest possible rights available under the law, including the power to exclude anyone for any reason, then the courts conclude 'it is necessary that native title is abolished in order that the rights or interests created by the law or act can be fully effective'.[39] But if a recipient of a more finite set of rights

[34] Ibid 487. He also referred to 'shades of inconsistency short of absolute inconsistency': at 503.

[35] Ibid 488. [36] Ibid. [37] Ibid 489. [38] See above n 18.

[39] *Western Australia v Ward* (2002) 213 CLR 1, 490.

can fully enjoy them without wiping out native title then there is no extinguishment:

> The law will recognise consequences on native title short of extinguishment, such as suspension of the enjoyment of some of the incidents dependent upon the holding of native title, in order to allow full scope for the enjoyment of the inconsistent rights or interests. A balance is thereby achieved which allows unhindered exercise of inconsistent rights or interests but permits native title to survive and permits the rights or interests dependent on holding native title to be enjoyed without interfering with countervailing rights or interests.[40]

It is not just the breadth or scope of interests granted that is relevant. Duration matters too, North J said, giving a hypothetical example of a one-day exclusive possession lease granted to enable a town to mark its anniversary with a country race day:

> The exclusive possession lease creates rights in the lessee which are temporarily inconsistent with some of the rights and interests dependent upon the existence of native title. The law could not hold that the inconsistent rights granted to the shire for one day bring to an end the native title of the aboriginal community dating back hundreds of years. Such a result is not necessary to achieve the protection of the granted rights. Rather, the exercise of rights under traditional aboriginal law dependent upon the holding of native title which are inconsistent with the granted rights are suspended for the day of the race meeting. Thereafter, those rights may be exercised again.[41]

The friction between an exclusive possession grant and native title is substantial, when the two sets of rights are compared. But it is possible to conclude that the friction is not fatal – that it does not compel an extinguishment conclusion – *if* extinguishment doctrine acknowledges that there are degrees of inconsistency and that duration is a factor that can be legitimately taken into account.

Justice North reinforced this co-existence approach by returning to *Mabo No 2* and the reliance of the majority there on the principle of racial non-discrimination and basic notions of justice in the common law treatment of property rights. In truth, even *Mabo No 2* had aspired to *somewhat more equal* treatment of Indigenous property rights rather

[40] Ibid.

[41] Ibid 489. Justice North pointed to examples of short-term, limited grants in the *Ward* litigation itself, such as a one-year lease of 8000 square metres for use as a campsite and 5.6 hectares leased for a year as a jetty and boat launch facility on the shore of Lake Argyle.

than full equivalence. The adoption of what I called the subordination principle or priority principle, which automatically favours rights derived from the Crown, showed that full equality was a bridge too far for the High Court, 204 years on from the assertion of British sovereignty and thousands of land grants down the track. But for North J, *Mabo No 2 pointed in the direction of* justice and non-discrimination, in common law approaches to native title, within the parameters imposed by history and legal pragmatism. Where government-given rights over land, created for a finite period, can be fully enjoyed by suspending ostensibly inconsistent native title rights for the duration necessary, then: 'To hold that in such circumstances the native title is abolished forever would neither accord full respect to the rights of the native title holders nor would it provide justice for them'.[42]

He later provided examples of how the common law applies a principle of suspension not extinguishment to non-native title property rights.[43]

Based on these principles of extinguishment and his view of native title as a holistic right to the land itself rather than merely an aggregation of standalone rights, North J rejected the doctrine of partial extinguishment. A pastoral lease for 30 years, to take a key example, was not permanently inconsistent with native title and therefore would merely regulate, albeit in some ways quite stringently, the exercise of co-existing native title rights, suppressing them to the extent necessary to give full legal effect to the rights of the pastoralist.

Justice North treated extinguishment as a possible legal conclusion – where the inconsistency is 'permanent or exhaustive of the full scope of native title'[44] – but a legal conclusion of last resort. Frequently, suppression of native title (typically referred to as 'regulation') is all that is needed to deliver legal certainty for holders of rights that derive from the Crown. A doctrine of partial extinguishment is superfluous. The practical consequences were large. Where the Miriuwung and Gajerrong peoples proved

[42] Ibid 491. At this point in the judgment, arguably North J flirted with danger in straying from precedent by referring to the 'suspension' of native title. Nowadays, judges who share a similar 'extinguishment as a last resort' mindset avert this danger by relying on the distinction between a native title right and its exercise: a law may prohibit the exercise of a right but not thereby extinguish the right itself. In substance, the distinction between a right and its exercise or enjoyment is not always as obvious as the High Court implies. Justice North could easily have reformulated this statement, as he did elsewhere in his judgment, to describe suspension of *the enjoyment of* native title rights, without diminishing the force of his argument. His choice of expression is perhaps a logical consequence of the belief that there can be degrees of inconsistency between rights.

[43] Ibid 510. [44] Ibid 490.

the maintenance of connection to country through their continued observance of traditional law and custom, their property rights survived in a stronger form and over a much wider area than would be the case under the approach adopted by the Full Federal Court majority and later the High Court on appeal.

VI A Great Dissent?

The High Court in *Mabo No 2* said that sovereign authority gave Parliament the power to expropriate *any* valuable legal interest.[45] New doctrine on when extinguishment might occur to *native title* was needed, however, because the Court had said the ordinary rule of non-derogation did not apply.[46] If a new body of law would permit harsher treatment – extinguishment by official action without a prior process of compulsory acquisition and absent a presumption of compensation at common law – the question was when such a conclusion of extinguishment was warranted. In addressing that existential question, should the Court lean as much as possible in the direction of non-discrimination, that is, towards equivalent treatment to non-Indigenous property rights? Or should it radically differentiate native title, with inevitably adverse consequences for Indigenous groups?

The Full Federal Court in *Ward*, and the High Court decision that followed, radically differentiated native title, emphasising its vulnerability to extinguishment. In his dissent, North J, like Lee J at trial, favoured co-existence where possible. Extinguishment was a legal conclusion of last resort, under an approach that stuck as closely as possible to the way that the common law would treat ordinary property rights subjected to official action.

I suggest that North J's judgment is a great dissent, for three reasons:

- he recognised the social and moral dimensions to the extinguishment inquiry, at this critical early stage in the evolution of native title doctrine;
- he asked a legal policy question that otherwise went unacknowledged, namely, what purpose should extinguishment doctrine serve; and
- he crafted a technically sound doctrine that better answered the demands of justice, fairness and the nature of the issue.

[45] (1992) 175 CLR 1, 63 (Brennan J), 110–11 (Deane and Gaudron JJ).
[46] Ibid 64 (Brennan J).

Social and Moral Dimensions

Mabo No 2 is recognised as one of the High Court's most significant decisions because of the gravity of the issue with which it dealt – the consequence of colonisation for the hundreds of thousands of people already in occupation under their own system of law and property, and for their descendants today. The High Court majority joint judgment in *Ward* was devoid of references to the seriousness of concluding that extinguishment has occurred. The clear and plain intention principle was mentioned only to disparage it, as 'apt to mislead'.[47] Given the novelty of the task confronting the courts, in constructing an Australian doctrine of native title extinguishment, this absence of context is odd and unsatisfactory.

Justice North, by contrast, acknowledged that fashioning extinguishment doctrine in Australia took judges into 'waters that are largely unchartered' and he asked how, then, 'should the Court approach the task of creating the charter'.[48] His answer started with a recognition that extinguishment is a technical finding in non-Aboriginal law with little or no resonance in Aboriginal law. That showed awareness of the bicultural context in which the courts were carrying out their task. It also signalled awareness that extinguishment law has a potential to be perceived as harsh and arbitrary. He illustrated that by explicitly drawing attention to the outcomes if respondent arguments were accepted. Limited tenures lasting 12 months or five years were enough to wipe out, in a legal sense, the Miriuwung-Gajerrong people's native title 'dating back hundreds of years'.[49] Justice North also considered it relevant to the question of how native title should be treated that non-Aboriginal property holders can be subject to severe restrictions on the exercise of their rights, without losing them forever.

Asking and Answering the Purpose Question: What Is Extinguishment Law For?

A disturbing consequence of the courts' general failure to acknowledge the novelty of their task in constructing extinguishment doctrine in the wake of *Mabo No 2*, is that no one, other than North J, sought to defend or explain the content of that doctrine by reference to an underlying

[47] *Western Australia v Ward* (2002) 213 CLR 1, 89 (Gleeson CJ, Gaudron, Gummow and Hayne JJ).

[48] *Western Australia v Ward* (2000) 99 FCR 316, 520. [49] Ibid 489.

legal purpose or rationale. It is as if, once more, Bill Stanner's Great Australian Silence about Aboriginal people and dispossession[50] returned, obscuring the choices being made. If an implicit impression was conveyed by the courts in developing extinguishment doctrine, it was of determinate answers yielded up by nothing more complicated than legal logic.

But it makes little sense to write a set of legal rules without explaining why the rule book is needed at all. Justice North stands apart in enunciating a purpose for extinguishment. It is legal certainty for holders of non-Indigenous property rights. However, he said that the rules of extinguishment should be proportionate to the achievement of that purpose. Thus fee simple grants extinguish native title, because the scope and permanence of that set of rights necessitate the abrogation of any pre-existing rights in the land. But the law can give certainty for rights, powers and obligations that are narrower in scope, or last for a finite period, without needlessly destroying the other set of rights that pre-existed them – through the principle of priority or subordination.

I suggest that when native title law goes beyond the example of an unqualified fee simple and starts identifying situations of total and partial extinguishment in dozens, indeed hundreds, of other situations and categories, there is no proportionality principle at work and injustice is bound to follow.

Or worse, the purpose is an unstated and darker one. That is, extinguishment law is not merely about achieving legal certainty for rights, powers and obligations conferred by the legislature or the executive in an immediate setting. Instead, it is about clearing from the landscape, once and for all, the prospect that native title will ever have to be dealt with on that land in the future. That may not be the intentional purpose behind the High Court's harsher approach in *Ward*. But, once duration is treated as irrelevant and 12-month 'permits to occupy' are sufficient to terminate ancient property rights, it is impossible to see such findings as serving the more limited purpose of priority or subordination in a proportionate way. And no other purpose or legal policy rationale for the ascendant version of extinguishment doctrine in *Ward* was ever publicly stated. It seems at the very least to be excessively unmindful of the consequences for groups who can otherwise prove native title by the maintenance of continuous connection with land through observance of traditional law and custom.

[50] W E H Stanner, *After the Dreaming* (Australian Broadcasting Commission, 1969).

Technically Sound Doctrine that Better Answers the Demands of the Situation

It is already clear, I think, why I regard the approach of North J as better answering the demands of justice and fairness. In addition, I believe it is technically superior to the alternative put forward, particularly in the High Court majority joint judgment that repudiated his approach. The courts made a terrible mistake in my view, in characterising inconsistency as an 'all or nothing' question. They thereby rejected North J's proposition that there are degrees of inconsistency and that only total and permanent inconsistency is relevant to extinguishment. That all or nothing approach to inconsistency created a straightjacket that led to strained reasoning and the exclusion of relevant considerations. It also paved the way for harsh results that sit uneasily with the common law's traditional respect for property rights and with the principle of legality in statutory interpretation.

The best illustration is the most recent native title decision by the High Court at the time of writing. In May 2015, in *Queensland v Congoo* ('*Congoo*'),[51] the question for the Court was whether five military declarations, by which the defence force took control of land during World War II, had permanently extinguished native title. The declarations conferred 'possession' on the Commonwealth for three years, before it relinquished its rights and departed the scene. The orders themselves expired in 1946. Almost 70 years later, the parties accepted that the Bar-Barrum people of the Atherton Tableland region in Far North Queensland had otherwise proved native title, through maintaining connection to the land under their traditional law and custom. The national security laws that authorised these declarations clearly contemplated that pre-existing property rights would subsist for the duration of the war and then once more take full effect. The question was whether the same could be said for the native title rights of the Bar-Barrum.

Recalling both the doctrine and the mindset displayed by the *Ward* majority of which he was a member, Hayne J in *Congoo* said that native title must be radically differentiated from other pre-existing rights in the land.[52] He interpreted the declarations as conferring 'exclusive' possession and that was the end of the matter – native title was completely extinguished. Two other judges joined him in that result (Kiefel and Bell JJ).

[51] (2015) 320 ALR 1.

[52] Ibid 23. See also Transcript of Proceedings, *Queensland v Congoo* [2014] HCATrans 273 (3 December 2015) 3545–53.

Within the framework established by *Ward* it is possible to understand how they reached this conclusion. The short duration of this particular land use decision was irrelevant – exclusive possession meant inconsistency under an all or nothing test.

But with proof of traditional connection established according to the high standard of continuity demanded under Australian law, the idea that such a transitory government measure 70 years earlier is enough to permanently wipe out native title is arbitrary and unjust.

Three other judges avoided that outcome. But two of them (French CJ and Keane J) in particular felt compelled to work entirely within the existing restrictive framework provided by *Ward*, putting some strains on the reasoning used. Because *any* inconsistency of rights is enough to result in annihilation of the native title right, inconsistency was denied, even where the impact of official action in the short term was severe (essentially total exclusion from the area, with bombardment and live fire training drills going on). This and other recent cases relied on a fine distinction between the effects of official action on the *existence* of a right versus effects on the *exercise* of that right. A factor that North J suggested was self-evidently relevant to whether official action has *permanently* ended a native title right – the *duration* of the official action – was excluded from consideration.[53]

In my view, the extinguishment doctrine and mindset bequeathed by *Ward* impeded the Court from taking a direct, logical approach to the question in *Congoo*. Back in 2000, North J in *Ward* had the insight that a rigid approach to inconsistency would lead to artificial reasoning as well as unnecessarily harsh outcomes. His approach of acknowledging degrees of inconsistency was technically better attuned to the nature of the problem being addressed.

VII Conclusion

An Aboriginal group that has maintained continuous connection with traditional territory through to the present day can be denied native title recognition (in full or in part) because, on a temporary basis, at some point in the distant past, official action prevented the full exercise of rights on that land. That is so, even in circumstances where ordinary

[53] Justice Gageler, who agreed in the result with French CJ and Keane J, appeared, by contrast, willing to take account of the temporary nature of the military declarations, in analysing their allegedly extinguishing effects: (2015) 320 ALR 1, 43, 45.

owners would resume full rights once the legally imposed restriction was lifted or could not suffer such non-consensual action on their land in the first place. That epitomises the potentially harsh and arbitrary nature of Australian native title extinguishment law.

The dissent of North J in *Western Australia v Ward* shows how the courts could have avoided this injustice in many situations. His dissenting judgment is a standing rebuke to some fundamental features of the Australian common law of extinguishment. It continues to speak directly to the legal challenges the judiciary confronts in the present day, the High Court having delivered judgment in a series of recent cases where traditional connection was established but a state government invoked temporary official action taken decades ago, in attempting to defeat native title recognition.

VIII Coda

The High Court judgment in *Ward* in 2002 did not resolve the litigation. With the applicants forced to accept substantial extinguishment of their native title rights across the claim area, the matter was referred back to the Full Federal Court and the parties engaged in court-supervised mediation. Eventually, nine years and eight months after the Miriuwung and Gajerrong peoples first lodged their application for native title recognition, a Federal Court bench sitting at Kununurra (including North J) made a determination of exclusive and non-exclusive native title over a reduced proportion of the claim area. By then the communities were also negotiating what became the Ord Final Agreement, a comprehensive native title settlement with the Western Australian Government, providing freehold title to some land, a charitable trust fund, 10 years of State financial support for the Miriuwung Gajerrong Corporation, and structured opportunities for economic participation.[54]

In the period 2013–15 many of the tensions present in the various *Ward* judgments resurfaced in the High Court. Some aspects of the *Ward* reasoning most damaging to native title remain undisturbed. But members of the Court appear to be hauling extinguishment law back from some of its earlier extremity. On four consecutive occasions in less than two years

[54] *About Us*, Yawoorroong Miriuwung Gajerrong Yirrgeb Noong Dawang Aboriginal Corporation, <mgcorp.com.au/about-us/background>; Land, Approvals and Native Title Unit, *Ord Final Indigenous Land Use Agreement* (1 June 2015) Government of Western Australia <www.dpc.wa.gov.au/lantu/Agreements/OrdFinal/Pages/Default.aspx>.

a state has argued for extinguishment but the Court has instead favoured regulation and co-existence.[55]

The most recent is *Congoo* where the Court split right down the middle along the lines described earlier. The 3:3 split meant that a very significant result hung in the balance, with apparently thousands of such military orders having been made across Australia during World War II. Because the matter had come on appeal from the Full Federal Court, s 23(2)(a) of the *Judiciary Act 1903* (Cth) determined the outcome in favour of the decision below, that is, in favour of the Bar-Barrum people. While one Federal Court judge had found extinguishment, a majority of two favoured regulation.

One of those two majority Federal Court judges was Justice Anthony North.

[55] See above n 5.

17

When Liberty Divides: Judicial Cleavages and their Consequences in *Al-Kateb v Godwin* (2004)

A J BROWN

I Introduction

Few issues lie as close to the heart of the rule of law in modern democracy, or the social and political legitimacy of independent courts, as the preservation of individual human liberty. So on 15 August 2002, when Justice Ronald Merkel of the Federal Court of Australia ordered the release of a Palestinian asylum-seeker from the notorious Woomera Immigration Detention Centre,[1] he opened up a controversy going to the core of the nation's legal and political systems. In fact, Akram Ouda Mohammed Al Masri, who arrived 'unlawfully' by boat in June 2001, had not been granted refugee status, and now was no longer seeking asylum as he had agreed to be deported back to Gaza. However, the Australian government was unable to secure his return, and yet was keeping him in detention – apparently forever – despite the growing impossibility of deporting him, and despite him having committed no crime nor representing any threat to the community. 'Extremely distressed' at his continuing detention,[2] Al Masri suffered anxiety and depression, self-harmed and was admitted to hospital. He asked to be released, promising to cooperate with attempts to deport him, yet in detention he remained – until Merkel J declared that this deprivation of liberty had become arbitrary and unjustified by law.

Was, and is, such indefinite administrative detention by an Australian government, without charge or trial or any process or purpose related to an individual's personal circumstances, permissible under law? This

[1] *Al Masri v Minister for Immigration and Multicultural and Indigenous Affairs* (2002) 192 ALR 609.

[2] See *Minister for Immigration and Multicultural and Indigenous Affairs v Al Masri* (2003) 126 FCR 54, 59 ('*Al Masri*').

question quickly played out in a trio of High Court cases, the most significant of which revolved around the plight of another young 'stateless' Palestinian asylum-seeker, Ahmed Ali Al-Kateb.[3] In April 2003, after the Full Federal Court upheld Merkel J's decision in *Minister for Immigration and Multicultural and Indigenous Affairs v Al Masri*('*Al Masri*'),[4] Al-Kateb was released from Baxter Immigration Detention Centre after 28 months in captivity, the last nine of them despite his willingness to return to any country where the Australian government could place him. By August 2003, his case was removed to the High Court, the final battleground for the Australian government's claim that it did possess this power of indefinite detention.[5] The decision on 6 August 2004 marked a 'watershed in Australian legal history'.[6] The High Court decided by a slim majority – four justices to three – that indefinite executive detention, without independent oversight by the courts, was indeed allowable under Australian law.

In many respects, it is unsurprising that such a notorious outcome, on such a deep principle, would generate at least one great dissenting judgment. Affirming the power of Parliament and executive to hold individuals in indefinite administrative detention went beyond the lawfulness of detaining stateless asylum-seekers for purposes of immigration control, to the heart of individual liberty in the Australian political system. As stated by the United States Supreme Court's Justice Scalia not long before, and quoted in *Al-Kateb v Godwin* ('*Al-Kateb*'), 'the very core of liberty secured by our Anglo-Saxon system of separated powers has been freedom from indefinite imprisonment at the will of the Executive'.[7] For many Australians, the view of the majority could simply not be right.[8] The

[3] *Al-Kateb v Godwin* (2004) 219 CLR 562 ('*Al-Kateb*'). See also *Minister for Immigration and Multicultural and Indigenous Affairs v Al Khafaji* (2004) 219 CLR 664; *Behrooz v Secretary, Department of Immigration and Multicultural and Indigenous Affairs* (2004) 219 CLR 486 ('*Behrooz*').

[4] (2003) 126 FCR 54.

[5] On 14 August 2003 the appeal from von Doussa J's judgment was removed from the Full Court of the Federal Court into the High Court by order of Gummow, Kirby and Hayne JJ, on the application of the Attorney-General for the Commonwealth under s 40 of the *Judiciary Act* 1903 (Cth): see *Al-Kateb* (2004) 219 CLR 562, 562.

[6] Peter Prince, 'The High Court and Indefinite Detention: Towards a National Bill of Rights?' (Current Issues Brief No 7, Parliamentary Library, Parliament of Australia, 2004–05) <http://www.aph.gov.au/binaries/library/pubs/cib/2004-05/05cib07.pdf>. See also Linda Tucker, 'High Court Decisions on Stateless Persons' [2004–05] (Summer) *Bar News* 17.

[7] *Hamdi v Rumsfeld*, 542 US 507, 554–5 (Scalia J) (2004), quoted in *Al-Kateb* (2004) 219 CLR 562, 612 (Gummow J).

[8] The four majority opinions were authored by McHugh, Hayne, Callinan and Heydon JJ.

former Commonwealth Solicitor-General, Gavan Griffith QC, described it as 'shameful' and a 'stain upon our public life'.[9] As pinpointed by the journalist David Marr, the High Court had experienced a line of deep fracture which would continue to resonate: 'the liberty divide'.[10] To the present day, the significance of the *Al-Kateb* decision, 'as a spectacular failure of rights protection, appears undiminished as the years go by':

> The shock goes not simply to the sense that a long-hallowed civil right – the right to personal liberty – has been effaced. There is a sense that something not easily reducible to any isolated right, a conception of human dignity or humanity, affirmed in the idea that those subject to the law should be entitled to its protection, has been undermined.[11]

What was remarkable about the *Al-Kateb* case was not that there were dissenting opinions, but the differences in character and power of the dissents, as well as the nakedness of the intellectual and personal inter-judicial battles that ultimately determined which opinions were thrown into 'dissent' and 'majority' categories. Appropriately for a case about arbitrary detention, rarely has the arbitrariness of the judicial process itself been laid so bare. Of the three dissenting opinions, that of Justice Michael Kirby arguably became most famous in wider public life. One of the most frequent dissenters in the history of the High Court of Australia, Kirby J has long been celebrated for his judicial and public advocacy for protection of universal human rights. But in fact, in legal substance the Kirby dissent added little compared with the separate minority opinion of Chief Justice Murray Gleeson, whose articulation of the role of the courts in protecting the common law right to liberty stands likely to win the test of time. These views were endorsed by the dominant workhorse of the court at the time, Justice William Gummow, leading to strong convictions that together these dissents spelt out the correct and preferable answer. As Gleeson's biographer wrote, the simple composition of the minority seemed to prove that the majority must be wrong.[12] These convictions were reinforced by the key, last judgment which tipped the court into its

[9] Gavan Griffith quoted in Gavan Griffith and Graeme Hill, 'Constitutional Law: Dissents and Posterity' in Ian Freckelton and Hugh Selby (eds), *Appealing to the Future: Michael Kirby and His Legacy* (Thomson Reuters, 2009) 217, 238.

[10] David Marr, 'Liberty Is Left in Shaky Hands when the High Court No Longer Defends It', *The Sydney Morning Herald* (Sydney), 31 March 2005.

[11] Rayner Thwaites, *The Liberty of Non-Citizens: Indefinite Detention in Commonwealth Countries* (Hart Publishing, 2014) 10–11.

[12] See Michael Pelly, *Murray Gleeson: The Smiler* (Federation Press, 2014) 217.

result, in which Justice Michael McHugh, despite being in the majority, affirmed that the Court's decision entailed a 'tragic' outcome.

This chapter explores differences in the character and dynamics of judicial dissent, by examining the ways in which these opinions have contributed to the fundamental question of human rights protection in Australia. It reviews each of the three most influential opinions: Kirby J's famous pro-rights dissent; the pained judgment of his antagonist, McHugh J, which fulfilled the function of a dissent despite falling into the majority; and the quiet, surgically precise dissent of Gleeson CJ. These opinions highlight the different ways in which judicial dissent serves its purposes in the legal and political system: by helping express and galvanise public discourses and debates on issues of fundamental principle; by exposing weaknesses in constitutional arrangements, practices and cultures; and by charting the adaptability of existing legal principles to help resolve vital challenges, if not now, then in the future. Which opinion qualifies as the 'greatest' dissent depends in large part on what value is attached to each different purpose. On one hand, lawyers may conclude that the Gleeson dissent 'wins' as the most persuasive and accurate guide to the real, and likely future state of the law. On the other, the longer term significance and impacts of the judicial exchanges between Kirby J and McHugh J, for the larger cause of human rights protection in Australia, remain difficult to overstate. Ultimately, all three can be seen as 'great dissents', where not in their terms, then in their wider effects.

II *Al-Kateb*, Liberty and Human Rights in Australia

Ahmed Ali Al-Kateb was a second-generation refugee, born in 1976 in Kuwait to Palestinian exiles. As a young man he scraped together US$4000 during an illegal stay in Jordan, to pay people-smugglers for a passage to what he hoped to make his distant new home: Australia. In December 2000, the Australian Navy rescued him from the wreck of an Indonesian fishing boat on Ashmore Reef.[13] Under ss 189 and 196 of the *Migration Act 1958* (Cth) ('*Migration Act*'), Australia's policy of mandatory detention of any 'alien' who arrives or remains in Australia without a visa (an 'unlawful non-citizen') required that he be detained while his status and visa or other claims were determined, and if rejected, then to facilitate his deportation or removal. However, after Al-Kateb agreed to leave Australia in June

[13] Al-Kateb as interviewed by David Marr, 'Escape from a Life in Limbo', *The Sydney Morning Herald* (Sydney), 27 October 2007.

2002, it became increasingly questionable that this detention was serving any of these purposes. Like Al Masri before him, Al-Kateb was found by the Federal Court to have 'no real likelihood or prospect of removal in the reasonably foreseeable future',[14] because no home could be found. His release meant he was able to sit and hear arguments in the High Court, in November 2003, by which time he was still only 26 years old; but if the Australian government won, it would mean confirmation of its power to place him and others back in 'administrative' detention, irrespective of personal circumstances and for an indefinite period – possibly, for the term of their natural lives.

Al-Kateb's case came as one of a trio of cases which aired the fundamental legal issues of Australia's detention policy. Alongside him, Abbas Mohammad Hasan Al Khafaji had been an Iraqi refugee in Syria since he was just a child, and had been kept in detention in Australia for even longer (39 months) despite his similar willingness to try to go back. As well, an Iranian asylum-seeker, Mahran Behrooz, had been detained at Woomera for almost two years when he committed the offence of 'escaping' from immigration detention, and was now appealing to the High Court that this detention was so inhumane and harsh, it amounted to the type of punishment which could only be imposed by a proper judicial process – not the blind will of the executive. Previously, the High Court had confirmed that mandatory administrative detention was lawful, because it was 'reasonably capable of being seen as necessary for the purposes of deportation or necessary to enable an application for an entry permit to be made and considered',[15] and that as long as these limited purposes were being served, the authority to detain was neither 'punitive in nature' nor an exercise of 'the judicial power of the Commonwealth' of the kind requiring normal judicial oversight.[16] However, the government's claim that it could continue to impose this kind of detention indefinitely was now pushing this licence to, if not beyond, the absolute limit of its power. It was becoming painfully clear that, as reported to the United Nations High Commissioner for Human Rights by the visiting former Chief Justice of India, P N Bhagwati, the 'virtual prison-like conditions' of immigration

[14] *SHDB v Goodwin* [2003] FCA 300 (3 April 2003) [9] (von Doussa J).

[15] *Chu Kheng Lim v Minister for Immigration, Local Government and Ethnic Affairs* (1992) 176 CLR 1('*Lim*'), 33 (Brennan, Deane and Dawson JJ), 10 (Mason CJ agreeing). See Adrienne Stone, 'Australia's Constitutional Rights and the Problem of Interpretive Disagreement' (2005) 27 *Sydney Law Review* 29, 34 n 26 and accompanying text.

[16] *Lim* (1992) 176 CLR 1, 32 (Brennan, Deane and Dawson JJ).

detention were now home to 'a great human tragedy'.[17] In his opinion in *Al-Kateb*, even Justice Kenneth Hayne conceded that immigration detention was 'confinement having many, if not all' of the features of prisons, making it 'easy to equate confinement in such a place with punishment' despite its technically different legal character.[18]

One issue, therefore, was the arbitrary nature of the detention, irrespective of whether it was technically 'punitive' or 'administrative', because it had become quarantined from independent judicial review regarding the merits in each individual case.[19] The second, compounding issue was whether it could truly be indefinite, when not even punitive detention ever normally had that character. As far back as 1949, the High Court had noted that immigration detention powers did 'not create or purport to create a power to keep a deportee in custody for an unlimited period' – rather, they implied that 'unless within a reasonable time [the deportee] is placed on board a vessel he would be entitled to his release'.[20]

Deciding all three cases in favour of the government, the four majority judges effectively sidestepped both these issues – concluding that the legislation requiring detention remained valid, that the conditions of detention were not relevant to this question, and that continuing detention still served the lawful purpose of facilitating the refugees' removal. Quoting minority opinions of the United States Supreme Court in *Zadvydas v Davis*,[21] Callinan J argued it was impossible to know that the purpose of

[17] Justice P N Bhagwati, 'Human Rights and Immigration Detention in Australia: Report of Justice P N Bhagwati, Regional Advisor for Asia and the Pacific of the United Nations High Commissioner for Human Rights, Mission to Australia, 24 May to 2 June 2002' (2002), quoted in Tania Penovic, 'Immigration Detention of Children: Arbitrary Deprivation of Liberty' (2003–04) 7(2) *Newcastle Law Review* 56, 65.

[18] (2004) 219 CLR 562, 650.

[19] This issue was a cornerstone of Gummow J's dissent in *Al-Kateb*. The 'punitive/non-punitive distinction' could not be the basis for triggering independent judicial oversight, because even if administrative detention was not permitted to have punitive purposes, court-ordered detention often involved a mix: 'not only the punitive purposes of deterrence, retribution and reform, but also what may be seen as the non-punitive purpose of protection of society. . . . It is primarily with the deprivation of liberty that the law is concerned, not with whether that deprivation is for a punitive purpose': *Al-Kateb* (2004) 219 CLR 562, 612 (Gummow J). Accordingly, it was the job of the judiciary to decide whether the *Constitution* authorised specific types of laws, and whether administrative actions were then faithful to those laws – not the executive to be the arbiter of its own power with respect to whether or when the circumstances requiring deportation or release had been met.

[20] *Koon Wing Lau v Calwell* (1949) 80 CLR 533, 556, 581, quoted in *Al-Kateb* (2004) 219 CLR 562, 598–9 (Gummow J). See Prince, above n 6.

[21] 533 US 678 (2001).

removal might *not* suddenly be able to be fulfilled, and that even if 'no current prediction' as to a date and place of removal could be made, this did not mean the purpose had been abandoned.[22] For all majority judges, the determinative issue was whether the Commonwealth Parliament had shown an 'unmistakably clear' intention to allow this form of arbitrary, indefinite detention, even if it meant interfering with a person's normal fundamental right to liberty.[23] According to Hayne J, ss 189, 196 and 198 of the *Migration Act* made this intention unmistakably clear to the point of being 'intractable',[24] while McHugh J saw it as 'unambiguous'.[25]

The *Al-Kateb* decision sent shockwaves through many parts of the Australian community, given the extent of the power the High Court seemed prepared to grant the Australian government to detain persons – including, potentially, its own citizens – who had been convicted of no crime. Some commentators were comfortable with the decision, arguing it was undesirable to see judges overstep their role by getting involved in trying to protect fundamental human rights.[26] But far more agreed with the constitutional lawyer Gavan Griffith QC, cited earlier, or the human rights lawyer Julian Burnside AO QC, that the decision helped Australia's immigration policy make 'a mockery of human dignity', ensuring that 'a voiceless few who risked their lives in leaky vessels to find freedom in a just and decent society' instead found 'years of emotional and dehumanising abuse brought about through mandatory detention': 'What does this say about the quality of our society?'[27] Internationally, the case stood out as an unprecedented extension of power for a national government, by its highest court, with or without a bill of rights.[28]

Indeed, having gone unrestrained by the majority of the High Court, the Australian government itself proceeded to act in ways which indicated

22 *Al-Kateb* (2004) 219 CLR 562, 658–9, 660.

23 The 'principle of legality' described in *Coco v The Queen* (1994) 179 CLR 427, 436–8 (Mason CJ, Brennan, Gaudron and McHugh JJ); *Daniels Corporation International Pty Ltd v Australian Competition and Consumer Commission* (2002) 213 CLR 543, 553 (Gleeson CJ, Gaudron, Gummow and Hayne JJ), cited in *Al-Kateb* (2004) 219 CLR 562, 643 (Hayne J).

24 *Al-Kateb* (2004) 219 CLR 562, 643 (Hayne J).

25 Ibid 581 (McHugh J). See also at 638–40 (Hayne J), 658–62 (Callinan J), 663 (Heydon J agreeing with Hayne J).

26 See, eg, James Allan, '"Do the Right Thing" Judging? The High Court of Australia in Al-Kateb' (2005) 24 *University of Queensland Law Journal* 1, 2.

27 Julian Burnside AO QC, 'Borderline Justice: Dignity and Decency outside the Margins' (2012) 1 *Griffith Journal of Law & Human Dignity* 37, 37.

28 Thwaites, above n 11, 10–11.

that, 'despite winning the cases', it felt some 'discomfort with the High Court's position'.[29] The Immigration Minister did not exercise her power to return Al-Kateb and Al Khafaji to detention, instead ordering a review of all long-term detention, stating: 'It is not for life'.[30] Both men were issued bridging visas and given temporary permission to live in the Australian community (although others remained in detention, including one asylum-seeker who had been there for six years).[31] Al-Kateb is now not only free, but an Australian citizen, resident in Sydney. Further, the following year, amendments were made to the *Migration Act* to render the process less arbitrary and reduce the likelihood of any such cases arising again – while judicial oversight remained excluded, the Ombudsman was required to review all cases of detention extending longer than two years, and empowered to recommend release or alternative residence arrangements, which the Minister could implement via a new 'public interest' visa category.[32] Contrary to later claims by Hayne J that the Parliament had taken 'no step' to amend the mandatory detention provisions 'in any relevant way', thus confirming its intention to abrogate the fundamental right to liberty,[33] that is exactly what it did.

Most importantly of all, the case came to occupy 'a central importance' in political and legal deliberations over the need for strengthened human rights protection in Australia – in particular, the merits of a Bill or Charter of Rights, such as existed then (and now) only in Victoria and the Australian Capital Territory, to make up for the apparent inability of existing institutions to safeguard human liberty.[34] Four years later, the report of Australia's national consultation on human rights protection, led by social justice lawyer and cleric Frank Brennan, referenced *Al-Kateb* prominently

[29] Prince, above n 6, 3.

[30] Kate Gauntlett, 'Vanstone Offers Detainees Hope', *West Australian* (Perth), 10 August 2004, 15.

[31] Meaghan Shaw, 'Stateless Detainees Get Bridging Visas in Review', *The Age* (Melbourne), 1 September 2004, 7. See also Senator Amanda Vanstone, '*Al-Masri* Decisions' (Media Release, VPS 126.04, 31 August 2004). See Prince, above n 6.

[32] *Migration Amendment (Detention Arrangements) Act 2005* (Cth), inserting ss 195A, 197AB–197AG (residence determination) and pt 8C (reports on persons in detention for more than two years).

[33] *Plaintiff M76/2013 v Minister for Immigration, Multicultural Affairs and Citizenship* (2013) 251 CLR 322, 345 ('*Plaintiff M76*').

[34] Dan Meagher, 'The Significance of *Al-Kateb v Godwin* for the Australian Bill of Rights Debate' (2010) 12 *Constitutional Law and Policy Review* 15, 22–3. For an overview of the immediate public commentary to this end at the time, see Prince, above n 6, 12–14.

in its arguments in support of a statutory national bill of rights.[35] All this also happened in a context where the Australian government had begun severely tightening controls on not only unlawful refugee arrivals, but anything else that could be linked to the post-September 11, 2001 'war on terror', both of which combined to construct 'border protection' as the then-government's most potent vote winner.[36] Later, having not disclosed his reasoning in *Al-Kateb* but rather having simply agreed with Hayne J, Heydon J rejected a further attempt to revisit indefinite detention in terms that confirmed that the explicit purposes of detention in the *Migration Act* – to support non-citizens' visa processing and/or removal – were not the only, nor most important ones.[37] It became clearer that the detention policy, and other associated measures, also had domestic political motives linked to other issues of social control, as well as broader motives of deterrence against irregular arrival attempts. This actually meant that the worse the perceived human rights treatment of irregular asylum-seeker arrivals, the more successful the policy became.

Consequently, the implications of *Al-Kateb* and its authorisation of 'administrative' detention and control regimes over non-citizens or citizens in the name of other policy reasons, such as counter-terrorism, keep this broader debate about the need for human rights protection firmly alive.[38] In turn, this debate provides fertile ground for dissenting judicial opinions to have an important role and ongoing impact. But what roles, and what impacts should be considered the 'greatest'? The answers help clarify not only the different purposes served by judicial dissent, but the volatile ways in which the status of judicial majorities and dissents may be determined, and ongoing questions about the best ways in which Australia's democratic institutions might seek to preserve and protect human rights.

35 National Human Rights Consultation Committee, 'Report on the Consultation into Human Rights in Australia' (September 2009) 268. See generally at ch 12.

36 For a detailed account, see David Marr and Marian Wilkinson, *Dark Victory* (Allen & Unwin, 2003). See especially at 277–86.

37 Plaintiff M47/2012 v Director General of Security (2012) 251 CLR 1, 105–6, 131–2, 135–6, 136–7 ('*Plaintiff M47*').

38 See David Dyzenhaus, 'Cycles of Legality in Emergency Times' (2007) 19 *Public Law Review* 165, 178–83; H P Lee, 'Salus Populi Suprema Lex Esto: Constitutional Fidelity in Troubled Times' in H P Lee and Peter Gerangelos (eds), *Constitutional Advancement in a Frozen Continent: Essays in Honour of George Winterton* (Federation Press, 2009) 53, 70–3; Thwaites, above n 11.

III Justice Kirby: Dissent as Symbolic Political Communication

Among the opinions expressed in *Al-Kateb*, the longest and most impassioned argument in favour of the priority of fundamental human rights stemmed from Kirby J, who described the majority view as having 'grave implications for the liberty of the individual in this country which this Court should not endorse'.[39] Indeed, in response to Behrooz's claim, it was Kirby J, in sole dissent, who argued that the punitive conditions of detention were relevant, and that a trial judge in a criminal case should be entitled to assess whether, as a question of fact, the incarceration exceeded the legislated purposes of immigration detention.[40] Kirby J wrote with typical force, that 'there remained a considerable body of disturbing evidence... from which inferences might be drawn that the conditions of supposed "detention"... were inhuman and intolerable': 'Courts in other lands might turn a blind eye to such materials. But the independent courts of the Australian Judicature are not so indifferent to such evidence as to reject the inferences that reasonably arise from it'.[41]

These stances were surprising to few. Long before joining the High Court in 1996, as President of the New South Wales Court of Appeal, Kirby had first announced his support for a national Bill of Rights in 1984,[42] and in 1988 had participated in a famous Commonwealth colloquium on the domestic application of international human rights norms in Bangalore, India.[43] The key 'Bangalore Principle' to emerge was that, even though a legislature could make clear that it did *not* want its law to protect particular human rights, in all other cases it was proper for judges to use internationally recognised rights to remove any 'ambiguity or uncertainty from national constitutions, legislation or common law'.[44] Thereafter, Kirby J became Australia's foremost judicial proponent of a pro-rights approach to constitutional and statutory interpretation, as well as a public advocate for incorporation of human rights into Australian law, and stronger, independent rights protection mechanisms.[45]

[39] *Al-Kateb* (2004) 219 CLR 562, 615–16.

[40] *Behrooz* (2004) 219 CLR 486, 528–9. [41] Ibid 519–20.

[42] Michael Kirby, 'Human Rights, Racial Discrimination and People of the Book' (Speech delivered at the Annual B'Nai B'Rith Oration, Melbourne, 9 December 1984).

[43] Commonwealth Secretariat, 'Judicial Colloquium in Bangalore, 24–26 February 1988 – Developing Human Rights Jurisprudence: The Domestic Application of International Human Rights Norms' (Human Rights Unit, Commonwealth Secretariat, 1988).

[44] Ibid.

[45] Michael Kirby, 'The Right to An Interpreter: A Damascus Road Conversion' (Speech delivered at the National Accreditation Authority for Translators and Interpreters Lunch,

His prominent and sometimes controversial attempts to interpret the *Constitution* by reference to such international legal principles were well known.[46]

By 2004, and the arrival of the 'liberty divide', it was no surprise that Kirby J might fall into vigorous dissent in *Al-Kateb*. He was emerging as the most frequent dissenter among an increasingly conservative group of judges, and by the next year, had become 'the greatest outlier in the history of the High Court'.[47] The powerful, accessible prose that characterised most of his dissents was increasingly winning praise from like-minded jurists as attempts to appeal 'directly to the readers and, through them, to posterity'[48] on important issues of principle. His opinion in *Al-Kateb* followed Gummow J in calling on the famous *Australian Communist Party v Commonwealth* ('*Communist Party Case*')[49] for the principle that the 'validity of a law or of an act of the Executive' should not depend on 'the conclusive assertion or opinion of the Parliament . . . [nor] of an officer of the Executive' itself, in the manner suggested by the majority; rather that it remained for the judiciary in each contested case to interpret the applicable law, 'an important, even vital, protection for individual liberty'.[50] Subsequent dissents would make the same plea in even stronger terms.[51] The bulk of Kirby J's 51 paragraphs were

Sydney, 28 July 1988); M D Kirby, 'The Australian Use of International Human Rights Norms: From Bangalore to Balliol – A View from the Antipodes' (1993) 16 *University of New South Wales Law Journal* 363, 364. See generally Rod Pitty, 'Michael Kirby: Speaking for Human Rights' in Geoffrey Stokes, Roderic Pitty and Gary Smith (eds), *Global Citizens: Australian Activists for Change* (Cambridge University Press, 2008) 162; A J Brown, *Michael Kirby: Paradoxes & Principles* (Federation Press, 2011) 221–46.

46 Stone, above n 15, 40 n 75 and accompanying text.

47 ABC Radio National,'2005: The Year that Was', *ABC Radio National*, 13 December 2005 (Damien Carrick, Interview with George Williams).

48 Gavan Griffith and Graeme Hill, 'Constitutional Law: Dissents and Posterity' in Ian Freckelton and Hugh Selby (eds), *Appealing to the Future: Michael Kirby and His Legacy* (Thomson Reuters, 2009) 217, 217. See also Sir Anthony Mason AC KBE 'Book Launch – *Appealing to the Future: Michael Kirby and His Legacy*' (Speech delivered at the Launch of *Appealing to the Future: Michael Kirby and His Legacy*, The State Library of New South Wales, 5 February 2009).

49 (1951) 83 CLR 1.

50 *Al-Kateb* (2004) 219 CLR 562, 618 (Kirby J). For Gummow J, similarly, continued detention could not be justified 'by the hope of the Minister, triumphing over present experience' that at some time in the future some country might accept the detainees, as this would allow the executive government to declare that detention was still for the constitutionally permissible purpose of deportation, irrespective of the reality: at 599, 613.

51 See, eg, *Thomas v Mowbray* (2007) 233 CLR 307. See also George Williams, '"Lone, Vehement and Incredulous": Chief Justice Latham in the *Communist Party Case* (1951)' in ch 6 of this book.

devoted to explaining the applicability and usefulness of rights-protective principles, concluding with a final bid for the *Migration Act* to be interpreted consistently with 'the principles of the international law of human rights and fundamental freedoms that illuminate our understanding both of the provisions of the Act and of the *Constitution* applicable to this case'.[52]

Just as important is the supporting role that Kirby J's dissent played in the public advocacy that followed, across Australia, convincing an increasing number of citizens that more must be done to protect human rights. Indeed, Kirby J himself used the case, and Al-Kateb, as a public symbol of the reality that such rights should not be left to chance. Three years later, one year before judicial retirement, he met Al-Kateb personally at the request of the New South Wales Asylum Seekers Centre, accepting the invitation with the reply: 'And I think God will also be with us'.[53] Justice Kirby went on to speak publicly about the note that Al-Kateb presented him, written in large Arabic script: 'Thank you for your humanity',[54] and, ultimately, left the note pasted in the *Commonwealth Law Report* of the case in his Canberra chambers, for every judge that followed thereafter. In February 2009, at a dinner at the University of Sydney to mark his retirement, Kirby J met Al-Kateb again, and publicly applauded the 'combination of decisions of the Courts, of decisions of elected politicians, and decisions of good Australian citizens to stand with you in what they saw as a human ordeal', ultimately leading to his acceptance 'into our midst as an honoured citizen'.[55] The University of Sydney Union President, Ruchir Punjabi, spoke of Kirby J's contribution to human rights by introducing him as 'an extraordinary individual, a personal hero, a living legend': 'few of us actually have the passion, dedication and the determination to be the change agent . . . still fewer of us are able to do it with such humility, dignity and poise'.[56]

For all the power and impact that Kirby J's dissent in the case came to possess, it is nevertheless clear that his opinion was far from his greatest.

[52] *Al-Kateb* (2004) 219 CLR 562, 630.

[53] Email from Edward Brockhoff to Tamara Domicelj, New South Wales Asylum Seekers Centre, 19 March 2008 (on file with author).

[54] Michael Pelly, 'Rock Star of the Bench Performs and the Kids Lap it Up', The Australian (Sydney), 15 August 2008.

[55] Michael Kirby and the University of Sydney, *Transcript of Michael Kirby's Talk* (28 February 2009) <http://sydney.edu.au/news/84.html?newsstoryid=3089>.

[56] Ibid.

As a piece of legal analysis and reasoning it was not his most fluent or persuasive, and instead was relatively contorted. From rare evidence in his own archives about the sequence in which the seven Justices circulated their draft opinions within the High Court, we know some of the reasons for this – with implications for how we should understand the final result reached, as well as the dynamics of majority and dissent. As already indicated, much of the substance of Kirby J's opinion represented mere endorsement of analysis stated by Gummow J, who was the first dissenter to circulate his draft, following two Justices who proposed to decide the other way (Hayne J and Callinan J).[57] In fact, Kirby J's first draft was a mere seven paragraphs, agreeing with Gummow J and making relatively scant reference to human rights:

> Gummow J's conclusion is further supported, in my view, by considerations of international law and the common law presumption in favour of personal liberty. In my opinion, the *Constitution* and the Act are to be read in the light of these abiding values. The conclusion of Gummow J is one defensive of individual liberty. It is also in conformity with the obligations binding upon Australia under international law. The common law has a strong presumption in favour of liberty, and against indefinite detention.[58]

Justice Kirby later joked that it was, for him, 'a brilliantly short and pithy decision . . . Lawyers present will know that my reasons for judgment, though wonderful, lucid and useful and helpful, are not noted for their brevity'.[59] Thus it remained when Gleeson CJ's draft opinion was circulated, written not as a dissent, but as the judgment that at that stage, tipped the balance in Al-Kateb's favour (three judges to two).[60] But there were two judges to go; and Heydon J circulated his two paragraphs against Al-Kateb, and agreeing with Hayne J. This left the outcome squarely in the hands of the last of the seven, McHugh J. It was only in response to what happened next, that Kirby J extended his brief draft into a longer dissent – one that had come within a hair's breadth of not being a dissent at all,

[57] High Court Draft Judgments Lists ('Tick Lists') 12 February 2004 and 29 March 2004 (National Archives of Australia Series M4101, box 2, items 592–7, Assorted Correspondence 2003–2004, National Archives of Australia Deposit 14 June 2007).

[58] *Al-Kateb* (2004) 219 CLR 562, 616–17.

[59] Kirby and the University of Sydney, above n 55.

[60] High Court Draft Judgments List ('Tick List') 3 May 2004 (National Archives of Australia Series M4101, box 2, items 592–7, Assorted Correspondence 2003–2004, National Archives of Australia Deposit 14 June 2007).

but rather part of a majority decision against indefinite administrative detention.

IV Justice McHugh: Majority Judge as Pained Dissenter

When circulated and later when published, McHugh J's opinion stood out for two reasons that would make it both famous and notorious. While tipping the result against Al-Kateb and liberty in this case, McHugh J did so in terms that nakedly affirmed the 'tragic' nature of this outcome for Al-Kateb, Al Khafiji and others in their position.[61] This explicit confirmation from the Court's longest serving member, that its decision was unjust, immediately did more than all else to fuel public realisation that basic human rights were not safe in Australia. Commentators grasped McHugh J's remarks as 'a dismal yet accurate reflection on the way in which the common law of Australia has failed to protect human rights', driving the debate further than it had ever gone.[62] Justice McHugh's comments were also interpreted quite differently from the conventionally apersonal (some might say, typically heartless) analyses of the other majority judgments – instead his comments displayed 'an acute interest in the welfare of Mr Al-Kateb, and a deep frustration that he [McHugh] [felt he] was powerless . . . to do anything about it'.[63] Indeed it was McHugh J, more than any minority judge, whose opinion directly fed the campaign for stronger rights protection by calling for a national bill of rights:

> Eminent lawyers who have studied the question firmly believe that the *Australian Constitution* should contain a Bill of Rights which substantially adopts the rules found in the most important of the international human rights instruments. It is an enduring – and many would say a just – criticism of Australia that it is now one of the few countries in the Western world that does not have a Bill of Rights. . . . If Australia is to have a Bill of Rights, it must be done in the constitutional way – hard though its achievement may be – by persuading the people to amend the *Constitution* by inserting such a Bill.[64]

[61] *Al-Kateb* (2004) 219 CLR 562, 581; *Minister for Immigration and Multicultural and Indigenous Affairs v Al Khafaji* (2004) 219 CLR 664, 668.

[62] Alice Rolls, 'Avoiding Tragedy: Would the Decision of the High Court in *Al-Kateb* have Been Any Different if Australia had a Bill of Rights like Victoria?' (2007) 18 *Public Law Review* 119. See also Dan Meagher, 'The "Tragic" High Court Decisions in *Al-Kateb* and *Al-Khafaji*: The Triumph of the "Plain Fact" Interpretive Approach and Constitutional Form over Substance' (2005) 7 *Constitutional Law and Policy Review* 69.

[63] Meagher, above n 34, 20.

[64] *Al-Kateb* (2004) 219 CLR 562, 594–5.

Justice McHugh went on to advocate publicly for a bill of rights solution as he moved into retirement. Speaking to law students in October 2005, he confirmed that he did see the mandatory detention provisions as having interfered with a 'basic civil right' in the *Al-Kateb* case, thus highlighting 'the inability of Australian judges to prevent unjust human rights outcomes' unless given authority to do so under a bill of rights, which he encouraged students to support.[65] Later, McHugh J's position changed, highlighting that under a limited 'dialogue model' of rights protection between the legislature and the courts, the most that a court could do when faced with such an 'unambiguous' intention to breach human rights, was issue a non-enforceable, advisory declaration that the law was incompatible. Accordingly, he argued 'there must be doubt . . . whether Mr Al-Kateb would have fared better in the High Court if [a bill of rights] had been in force as a federal enactment', since the legislature might well simply confirm the incompatibility it had always intended.[66] This issue will be further discussed below, but the special impetus that was given to the human rights debate by McHugh J's opinion is clear.

The second stand-out feature of McHugh J's opinion, however, revealed even more about the inner dynamics of how and why this perverse outcome was reached. Professor George Williams, once an associate to McHugh J, described the case as remarkable for the level of disagreement that erupted through the opinions between just two individuals, McHugh J and Kirby J, 'on an amazing array of things'.[67] Williams noted, 'I'm not aware of any High Court case that's had such a direct level of disagreement and if you like, difference on key matters so publicly expressed'.[68] Indeed, Williams described McHugh J's reaction against Kirby as 'unparalleled in High Court history'.[69] Having known Kirby J and worked with him for much of the previous three decades, as barristers and judges, McHugh J later said the *Al-Kateb* exchange never affected their friendship 'in the slightest',[70] while Kirby J told journalists not to 'get too anxious about

[65] M H McHugh, 'The Need for Agitators – The Risk of Stagnation' (Speech delivered at the Sydney University Law Society Public Forum, Sydney, 12 October 2005) 23 <http://www.hcourt.gov.au/publications/speeches/former/speeches-by-the-hon-michael-mchugh>.

[66] Michael McHugh AC QC, 'A Human Rights Act, the Courts and the Constitution' (2009) 11 *Constitutional Law and Policy Review* 86; see generally Meagher, above n 34.

[67] ABC Radio National, 'David Hicks; Sexual Assault; Indefinite Detention', *The Law Report* (31 August 2004) <http://www.abc.net.au/radionational/programs/lawreport/david-hicks-sexual-assault-indefinite-detention/3416830>.

[68] Ibid. [69] ABC Radio National, above n 47.

[70] Quoted in David Marr, 'Now History Will Be the Judge', *The Sydney Morning Herald* (Sydney), 31 January 2009.

it all', noting that heated exchanges were 'the mark of honest judges and strong institutions'.[71]

Nevertheless, the explosion was real and direct, with McHugh J embarking on a multi-page assault against his assessment of Kirby J's 'heretical' position. The fact that Kirby J had, unusually, only offered a seven-paragraph target, made clear that McHugh J's reaction was less against the principles in this particular case, than against Kirby J's wider views over a much longer period. It seemed that just one small word in Kirby J's draft – his reference to international human rights norms as 'binding' on Australia – had been enough to set McHugh J off. Four years earlier, McHugh J had joked that Kirby J's ideas that constitutions and statutes should be interpreted in a pro-rights manner, as defined by international instruments and practices not formally incorporated into Australian legislation, amounted to a 'loose-leaf theory of the *Constitution*';[72] now he stated this outright.[73] For 12 years, Kirby J had been citing McHugh J publicly as an example of a judge who was proving his own theories of legal change by using international norms to decide the content of Australia's fundamental laws, including in the famous decision in *Mabo v Queenland [No 2]*[74] – but McHugh J had suffered this without ever publicly correcting him. Now he did so in unequivocal terms:

> It is not for courts, exercising federal jurisdiction, to determine whether the course taken by Parliament is unjust or contrary to basic human rights. The function of the courts in this context is simply to determine whether the law of the Parliament is within the powers conferred on it by the *Constitution*.[75]

It was only in response to this sustained, long overdue attack – and the confirmation that he, Gleeson CJ and Gummow J had been pushed into the minority – that Kirby J rewrote his draft opinion as a dissenter's appeal to history, extending it from seven to 51 paragraphs. Thus emerged a blow-by-blow counter-attack against each of McHugh J's points, many of which had little direct relevance to the case, accusing McHugh J of disingenuous inconsistency and an isolationism 'doomed to fail', and predicting that history would look back on McHugh J's position with 'curiosity and

71 Quoted in A Fraser, 'The Legal-Eye View: Michael Kirby's Perspective on Life', *The Canberra Times* (Canberra), 23 April 2005, B1, B6–B7.

72 Transcript of Proceedings, *Brownlee v The Queen* [2000] (High Court of Australia, S82/1998, McHugh J, 17 November 2000).

73 *Al-Kateb* (2004) 219 CLR 562, 595.

74 (1992) 175 CLR 1.

75 *Al-Kateb* (2004) 219 CLR 562, 592.

embarrassment'.[76] Later, McHugh J would describe such 'kicks' in Kirby J's dissenting opinions as having grown out of 'resentment and impulsive statement rather than a studied position'.[77] But it was McHugh J who first exploded so vigorously, in such a pent-up fashion against things that Kirby J had said previously, and not in this case; and it was he who decided the case on the basis of a supposedly 'unambiguous' clarity of parliamentary intent, without engaging directly with the contrary analyses laid out by Gleeson CJ and Gummow J. For example, his reaction against the relevance of the *Communist Party Case* was directed only at Kirby J, with dubious accuracy, and no apparent recognition of Gummow J's more detailed reasoning on the same point. All these things suggest that it was actually McHugh J's turn to hit a blind spot.

On one hand, therefore, McHugh J had arrived at a judgment that, more than any other, fulfilled the function of a great dissent by powerfully highlighting the inadequacy of the outcome and the state of the law, on one of society's most fundamental issues. On the other hand, the circumstances, reasoning and apparent trigger of this decision fuelled doubts as to its logic, objectivity and wisdom. Indeed, in his speech to law students in October 2005, McHugh J undermined his own claim that the Parliament's intent to abrogate the right to liberty was so 'unambiguous' that it could not be disturbed, by saying that in fact, 'the legislature *probably did not intend* to interfere' with such a basic civil right to that extent[78] – directly contradicting his judicial opinion, 14 months earlier.

Had McHugh J not been so clearly provoked by his frustrations over Kirby J's views, would he have seen the issues differently and decided the other way – if not agreeing with Kirby J, then at least following Gleeson CJ or Gummow J? Had Kirby J not gilded the lily about McHugh J's supposed exemplification of his own preferred approach, in so many years of advocacy over the Bangalore Principles, would McHugh J have reacted so forcefully in the other direction? In either case, the result may have been that all the opinions discussed here would have united in the majority, rather than standing as expressions and triggers of dissent. The reality that the dynamics of dissent can be influenced not only by the substantive arguments involved, but by such personal, arbitrary factors,

76 Ibid 629.

77 Michael Pelly, 'Michael Kirby: A Career Shaped by a Secret', *The Australian* (Sydney), 13 December 2008. See also Michael Pelly, 'Kirby Concludes: I'll Be Vindicated', *The Australian* (Sydney), 6 February 2009, 27.

78 McHugh, above n 65, 23 (emphasis added). Cf McHugh J's later analysis of the extent to which a bill of rights would solve the case: see Meagher, above n 34; McHugh, above n 66.

reinforces the complexity of artificial criteria for objectively assessing particular opinions as 'great' – even when they turn on great issues, reflect great passion and human concern, and have great effects on public consciousness and debate.

V Chief Justice Gleeson: Precision, Vindication and Limits

The third and final candidate for a great dissenting opinion in *Al-Kateb* is that of Gleeson CJ. As already noted, his succinct 30-paragraph reasons were circulated after those of Gummow J and Kirby J, at a point where it was likely they would define the majority outcome. Despite ending up in dissent, and perhaps for the wrong reasons, there was no rewrite in an impassioned appeal to posterity. Instead, the opinion remained a tight combination of precise statutory construction as to the powers available to the Australian government under the *Migration Act*, and traditional, but high common law principle regarding the responsibility of the courts to enforce the 'principle of legality', or presumption against unnecessary erosions of fundamental rights. Chief Justice Gleeson endorsed Gummow J's technical analysis that once there was no reasonable prospect of a person being removed from Australia, the purposes of detention as defined by the *Migration Act* were 'spent'; the gap in the legislative scheme – that is, what to do if a person could not be removed – could not be overcome by general words.[79] Not only did this leave the Australian government without a clear power to detain, but brought the opposing, higher principle into play:

> Courts do not impute to the legislature an intention to abrogate or curtail certain human rights or freedoms (of which personal liberty is the most basic) unless such an intention is clearly manifested by unambiguous language, which indicates that the legislature has directed its attention to the rights or freedoms in question, and has consciously decided upon abrogation or curtailment.[80]

[79] *Al-Kateb* (2004) 219 CLR 562, 607–8 (Gummow J), 577–8 (Gleeson CJ).

[80] Ibid 577 (Gleeson CJ); see also at 616–17 (Kirby J). For an extended account of Australian authority on the principle, see *Plaintiff M47* (2012) 251 CLR 1, 154 (Crennan J): 'authorities which provide that there must be "express authorization of an abrogation or curtailment of a fundamental right [or] freedom" such as the right to personal liberty', quoting *Coco v The Queen* (1994) 179 CLR 427, 437 (Mason CJ, Brennan, Gaudron and McHugh JJ). See *Annetts v McCann* (1990) 170 CLR 596, 598 (Mason CJ, Deane and McHugh JJ); *R v Home Secretary; Ex parte Simms* [2000] 2 AC 115, 131 (Lord Hoffmann); *Plaintiff S157/2002 v Commonwealth* (2003) 211 CLR 476, 492; *Al-Kateb* (2004) 219 CLR 562, 577 (Gleeson CJ); *CTM v The Queen* (2008) 236 CLR 440, 497–8 (Heydon J). See also *South Australia v Totani* (2010) 242 CLR 1, 155–6 (Crennan and Bell JJ).

> It is submitted for the respondents that the terms of the statute are general, but tolerably clear, and that if there is a silence on the particular problem raised by the case of the appellant, that is only because it is sufficiently covered by the general words. I am unable to accept that submission.... The Act does not say what is to happen if, through no fault of his own or of the authorities, he cannot be removed. It does not, in its terms, deal with that possibility. The possibility that a person, regardless of personal circumstances, regardless of whether he or she is a danger to the community, and regardless of whether he or she might abscond, can be subjected to indefinite, and perhaps permanent, administrative detention is not one to be dealt with by implication.[81]

Justice Gummow had approached the question of the government's power simply as a question of statutory construction, along with protecting the role of the courts against a usurping executive. Even Kirby J had primarily agreed with that approach, only raising respect for fundamental rights as a supportive and somewhat secondary issue – at least initially. Similarly, while Kirby J's original and then redrafted opinion made reference to analogous decisions in foreign courts, it was Gleeson CJ who first pointed out specifically that the Full Federal Court's answer to the problem of indefinite detention of stateless persons, as reached in *Al Masri*, should be considered logical not only on principle, but because it aligned with the 'similar answer . . . given in the United Kingdom, the United States, and Hong Kong'.[82] It was thus Gleeson CJ who most squarely raised, and relied on, the fundamental common law presumption in favour of basic rights. Indeed, revisiting the issue in 2012, prior to his retirement, Gummow J cited and supported the correctness of Gleeson CJ's approach, rather than focusing on his own.[83] For his part, not only did Kirby J *not* update his final opinion to draw more directly on Gleeson CJ's application of the principle of legality, but despite cross-referencing the opinions of Gummow J, McHugh J and Callinan J, he made no reference to Gleeson CJ's opinion at all.

For lawyers, the claim for Gleeson CJ's opinion as the 'greatest' of these dissents is clear, and twofold. First, as Associate Professor Dan Meagher has argued, it very precisely 'demonstrated the constitutional significance of the principle of legality and its capacity to provide meaningful rights protection at common law if judges are so minded'.[84] At no stage did the

[81] *Al-Kateb* (2004) 219 CLR 562, 577–8 (Gleeson CJ).

[82] Ibid 572.

[83] Plaintiff M47 (2012) 251 CLR 1, 60–1, 68.

[84] Meagher, above n 34, 15. See also Dennis Rose, 'The High Court Decisions in Al Kateb and Al Khafaji – A Different Perspective' (2005) 8 *Constitutional Law and Policy Review* 58, 58–60.

majority judges dispute the legitimacy or importance of this principle – simply the question of whether it applied to these facts and statutory provisions. Thus, 'Gleeson CJ's succinct articulation of the principle of legality and its centrality to the rule of law'[85] helps bypass the problems raised by uncertainties and conflicts over new models of constitutional or statutory rights protection, by highlighting 'the capacity and constitutional responsibility of the courts to protect rights, even without a bill of rights':[86]

> There is . . . no need or constitutional propriety in the courts waiting for the democratic mandate of a bill of rights before they can robustly employ principles of statutory interpretation in order to protect rights. The presumption is not merely a common sense guide to what a parliament in a liberal democracy is likely to have intended; it is a working hypothesis, the existence of which is known both to Parliament and the courts, upon which statutory language will be interpreted. The hypothesis is an aspect of the rule of law.[87]

This is all the more attractive, when there is uncertainty about the likely consequences and benefits of either constitutional rights or a bill of rights.[88] As reflected in McHugh J's later reconsideration of whether a separate judicially interpretable bill of rights would provide any better answer to the 'tragedy', Gleeson CJ's focus on the existing, traditional common law presumption helps prompt closer scrutiny of what Meagher calls the '*Al-Kateb* orthodoxy',[89] that the majority judges may have decided *Al-Kateb* differently if Australia had a bill of rights, like the *Human Rights Act 2004* (ACT), *Charter of Human Rights and Responsibilities Act 2006* (Vic) or the federal Bill of Rights proposed by the Brennan Committee.[90] In fact, according to Meagher, from the fact that the majority judges considered the language and meaning of the impugned provisions to be clear and unambiguous, it 'necessarily follows that the majority judges in *Al-Kateb* would reach the same decision under an Australian bill of

85 Meagher, above n 34, 21. 86 Ibid (emphasis altered). 87 Ibid 17–18.

88 Stone, above n 15, 34 n 26 and accompanying text. 89 Meagher, above n 34, 22.

90 Examples of this 'orthodoxy' cited by Meagher include Sir Gerard Brennan, 'The *Constitution*, Good Government and Human Rights' (Speech delivered at the Human Rights Resource Centre, Melbourne, 12 March 2008) 23–4 <http://www.hrlrc.org.au/content/topics/national-human-rights-consultation/sir-gerard-brennan>; Rolls, above n 62, 134; Chief Justice J J Spigelman AC, 'Statutory Interpretation and Human Rights' (Speech delivered at the McPherson Lectures, University of Queensland, Brisbane, 2008) 95; Catherine Branson QC, 'A Human Rights Act for Australia' (Speech delivered at the Dame Roma Mitchell Memorial Luncheon, Melbourne, 4 March 2009) <http://humanrights.gov.au/news/speeches/president-speech-human-rights-act-australia-dame-roma-mitchell-memorial-luncheon>.

rights'.[91] Simply reactivating the traditional common law role of the courts, through a greater preparedness to recognise when the real meaning and functioning of a statute's impacts on rights is uncertain and retrograde, may therefore represent a more efficient path to a suitable outcome.

Second, for lawyers, Gleeson CJ's approach to the indefinite detention dilemma is the most likely to provide a workable solution, if or when the question emerges for re-decision. The likelihood of identical facts repeating has been relieved by the 2005 reforms, reducing the arbitrariness of long-term detention and providing an administrative 'safety valve' against injustice. Indeed, it may be in response to an entirely different application of the Commonwealth's powers of indefinite detention that the fundamental question ends up returning. Nevertheless, on many accounts, the question will be ripe for review when these circumstances arise, and it will be Gleeson CJ's approach which is most likely to confirm that the Australian legal system 'had and has ample legal resources to support a ruling that indefinite detention is unlawful'.[92]

More than a decade after *Al-Kateb*, three decisions provide some indication of the trajectory. In *Plaintiff M47/2012 v Director General of Security* ('*Plaintiff M47*'), the High Court upheld a challenge by a detained Sri Lankan refugee to the regulation under which an adverse security assessment had precluded him from being granted an Australian protection visa.[93] Chief Justice French, Crennan J and Kiefel J concluded that since the invalidity of the security assessment regulation meant the plaintiff's visa application must now be reconsidered, his detention still had a clear purpose, and *Al-Kateb* did not arise. Chief Justice French and Crennan J kept their cards especially close to their chest by not referring to *Al-Kateb* at all.[94] However Gummow J affirmed Gleeson CJ's approach, as did Bell J, who dismissed as 'glib' the idea that the principles had already been conclusively decided without 'inconvenience'.[95] The *Plaintiff M47* result thus meant two judges for overturning the result in *Al-Kateb* (Gummow J and Bell J), two against (Hayne J and Heydon J), and three yet to show their hand.

In *Plaintiff M76/2013 v Minister for Immigration, Multicultural Affairs and Citizenship* ('*Plaintiff M76*'),[96] the High Court upheld a claim by

[91] Meagher, above n 34, 19. [92] Thwaites, above n 11, 11. See especially at chs 3–4.

[93] (2012) 251 CLR 1. The Court was French CJ, Gummow, Hayne, Heydon, Crennan, Kiefel and Bell JJ.

[94] Ibid 31–2 (French CJ), 155 (Crennan J). [95] Ibid 190–3 (Bell J).

[96] (2013) 251 CLR 322, 369.

another detained Sri Lankan asylum-seeker that there had been an error of law in the Minister's consideration of her request for permission to apply for a visa, and so again concluded that since those processes were incomplete, her challenge to indefinite detention did not need to be heard.[97] While three judges (Hayne J and Kiefel and Keane JJ) nevertheless went out of their way to defend the *Al-Kateb* result, French CJ again remained silent, and the joint judgment of Crennan, Bell and Gageler JJ found that a return to the question 'can and should await another day'.[98] Most recently, *Plaintiff S4/2014 v Minister for Immigration and Border Protection* saw a unanimous High Court, comprising French CJ, Hayne, Crennan, Kiefel and Keane JJ, confirm that detention under those provisions can only be for purposes of the *Migration Act*, with the requirement to remove a non-citizen 'as soon as reasonably practicable' as the leading purpose, to which others are subordinate.[99] Since then Hayne J, the last veteran of the original *Al-Kateb* decision, has retired; of the Court's current membership there are two judges who support leaving *Al-Kateb* alone, one for overturning it, and four whose stance on *Al-Kateb* remains unknown.[100]

While Gleeson CJ's precise focus on the principle of legality offers the most ready solution, is consistent with longstanding institutional relationships, and helps to provoke a more nuanced debate about how best to protect human rights, it remains open to debate whether that solution is the ultimate or 'greatest' one. How good is the common law principle of legality as a protection of fundamental rights, when the number and nature of those rights remains unclear, questions remain as to when the parliamentary intent to abrogate them is unambiguous, and – perhaps most of all – there is no guarantee that a majority of judges will be willing to exercise the necessary courage to tell the political arms of government that their laws or actions do not pass these tests? Chief Justice Gleeson's great legal dissent confirms the availability of a viable 'backstop', but should it only be by resort to a 'backstop', when all else fails and breaches of rights become unambiguously egregious, that remedies

97 See Simon Thornton and Andrew Buckland, 'Validity of Immigration Detention Revisited' (Litigation Note No 24, Australian Government Solicitor, December 2014) 19–22.

98 *Plaintiff M76* (2013) 251 CLR 322, 365–7 (Hayne J), 381 (Kiefel and Keane JJ). Justices Kiefel and Keane stated 'it is difficult to accept that [the majority's construction in *Al-Kateb*] is not the better view of the relevant provisions of the Act'. See also at 334–5, 344 (French CJ), 568–9 (Crennan, Bell and Gageler JJ).

99 (2014) 253 CLR 219.

100 See Rohan Nanthakumar, 'Immigration Detention in Australia – An Indefinite Future for Indefinite Detention: Plaintiff M76's Case' (2014) 33 *University of Tasmania Law Review* 165.

for basic civil rights abuses become available? These challenges confirm the significance of other options, whether the more ambitious judicial activism suggested by Kirby J, or the formal bill of rights advocated for a period by McHugh J. They also confirm, in a great case like *Al-Kateb*, the different goals and purposes of major dissents.

VI Conclusions: Alternative Visions of Greatness

This chapter has focused on *Al-Kateb*, in which a majority of 4:3 infamously decided that Al-Kateb, a stateless asylum-seeker unable to be deported could be held indefinitely in immigration detention by the Australian government. Together, the contrasting and conflicting opinions of Gleeson CJ, Kirby J and McHugh J highlight the different ways in which judicial dissent serves its purposes in the legal and political system: by helping express and galvanise public discourses and debates on issues of fundamental principle; by exposing weaknesses in constitutional arrangements, practices and cultures; and by charting the adaptability of existing legal principles to help resolve vital challenges, if not now, then in the future. While Kirby J's views come with the mantle of one of the High Court's most frequent and greatest ever dissenters, it was and is his broader public advocacy of human rights protection using the case, rather than through its reasoning, that has had the greatest impact. While McHugh J's opinion was in the majority, it strongly fulfilled a function normally attributed to dissent by exposing what its author saw as the inadequate state of Australian law and institutions. It arguably did even more than Kirby J's opinion to galvanise public concern and attention, but McHugh J's reasons ultimately offered little by way of coherent solution to an abiding problem, being caught up instead in the interpersonal dynamics of judicial relationships on the High Court. Chief Justice Gleeson's dissent – the strongest in legal terms – has gone on to have greatest impact on the thinking of later judges, and is most likely to be vindicated, but whether it represents an ultimate solution is another question.

In these ways, *Al-Kateb* illuminates our appreciation of the relational nature of dissent in the collective decision-making of final courts. Had circumstances been slightly different, the three minority views which ultimately appeared as dissents may have formed the core of a majority decision. It is possible that had the court's internal dialogue (and McHugh J's relationship with Kirby J) played out differently at that time, McHugh J would have agreed with one or more of the 'dissenting' judges thus causing the High Court's decision to go the other way – and meaning none of these opinions would have been dissents at all. Overall, which opinion qualifies as the 'greatest' depends on how much value is attached to each different purpose. While lawyers may conclude that the Gleeson dissent is the most persuasive and accurate guide to the real, and likely future state of the law, the longer term political significance and impacts of the judicial exchange between Kirby J and McHugh J, over the larger cause of human rights protection in Australia, remain difficult to overstate. Ultimately, all three can be seen as 'great dissents', whether in their terms or their wider effects.

18

He Who Would Not Be Muzzled: Justice Heydon's Last Dissent in *Monis v The Queen* (2013)

GABRIELLE APPLEBY AND HEATHER ROBERTS

I Introduction

By 2013, the time of his final judgment in *Monis v The Queen* ('*Monis*'),[1] Heydon J had established a reputation for being a lone and somewhat curmudgeonly dissenting voice on the High Court. At his retirement, his disagreement and disappointment with the Court's increasing departure from traditional, formalistic judicial method[2] was well documented in a series of increasingly acerbic judgments. This was not the voice that had first spoken from the bench in 2003, at a time when there was a movement towards formalism and away from the reasoning and doctrines of the Mason and Brennan Courts.

Justice Heydon's judgment in *Monis* is remarkable.[3] In Part II we explain how Heydon J executed his judgment in *Monis* with literary and dramatic techniques designed to command the reader's attention, before sowing the seeds of the arguments an advocate might employ to overturn the implied freedom of political communication (in Heydon J's opinion, the

1 (2013) 249 CLR 92.

2 Justice Heydon's pattern of dissents can be understood, fundamentally, as driven by disagreement on 'the institutional constraints of the judicial function': John Alder, 'Dissents in Courts of Last Resort: Tragic Choices?' (2000) 20 *Oxford Journal of Legal Studies* 221, 228–30.

3 The Court's decision in *Monis* is more generally notable for two other reasons. First, it was the first time the Court divided on gender lines: see further Helen Irving, 'Constitutional Interpretation: A Woman's Voice?' on *A Woman's Voice* (20 March 2013) <http://blogs.usyd.edu.au/womansconstitution/2013/03/constitutional_interpretation_1.html>; Gabrielle Appleby and Ngaire Naffine, 'Civility, Gender and the Law: Critical Reflections on the Judgments in Monis v The Queen' (2015) 24 *Griffith Law Review* 616. Second, the case is now one of notoriety by virtue of the events of 15–16 December 2014, when Man Haron Monis held hostage 18 people in a café in central Sydney, leading to his death and that of two hostages.

worst of the excesses of the Mason era). These distinctive stylistic elements of the decision set it apart from the standard High Court reasoning, and, indeed, from other dissenting judgments featured in this book. However, it is not because of these striking literary elements that we submit that the *Monis* decision is a 'great dissent'. Nor is it because we regard Heydon J's judgment as representing a persuasive answer to the legal questions raised in the case. In our view Heydon J's approach in *Monis* is persuasive neither in substance, nor in form. Rather, we argue that the judgment can be read as a 'great' example of conscious and strategic use of dissent. That is, the *Monis* judgment represented for Heydon J the final and authoritative crescendo in his years of advocacy on and off the bench to return the Court to 'proper' judicial method.

Part III explains the judicial philosophy of Heydon J, as evidenced in his judgments and extra-curial writings. It explores the journey he took as a judge appointed to a generally conservative court in 2003, in which he found himself in the mainstream of opinion, to having become an outlying and dissenting voice by 2013. We conclude by placing Heydon J's judgment in *Monis* in this context, as demonstrating the transformative effect that the High Court's trajectory had on him, and as his final opportunity on the bench to record arguments for returning the Court to proper judicial method and process, at a time when the opportunity for him to lead that revival had passed.

II *Monis*: A Judgment in Two Acts

In *Monis*, the Court considered whether a provision of the *Criminal Code* (Cth) breached the freedom to communicate about government and political matters, an implied constitutional limitation first recognised by the Mason Court in 1992.[4] The case arose from the prosecution of Man Haron Monis and Amirah Droudis under s 471.12 of the *Criminal Code*, a provision that criminalised the use of the postal service in ways that 'reasonable persons would regard as being, in all the circumstances, menacing, harassing or offensive'. Monis had sent a number of letters to the families of soldiers who had been killed while serving in Afghanistan, letters that expressed his condolences but went on to criticise Australia's military involvement in Afghanistan, and referred to the deceased solders

[4] *Australian Capital Television v Commonwealth* (1992) 177 CLR 106; *Nationwide News Pty Ltd v Wills* (1992) 177 CLR 1.

in what Bathurst CJ of the New South Wales Court of Criminal Appeal described as a 'denigrating and derogatory fashion'.[5]

Unusually, only six judges sat in the *Monis* appeal,[6] and more unusually, the High Court split 3:3. Pursuant to s 23(2)(a) of the *Judiciary Act 1903* (Cth), the decision of the Court below (upholding the constitutional validity of s 471.12 of the *Criminal Code*) was affirmed. All of the judges agreed that the provision placed a burden on political and government communication. Where the judgments diverged was on the second question asked in testing for a breach of the constitutional implication. This was whether the law was nonetheless valid because it was:

> reasonably appropriate and adapted to serve a legitimate end in a manner which is compatible with the maintenance of the constitutionally prescribed system of representative and responsible government and the procedure prescribed by section 128 of the *Constitution* for submitting a proposed amendment to the *Constitution* to the informed decision of the people.[7]

Chief Justice French and Hayne and Heydon JJ would have struck down the provision. Chief Justice French and Hayne J found that the objective of s 471.12 was to prevent the use of the post in an offensive way, and that this objective was inconsistent with the maintenance and operation of robust representative government in Australia.[8] As we explain below, Heydon J agreed with their reasoning on these points. Justices Crennan, Kiefel and Bell upheld the constitutionality of the provision. They construed the objective behind the provision differently, accepting that its purpose extended beyond ensuring general civility of discourse, to protecting individuals 'from intrusion into their personal domain of unsolicited material which is seriously offensive'.[9]

It is apparent from Heydon J's judgment that he was aware of the position taken by his colleagues at the time he wrote it. He might have provided an opinion that concurred in the orders made by Crennan, Kiefel and Bell JJ. Doing so would have been consistent both with his stance in the earlier case of *Coleman v Power*, where he defended the value of civility in Australian political discourse,[10] and with objections he

5 *Monis v The Queen* (2011) 256 FLR 29, 30 (Bathurst CJ).

6 Justice Gummow did not sit pending his retirement.

7 *Lange v Australian Broadcasting Corporation* (1997) 189 CLR 520, 567–8 ('*Lange*'); *Coleman v Power* (2004) 220 CLR 1, 50 (McHugh J).

8 *Monis* (2013) 249 CLR 92, 133–4 (French CJ), 139–40, 173 (Hayne J).

9 Ibid 205.

10 *Coleman v Power* (2004) 220 CLR 1.

voiced in *Monis* regarding a broad operation of the implied freedom. But with the effect of s 23(2)(a) of the *Judiciary Act* being to ensure that the joint judgment of his female colleagues would prevail regardless, Heydon J knew that, ultimately, his position would make no difference to the outcome in the case. This gave him a freedom to use his judgment in an entirely strategic manner, to leave a stain on the High Court's implied freedom jurisprudence.

The resulting judgment is in two acts: the first act drawing the reader into the grief and pride of the bereaved families, and the effect of Monis' letters, and the second compiling a set of arguments for overturning the implied freedom of political communication. Its literary invocation and brevity 'focuses and commands the reader's attention'.[11] Justice Heydon commenced with a two-paragraph prologue, providing an explanation of the issues, his conclusions on them, and his orders.[12] In these two paragraphs, Heydon J answered the questions posed in the case. He could have stopped there. Instead, over almost six more pages, Heydon J made his final and strategic stand against the implied freedom of political communication, and what he regarded as the evils of judicial activism more generally.

Act I: Sadness, Grief and a Poem

Act I consists of just five paragraphs.[13] Justice Heydon commences by foreshadowing of Act II: that his conclusion (upholding the validity of the legislation) was 'so extraordinary as to cast doubt, and perhaps more than doubt, on the fundamental assumption and the chain of reasoning which led to it'.[14] With a particularity not shared by the other members of the Court, he described the communications Monis and Droudis sent to the families. Justice Heydon rejected euphemism to neutralise the character of these communications for the reader, an approach that muted the impact on the families. Rather, he 'concentrate[d] on the actual language of the communications, unmediated by bland summary'.[15] He extracted the unpleasant and harsh phrases; he *showed* the reader the offence of which the other judgments only spoke of in the abstract.

Justice Heydon then demonstrated the *effect* of those communications by reminding the reader of the vulnerability of those who received them: parents grieving the death of a child. However, Heydon J observed that

[11] Richard Posner, *Law and Literature* (Harvard University Press, 3rd ed, 2009) 345.
[12] *Monis* (2013) 249 CLR 92, 178–9. [13] Ibid 179–80. [14] Ibid 179. [15] Ibid.

where that child has died in battle, this sadness is 'often assuaged by the feeling that the child's death was a necessary and a meritorious sacrifice'.[16] To demonstrate his point, Heydon J reproduced (without attribution) a Rudyard Kipling poem. Kipling wrote *My Boy Jack* after his 18-year-old son, a subaltern in the Irish Guards, was presumed dead after the Battle of Loos on 27 September 1915:

> *My Boy Jack*
> 1914–18
> 'Have you news of my boy Jack?'
> *Not this tide.*
> 'When d'you think that he'll come back?'
> *Not with this wind blowing, and this tide.*
> 'Has any one else had word of him?'
> *Not this tide.*
> *For what is sunk will hardly swim,*
> *Not with this wind blowing, and this tide.*
> 'Oh, dear, what comfort can I find!'
> *None this tide,*
> *Nor any tide,*
> *Except he did not shame his kind –*
> *Not even with that wind blowing, and that tide.*
> *Then hold your head up all the more,*
> *This tide,*
> *And every tide;*
> *Because he was the son you bore,*
> *And gave to that wind blowing and that tide!*

The use of literature to demonstrate the mingling of sadness and pride experienced by the families allowed Heydon J to make his point with heightened lyrical, visual and emotive force: at this moment in their lives, many families who received Monis' communications would have regarded them as 'sadistic, wantonly cruel and deeply wounding blows during the most painful days of their lives'.[17]

The poem set Heydon J's judgment in *Monis* apart. Invocation of literature is rare in Australian judgment writing.[18] Perhaps surprisingly

[16] Ibid.

[17] Ibid 180. On rhetoric in constitutional adjudication, see Sandra S Berns, 'Constituting a Nation: Adjudication as Constitutive Rhetoric' in Charles Sampford and Kim Preston (eds), *Interpreting Constitutions: Theories, Principles and Institutions* (Federation Press, 1996) 84.

[18] In constitutional jurisprudence, see, eg, the unusual illustrations in Deane J's decision in *Commonwealth v Tasmania* (1983) 158 CLR 1, 260 ('*Tasmanian Dam Case*'), referring to 'Tweedledee' and 'contrariwise' logic from Lewis Carroll's *Alice's Adventures in Wonderland*

then, literary illustration of the fears associated with the loss of a child arises twice in this book.[19] However, Heydon J's decision to include the poem in its entirety, retaining in full its poetic lines and form, was an especially dramatic departure from the Court's standard practice.[20] The poem also marked a distinctive break from Heydon J's own narrative style, even those judgments in which he had previously suggested (at first subtly and then increasingly less so)[21] that the time had come for the Court to be asked to reconsider the legitimacy of the implied freedom of political communication.

Justice Heydon transitioned to his Act II in *Monis* with a short paragraph.[22] In this bridge, having explained the victims' unique vulnerability to communications of this nature, Heydon J explained that it is the role of the democratically responsive (and responsible) legislator to make the choice whether the law should protect these people. It is a role that, in Act II, he contrasted against his view of the proper role of the Court.

Act II: The Legal Submissions

In Act II Heydon J provided his set of immutable reasons why the existence of the implied freedom of political communication should be doubted. He buttressed the credibility of this, his final Act, by referring to a number of High Court judgments (which he denotes as 'powerful' dissents)[23] and pieces of academic commentary that have developed similar reasons.[24] Maintaining his commitment to proper judicial process to the end, he

and Through the Looking Glass. See also the first line in the joint judgment in *Zhu v Treasurer (NSW)* (2004) 218 CLR 530, 535 (Gleeson CJ, Gummow, Kirby, Callinan and Heydon JJ), taken from Jane Austen's *Pride and Prejudice*, all the more exceptional for being contained in a joint judgment. See generally Michael Kirby, 'Creative Literature in the Desert of Australian Law' (Speech delivered at the 34th Annual Dinner of the Foundation for Australian Literary Studies, James Cook University, Townsville, Queensland, 16 October 2000).

19 See Barbara McDonald, 'Justice Evatt and the Lost Child in *Chester v Waverley Corporation* (1939)' in ch 4 of this book.

20 See generally Michael Kirby 'Literature in Australian Judicial Reasoning' (2001) 75 *Australian Law Journal* 602.

21 *Roach v Electoral Commissioner* (2007) 233 CLR 162, 223–4 n 179 ('*Roach*'); *Wotton v Queensland* (2012) 246 CLR 1, 18.

22 *Monis* (2013) 249 CLR 92, 180–1.

23 *Australian Capital Television Pty Ltd v Commonwealth* (1992) 177 CLR 106, 177–91 (Dawson J); *Australian Broadcasting Corporation v Lenah Game Meats Pty Ltd* (2001) 208 CLR 199, 298–309, 330–9 (Callinan J).

24 Citing, eg, Jeffrey Goldsworthy, 'Constitutional Implications and Freedom of Political Speech: A Reply to Stephen Donaghue' (1997) 23 *Monash University Law Review* 363;

presented this set of reasons as 'a miscellany of additional or overlapping points calling for inquiry';[25] points that would require analysis *should* a *future litigant* apply for, and be granted, leave to overrule the relevant authorities.[26] Through this second act, Heydon J employs his judgment to protest against the High Court's implied freedom jurisprudence.

Justice Heydon challenged two aspects of the reasoning in the implied freedom cases. First was the reasoning that led the Court to find a guarantee implied in the *Constitution*, and second was that which the Court must employ in applying the implied freedom to the facts of any given case. On the first, Heydon J criticised the value judgments of the Court, specifically the privilege the Court had given political communication over the most fundamental of rights, that of dignity. Indeed, he noted the freedom was even 'capable of injuring that right'.[27] The freedom's existence, he claimed, had never enjoyed unanimous support or consistent articulation.[28] It was neither necessary to make the constitutional structures of representative and responsible government work, nor would it have been intended by the framers.[29] On the second, Heydon J criticised the semantics of the Court's proportionality test as 'mysterious':[30] tautologous and nonsensical. More fundamentally, he asked: 'How does the application of so amorphous a test avoid the dangers of judicial legislation?'[31] While Heydon J's attacks on the freedom thus rest on different bases, at their core was a critique of the Court's activism in creating the limitation, and also that which is necessary to apply it.

Many of the points that Heydon J raised in *Monis* were not new. Indeed, he even referred to his own previous judgments to support his propositions.[32] But *Monis* was the only time Heydon J systematically gathered in one place the set of reasons that, in his view, undermined the freedom. It is unlikely to be a coincidence that this appeared in his last judgment, his final opportunity to secure the inclusion of such a list in the *Commonwealth Law Reports.*

III The Journey to *Monis*

Monis contains Heydon J's final words from the bench, the culmination of a carefully constructed judicial philosophy spanning his decade's service

Adrienne Stone, 'Freedom of Political Communication, the Constitution and the Common Law' (1998) 26 *Federal Law Review* 219.

25 *Monis* (2013) 249 CLR 92, 181. 26 Ibid 184. 27 Ibid 182. 28 Ibid.

29 Ibid. 30 Ibid. 31 Ibid. 32 See, eg, ibid 182 nn 293–4.

as a High Court Justice. In order to appreciate the craftsmanship of his dissent in *Monis*, it is essential to explore key elements of that context. This part of the chapter tells that story.

In the Beginning: Justice Heydon's Vision for the Court

On 30 October 2002, Dyson Heydon made his (in)famous speech, 'Judicial Activism and the Death of the Rule of Law'.[33] Delivered shortly after news of Justice Mary Gaudron's decision to take early retirement from the Court, the speech quickly earned the moniker 'Heydon's job-application'.[34] In it Heydon called out the 'hero judge' as the 'enemy' of the rule of law in Australia.[35] He painted the hero judge as ruled not by judicial process and strict legal reasoning, but rather by 'individual judicial whim'[36] and idiosyncratic personal values. Heydon then lambasted what he portrayed as the excesses of the High Court under the leadership of Mason CJ, and the legal chaos he perceived was created by its 'judicial activism'.

Heydon's emphasis on judicial deference to Parliament and 'legalism' would have been received sympathetically by the Commonwealth government of the day, whose commitment to filling the High Court with 'Capital C Conservative' judges was well known.[37] Rosalind Dixon and Sean Lau have observed that the politically conservative government of Prime Minister John Howard was actively '*looking*' for judges who

[33] The paper was later published in numerous journals under the same title: J D Heydon 'Judicial Activism and the Death of the Rule of Law' (2003) 23 *Australian Bar Review* 110; (2003) 47 *Quadrant* 9; (2003) 14 *Australian Intellectual Property Journal* 78; (2003) 10 *Otago Law Review* 493. All citations to 'Death of the Rule of Law' in this chapter are to the *Australian Bar Review* version.

[34] A J Brown, *Michael Kirby: Paradoxes and Principles* (Federation Press, 2011) 350. See also, regarding the 'job application' moniker, Cynthia Banham, 'Arise Justice Heydon: Capital-C Conservative Elevated to High Court', *The Sydney Morning Herald* (Sydney), 18 December 2002.

[35] Heydon, above n 33, 119, taking the use of this term from John Gava, 'The Rise of the Hero Judge' (2001) 24 *University of New South Wales Law Journal* 747. See also Andrew Lynch, 'Judicial Dissent and the Politics of the High Court' in Rosalind Dixon and George Williams (eds), *The High Court, the Constitution and Australian Politics* (Cambridge University Press, 2015) 58, 68.

[36] Heydon, above n 33, 116.

[37] See, eg, 'Howard Stamp on High Court', *The Sydney Morning Herald* (Sydney), 21 December 2002. The phrase 'Capital C Conservative' judges was coined by Tim Fischer in response to the High Court's decision in *Wik Peoples v Queensland* (1996) 187 CLR 1. See further Brown, above n 34, 283.

embodied a mix of legal and political conservatism.[38] In that sense, 'Death of the Rule of Law' can be read as perfectly pitched. Certainly, if it were a 'job application', it was successful. However, a study of Heydon's judicial and extra-judicial writing suggests that the motivation for the speech was much broader – it was a manifesto for a conservative revival in judicial reasoning.

Critics of 'Death of the Rule of Law' questioned the intellectual honesty of the philosophy Heydon defended.[39] Professor Allan Hutchinson argued that Heydon's professed 'legalism' was no less infused by judicial values than that of the 'hero' (or 'activist') judge; rather, the 'legalist' judge was motivated by socially conservative values shielded from scrutiny by the adherence to 'legalism'.[40]

Justice Heydon at the Centre of the Court

Justice Heydon's appointment in 2003 occurred at the midpoint of the Howard Government's term, at a time when Prime Minister Howard was confidently and successfully pursuing his agenda to return Australia to traditional, conservative social values.[41] His appointment came almost in the middle of the Howard appointments to the High Court: preceded by Kenneth Hayne in 1997 and Murray Gleeson and Ian Callinan in 1998; and followed by Susan Crennan in 2005 and Susan Kiefel in 2007. In 2003, it would not have been unreasonable for Heydon J, and others, to predict that his appointment might herald a change in the Court's jurisprudential and methodological trajectory back to the traditional formalism that he so revered.

38 Rosalind Dixon and Sean Lau, 'The Gleeson Court' in Rosalind Dixon and George Williams (eds), *The High Court, the Constitution and Australian Politics* (Cambridge University Press, 2015) 284, 304 (emphasis in original).

39 See Allan C Hutchinson, '"Heydon" Seek: Looking for Law in all the Wrong Places' (2003) 29 *Melbourne University Law Review* 87; Frank Carrigan 'The Parallel Intellectual Universes of Justice Heydon and Keith Windschuttle: A Meeting of Minds?' (2008) 29 *Adelaide Law Review* 79.

40 Hutchinson, above n 39; see also Sir Anthony Mason, 'Legislative and Judicial Law-Making: Can We Locate an Identifiable Boundary?' (2003) 24 *Adelaide Law Review* 15. Such criticisms of legalism were not new in 2002. In 2000, when Chief Justice Murray Gleeson had extolled the virtues of Dixonian legalism, similar questions had been raised: see, eg, Leslie Zines, 'Chief Justice Gleeson and the Constitution' in H P Lee and P Gerangelos (eds), *Constitutional Advancement in a Frozen Continent: Essays in Honour of George Winterton* (Federation Press, 2010) 269.

41 See Michelle Grattan, 'John Winston Howard' in Michelle Grattan (ed), *Australian Prime Ministers* (New Holland, revised ed, 2008) 436, 454–5.

In the early years of Heydon J's High Court career, Heydon J sat at the 'centre'[42] of a Court that Andrew Lynch and George Williams described as evincing 'a remarkable level of consensus' in constitutional decisions.[43] Excepting Kirby J, among the remaining six judges a pattern quickly emerged in which Heydon J frequently joined with Gleeson CJ, Gummow and Hayne JJ,[44] converting the earlier dominance of these three judges into an unassailable majority bloc. Reflecting in 2007 on Heydon J's early voting patterns, Lynch and Williams also observed that in 2004 not only was Heydon J joining with these judges most frequently, but also that Heydon J had been the most frequent collaborator for each of Gleeson CJ, Gummow, McHugh, and Callinan JJ.[45] These statistics reinforce Heydon J's status as a key figure at the 'centre' of the Court. Finding himself so quickly as a member of a dominant majority, Heydon J might have therefore justifiably felt quite comfortable that the Court's future was likely to be aligned with his view of its role.

Losing the Court

By the time of French CJ's appointment in 2008, Heydon J's confidence in the commitment of even the Court's conservative appointees to a return to formalism must have been receding. Drawing on their annual statistical analysis of the 2007 term, Lynch and Williams observed that in contrast to Heydon J's early years, by 2007 his status as the most frequent collaborator was waning.[46]

The narrative of Heydon J's judgments after 2008 also reveals an increasing despair at his brethren's failure to right the wrongs of the judicial activism of the 1990s, and most particularly its incarnation in the 'tactical compromise' in *Lange v Australian Broadcasting Corporation* ('*Lange*').[47] This shift in tone, particularly in the decision in *Roach v Electoral Commissioner* ('*Roach*'),[48] discussed below, led James Allan to suggest that

[42] Andrew Lynch and George Williams, 'The High Court on Constitutional Law: The 2004 Statistics' (2005) 28 *University of New South Wales Law Journal* 14, 28.

[43] Andrew Lynch and George Williams, 'The High Court on Constitutional Law: The 2003 Statistics' (2004) 27 *University of New South Wales Law Journal* 88, 95.

[44] Lynch and Williams, above n 42, 28; Andrew Lynch, 'The Gleeson Court on Constitutional Law: An Empirical Analysis of Its First Five Years' (2003) 26 *University of New South Wales Law Journal* 32, 62.

[45] Andrew Lynch and George Williams 'The High Court on Constitutional Law – The 2007 Statistics' (2008) 31 *University of New South Wales Law Journal* 238, 250.

[46] Ibid. [47] (1997) 189 CLR 520. See Heydon, above n 33, 123.

[48] (2007) 233 CLR 162.

Heydon J's decisions evince a 'real anger' at the direction the majority judgments were taking Australian constitutional law.[49]

A Lone(ly) and Dissenting Voice on the Bench

It was after the 2007 High Court judgment in *Roach* that Heydon J found his voice more frequently alone, and in dissent – not just on outcome, but on fundamental issues about approach to the judicial role. At some point along this timeline, his mission to return the court to its proper role during his term became quixotic.

Roach did not merely apply *Lange*, but saw Gleeson CJ, Gummow, Kirby and Crennan JJ *expand* the implied limitations on legislative power based on the text of ss 7 and 24 of the *Constitution*, an approach criticised by some commentators as departing from accepted (traditional) legal method.[50] While Heydon J's judgment in *Roach* noted his agreement with Hayne J's dissenting reasons, he provided seven paragraphs of 'additional points' directed at his disappointment with *Lange* and the arguments made (and accepted) in *Roach*. In these paragraphs, Heydon J drew attention to a number of significant concessions by the Commonwealth Solicitor-General, particularly, a concession as to the correctness of *Lange*.[51] In accord with his conception of proper legal process, Heydon J considered himself bound by these concessions. But, in a point that he would also identify in *Monis*, Heydon J highlighted in *Roach* that:

> [*Lange*] may serve as a warning about the difficulties of tests turning on whether legislation is 'reasonably appropriate and adapted' to fulfillment of a particular purpose, . . . and a warning against too readily detecting tests of that kind in the *Constitution*.[52]

Justice Heydon's judgment in *Roach* reinforced the distinction he had drawn previously in 'Death of the Rule of Law' between the role of the *courts* and the role of the *legislature* in a liberal democratic regime.[53] He also issued a strong warning about relying upon international and foreign instruments and decisions in Australian constitutional interpretation; 'calling out' Kirby J as the only judge in the High Court's history who had ever countenanced this approach.[54] By isolating Kirby

[49] James Allan, 'The Three "Rs" of Recent Australian Judicial Activism: Roach, Rowe and (No) "Riginalism"' (2012) 36 *Melbourne University Law Review* 744, 776–7.

[50] Ibid; Anne Twomey, 'Rowe v Electoral Commissioner: Evolution or Creationism?' (2012) 31 *University of Queensland Law Journal* 181.

[51] *Roach* (2007) 233 CLR 162, 223–4 n 179.

[52] Ibid.

[53] Heydon, above n 33, 124 ff.

[54] *Roach* (2007) 233 CLR 162, 225 n 182.

J, Heydon J appeared to carefully insulate his own dissenting position from any charge of radicalism, signalling that although he may have found himself, somewhat to his surprise, in dissent, *he was not a radical judge.*[55]

When the Court returned to the implied right to vote in the 2010 decision of *Rowe v Electoral Commissioner*,[56] Heydon J, again along with Hayne J, still refused to accept the majority position in *Roach*.[57] By this time Heydon J's judgments were losing their diplomatic language.[58] Graeme Orr describes Heydon J's judgment in *Rowe v Electoral Commissioner* as 'resigned' to the fact that more traditional approaches to constitutional interpretation were out of contemporary favour.[59] By February 2012, in *Wotton v Queensland*, Heydon J had completely abandoned any diplomacy in his treatment of *Lange*.[60]

Justice Heydon's isolation was at its most stark in the cases of *Pape v Commissioner of Taxation* (2009), *South Australia v Totani* (2010) and *Williams v Commonwealth* (2012). In each of these cases he commenced with the pugnacious and irrefutably terse statement: 'I dissent'.[61] In each case his was a lone voice in dissent on all of the issues; in each case he emphasised the majority judges' departure from proper legal process.

It would be wrong to conclude that upon French CJ's appointment in 2008, Heydon J immediately abandoned his attempt to persuade the rest of the Court. While he increasingly became an outsider, and isolated on many constitutional doctrines, in his Chapter III jurisprudence Heydon J remained in the majority on many cases. Justice Heydon's vision of the proper role of the judge and Court was tightly bound up with the maintenance of proper judicial process. As such, Chapter III protections of judicial process were perhaps naturally an area in which Heydon J was less likely to oppose judicial expansion, and so, for a number of years, he joined judgments that saw the Court expand the scope of constitutional protections of judicial process,[62] even where these

[55] But see Lynch, above n 35, 68. [56] (2010) 243 CLR 1. [57] Ibid 94, 96–7.

[58] Cf Heydon J's reasoning in *Coleman v Power* (2004) 220 CLR 1, 124.

[59] Graeme Orr, 'The Voting Rights Ratchet: Rowe v Electoral Commissioner' (2011) 22 *Public Law Review* 83, 87.

[60] (2012) 246 CLR 1, 17–18.

[61] *Pape v Commissioner of Taxation* (2009) 238 CLR 1, 134; *South Australia v Totani* (2010) 242 CLR 1, 93; *Williams v Commonwealth* (2012) 248 CLR 156, 282.

[62] *K-Generation Pty Ltd v Liquor Licensing Court* (2009) 237 CLR 501 (writing with Gummow, Hayne, Crennan and Kiefel JJ; French CJ, in majority, writes alone); *Lane v Morrison* (2009) 239 CLR 230 (Heydon J joining with Hayne, Crennan, Kiefel and Bell JJ).

expansions sat oddly with his avowed legalistic approach.[63] Despite these initial glimpses of a more conciliatory approach to Chapter III jurisprudence, even in this area Heydon J would come to find himself alone and in dissent.

By the 2010 case of *South Australia v Totani*,[64] Heydon J expressed doubts about the *Kable* principle. Although the principle was 'difficult to understand', Heydon J continued to apply it because 'no counsel has ever sought leave to argue that [it] be overruled'.[65] Yet, in 2011, in *Momcilovic v The Queen*, Heydon J invalidated the *Charter of Rights and Responsibilities Act 2006* (Vic) as breaching the *Kable* principle.[66] What worried Heydon J in *Momcilovic v The Queen* was what the *Charter* (adopting a judicial dialogue model of rights protection) asked of the judges in terms of judicial *method*. This concern trumped even his concern about the *Kable* principle itself. Just over a year later in *Public Service Association and Professional Officers' Association Amalgamated (NSW) v Director of Public Employment* ('*PSA*'), Heydon J launched another scathing attack on the *Kable* principle for its own vagueness and uncertainty.[67]

His about-face on the *Kable* principle might be explained by reference to an omnipresent determination to ensure fidelity to traditional legal method. He may always have held concerns that *Kable*, like *Lange*, might cut across this commitment. But in earlier *Kable* cases, he was confronted with legislation cutting across his commitment to the protection of judicial process, independence and method. By the time of *PSA* Heydon J was no longer willing to accept the fundamental flaws of the *Kable* principle, even if in the past he had been persuaded by the specific results it might enable.

Justice Heydon's Dissent in Statistics

A statistical snapshot of the Court from 2009 until Heydon J's 2013 retirement reinforces his increasingly frequent and individualised dissent. In 2009, with the retirement of Kirby J, Heydon J became the Court's most frequent dissenter, issuing dissents in 14.89 per cent of all matters.[68] In

[63] *International Finance Trust Co Ltd v New South Wales Crime Commission* (2009) 240 CLR 319; *Kirk v Industrial Court of New South Wales* (2010) 239 CLR 531.

[64] (2010) 242 CLR 1. [65] Ibid 95–6.

[66] *Momcilovic v The Queen* (2011) 245 CLR 1. On the *Kable* principle, see *Kable v DPP (NSW)* (1996) 189 CLR 51.

[67] (2012) 250 CLR 343, 369–70.

[68] This was not his highest level of dissent, which was 15.52 per cent in 2006. See Lynch and Williams, above n 45, 246, 253.

2009, his dissent rate in constitutional matters also rose to its highest to that point: 30 per cent. In 2010, he was again the Court's most frequent dissenter. He dissented in 14.63 per cent of all cases and 44.44 per cent of constitutional cases.[69] In 2010 he was also increasingly individualised. He was every other judge's least frequent co-author in joint judgments, and he joined in opinions at a lower rate than others on the bench,[70] a striking contrast to his status as *most* frequent co-author of Gleeson CJ, Gummow, McHugh, and Callinan JJ in 2004. By 2011, Heydon J's dissent rate in all cases reached 45.45 per cent and in constitutional cases 50 per cent.[71] He became a more frequently lone voice generally, increasing not only the frequency of his sole-authored dissents, but the frequency of his sole-authored concurring judgments.[72] His rates of dissent in 2012 were slightly lower against his own standards but still the highest on the bench. He dissented in 40.43 per cent of total cases and 28.57 per cent of constitutional cases.[73] His 'pronounced degree of individualism' was even more striking in 2012,[74] as he did not join with any other judge.[75] Lynch and Williams commented that, since they commenced their statistical surveys in 2003, 'a complete lack of co-authorship [was] something never observed before'.[76]

Off the Court: Self-Justification of the 'Counter-Hero' Judge

Justice Heydon's conviction in the correctness of his vision for the Court's role and proper legal method is increasingly evident, not just in his judgments, but in his extra-judicial speeches and writings. In this respect, and others, it is difficult to resist the parallels between Heydon J's actions and those of conservative dissentient Justice Antonin Scalia of the United States Supreme Court. Justice Scalia's development and defence of a conservative, restraint-focused judicial ideology, coupled with the withering

[69] Although, as Lynch and Williams observed, Heydon J's dissent rates are low when compared to dissent rates of McHugh and Callinan JJ on the Gleeson Court: Andrew Lynch and George Williams, 'The High Court on Constitutional Law: The 2010 Statistics' (2011) 34 *University of New South Wales Law Journal* 1030, 1039–40.

[70] Ibid 1042.

[71] Andrew Lynch and George Williams, 'The High Court on Constitutional Law: The 2011 Statistics' (2012) 35 *University of New South Wales Law Journal* 846, 855–7.

[72] Ibid 856.

[73] Andrew Lynch and George Williams, 'The High Court on Constitutional Law: The 2012 Statistics' (2013) 36 *University of New South Wales Law Journal* 514, 522–3.

[74] Ibid 526. [75] Ibid.

[76] Ibid. The statistical surveys have been conducted by Lynch and Williams since 2003.

attacks on his judicial colleagues, have brought him a level of notoriety rarely achieved by jurists.[77]

By 2007, Heydon J had already started to develop the concept of what may be described as the 'counter-hero' judge: an individual adherent to 'true' legal method who will not be pressured by another judge. By 2012, his writings unambiguously championed the counter-hero. These writings may be read as self-justificatory appeals made to the legal profession. Now labelled the Court's great dissenter, Heydon J used his extra-judicial remarks to distinguish his form of dissent from that of the progressive dissenter.

Justice Heydon's celebration of the integrity and courage of his counter-hero judge, and particularly the invocation of 'truth', has many resonances with the academic celebration of the 'intellectual'. In 1928, Julien Benda wrote passionately of the 'betrayal of the intellectuals', when intellectuals abandon their calling and compromise their principles.[78] In his 1993 Reith Lectures, Edward Said described Julien Benda's intellectual as willing 'to risk being burned at the stake, ostracized, or crucified. . . . They have to be thoroughgoing individuals with powerful personalities'.[79] For Said, the intellectual speaks to and for the public,[80] not simply because the things of which they speak are perceived as true to them, but because they seek to persuade.[81] The intellectual takes a public stand, speaks truth to power,[82] 'even though it doesn't make one particularly popular'.[83] Similarly, Heydon J's counter-hero judge speaks truth to power, although in a different sense to that of the progressive hero judge that speaks truth to government power and its abuse. The counter-hero speaks truth to the hero judge, to the abuse of judicial power.

Even in Heydon's earlier speeches, this admiration of the counter-hero judge is evident. In 'Death of the Rule of Law', he defended Sir Owen Dixon's reverence for the 'strict logic and high technique' of the common law,[84] and he praised Viscount Haldane as a subscriber to this method.[85] In his 2004 speech titled 'Outstanding Australian Judges',

77 Conor Clarke, 'How Scalia Lost His Mojo: Why the Supreme Court's Most Exciting Justice is Becoming Much Less Fun to Read', *Slate* (online), 5 July 2006 <http://www.slate.com/articles/news_and_politics/jurisprudence/2006/07/how_scalia_lost_his_mojo.html>.

78 Julien Benda, *The Betrayal of the Intellectuals* (Beacon Press, first published 1928, 1955 ed).

79 Edward Said, *Representations of the Intellectual: The 1993 Reith Lectures* (Vintage Books, 1994) 7.

80 Ibid 11. 81 Ibid 12. 82 Ibid ch 5. 83 Ibid 23.

84 Heydon, above n 33, 114. See generally at 113–16. 85 Ibid 115.

he cited Windeyer, Glass and Wells JJ as 'judges of *ability* and *character* who preserve the rule of law'.[86] While integrity featured highly in Heydon's litany of their exemplary characteristics, it was their judicial restraint,[87] and internal rigour, and 'right judicial method'[88] – essential attributes for a counter-hero judge – which for Heydon were key markers of their ability.[89]

In 2006, Heydon also returned to the theme of true legal method, through his Inaugural Sir Harry Gibbs Memorial Oration.[90] In 'Death of the Rule of Law', he had spoken of the danger of judgments being ruled by 'individualised whim'.[91] Justice Heydon's Gibbs Oration also featured a recurring character in his extra-judicial speeches: the individual judge, often in dissent, refusing to depart from the true legal method, and steadfastly continuing to advocate for that truth. Thus in his Gibbs Oration, Heydon recast judicial individualism in a positive light, provided it remained independence 'rooted in principle',[92] and not used to further 'one's own idiosyncratic views of justice'.[93] On constitutional interpretation, he recalled Gibbs CJ's 'fundamental warning' that '[t]he function of this Court is to consider not what the *Constitution* might best provide but what, upon its proper construction, it does provide'.[94]

Heydon thus concluded by describing Gibbs CJ as:

> a sturdy and forceful and unselfconscious expounder of plain truths as he saw them. He confronted opposing views directly, head-on, without flinching. To use the words he used of Sir Samuel Griffith, he was 'an exemplar of unselfish dedication to the law'.[95]

In 2011, Heydon authored two pieces which further developed his views of the counter-hero judge. In the *Australian Law Journal*, he wrote of Justice Radhabinod Pal, who sat on the Tokyo War Tribunals from

[86] J D Heydon, 'Outstanding Australian Judges' (2005) 7 *The Judicial Review* 255, 292. See also at 265.

[87] Ibid 280; see also at 280–3. See in relation to Wells J at 286–7.

[88] Ibid 286, quoting *Amoco Australia Pty Ltd v Rocca Bros Motor Engineering Co Pty Ltd* (1973) 133 CLR 288, 296 (Menzies J).

[89] Heydon, above n 86, 277.

[90] Dyson Heydon, 'Chief Justice Gibbs: Defending the Rule of Law in a Federal System' (Speech delivered at the Inaugural Sir Harry Gibbs Memorial Oration, Canberra, 26 May 2006).

[91] Heydon, above n 33, 116.

[92] Heydon, above n 90, x.

[93] Ibid x, quoting 'NSW Bar Honours Sir Harry Gibbs' [1987] (Autumn) *Bar News* 9, 12.

[94] Heydon, above n 90, xvii, quoting *Western Australia v Commonwealth* (1975) 134 CLR 201, 249.

[95] Heydon, above n 90, xvii, quoting Sir Harry Gibbs, *Sir Samuel Walker Griffith Memorial Lecture: 30 April 1984*, 1.

1946–48, and, in sole dissent, acquitted all of the Japanese defendants. Justice Pal reached his decision based on his concern against the retroactive application of crimes against peace.[96] Heydon praised Pal J's moral courage: to disagree with his colleagues after a gruelling trial where dissenting opinions had been discouraged as 'marring' the Tribunal's judgment; to acquit the defendants when the international community and his own government were fervently calling for conviction and punishment.[97] Heydon continued: 'A key function of courts, sometimes, is to stand out not only against public opinion, but also the opinion of elites and executive governments, if they think it right to do so . . . It can take some courage not to join the herd on those occasions'.[98]

Then on 18 August 2011, Heydon gave the Inaugural R P Meagher Lecture.[99] In it, he developed his vision of the virtuous judge as independent *from* his or her fellow judges, and standing against pressures of judicial 'bargaining' to produce unanimous or majority opinions.[100] Here again, he revered Meagher as the epitome of the counter-hero judge:

> The instincts of the herd never affected him. No one was less likely than him to suffer the fate of the Gadarene swine. He saw his duty as being to hear full argument from counsel and then to concentrate on trying to formulate his personal view of what should be the just outcome of the controversy according to law. In those qualities lie the sources of his greatness.[101]

Through his extra-judicial writings, Heydon expounded an image of himself, and others before him, in similar terms: maintaining commitment to true legal method and the judicial oath in the face of what he would ultimately identify as the 'enemy within' – the quelling of independent thought by the majority or the 'herd'.

Famously, a year before his retirement, Heydon delivered a speech to the Cambridge Law Faculty, and then to the Inner Temple and Herbert Smith & Co, titled 'Threats to Judicial Independence: The Enemy Within'.[102] It would be published upon his retirement and receive significant publicity

[96] J D Heydon 'Japanese War Crimes, Retroactive Laws and Mr Justice Pal' (2011) 85 *Australian Law Journal* 627.

[97] Ibid 666–7. [98] Ibid 667.

[99] J D Heydon 'Varieties of Judicial Method in the Late 20th Century' (2012) 34 *Sydney Law Review* 219.

[100] Ibid 237. [101] Ibid.

[102] J D Heydon, 'Threats to Judicial Independence: The Enemy Within' (2013) 129 *Law Quarterly Review* 205.

in Australia.[103] In it, Heydon provided a robust defence of his legacy and the position he ultimately took against his own court, which reached its crescendo in his judgment in *Monis*. The 'enemy within' that he refers to are the threats posed *by judges* to their own independence:[104] the pressure to participate in joint judgments and the elevation of consensus as a value over individual intellectual integrity. He explains that '[j]udicial independence can be threatened when judicial majorities attempt to muzzle minorities'.[105] Apart from the influence of 'excessively dominant judicial personalities',[106] he also warned against the 'herd instinct', a fundamental instinct of human nature in which the 'cascade effect' causes people to flow along with what they perceive to be the majority opinion.[107] He emphasised that '[t]he function of independent judges is to concentrate on their personal view of what constitutes a just outcome according to law after full argument from counsel'.[108]

Heydon explained the courage and independence the counter-hero judge requires to remain true to this function:

> Judges need another sort of independence. It lies in the willingness and ability to work out and say what they think is right – irrespective of what advocates agree on, what academic lawyers urge, what pressure groups desire, what media groups demand, what their colleagues seem to think or what their colleagues want them to say.[109]

Justice Heydon's railing against the Court's departure from his vision of the true legal method on and off the bench, and his extra-curial statements pertaining to the 'muzzling' of judges by their peers, might lead an outside observer to remark that it was *his* comments that risked undermining the reputation of the Court on which he sat. But, from Heydon J's point of view, *his* judgments and statements did not risk the reputation of the Court. Rather, it was the failures in judicial method, process and independence occasioned by the remainder of the Court that risked the enduring reputation of the Court as the non-political, independent, branch of government.

[103] See, eg, Andrew Lynch, 'Heydon's Push for Judicial Individualism Admirable, but Will it Catch On?' *The Australian* (Sydney), 22 March 2013; Richard Ackland, 'The Great Dissenter Warns of the Judiciary's Worst Enemy: Itself', *The Sydney Morning Herald* (Sydney), 22 March 2013.

[104] Heydon, 'The Enemy Within' above n 102, 206. [105] Ibid 208–9. [106] Ibid 215.

[107] Ibid 216. [108] Ibid 219. [109] Ibid 210.

IV Conclusion: *Monis* as a Strategic Dissent

Justice Heydon's 'The Enemy Within' set off a series of responses: speeches and writings by current and former judges, including his colleagues on the High Court,[110] on judgment writing and independence. In 2014, for example, Kiefel J delivered an address, 'The Individual Judge', in which she challenged judges to ask themselves: for what reason am I writing separately?[111] We submit that to fully understand Heydon J's reasons for writing separately, *in dissent*, in *Monis*, the decision must be read in light of the history of his views which we have detailed in this chapter.

In *Coleman v Power*, a decade before *Monis*, Heydon J concluded that legislation restricting the use of insulting words in public spaces was consistent with the constitutional guarantee. Restricting the use of insulting words was not censorship of political debate, he argued, as it left 'full, compelling, trenchant, robust, passionate, indecorous, acrimonious and even rancorous debate' untouched.[112] For Heydon J in *Coleman v Power*, insulting words were 'alien to the virtues of free and informed debate'.[113] Such words were incapable of informing electors, and therefore inconsistent with the very premise of the implied freedom as they were 'so unreasonable, so irrational, so much an abuse of the occasion' as to 'retard' political communication in Australia.[114] In *Monis*, Heydon J was equally trenchant regarding the value of the offensive letters to Australian political communication; he had not changed his view on the importance of civility and dignity in Australian life. And yet Heydon J endorsed the dissenting reasoning of French CJ and Hayne J in *Monis* and thereby took a broad reading of the provision – a reading which was in his view so 'extraordinary' that it then enabled him to 'cast doubt, and perhaps more than doubt'[115] on the validity of the implied freedom.

This, we submit, was Heydon J's purpose for writing in dissent, rather than concurring with the joint opinion's narrowing of the implied freedom's operation. *Monis* was Heydon J's 'swansong' judgment, his final

[110] See, eg, Stephen Gageler, 'Why Write Judgments?' (2014) 36 *Sydney Law Review* 189; Peter Heerey, 'The Judicial Herd: Seduced by Suave Glittering Phrases?' (2013) 87 *Australian Law Journal* 460; Sir Anthony Mason, 'Reflections on the High Court: Its Judges and Judgments' (2012) 37 *Australian Bar Review* 102; Susan Kiefel, 'The Individual Judge' (2014) 88 *Australian Law Journal* 554; P A Keane 'The Idea of the Professional Judge: The Challenges of Communication' (Speech delivered at the Judicial Conference of Australia Colloquium, Noosa, 11 October 2014) <http://www.jca.asn.au/wp-content/uploads/2013/11/P01_14_02_28_1-Justice-P-A-Keane.pdf>.

[111] Kiefel, above n 110, 560. [112] *Coleman v Power* (2004) 220 CLR 1, 104.

[113] Ibid 105. [114] Ibid. [115] *Monis* (2013) 249 CLR 92, 179.

occasion to be read in the authorised reports of the High Court of Australia. In *Monis*, Heydon J shifted from the position he had taken in *Coleman v Power*, to enable him to employ his 'swansong'[116] judgment for a broader purpose. He wrote his *Monis* dissent to grab his audience's attention and direct them to future action. In *Monis*, Heydon J performed his final act as a counter-hero judge. For a decade, Heydon J had spoken from the bench inviting the overturning of the implied freedom; inviting an attack on the doctrines that stand as the signature achievements of the preceding era of judicial activism. His more diplomatic attempts, at a time when the Court was more likely to be sympathetic, had not delivered change. By *Monis*, Heydon J was out of time. It must, therefore, be different from his previous dissents.

It is unlikely that upon his appointment to the Court in 2003, Heydon J would have imagined that his final judgment would need to be an emotive appeal made to the future bar and Court to return to proper judicial method. In 2003 he presented as confident in joining a Court that was already on its way to reversing the perceived excesses of the Mason era.

While that future proved elusive, Heydon never abandoned his commitment to what he believed to be the true method for the judge, unwavering in the face of pressure to compromise and adopt more popular and progressive method and doctrine. He refused to be muzzled.[117] In his writings on and off the bench, he carefully crafted and cultivated the self-justifying myth of the counter-hero judge. As his final words to be recorded in the *Commonwealth Law Reports*, Heydon J's reasons in *Monis* appear to have been crafted to ensure that they were *noticed, read* and *remembered.* Thus, *Monis* emerges as a precisely executed performance, and a 'great' dissent, left to wait for the next generation of courageous counter-heroes.

[116] In this respect, this chapter forms part of Heather Roberts' broader research into the phenomenon of 'swansong' judgments in the High Court.

[117] Heydon had written '[j]udicial independence can be threatened when judicial majorities attempt to muzzle minorities': Heydon, above n 102, 208.

INDEX

For EU product safety concerns, contact us at Calle de José Abascal, 56–1°,
28003 Madrid, Spain or eugpsr@cambridge.org.

www.ingramcontent.com/pod-product-compliance
Lightning Source LLC
LaVergne TN
LVHW011529200926
848484LV00001B/208
9781107158535